SCRIPTING YOUR WORLD

THE OFFICIAL GUIDE TO SECOND LIFE® SCRIPTING

Dana Moore

Michael Thome

Dr. Karen Zita Haigh

Wiley Publishing, Inc.

Senior Acquisitions Editor: **Willem Knibbe**

Development Editor: **Candace English**

Technical Editor: **Richard Platel**

Production Editor: **Patrick Cunningham**

Copy Editor: **Candace English**

Production Manager: **Tim Tate**

Vice President and Executive Group Publisher: **Richard Swadley**

Vice President and Executive Publisher: **Joseph B. Wikert**

Vice President and Publisher: **Neil Edde**

Book Designer and Compositor: **Patrick Cunningham**

Proofreader and Indexer: **Asha Johnson**

Project Coordinator, Cover: **Lynsey Stanford**

Cover Designer: **Ryan Sneed**

Cover Image: **Michael Thome**

Library of Congress Cataloging-in-Publication Data

```
Moore, Dana, 1947-
  Scripting your world: the official guide to second life scripting / Dana Moore, Michael Thome, Karen Haigh.
  -- 1st ed.
     p. cm.
  ISBN 978-0-470-33983-1 (paper/website)
1. Entertainment computing. 2. Scripting languages (Computer science) 3. Second Life (Game)
  I. Thome, Michael, 1965- II. Haigh, Karen, 1970- III. Title.
  QA76.9.E57M66 2008
  790.20285—dc22
                                        2008027400
```

FOREWORD

In 2008 the virtual world of *Second Life* celebrated five years of existence. During that time, we have been participants in the creation of something truly extraordinary—a completely new realm in the Internet, a cyberspace unlike any other. Linden Lab and the residents of *Second Life* are the creative forces at work bringing this new metaverse, this three-dimensional world we can visit together via the Web, to life.

We think of *Second Life* as a place, although paradoxically, aside from a large set of servers and code, this new place has no physical existence outside the consensual agreement amongst a million human minds that here we dwell together in the three-dimensional Internet, the virtual world that is *Second Life*. For the hundreds of thousands who visit here occasionally and for those who reside and do business here daily, this place of the mind exerts a pull as real as anywhere in the physical world. For the avant-garde thinkers, creators, and entrepreneurs who live at least a portion of their lives here, making tools, artifacts, environments, experiences, and even earning a living, this is our world.

Consisting of a series of sophisticated content-creation, land-management, transactional and scripting tools, the *Second Life* Grid is the technology platform used to power *Second Life*. The Linden Scripting Language (LSL), embedded in all objects created in-world, enables object interactivity. LSL is a compact programming language made for virtual-world creation. Programmers and nonprogrammers alike are capable of creating in *Second Life*; LSL is easy to learn and well-supported by in-world and real-world tools. With scripting, any element in *Second Life* can move, react, sense, change appearance and state. Without it, even the most detailed objects are akin to museum sculptures—inherently static.

In this Official Guide, thoroughly explained examples will prepare you to awaken objects' potential through scripting. Three seasoned software professionals coach the reader through their approach to understanding a new computer language for virtual creation in *Second Life* and on the Web.

As the new 3D world of *Second Life* begins to replace familiar software like the browser, the Java VM, or Windows, a new generation of software developers will inevitably emerge. This book is written with them in mind as well as the common *Second Life* resident, for the future extends beyond technical specifications and interface standards—it affects virtual objects, characters, and their interactions. We at Linden Lab believe this book serves as an educational travel companion for exploration of the innovative, virtual world.

Joe Miller,
Vice President of Technology and Platform Development

Dedication

Acknow-
ledgments

About the
Authors

Introduction

Contents

 DEDICATION

*To all the amazingly creative people of **Second Life**, making and continuously remaking the world.*

ACKNOWLEDGMENTS

We could not have written this book without the assistance and support of many people, both in the real world and in **Second Life**. First we need to thank our families for picking up the slack while we were immersed in writing: Kelly and Alicia Thome; Robert, Sonia, and Rachael Driskill; Jane and Caitlin Moore.

We would like to thank our reviewers, Aaron Helsinger, Robert Driskill, Trouble Streeter, and Roisin Hotaling for their time and patience. Also, many thanks to the scripting experts on the **SL** forums, scripting groups, mailing lists, and wikis—you might not *know* that you helped, but your conversations and documentation were invaluable in gaining the breadth of knowledge we needed to produce this book. Specific callouts to Strife Onizuka, Timeless Prototype, Delta Czukor, Adam Marker, Talin Sands, and Morrigan Mathilde.

Finally, a vigorous nod to our **SL** friends and cohorts, who have not only been interested and supportive during the writing process, but together have been a source of creativity, enthusiastic instigators for scripting projects, and tolerant models for screenshots. We would like to specifically thank Anu, Siv, Slade, Shel, Harper, Dillon, Amee, Jac, Midlou, Robert, and the Wellstone regulars. ElectricSheep would like to thank Morrigan for her friendship and conversations during the book-writing process.

Of course the book wouldn't be possible at all without the Sybex team. We would especially like to thank Willem Knibbe, our acquisitions editor, for investing the faith in this project, and of course our gratitude to the editorial and production staff for helping to produce a high quality work: Candace English, Patrick Cunningham, Pete Gaughan, and Richard Platel.

And no book on **Second Life** can fail to acknowledge the wizards behind Linden Lab, especially Philip Rosedale (Philip Linden) and Cory Ondrejka (Cory Linden).

ABOUT THE AUTHORS

Michael Thome (Vex Streeter) has been a computer scientist with BBN Technologies for over 20 years, and currently specializes in scalable computing technologies including parallel, distributed, and agent-based computing. Michael has degrees in cognitive science from the University of Rochester and Boston University, with specialties in computational models of human neurological systems. His interest in gaming started while he was in high school, building cellular automata systems to create terrains for the *PSL Empire* computer game, writing video games, and collaborating on one of the very first open source computer games, *LSRHS Hack* (the antecedent to the now-venerable *NetHack*). His first *Second Life* avatar was rezzed in late 2006, but he's been a true active *Second Life* resident as Vex since only mid 2007. He currently lives in the Boston area with his real-life family, and also on a small desert island in Camembert.

Dr. Karen Zita Haigh's (Karzita Zabaleta) research is in machine learning for physical systems—she builds brains for robots. Karen has a Ph.D. in computer science from Carnegie Mellon University. She has worked in a variety of domains, including networking, cyber security, oil refineries, jet engines, and—far and away the most fun—the homes of elders. She was one of the analysts who looked at Space Shuttle *Colombia*'s data after the explosion. Computer gaming in general never particularly interested her, but *Second Life* was different; it had just the right mix of elements—the ability to create content, stretch the limits of reality, and have fun without shooting everything she encountered. She was born in Kenya, lived in six countries, and holds citizenships in Canada, Great Britain, and the USA. Karen speaks fluent French and Mandarin Chinese. She lives in Minnesota with her husband and two daughters.

Dana Moore is a division scientist with BBN Technologies and is an acknowledged expert in the fields of peer-to-peer and collaborative computing, software agent frameworks, and sensor-imbued environments. Prior to joining BBN, Dana was Chief Scientist for Roku Technologies, and a Distinguished Member of Technical Staff at Bell Laboratories. Dana is a popular conference speaker and a university lecturer. He has written articles for numerous computing publications and published several books on topics ranging from peer-to-peer computing to rich Internet applications. Although not a gamer, Dana finds enormous value in the potential transformative value of *Second Life*. Dana holds a Master of Science degree in engineering and a Bachelor of Science degree in industrial design from the University of Maryland. He lives in the Annapolis, Maryland, area with his family and also in a Tudor village in *Second Life*.

CHAPTER 1
CHAPTER 2
CHAPTER 3
CHAPTER 4
CHAPTER 5
CHAPTER 6
CHAPTER 7
CHAPTER 8
CHAPTER 9
CHAPTER 10
CHAPTER 11
CHAPTER 12
CHAPTER 13
CHAPTER 14
CHAPTER 15
APPENDICES

DEDICATION

ACKNOW-
LEDGMENTS

ABOUT THE
AUTHORS

INTRODUCTION

CONTENTS

INTRODUCTION

Learning the skills needed to activate and enliven *Second Life* has multiple benefits: You will be one of the rare folk able to lift the veil of mystery behind how things work in *Second Life*. And you may be able to turn your talents and newly gained prowess into a revenue stream. Additionally, you will gain the joy of creating things that other *Second Life* residents will use and enjoy, and may well marvel at. But there's a far greater benefit to becoming a *Second Life* scripter *par excellence*.

Years ago, most software-development challenges involved translating real-world actions, events, and objects into command-line arguments. Your creativity was severely tested due to the constraints and limits on both the computer and the user. Frankly, early interactive command-line applications were far from cool—in fact, they were exactingly tedious. This evolved into a long "Middle Ages" filled with desktop applications expressed in menus and windows—still a very frustrating experience from so many perspectives.

Skip ahead a few generations, and suddenly *Second Life* is on every pundit's radar. The overwhelming conclusion: *Second Life* begins to realize the promise of "cyberspace," a virtual place peopled with real humans interacting with virtual objects. Whether you are a hard-core software developer or simply an enthusiastic *Second Life* resident, this new 3D world gives you an opportunity to create things that operate like their real-world counterparts, or even more intriguingly, things that operate in ways that they never could in plain old reality. Scripting for *Second Life* affords you a whole new set of opportunities, bringing with it a whole new set of challenges and possibilities.

Second Life brings us new 3D development tools and, more importantly, a new 3D development perspective. The 3D development tools are both familiar (such as language constructs and events) and strange (such as coding the many possible interactions with an expressive, dynamic 3D object that responds to real-world inputs such as touch, gravity, proximity to other objects and avatars, and conversation). *Second Life* development perspectives are strangely familiar—all of us live our "first life" in a 3D world but until recently we painfully translated our surroundings to a flat, 2D computing world; think menus and windows. We humans are most comfortable living in 3D, and thanks in part the way that humans interact with computers and through computers to *Second Life*, the future of computers and the Web will be an experience of sights, sounds, and sensation that are inherently 3D!

The emerging 3D Web will offer the benefits of useful, natural metaphors to interact, exchange information, run businesses, and the like. *Second Life*—as the premiere 3D immersive web of people, places, and things—offers vast new opportunities. But it also creates development challenges that will demand a whole new set of skills and perspectives. This book gives you the insights, tools, and skills to take full advantage of this new 3D computing world by enabling you to build in *Second Life*. We provide useful, working examples that you can implement and see in action in our 3D world.

Who Should Buy This Book

Most people, on becoming *Second Life* residents, spend their first few hours and days (once they've figured out how to maneuver and get to a sim of interest) socializing, dancing, buying sporty outfits, exploring alternate aspects of their personality, and doing sundry things analogous to their real-life activities. That's their primary filter for understanding what *Second Life* is and what it offers. Their first reaction is often, "Wow, look at all the neat things I can participate in and do. *I wonder how many ways I can have fun?*"

As their comfort and experience level grows, many people begin to think, "Wow, look at all the nifty gadgets. *I wonder how they work?*" Initially residents look at poofers and dance pads, jukeboxes and media players, windmills and waterfalls, admiring their functionality or their beauty; later these same people look at the same artifacts and wonder how they were made and whether they could create a better version. In fact, in many cases they are **convinced** they could create a better version. If this description captures your experience even a little, congratulations! You've come to the right place. You are our audience.

As we wrote, we assumed the following about our readers:

- You are familiar with *Second Life* concepts. You don't need to be an expert, but you'll get lost pretty quickly if you haven't left Orientation Island.
- You understand basic *SL* building. Some of the scripting in this book requires some careful assembly of primitive objects, though more-complex examples are included in some of the other books in this series.
- You have played with scripts enough to know that you want to know more: you know how much scripting can add to the content you are creating. We don't assume you've attended a Scripting 101 class or read any scripting tutorials, but you'll have an easier time absorbing the book's ideas if you have.

You do not need to be a programmer, a mathematician, or a computer scientist—some parts of this book **will** be slow going if you haven't had any prior experience, but **don't worry**! Nothing here is rocket science, and it is easy to skip over the parts that you aren't interested in or that seem a little too difficult. You can always come back to them later.

One of the great things about scripting in *Second Life* is that it is extremely easy to play with even advanced concepts and quickly grasp how things work: you won't hurt anything if you get it wrong the first or even the 47th time, but you'll learn a huge amount as you experiment.

Above all, enjoy the process!

What's Inside

Here is a glance at each chapter's offerings:

Chapter 1: Getting a Feel for the Linden Scripting Language begins the book by describing LSL and the basic concepts of *Second Life* scripting. It may be used both as an in-depth introduction for novices and as reference material for more-advanced scripters. We recommend that you at least skim Chapter 1 before diving into the chapters that interest you most.

Chapter 2: Making Your Avatar Stand Up and Stand Out includes some of the most basic and common scripted objects in *Second Life*, with particular attention to scripting used to enhance avatars' appearance and behavior.

Chapter 3: Communications describes a variety of ways that scripts can communicate and interact with avatars and with other scripts.

Chapter 4: Making and Moving Objects covers various ways to create new objects and manipulate existing objects under script control.

Chapter 5: Sensing the World includes a variety of examples and projects that focus on using scripts to react automatically to their surroundings, including objects, avatars, and the environment.

Chapter 6: Land Design and Management illustrates how to manipulate the basic structure of the *Second Life* landscape, how to enable land security, and how to learn more about the land around you.

Chapter 7: Physics and Vehicles covers the *Second Life* simulation of physics, and the details of how to build basic vehicles. It includes a brief description of how to make flexiprims interact with physics.

Chapter 8: Inventory discusses how scripted objects can manipulate and manage their own inventory of objects, giving them to and accepting them from avatars and other objects.

CHAPTER 1
CHAPTER 2
CHAPTER 3
CHAPTER 4
CHAPTER 5
CHAPTER 6
CHAPTER 7
CHAPTER 8
CHAPTER 9
CHAPTER 10
CHAPTER 11
CHAPTER 12
CHAPTER 13
CHAPTER 14
CHAPTER 15
APPENDICES

DEDICATION

ACKNOW-
LEDGMENTS

ABOUT THE
AUTHORS

 INTRODUCTION

 CONTENTS

Chapter 9: Special Effects uses the particle system, texture animation, and lighting to generate fireworks, fire, and lighting effects.

Chapter 10: Scripting the Environment describes scripting solutions to react to the *Second Live* environmental simulation, including wind, water, and time.

Chapter 11: Multimedia brings music, audio, video, and web content into the mix, describing how to present multimedia to *SL* users.

Chapter 12: Reaching Outside *Second Life* introduces communications between *SL* scripts and the outside world.

Chapter 13: Money Makes the World Go Round describes how to make your scripts deal with money, including building tip jars and vendor devices.

Chapter 14: Dealing with Problems discusses the sorts of scripting problems you are likely to see and their causes, and provides hints on how to fix them. It also discusses where and how to get and give help.

Chapter 15: New and Improved describes some newly implemented features and issues that scripters will be interested in, including the new Mono virtual machine.

Appendix A: Setting Primitive Parameters is a reference for the complexities of the `llPrimitiveParams()` family of functions. It describes the parameters themselves and what they do.

Appendix B: The Particle System details all of the options of the LSL function `llParticleSystem()`.

Appendix C: *SL* Community Standards lists the standards of behavior expected of *Second Life* residents.

Once you understand a given chapter's content, you should be well-equipped to attack any similar scripts. You can always go back to Chapter 1 to review, and the appendices are organized to be complete references.

We've written a whole lot more content than could be squeezed into the book. There are several bonus chapters, additional examples, and LSL resources that you can download from either the book's companion website (`http://syw.fabulo.us/`) or the publisher's website for the book at `http://www.sybex.com/WileyCDA/SybexTitle/productCd-0470339837.html`. The authors also maintain a headquarters inside *Second Life* at Hennepin <38,136,108>; you can also find it by searching for SYWHQ, where you can see and get demonstrations of just about everything in this book and the components on the website.

BUILD NOTE

Build Notes (which look like this!) contain special instructions for how to build the objects that go with the nearby scripts whenever special tricks or building pitfalls are present.

How to Contact the Authors

We welcome feedback from you about this book or about books you'd like to see from us in the future. You can reach us by writing to `authors@syw.fabulo.us`.

Sybex strives to keep you supplied with the latest tools and information you need for your work. Please check their website at `www.sybex.com`, where we'll post additional content and updates that supplement this book should the need arise. Enter ***Scripting Your World*** in the Search box (or type the book's ISBN—**9780470339831**), and click Go to get to the book's update page.

◼ CONTENTS

CHAPTER 1: GETTING A FEEL FOR THE LINDEN SCRIPTING LANGUAGE   2

SCRIPTING STRUCTURE 101   4

TYPES   8

     Integer   9

     Float   10

     Vector   10

     Rotation   12

     Key   13

     String   14

     List   15

VARIABLES   19

FLOW CONTROL   20

OPERATORS   21

FUNCTIONS   23

EVENTS AND EVENT HANDLERS   25

STATES   26

     When to Use Multiple States (or Not!)   28

MANAGING SCRIPTED OBJECTS   29

     Losing Moving Objects   29

     Multiple Scripts   30

     Resetting Scripts   31

AN LSL STYLE GUIDE   32

     Cleanliness   33

     Modularity   34

SUMMARY   35

CHAPTER 2: MAKING YOUR AVATAR STAND UP AND STAND OUT   36

MOVING YOUR AVATAR AROUND THE WORLD   38

     Sitting   38

     Teleporting   41

CHAPTER 1
CHAPTER 2
CHAPTER 3
CHAPTER 4
CHAPTER 5
CHAPTER 6
CHAPTER 7
CHAPTER 8
CHAPTER 9
CHAPTER 10
CHAPTER 11
CHAPTER 12
CHAPTER 13
CHAPTER 14
CHAPTER 15
APPENDICES

ATTACHMENTS — 46

Flip Tag — 47

Face Light — 48

Wind Me Up! — 50

Discovering whether Objects Are Attached — 53

ANIMATION — 57

Animation Overrides — 58

Typing Animator — 61

CONTROLLING YOUR ATTACHMENTS — 64

SUMMARY — 65

CHAPTER 3: COMMUNICATIONS — 66

TALKING TO AN OBJECT (AND HAVING IT LISTEN) — 68

A Practical Joke: Mimic! — 75

DIALOGS — 77

CREATING OBJECTS THAT COMMUNICATE WITH EACH OTHER — 79

Chat Relay — 82

USING LINK MESSAGES FOR PRIM-TO-PRIM COMMUNICATION INSIDE AN OBJECT — 83

Associating Prims with Their Link Numbers — 88

EMAIL AND INSTANT MESSAGING — 89

Send Me Some Email — 89

Object-to-Object Email — 94

SUMMARY — 96

CHAPTER 4: MAKING AND MOVING OBJECTS — 98

THE PRESTO, ABRACADABRA OF REZZING — 100

Loop Rezzers — 100

A Temporary Rezzer — 106

A Less-Temporary Temporary Rezzer — 108

Other Object-Manipulation Functions — 111

DEDICATION

ACKNOW-
LEDGMENTS

ABOUT THE
AUTHORS

INTRODUCTION

CONTENTS

CONTROLLING MOTION OF NONPHYSICAL OBJECTS 112

Controlling Position 112

Rotation with Target Omega 113

Using Quaternions 115

Sun, Earth, and Moon (Combining Target Omega and Quaternions) 122

SUMMARY 123

CHAPTER 5: SENSING THE WORLD 124

BUILDING SENSORS 126

Open Up! A Simple Automated Door Slider 127

Outdoors: The Birds and the Bees 128

Indoors: Roomba 130

DETECTION WITH COLLISIONS 134

USING GREETERS TO WELCOME VISITORS 136

A Personalized Memory Greeter 137

SUMMARY 139

CHAPTER 6: LAND DESIGN AND MANAGEMENT 140

A WATERFALL 142

SHAPING THE LAND BY TERRAFORMING 145

LAND SECURITY—ARE YOU ON THE LIST? 147

Access-Controlled Teleports 148

A Land Monitor and Ejector 150

LAND INFORMATION FUNCTIONS 152

SUMMARY 155

CHAPTER 7: PHYSICS AND VEHICLES 156

PHYSICAL OBJECTS 158

Working with Acceleration 160

Physical Functions 162

Optical Illusions 165

A Human Cannon Ball 167

Damage 169

Pushing Objects: Flight Assist 170

Energy Drain 175

CHAPTER 1
CHAPTER 2
CHAPTER 3
CHAPTER 4
CHAPTER 5
CHAPTER 6
CHAPTER 7
CHAPTER 8
CHAPTER 9
CHAPTER 10
CHAPTER 11
CHAPTER 12
CHAPTER 13
CHAPTER 14
CHAPTER 15
APPENDICES

VEHICLES 176

   Vehicle Properties 178

   Vehicle Flags 181

   Cameras and Mouselook 182

SUMMARY 185

CHAPTER 8: INVENTORY 186

INVENTORY PROPERTIES 188

GIVING INVENTORY 189

   Please Take a Note(card) 189

   Inventory List: Giving Folders 192

TAKING INVENTORY 193

PERMISSIONS 195

SUMMARY 197

CHAPTER 9: SPECIAL EFFECTS 198

PARTICLE EFFECTS 200

   Fireworks 201

   A Rainbow 205

   Kite String 207

TEXTURE ANIMATION 211

   Texture Animation Modes 212

   Picture Frame 218

LIGHT 221

   Creating Lights 222

   Reflecting Light 226

SUMMARY 227

CHAPTER 10: SCRIPTING THE ENVIRONMENT 228

TIME 230

   Script Time: Elapsed Time 230

   Real-World Time: Analog Clock 230

   Sim Time: Day, Night, and Shadows 232

DEDICATION

ACKNOW-
LEDGMENTS

ABOUT THE
AUTHORS

INTRODUCTION

CONTENTS

AIR, EARTH, WATER, AND WEATHER   236

    Air: Weather Vane   236

    Earth and Water: A Floating Bottle   237

    Weather: Snowfall   240

SUMMARY   240

CHAPTER 11: MULTIMEDIA   242

WORKING WITH SOUND   244

    Ambient-Sound Automation: Northern Winds   244

    Sound Orchestration: Rain and Thunder   247

STREAMING MEDIA   251

    Streaming Video   253

SUMMARY   256

CHAPTER 12: REACHING OUTSIDE SECOND LIFE   258

LOADING WEB PAGES IN-WORLD   260

USING HTTP REQUESTS TO GET DATA FROM THE WEB   261

    Getting Data from a Web Server   261

    Using the Web for Persistent Storage: name2Key   263

    Constructing Both Sides of a Request: Message in a Bottle   265

    RSS Feeds in *Second Life*   268

USING XML-RPC TO CONTROL SL FROM THE OUTSIDE   272

    The Server Side (LSL): Receiving Instructions from Out-World   273

    The Client Side (Perl): Send Instructions into *SL*   276

SUMMARY   277

CHAPTER 13: MONEY MAKES THE WORLD GO 'ROUND   278

TRANSACTION BASICS   280

REDISTRIBUTING WEALTH   281

    Tip Jars   281

    A Shared Tip Jar   285

    Charity Collectors   288

    Going on the Dole: Money Trees   291

CHAPTER 1
CHAPTER 2
CHAPTER 3
CHAPTER 4
CHAPTER 5
CHAPTER 6
CHAPTER 7
CHAPTER 8
CHAPTER 9
CHAPTER 10
CHAPTER 11
CHAPTER 12
CHAPTER 13
CHAPTER 14
CHAPTER 15
APPENDICES

Dedication
Acknow-
ledgments
About the
Authors
Introduction
Contents

SELLING IT! — 294

A Simple Vendor — 295

A Multiproduct Vendor — 296

Networked Vendors — 300

RENTALS AND SERVICES — 301

A Ticket to Ride — 301

Land Rentals — 303

Campers — 305

GAMBLI...UH...GAMES OF SKILL — 307

SUMMARY — 308

CHAPTER 14: DEALING WITH PROBLEMS — 310

WHAT COULD POSSIBLY GO WRONG? — 312

Compiler Errors — 312

Runtime Errors — 313

Logic Errors — 314

Memory — 315

TOO SLOW? — 316

Lag — 317

Linear Execution Speed — 317

Algorithms — 318

Time Dilation — 319

Script-Speed Governors — 319

Simultaneity — 319

BE PROACTIVE! — 320

Don't Be Overly Clever — 320

Debugging — 320

Backing Up Your Scripts — 322

Versioning — 322

Testing — 323

GETTING AND GIVING HELP   **324**

    Education   324

    In-World Locales   325

    Groups   328

    Mailing Lists and Forums   329

    Websites   329

    Script Libraries   330

    Bugs? In *Second Life*?!   330

PRODUCTIZING YOUR SCRIPT   **331**

SUMMARY   **332**

CHAPTER 15: NEW AND IMPROVED   **334**

THE *SECOND LIFE* VIRTUAL MACHINE: ON TO MONO!   **336**

RECENT CHANGES TO LSL   **337**

    Touch Position   337

    Avatar Information   339

    HTTP Server   339

ANNOUNCEMENTS OF NEW FEATURES   **340**

ONWARD!   **340**

APPENDICES   **342**

    Appendix A: Setting Primitive Parameters   344

    Appendix B: Particle System   356

    Appendix C: *SL* Community Standards   368

INDEXES   **370**

    Index A: Key Terms (Excluding LSL Code)   370

    Index B: Complete Listing of LSL Code   375

CHAPTER 1
CHAPTER 2
CHAPTER 3
CHAPTER 4
CHAPTER 5
CHAPTER 6
CHAPTER 7
CHAPTER 8
CHAPTER 9
CHAPTER 10
CHAPTER 11
CHAPTER 12
CHAPTER 13
CHAPTER 14
CHAPTER 15
APPENDICES

GETTING A FEEL FOR THE LINDEN SCRIPTING LANGUAGE

What is so compelling about *Second Life*? As Linden Lab Founder Philip Rosedale explained in an October 19, 2006 interview in *The New York Times*, in *Second Life* avatars can move around and do everything they do in the real world, but without constraints such as the laws of physics: "When you are at Amazon.com [using current web technology] you are actually there with 10,000 concurrent other people, but you cannot see them or talk to them," Rosedale said. "At *Second Life*, everything you experience is inherently experienced with others."

Much of the reason Rosedale can talk convincingly about shared experience is because of scripting in *Second Life*. To be sure, *Second Life* is a place of great physical beauty: in a well-crafted **SL** environment, a feeling of mood and cohesive appearance lend a level of credibility to the experience of existing and interacting in a specific and sometimes unique context. But consider how sterile *Second Life* would be without scripting. Builders and artists create beautiful vistas, but without interaction the world is *static*; little more than a fancy backdrop. Scripts give the world *life*, they allow avatars to be more realistic, and they enhance the residents' ability to react to and interact with each other and the environment, whether making love or making war, snorkeling, or just offering a cup of java to a new friend.

This chapter covers essential elements of scripting and script structure. It is intended to be a guide, and may be a review for you; if that's the case then skim it for nuggets that enhance your understanding. If you are new to *Second Life* scripting or even programming in general, consider this chapter an introduction to the weird, wonderful world of **SL** scripting and the Linden Scripting Language, LSL. If you don't understand something, ***don't worry***! You might find it easier to skip ahead and return here to get the details later.

NOTE

Throughout the book, you'll see references to the *LSL wiki*. There are actually several such wikis, of which `http://wiki.secondlife.com/wiki/LSL_Portal` is the "official" one, and `http://lslwiki.net` is one of many unofficial ones. Typing out the full URL is cumbersome and hard to read, so if you see a reference to the wiki, you'll see only the keyword. For example, if you see, "you'll find more about the particle system on the LSL wiki at llParticleSystem," it means `http://wiki.secondlife.com/wiki/LlParticleSystem`, `http://www.lslwiki.net/lslwiki/wakka.php?wakka=llParticleSystem` or `http://rpgstats.com/wiki/index.php?title=LlParticleSystem`. All of these wikis have search functions and convenient indexes of topics.

In general, all examples in this book are available at the *Scripting Your World* Headquarters (SYW HQ) in *Second Life* at Hennepin <38, 136, 108>* and on the Internet at `http://syw.fabulo.us`. There are also several extras that didn't get included in the book due to space limitations. Enjoy browsing!

_____

* Visit `http://slurl.com/secondlife/Hennepin/38/138/108/` or simply search in-world for "SYWHQ."

SCRIPTING
STRUCTURE 101

TYPES

VARIABLES

FLOW
CONTROL

OPERATORS

FUNCTIONS

EVENTS
AND EVENT
HANDLERS

STATES

MANAGING
SCRIPTED
OBJECTS

AN LSL
STYLE GUIDE

SUMMARY

SCRIPTING STRUCTURE 101

A script is a *Second Life* asset, much like a notecard or any other Inventory item. When it is placed in a *prim*, one of the building blocks of all simulated physical objects, it can control that prim's behavior, appearance, and relationship with other prims it is linked with, allowing it to move; change shape, color, or texture; or interact with the world.

 NOTE

A *prim* is the basic primitive building block of *SL*: things like cubes, spheres, and cylinders. An *object* is a set of one or more linked prims. When you link the prims, the *root* prim is the one that was selected last; the remaining prims are called *children*. The root prim acts as the main reference point for every other prim in the object, such as the name of the object and where it attaches.

Whether or not you've already begun exploring how to script, you've probably created a new object and then clicked the New Script button. The result is that a script with no real functionality is added to the prim's Content folder. Left-clicking on the script opens it in the in-world editor and you see the script shown in Listing 1.1. It prints `"Hello, Avatar!"` to your chat window and then prints `"Touched."` each time you click the object that's holding it.

Listing 1.1: Default New Script

```
default
{
    state_entry()
    {
        llSay(0, "Hello, Avatar!");
    }

    touch_start(integer total_number)
    {
        llSay(0, "Touched.");
    }
}
```

This simple script points out some elements of script structure. First of all, scripting in *SL* is done in the *Linden Scripting Language*, usually referred to as *LSL*. It has a syntax similar to the common C or Java programming languages, and is event-driven, meaning that the flow of the program is determined by events such as receiving messages, collisions with other objects, or user actions. LSL has an explicit *state model* and it models scripts as finite state machines, meaning that different classes of behaviors can be captured in separate states, and there are explicit transitions between the states. The state model is described in more detail in the section "States" later in this chapter. LSL has some unusual built-in data types, such as vectors and quaternions, as well as a wide variety of functions for manipulating the simulation of the physical world, for interacting with player avatars, and for communicating with the real world beyond *SL*.

The following list describes a few of the key characteristics of an LSL script. If you're new to programming, don't worry if it doesn't make much sense just yet; the rest of this chapter explains it all in more detail. The section "An LSL Style Guide" ties things together again.

CHAPTER I

CHAPTER 2
CHAPTER 3
CHAPTER 4
CHAPTER 5
CHAPTER 6
CHAPTER 7
CHAPTER 8
CHAPTER 9
CHAPTER 10
CHAPTER 11
CHAPTER 12
CHAPTER 13
CHAPTER 14
CHAPTER 15
APPENDICES

- All statements must be terminated by a semicolon (`;`).
- LSL is block-oriented, where blocks of associated functionality are delimited by opening and closing curly braces (`{ `*block*` }`).
- Variables are typed and declared explicitly: you must *always* specify exactly which type a variable is going to be, such as `string` or `integer`.
- At a bare minimum, a script must contain the `default` state, which must define at least one *event handler,* a subroutine that handles inputs received in a program, such as messages from other objects or avatars, or sensor signals.
- Scripts may contain user-defined functions and global variables.

Listing 1.2 shows a rather more complete script, annotated to point out other structural features. This script controls the flashing neon sign on the front of the *Scripting Your World* visitor center. **Do not be discouraged if you don't understand what is going on here!** Although this script is relatively complex, it is here to illustrate that you don't *need* to understand the details to see how a script is put together.

This first discussion won't focus on the function of the neon sign, but rather on the structure commonly seen in LSL scripts. A script contains four parts, generally in the following order:

- *Constants* (colored orange in Listing 1.2)
- *Variables* (green)
- *Functions* (purple)
- *States,* starting with `default` (light blue, with the event handlers that make a state in dark blue)

While common convention uses this order for constants, variables, and user-defined functions, they are permitted to occur in any order. They *must* all be defined before the `default` state, however. Additionally, you are required to have the `default` state before any user-defined states.

NOTE

Constants are values that are never expected to change during the script. Some constants are true for all scripts, and part of the LSL standard, including `PI` (3.141592653), `TRUE` (1), and `STATUS_PHYSICS` (which indicates whether the object is subject to the *Second Life* laws of physics). You can create named constants for your script; examples might include `TIMER_INTERVAL` (a rate at which a timer should fire), `COMMS_CHANNEL` (a numbered communications channel), or `ACCESS_LIST` (a list of avatars with permission to use the object).

Variables, meanwhile, provide temporary storage for working values. Examples might include the name of the avatar who touched an object, counts of items seen, or the current position of an object. The section "Variables" later in this chapter describes variables in more detail.

Functions are a mechanism for programmers to break their code up into smaller, more manageable chunks that do specific subtasks. They increase readability of the code and allow the programmer to reuse the same capability in multiple places. The section "User-Defined Functions" describes functions in more detail.

CHAPTER 1

Listing 1.2: Flipping Textures by Chat and by Timer

COMMENTS   CONSTANTS   VARIABLES   FUNCTIONS   STATES

EVENT HANDLERS

SCRIPTING
STRUCTURE 101

TYPES

VARIABLES

FLOW
CONTROL

OPERATORS

FUNCTIONS

EVENTS
AND EVENT
HANDLERS

STATES

MANAGING
SCRIPTED
OBJECTS

AN LSL
STYLE GUIDE

SUMMARY

```lsl
// Texture Flipper for a neon sign

// Constants
integer TIMER_INTERVAL   = 2;   // timer interval
string  NEON_OFF_TEXTURE = "bcf8cd82-f8eb-00c6-9d61-e610566f81c5";
string  NEON_ON_TEXTURE  = "6ee46522-5c60-c107-200b-ecb6e037293e";

// global variables
integer gOn   = TRUE;            // If the neon is burning
integer gSide = 0;               // which side to flip
integer gListenChannel = 989;    // control channel

// functions
fliptexture(string texture) {
    llSetTexture(texture, gSide);
}

usage(){
    llOwnerSay("Turn on by saying: /"+(string)gListenChannel+" sign-on");
    llOwnerSay("Turn off by saying: /"+(string)gListenChannel+" sign-off");
}

// states
default
{
    state_entry() {
        llSetTimerEvent(TIMER_INTERVAL);
        llListen( gListenChannel, "", llGetOwner(), "" );
    }

    listen(integer channel, string name, key id, string msg) {
        if (msg == "sign-on") {
            fliptexture(NEON_ON_TEXTURE);
            gOn = TRUE;
            llSetTimerEvent(TIMER_INTERVAL);  // start the timer
        } else if (msg == "sign-off") {
            fliptexture(NEON_OFF_TEXTURE);    // start the timer
            gOn = FALSE;
            llSetTimerEvent(0.0);
        } else {
            usage();
        }
    }

    timer() {
        if (gOn){
            fliptexture(NEON_OFF_TEXTURE);
            gOn = FALSE;
        } else {
            fliptexture(NEON_ON_TEXTURE);
            gOn = TRUE;
        }
    }
}
```

Two forward slashes (//) indicate a **comment**. The slashes and the entire rest of the line are completely ignored by **SL**. They remain part of the script but have no effect, so you can use them to add a copyright notice or a description of what's going on in the script, or even to disable lines when you are trying to debug a problem. Likewise, empty lines and extra spaces play no part in the execution of a script: indentation helps readability but **SL** ignores it.

Declarations of global constants and variables have script-wide scope; that is, the entire rest of the script can use them. Most programmers are taught that global variables are evil, but in LSL there is no other way to communicate information between states. Since most LSL scripts are fairly short, it's relatively easy to keep track of these beasties, eliminating one of the major reasons that global variables are discouraged in other languages. Although technically the LSL compiler does not distinguish between user-defined constants and variables, the examples in this book name constants with all capital letters, and global variables using mixed case beginning with the lowercase letter *g*.

Next you will notice a couple of code segments that seem to be major structural elements; these are called `fliptexture()` and `usage()`, respectively. These are user-defined functions. Functions are global in scope and available to all states, event handlers, and other user-defined functions in the same script. Functions can return values with a `return` command. The "Functions" section in this chapter provides considerably more detail. Linden Library functions are readily identifiable, as they (without exception) begin with the letters `ll`, as in `llSetTimerEvent()`.

The last elements of a script are the **states**. A state is a functional description of how the script should react to the world. For example, you could think of a car being in one of two states: when it is on the engine is running, it is making noises, it can move, it can be driven. When it is off it is little more than a hunk of metal; it is quiet, immobile, and cannot be driven. An LSL script represents an object's state of being by describing how it should react to events in each situation. Every script must have at least the one state, `default`, describing how it behaves, but you can define more states if it makes sense. An **event** is a signal from the **Second Life** simulation that something has happened to the object, for example that it has moved, been given money, or been touched by an avatar. When an event happens to a **Second Life** object, each script in the object is told to run the matching **event handler**: As an example, when an avatar touches an object, **SL** will run the `touch_start()`, `touch()`, and `touch_end()` event handlers in the active state of each script in the object, if the active state has those handlers. LSL has defined a set number of event handlers. (The SYW website has a complete list of event handlers and how they are used.) The three event handlers in Listing 1.2, `state_entry()`, `listen()`, and `timer()`, execute in a finite state machine managed by the simulator in which the object exists. More details on the state model are presented in the section "States," as it is one of the more interesting aspects of LSL.

You may well ask, "So what does this script do?" It's really pretty simple. Whenever a couple of seconds tick off the clock (the time interval defined by the constant `TIMER_INTERVAL`), the timer event fires, and the texture on the front face of the object is replaced either with the "on" texture referenced by the key in the string `NEON_ON_TEXTURE` or with the "off" texture, `NEON_OFF_TEXTURE`. The script also listens for input by anyone who knows the secret channel to talk to the object (989, declared as the variable *gListenChannel*). If the object hears anyone chat **sign-off** or **sign-on** on the secret channel*, it will activate or deactivate the sign. Come by SYW HQ and tell our sign to turn off (or on, as the case may be). Figure 1.1 shows the script in action. Chapter 3, "Communications," talks more about channels and how to communicate with objects.

CHAPTER 1

CHAPTER 2
CHAPTER 3
CHAPTER 4
CHAPTER 5
CHAPTER 6
CHAPTER 7
CHAPTER 8
CHAPTER 9
CHAPTER 10
CHAPTER 11
CHAPTER 12
CHAPTER 13
CHAPTER 14
CHAPTER 15
APPENDICES

---

* When typing in the chat window, the channel number is preceded by a slash, as in */989 **sign-off.**

CHAPTER 1

Scripting
Structure 101

Types

Variables

Flow
Control

Operators

Functions

Events
and Event
Handlers

States

Managing
Scripted
Objects

An LSL
Style Guide

Summary

Figure 1.1: Texture-flipping in action

TYPES

A *type* is a label on a piece of data that tells the computer (and the programmer) something about what kind of data is being represented. Common data types include integers, floating-point numbers, and alphanumeric strings. If you are familiar with the C family of languages (C, C++, C#, Java, and JavaScript) you'll notice similarities between at least a few of them and LSL. Table 1.1 summarizes the valid LSL variable types. Different data types have different constraints about what operations may be performed on them. Operators in general are covered in the "Operators" section of this chapter, and some of the sections that cover specific types also mention valid operations.

Because all variables in LSL are typed, type coercion is awkward. Most coercion must be done manually with *explicit casting*, as in

```
integer i=5;
llOwnerSay((string)i);
```

In many cases, LSL does the "right thing" when coercing (*implicit casting*) types. Almost everything can be successfully cast into a string, integers and floats are usually interchangeable, and other conversions usually result in the null or zero-equivalent. The discussion later, in Table 1.7, of `llList2<type>()` functions gives a good overview of what happens. Look on the Types page of the LSL wiki for an expanded example of coercion.

TABLE 1.1: LSL VARIABLE TYPES

Data Type	Usage
integer	Whole number in the range –2,147,483,648 to 2,147,483,647.
float	Decimal number in the range 1.175494351E-38 to 3.402823466E+38.
vector	A three-dimensional structure in the form <x, y, z>, where each component is a float. Used to describe values such as a position, a color, or a direction.
rotation quaternion	A four-dimensional structure consisting of four floats, in the form <x, y, z, s>, that is the natural way to represent rotations. Also known as a *quaternion*, the two type names are interchangeable.
key	A UUID (specialized string) used to identify something in *SL*, notably an agent, object, sound, texture, other inventory item, or data-server request.
string	A sequence of characters, limited only by the amount of free memory available to the script (although many functions have limits on the size they will accept or return).
list	A heterogeneous collection of values of any of the other data types, for instance [1, "Hello", 4.5].

NOTE

The value of a variable will never change unless your code reassigns it, either explicitly with = or implicitly with an operator such as ++, which includes a reassignment:

```
a = "xyzzy";
b = a;         // b is also "xyzzy"
a = "plugh";   // a is now "plugh" but b is still "xyzzy"!
```

This holds true for all types, including lists! In keeping with this immutability, all function parameters are pass-by-value (meaning only the value is sent) in LSL.

INTEGER

Integers are signed (positive or negative) 32-bit whole numbers. LSL does not provide any of the common variations on integer types offered in most other languages. Integers are also used to represent a few specific things in LSL:

- *Channels* are integer values used to communicate in "chat" between both objects and avatars. See the section "Talking to an Object (and Having It Listen)" in Chapter 3 for a deeper discussion of channels and their use.

- *Booleans* are implemented as integer types with either of the constant values: TRUE (1) or FALSE (0).

- *Event counters* are integer arguments to event handlers that indicate how many events are pending. Inside such an event handler, the llDetected*() family of library functions can be used to determine which avatars touched an object, which other objects collided with yours, or which objects are nearby.

- *Listen handles* are returned by llListen() and enable code to have explicit control over the listen stream. (Other things you might think would be handles are actually returned as keys.) See Chapter 2, "Making Your Avatar Stand Up and Stand Out," for examples of llListen().

- *Bit patterns* (or *bit fields*) are single integers that represent a whole set of Boolean values at once. Different bits can be combined to let you specify more than one option or fact at once. For instance, in the `llParticleSystem()` library function, you can indicate that particles should bounce and drift with the wind by combining the constant values `PSYS_PART_BOUNCE_MASK` and `PSYS_PART_WIND_MASK` by saying

```
PSYS_PART_BOUNCE_MASK | PSYS_PART_WIND_MASK
```

Scripting
Structure 101

 Types

Variables

Flow
Control

Operators

Functions

Events
and Event
Handlers

States

Managing
Scripted
Objects

An LSL
Style Guide

Summary

 FLOAT

A `float` in LSL is a 32-bit floating-point value ranging from ±1.401298464E−45 to ±3.402823466E+38. Floats can be written as numbers, such as 1.0 or 9.999, and they can be written in scientific notation, as in 1.234E−2 or 3.4E+38, meaning 1.234×10^{-2} and 3.4×10^{38}.

A `float` has a 24-bit signed *mantissa* (the number), and an 8-bit signed *exponent*. Thus for a float 1.2345E+23, the number 1.2345 is the mantissa, and 23 is the exponent.

Because one bit represents the sign of the number (positive or negative), a 23-bit mantissa gives a precision equivalent to approximately 7 decimal digits—more precisely $\log_{10}(2^{23})$. This means values are rarely stored exactly. For example, if you do something like

```
float foo = 101.101101;
```

and print the result, it will report 101.101105, so you should expect some rounding inaccuracy. Even 10E6 × 10E6 isn't 10E12, instead printing 100000000376832.000000. Often more disturbingly, addition or subtraction of two numbers of vastly different magnitudes might yield unexpected results, as the mantissa can't hold all the significant digits.

When an operation yields a number that is too big to fit into a float, or when it yields something that is not a number (such as `1.0 / 0.0`), your script will generate a run-time Math Error.

VECTOR

Vectors are *the* currency of three-dimensional environments, and so are found throughout LSL code. In addition, anything that can be expressed as a triplet of `float` values is expressed in a `vector` type. If you were guessing about the kinds of concepts readily expressed by a set of three values, you'd probably come up with positioning and color, but there are also others, shown in Table 1.2.

TABLE 1.2: COMMON USES FOR VECTORS AND WHAT THEY REPRESENT

Vector Concept	What Vector Represents
Position	Meters. Always relative to some base positioning (the sim, the avatar, or the root prim).
Size	Meters, sometimes also called scale.
Color	Red, green, blue. Each component is interpreted in a range from 0.0 to 1.0; thus yellow is `vector yellow = <1.0, 1.0, 0.0>;`
Direction	Unitless. It is usually a good idea to normalize directions (see `llVecNorm()`); since directions are often multiplied with other values, non-unit direction vectors can have an unexpected proportional effect on the results of such operations.
Velocity	An offset from a position in meters traveled per second. You can also think of velocity as a combination of direction and speed in meters per second.
Acceleration	Meters per second squared.
Impulse	Force (mass × velocity).
Rotation	Radians of yaw, pitch, and roll. Also known formally as the *Euler* form of a rotation.

The x, y, and z components of a vector are floats, and therefore it is slightly more efficient to write a vector with float components—for instance, <0.0, -1.0, 123.0>—than with integer components. Here are some examples of ways to access vectors, including the built-in constant ZERO_VECTOR for <0.0,0.0,0.0>:

CHAPTER 1

CHAPTER 2
CHAPTER 3
CHAPTER 4
CHAPTER 5
CHAPTER 6
CHAPTER 7
CHAPTER 8
CHAPTER 9
CHAPTER 10
CHAPTER 11
CHAPTER 12
CHAPTER 13
CHAPTER 14
CHAPTER 15
APPENDICES

```
vector aVector = <1.0, 2.0, 3.0>;
float xPart = 1.0;
vector myVec = <xPart, 2.0, 3.0>;
float yPart = myVec.y;
float zPart = myVec.z;
myVec.y = 0.0;
vector zeroVec = ZERO_VECTOR;
llOwnerSay("The empty vector is "+(string)ZERO_VECTOR);
```

Vectors may be operated on by scalar floats (regular numbers); for instance, you could convert the yellow color vector in Table 1.2 to use the Internet-standard component ranges of 0 to 255 with the expression <1.0, 1.0, 0.0>*255.0. Vector pairs may be transformed through addition, subtraction, vector dot product, and vector cross product. Table 1.3 shows the results of various operations on two vectors:

```
vector a = <1.0, 2.0, 3.0>;
vector b = <-1.0, 10.0, 100.0>;
```

TABLE 1.3: MATHEMATICAL OPERATIONS ON VECTORS

Operation	Meaning	Vector
+	Add	a+b = < 0.0, 12.0, 103.0 >
-	Subtract	a-b = < 2.0, -8.0, -97.0>
*	Vector dot product	a*b = 319.0 (1 * -1) + (2 * 10) + (3 * 100)
%	Vector cross product	a%b = < 170.0, -103.0, 12.0 > <(2 * 100) - (3 * 10), (3 * -1) - (1 * 100), (1 * 10) - (2 * -1) >

Coordinates in **SL** can be confusing. There are three coordinate systems in common use, and no particular annotation about which is being used at any given time.

- **Global coordinates**. A location anywhere on the *Second Life* grid with a unique vector. While not often used, every place on the grid has a single unique vector value when represented in global coordinates. Useful functions that return global coordinates include llGetRegionCorner() and llRequestSimulatorData().

- **Region coordinates**. A location that is relative to the southwest corner of the enclosing sim (eastward is increasing x, northward is increasing y, up is increasing z), so the southwest corner of a sim at altitude 0 is <0.0, 0.0, 0.0>. The position or orientation of objects, when not attached to other prims or the avatar, is usually expressed in terms of regional coordinates.

  A region coordinate can be converted to a global coordinate by adding to it the region corner of the simulator the coordinate is relative to:

  ```
  vector currentGlobalPos = llGetRegionCorner() + llGetPos();
  ```

Scripting
Structure 101

 Types

Variables

Flow
Control

Operators

Functions

Events
and Event
Handlers

States

Managing
Scripted
Objects

An LSL
Style Guide

Summary

- **Local coordinates**. A location relative to whatever the object is attached to. For an object in a linkset, that means relative to the root prim. For an object attached to the avatar, that means relative to the avatar. For the root prim of the linkset, that value is relative to the sim (and therefore the same as the region coordinates). If the attachment point moves (e.g., the avatar moves or the root prim rotates), the object will move relative to the attachment, even though local coordinates do not change. For example, if an avatar moves her arm, her bracelet will stay attached to her wrist; the bracelet is still the same distance from the wrist, but not in the same place in the region.

Useful functions on vectors include `llVecMag(vector v)`, `llVecNorm(vector v)`, and `llVecDist(vector v1, vector v2)`. `llVecMag()` calculates the magnitude, or length, of a vector—it's Pythagoras in three dimensions. These functions are really useful when measuring the distance between two objects, figuring out the strength of the wind or calculating the speed of an object. `llVecNorm()` normalizes a vector, turning it into a vector that points in the same direction but with a length of 1.0. The result can be multiplied by the magnitude to get the original vector back. `llVecNorm()` is useful for calculating direction, since the result is the simplest form of the vector. `llVecDist(v1,v2)` returns the distance between two vectors *v1* and *v2*, and is equivalent to `llVecMag(v1-v2)`.

 ROTATION

There are two ways to represent rotations in LSL. The native rotation type is a *quaternion*, a four-dimensional vector of which the first three dimensions are the axes of rotation and the fourth represents the angle of rotation. `quaternion` and `rotation` can be used interchangeably in LSL, though `rotation` is much more common.

Also used are *Euler* rotations, which capture yaw (x), pitch (y), and roll (z) as `vector` types rather than as `rotation` types. The LSL Object Editor shows rotations in Euler notation. Euler notation in the Object Editor uses degrees, while quaternions are represented in radians; a circle has 360 degrees or `TWO_PI` (6.283) radians.

Euler vectors are often more convenient for human use, but quaternions are more straightforward to combine and manipulate and do not exhibit the odd discontinuities that arise when using Euler representation. For instance, in the *SL* build tools, small changes in object rotation can make sudden radical changes in the values indicated. Two functions convert Euler representations into quaternions (and vice versa): `llEuler2Rot(vector eulerVec)` and `llRot2Euler(rotation quatRot)`. Many of your scripts can probably get away with never explicitly thinking about the guts of quaternions:

```
// convert the degrees to radians, then convert that
// vector into a quaternion
rotation myQuatRot = llEuler2Rot(<45.0, 0.0, 0.0> * DEG_TO_RAD);
// convert the rotation back to a vector
// (the values will be in radians)
vector myEulerVec = llRot2Euler(myQuatRot);
```

The above code snippet converts the degrees to radians by multiplying the vector by `DEG_TO_RAD`. Two other constants—`ZERO_ROTATION` and `RAD_TO_DEG`—are useful for rotations. These constants are defined in Table 1.4.

TABLE 1.4: CONSTANTS USEFUL FOR MANIPULATING ROTATIONS

Constant	Value	Description
ZERO_ROTATION	<0.0, 0.0, 0.0, 1.0>	A rotation constant representing a Euler angle of <0.0, 0.0, 0.0>.
DEG_TO_RAD	0.01745329238	A float constant that, when multiplied by an angle in degrees, gives the angle in radians.
RAD_TO_DEG	57.29578	A float constant that, when multiplied by an angle in radians, gives the angle in degrees.

CHAPTER 1

CHAPTER 2
CHAPTER 3
CHAPTER 4
CHAPTER 5
CHAPTER 6
CHAPTER 7
CHAPTER 8
CHAPTER 9
CHAPTER 10
CHAPTER 11
CHAPTER 12
CHAPTER 13
CHAPTER 14
CHAPTER 15
APPENDIXES

You will find much more in-depth discussion and some examples for using rotations in Chapter 4, "Making and Moving Objects."

 KEY

A **key** is a distinctly typed string holding the UUID for any of a variety of relatively long-lived **SL** entities. A UUID, or Universal Unique Identifier, is a 128-bit number assigned to any asset in **Second Life**, including avatars, objects, and notecards. It is represented as a string of hex numbers in the format "00000000-0000-0000-0000-000000000000", as in "32ae0409-83d6-97f5-80ff-6bee5f322f14". NULL_KEY is the all-zero key. A key uniquely identifies each and every long-lived item in **Second Life**.

In addition to the unsurprising use of keys to reference assets, keys are also used any time your script needs to request information from a computer other than the one it is actually running on, for instance to web servers or to the **SL** dataserver, to retrieve detailed information about **SL** assets. In these situations, the script issues a request and receives an event when the response is waiting. This model is used to ask not just about avatars using the llRequest*Data() functions, but also to do things like read the contents of notecards with llGetNotecardLine(). Asynchronous interactions with the outside world might include HTTP requests, llHTTPRequest(), and are identified with keys so that the responses can be matched with the queries.

Numerous LSL functions involve the manipulation of keys. Some of the main ones are shown in Table 1.5.

TABLE 1.5: SAMPLE FUNCTIONS THAT USE KEYS

Function Name	Purpose
key llGetKey()	Returns the key of the prim.
key llGetCreator()	Returns the key of the creator of the prim.
key llGetOwner()	Returns the key of the script owner.
key llDetectedKey()	Returns the key of the sensed object.
string llKey2Name(key *id*)	Returns the name of the object whose key is *id*.
key llGetOwnerKey(key *id*)	Returns a key that is the owner of the object *id*.

Note that there is no built-in function to look up the key for a named avatar who is not online. However, there are a number of ways to get this information through services, such as llRequestAgentData().

Scripting
Structure 101

 Types

Variables

Flow
Control

Operators

Functions

Events
and Event
Handlers

States

Managing
Scripted
Objects

An LSL
Style Guide

Summary

↘ STRING

Strings are sequences of letters, numerals, and other characters, collected as a single value. You can specify a constant string in LSL by surrounding the sequence of characters you want with double quotes ("). You can include a double-quote symbol in a string by prefixing it with a backslash (\). Similarly, you can include a backslash with \\, a sequence of four spaces with \t, and a newline with \n. Table 1.6 shows the set of string-manipulation functions provided by LSL.

String indexes are zero-based, ranges are always inclusive of the start and end index, and negative indexes indicate counting positions backwards from the end of the string (–1 is the last character of the string). Consider this example:

```
string test = "Hello world! ";
llGetSubString(test,0,0);     // "H"
llGetSubString(test,0,-1);    // "Hello world! "
llGetSubString(test, -6,-2);  // "world"
```

String values, like all other LSL values, are *immutable*; that is, no function will modify the original string. Rather, functions return brand-new strings that contain transformed versions. For example, the variable *test* in the following snippet does not change when a word is inserted into the string:

```
string test = "Hello world! ";
string x = llInsertString(test, 6, "cruel ");
// x = "Hello cruel world! ", test is unchanged
```

TABLE 1.6: FUNCTIONS THAT MANIPULATE STRINGS

Function Name	Purpose
integer llStringLength(string *s*)	Gets the length of a string.
string llToLower(string *s*)	Converts a string to lowercase.
string llToUpper(string *s*)	Converts a string to uppercase.
integer llSubStringIndex(string *s*, string *pattern*)	Finds the integer position of a string in another string.
string llGetSubString(string *s*, integer *start*, integer *end*)	Extracts a part of a string; returns the part.
string llDeleteSubString(string *s*, integer *start*, integer *end*)	Returns a copy of the original minus the specified part.
string llInsertString(string *s*, integer *pos*, string *snippet*)	Inserts a string snippet into a string starting at the specified position.
string llStringTrim(string *s*, integer *trimType*)	Trims leading and/or trailing whitespace from a string. Trim types are STRING_TRIM_HEAD for the leading spaces, STRING_TRIM_TAIL for the trailing spaces, and STRING_TRIM for both leading and trailing spaces.
string llEscapeURL(string *url*)	Returns the string that is the URL-escaped version of *url* (replacing spaces with %20, etc).
string llUnescapeURL(string *url*)	Returns the string that is the URL unescaped version of *url* (replacing %20 with spaces, etc).

LIST

Lists in LSL are collections of values of any other types. Lists are **heterogeneous**: they may contain any mixture of values of any type except other lists. This makes it important to keep track of what is stored in your lists to avoid getting into trouble, but you can type-check elements at runtime if you need to. For instance, the following code extracts elements from a list:

CHAPTER I

CHAPTER 2
CHAPTER 3
CHAPTER 4
CHAPTER 5
CHAPTER 6
CHAPTER 7
CHAPTER 8
CHAPTER 9
CHAPTER 10
CHAPTER 11
CHAPTER 12
CHAPTER 13
CHAPTER 14
CHAPTER 15
APPENDICES

```
list mylist = [1, 2.3, "w00t", <1.0, 0.0, 0.0>];
integer count = llList2Integer(mylist, 0);
float value = llList2Float(mylist, 1);
string exclamation = llList2String(mylist, 2);
vector color = llList2Vector(mylist, 3);
```

To access the individual elements, use the `llList2<type>()` functions, shown in Table 1.7.

You can use `llGetListEntryType()` to find out the type of the element. For example, `llList2Float(list src, integer index);` returns the float value at the specified index in the list. Thus Listing 1.3 prints 4.000000 when the object is touched. Note that it is implicitly casting the original `integer` value into a `float`.

TABLE 1.7: FUNCTIONS THAT EXTRACT INDIVIDUAL LIST ELEMENTS

FUNCTION NAME	PURPOSE
`string llList2String(list l, integer index)`	Returns a string element. All other types are appropriately coerced into a string.
`integer llList2Integer(list l, integer index)`	Returns an integer element. If the element is not coercible to an integer, it will return 0.
`float llList2Float(list l, integer index)`	Returns a float element. If the element is not coercible to a float, it will return 0.0.
`key llList2Key(list l, integer index)`	Returns a key element. If the element is a regular string, it is returned unchanged. Other non-key elements return `NULL_KEY`.
`vector llList2Vector(list l, integer index)`	Returns a vector element. If the element is not coercible to a vector, it will return `ZERO_VECTOR`
`rotation llList2Rot(list l, integer index)`	Returns a rotation element. If the element is not coercible to a rotation, it will return `ZERO_ROTATION`.
`integer llGetListEntryType(list l, integer index)`	Gets the type of entry of an element in the list. Returns an integer constant `TYPE_INTEGER`, `TYPE_FLOAT`, `TYPE_STRING`, `TYPE_KEY`, `TYPE_VECTOR`, `TYPE_ROTATION`, or `TYPE_INVALID`. Invalid occurs when the index was out of range.

Listing 1.3: Coercing an Element of a List into a Float

```
list gMyNumList=[1,2,3,4,5];
default
{
    touch_start(integer total_number) {
        float f = llList2Float(gMyNumList,3);
        llOwnerSay((string)f);
    }
}
```

The upside of heterogeneous lists in the LSL context is that you can imitate **associative arrays** (for instance, dictionaries or reference tables) with careful searches. If you keep your lists well-structured, you're very likely to know your list contents and their types very well, even when the contents are a mixed bag. The first element in a list is at index 0, and negative indexes reference elements counting backwards from the end of the list, with −1 indicating the last one. Table 1.8 shows some of the basic list-manipulation functions.

CHAPTER 1

SCRIPTING
STRUCTURE 101

TYPES

VARIABLES

FLOW
CONTROL

OPERATORS

FUNCTIONS

EVENTS
AND EVENT
HANDLERS

STATES

MANAGING
SCRIPTED
OBJECTS

AN LSL
STYLE GUIDE

SUMMARY

TABLE 1.8: SOME CORE FUNCTIONS TO MANIPULATE LISTS

FUNCTION NAME	PURPOSE
integer llGetListLength(list *l*)	Gets the number of elements in a list.
integer llListFindList(list *l*, list *test*)	Returns the index of the first instance of *test* in *l*, or –1 if it isn't found.
list llList2List(list *l*, integer *start*, integer *end*)	Returns the portion of a list, with the specified elements (similar to substring).
list llDeleteSubList(list *l*, integer *start*, integer *end*)	Removes a portion of a list, returns the list minus the specified elements.
list llListInsertList(list *dest*, list *snippet*, integer *pos*)	Inserts a list into a list. If *pos* is longer than the length of *dest*, it appends the snippet to the *dest*.
list llListReplaceList(list *dest*, list *snippet*, integer *start*, integer *end*)	Replaces a part of a list with another list. If the snippet is longer than the *end-start*, then it serves to insert elements too.
float llListStatistics(integer *operation*, list *input*)	Performs statistical operations, such as min, max, and standard deviation, on a list composed of integers and floats. The *operation* takes one of ten LIST_STAT_* constants, which are described fully on the SYW website.

You can use + and += as concatenation operators:

```
list a = [1,2];
a = a + [3];    // a now contains [1, 2, 3]
a += [4];       // a now contains [1, 2, 3, 4]
```

While you can't make nested lists, you can insert a list into another:

```
list myL = ["a", "b"];
list myLL = llListInsertList(myL,[1,2,3,4],1);
// myLL contains [a, 1, 2, 3, 4, b]
```

Perhaps the most interesting set of string functions deals with converting back and forth between lists and strings, listed in Table 1.9. For example, the function llDumpList2String() concatenates the items in a list into a string with a delimiter character sequence separating the list items; llDumpList2String([1,2,3,4,5], "--") prints "1--2--3--4--5". The function llList2CSV() is a specialized version, using only commas as separators.

TABLE 1.9: FUNCTIONS THAT CONVERT LISTS TO STRINGS

FUNCTION NAME	PURPOSE
string llDumpList2String(list *source*, string *delimiter*)	Turns a list into a string, with the *delimiter* between items.
list llParseString2List(string *s*, list *delimiters*, list *spaces*)	Turns a string into a list, splitting at *delimiters* and *spaces*, keeping *spaces*. Consecutive *delimiters* are treated as one delimiter. Listing 1.4 shows an example of how to use this function.
list llParseStringKeepNulls(string *s*, list *delimiters*, list *spaces*)	Turns a string into a list; consecutive *delimiters* are treated separately.
list llCSV2List(string *csvString*)	Converts comma-separated values (CSVs) to a list. For instance, if *csvString* is a string "1,2,3" then the list will be [1, 2, 3].
string llList2CSV(list *l*)	Converts a list to a string containing comma-separated values (CSVs).

The llParseString2List() is particularly useful because it converts a string's elements to a list of strings. Listing 1.4 shows an example of how you would call it to break a string into separate items and then print them to the chat window.

Listing 1.4: `llParseString2List()` Example

```
default
{
    touch_start(integer total_number) {
        list l = llParseString2List("The answer to Life, the Universe"➨
                                  + " and Everything is 42", [" "], []);
        integer i;
        integer len = llGetListLength(l);
        for (i = 0; i < len; i++){
            llOwnerSay("item==>"+ llList2String(l, i));
        }
    }
}
```

While not totally symmetrical to `llDumpList2String()`, it still produces useful results:

```
[8:31]   Object: item==>The
[8:31]   Object: item==>answer
[8:31]   Object: item==>to
[8:31]   Object: item==>Life,
[8:31]   Object: item==>the
[8:31]   Object: item==>Universe
[8:31]   Object: item==>and
[8:31]   Object: item==>Everything
[8:31]   Object: item==>is
[8:31]   Object: item==>42
```

  ## WARNING

If a list came from parsing a string using `llParseString2List()`, be aware that using `llList2<type>()` won't work. Instead you have to use an *explicit cast*, indicating that you want to change the type as in (*sometype*) `llList2String()`. The following snippet shows an example:

```
list components = llParseString2List(message, ["|"], []);
float gAngle = (float)llList2String(components,0),
vector gPosition = (vector)llList2String(components,1);
```

You can imitate objects or compound structures by using a ***strided list***, wherein the series of contained objects is repeated in a nonvarying sequence. The ***stride*** indicates how many elements are in each compound structure. Listing 1.5 creates a strided list, with a stride of 2, populating it with a string representation of the color name paired with the LSL vector of RGB values representing that color. It prints all the color names that occur between elements 2 and 4 of the list, namely green and blue.

Listing 1.5: Small Strided-List Example

```
list COLORS = ["red", <1., 0., 0.>, "green", <0., 1., 0.>,
               "blue", <0., 0., 1.>, "yellow", <1., 1., 0.>,
               "purple", <1., 0., 1.>, "cyan", <1., 0., 1.>];
integer STRIDE = 2;
default
{
    touch_start(integer total_number) {
        list keys = llList2ListStrided(COLORS, 2, 4, STRIDE);
        llOwnerSay(llDumpList2String(keys, ", "));
    }
}
```

CHAPTER 1

CHAPTER 2

CHAPTER 3

CHAPTER 4

CHAPTER 5

CHAPTER 6

CHAPTER 7

CHAPTER 8

CHAPTER 9

CHAPTER 10

CHAPTER 11

CHAPTER 12

CHAPTER 13

CHAPTER 14

CHAPTER 15

APPENDICES

There are some provisions for manipulating strided lists in LSL, including sorting and extracting elements such as keys, shown in Table 1.10. However, you will still need to have a few more utility functions. Put Listing 1.6 on your "save for later" pile—create the script and store it in your Inventory folder under Scripts. It contains a group of utility functions that enable the fetching, update, and deletion of a specific record.

SCRIPTING
STRUCTURE 101

TYPES

VARIABLES

FLOW
CONTROL

OPERATORS

FUNCTIONS

EVENTS
AND EVENT
HANDLERS

STATES

MANAGING
SCRIPTED
OBJECTS

AN LSL
STYLE GUIDE

SUMMARY

TABLE 1.10: FUNCTIONS THAT MANIPULATE STRIDED LISTS

FUNCTION NAME	PURPOSE
list llList2ListStrided(list *src*, integer *start*, integer *end*, integer *stride*)	Returns a list of all the entries whose index is a multiple of *stride*, in the range of *start* to *end* inclusive.
list llListSort(list *l*, integer *stride*, integer *ascending*)	Sorts a list ascending (**TRUE**) or descending (**FALSE**), in blocks of length *stride*. Works unreliably for heterogeneous lists.
list llListRandomize(list *l*, integer *stride*)	Randomizes a list in blocks of length *stride*.

Listing 1.6: Managing Records in a Strided List

```
list gColors = ["red", <1.0, 0.0, 0.0>,
                "green", <0.0, 1.0, 0.0>,
                "blue", <0.0, 0.0, 1.0>];
integer STRIDE = 2;

integer getPosition(integer recordNumber)
{
    return recordNumber * STRIDE;
}
list getRecord(integer recordNumber)
{
    integer pos = getPosition(recordNumber);
    if (pos < (llGetListLength(gColors) + STRIDE - 1))
        return llList2List(gColors, pos, pos + STRIDE - 1);
    else
        return [];
}
deleteRecord(integer recordNumber)
{
    integer pos = getPosition(recordNumber);
    if (pos < (llGetListLength(gColors) + STRIDE - 1)) {
        gColors = llDeleteSubList(gColors, pos, pos + STRIDE - 1);
    }
}
updateRecord(integer recordNumber, list newRecord)
{
    integer pos = getPosition(recordNumber);
    if (pos < (llGetListLength(gColors) + STRIDE - 1)) {
        gColors = llListReplaceList(gColors, newRecord, pos,
                        pos + STRIDE - 1);
    }
}
default
{
    // embed some test code in a touch_start event handler
    // get record # 2
    touch_start(integer total_number) {
        integer i = 0;
        list l = getRecord(2);
        llOwnerSay(llDumpList2String(l, " + "));
    }
}
```

VARIABLES

Variables provide a place to store temporary working values. Variables can be both **global** and **local**. Global variables are available to everything in the script, while local variables are available only to the block they were defined in. A variable name must start with an ASCII letter or an underscore. Numerals may be part of a variable name after the first character, and non-ASCII letters, while allowed, are **ignored**. Thus, valid declarations include the following:

```
integer x;
integer y1;
integer _z;
integer thisIs_ALongComplicatedVariable_42;
integer enumerator;
integer _enumerator;
integer énumérateur;   // same as numrateur
```

However, you can not **also** declare an `integer numrateur` because LSL ignores the é, and thus thinks the name has previously been declared in scope; that is, *numrateur* is the same variable as *énumérateur*.

Global variables (and constants) must be defined before the `default` state, as shown in the following code:

```
integer gFoo = 42;
default
{
    on_rez(integer start_param) {
        llOwnerSay("gFoo is "+(string)gFoo);
    }
}
```

Variables can **not** be defined directly inside states (they must appear inside blocks, functions, or event handlers). Thus, a slight rearrangement of the preceding code will generate a syntax error:

```
default
{
    integer gFoo = 42;
    on_rez(integer start_param) {
        llOwnerSay("gFoo is "+(string)gFoo);
    }
}
```

Local variables must always be declared within the **scope** (enclosing curly braces) of a function or event handler but needn't be declared before the first executable statement. Just declare it prior to its first use and you'll be fine. Consider the following example:

```
foo() {
    integer bar = 0;
    llOwnerSay("bar is "+(string)bar);
    integer baz = 0;
    llOwnerSay("baz is "+(string)baz);
}
```

SCRIPTING
STRUCTURE 101

TYPES

VARIABLES

FLOW
CONTROL

OPERATORS

FUNCTIONS

EVENTS
AND EVENT
HANDLERS

STATES

MANAGING
SCRIPTED
OBJECTS

AN LSL
STYLE GUIDE

SUMMARY

Using a local variable before it has been declared will generate the error "Name not defined in scope." Variables are scoped to the closest enclosing code block. Variables are not accessible outside this scope. After the function `foo()` returns, the variables **bar** and **baz** are unavailable. Thus, in the following code snippet the variable **baz** is not available outside the `else` branch of the `if (gBoolean)` test:

```
integer gBoolean = TRUE;
foo() {
    string bar = "Ford Prefect";
    if (gBoolean) {
        string bar = "Slarty Bartfast";
        llOwnerSay(bar);
    } else {
        string baz = "Zaphod Beeblebrox";
        llOwnerSay(baz);
    }
}
```

The snippet also demonstrates that you can *shadow* a variable from an outer code block with a redefinition of the same name. The innermost wins; that's why in this code example, `llOwnerSay(bar)` will always tell you "Slarty Bartfast" and ignore poor "Ford Prefect."

It is also useful to know that global variables can be *set* to the value returned by a function, but they can not be *intialized* to the value of a function. Similarly, LSL does not allow any code evaluation outside blocks, generating a syntax error for the following snippet:

```
float gHalfPi = PI/2;
default
{
}
```

FLOW CONTROL

Flow control is the process of directing the computer through your program in ways other than simply executing each line one after the other. If you have some experience with other computer languages, LSL flow control will come naturally to you, as most of the familiar constructs are here.

Conditionals are represented with `if...else` statements: they allow the *conditional* execution of code depending on the value of the expression following the word `if`:

- `if ( condition ) trueBranch`
- `if ( condition ) trueBranch else falseBranch`

The branches can be single statements; block statements (enclosed in braces, `{block}`); or null statements (empty or just a semicolon "`;`"). There is no LSL equivalent to the `switch` or `case` statements found in many other languages.

LSL provides a standard set of loop statements as well: `for`, `do...while`, and `while`:

- `do { loop } while ( condition );`
- `for ( initializer; condition; increment ) { loop }`
- `while ( condition ) { loop }`

Loop statements may also be single statements, block statements, or the empty statement ";". Loops may not declare variables in the initializer. That is, the following snippet is *not* allowed:

```
for (integer i=0; i<10; i++) {
    // loop
}
```

You can declare variables inside a loop block:

```
integer i;
for (i=0; i<10; i++) {
    float f=3.0;
    llOwnerSay((string)i+". "+(string)f);
}
```

A do...while loop is slightly faster than a while or for loop, and also requires fewer bytes of memory.

The flow statement state is described in the "States" section later in this chapter. return is used to return a value from a function, described in the section "User-Defined Functions." jump is just like the goto statement of many other languages, allowing direct jumping around the code of your script, and should generally be avoided. It is not uncommon in LSL for jump to be used to break out of loops:

```
integer i;
integer bigNumber = 1000;
for (i=0; i<bigNumber; i++) {
    if (weFoundOurNumber(i)) {
        jump doneWithIt;
    }
}
@doneWithIt;
llOwnerSay("Done after "+(string)i+"steps");
```

OPERATORS

Mathematical operators are the usual suspects (arithmetic, comparison, and assignment), with approximately the same precedence as you'd expect, such as multiplication and division before addition and subtraction. The exclamation point, !, denotes negation (returns TRUE for a FALSE value and vice versa). The tilde, ~, is the bitwise complement, flipping each bit of the integer it is applied to. The plus sign, +, can be used for a variety of things, including addition, string concatenation, and list appending.

NOTE

Unlike in most modern computer languages, Boolean operators in LSL do not "short-circuit" the calculation of an expression. If you were expecting short-circuiting, your code can have unexpected inefficiencies or broken logic.

CHAPTER 1

CHAPTER 2
CHAPTER 3
CHAPTER 4
CHAPTER 5
CHAPTER 6
CHAPTER 7
CHAPTER 8
CHAPTER 9
CHAPTER 10
CHAPTER 11
CHAPTER 12
CHAPTER 13
CHAPTER 14
CHAPTER 15
APPENDICES

Table 1.11 shows the operators, in approximate order of precedence. Empty cells will generate a compiler error with a type mismatch. Lists and strings are not in this table because they only support the addition operators + and +=, indicating concatenation. Note specifically that lists may not be compared with any operator, while strings can be compared with only == and != (but they compare only list **length**, not list **contents**). Table 1.12 lists the math-related library functions.

CHAPTER 1

SCRIPTING
STRUCTURE 101

TYPES

VARIABLES

FLOW
CONTROL

 OPERATORS

 FUNCTIONS

EVENTS
AND EVENT
HANDLERS

STATES

MANAGING
SCRIPTED
OBJECTS

AN LSL
STYLE GUIDE

SUMMARY

WARNING

There have been reports of unexpected (and unexplainable) precedence calculations in the expression parser, so use parentheses liberally.

TABLE 1.11. OPERATORS AND THEIR SEMANTICS FOR DIFFERENT TYPES

Operator	Integer (and Boolean)	Float	Vector	Rotation
.			Dot	Dot
!	Not			
~	Bitwise complement	Bitwise complement		
++ --	Increment, decrement	Increment, decrement		
* / %	Multiply, divide, modulus	Multiply, divide, modulus	Dot product, N/A, cross product	Addition, subtraction, N/A
+ -	Add, subtract	Add, subtract	Add, subtract	Legal, but semantically unlikely
<< >>	Left / right shift			
< <= > >=	Less than, less than or equal to, greater than, greater than or equal to	Less than, less than or equal to, greater than, greater than or equal to		
== !=	Comparison equal, comparison not equal	Comparison equal, comparison not equal		
& ^ |	Bitwise AND, XOR, OR			
|| &&	Comparison OR, AND			
= += -= *= /= %=	Assignment, with above semantics	Assignment	Assignment	Assignment

TABLE 1.12: LSL MATH FUNCTIONS

Function	Behavior
integer llAbs(integer *val*)	Returns an integer that is the positive version of the value *val*.
float llFabs(float *val*)	Returns a float that is the positive version of *val*.
integer llRound(float *val*)	Returns an integer that is *val* rounded to the closest integer. 0.0 to 0.499 are rounded down; 0.5 to 0.999 are rounded up.
integer llCeil(float *val*)	Returns the closest integer larger than *val*.
integer llFloor(float *val*)	Returns the closest integer smaller than *val*.

CHAPTER 2
CHAPTER 3
CHAPTER 4
CHAPTER 5
CHAPTER 6
CHAPTER 7
CHAPTER 8
CHAPTER 9
CHAPTER 10
CHAPTER 11
CHAPTER 12
CHAPTER 13
CHAPTER 14
CHAPTER 15
APPENDICES

FUNCTION	BEHAVIOR
`float llFrand(float max)`	Returns a float that is a pseudorandom number in the range [0.0, *max*) or (*max* , 0.0] if *max* is negative. That is, it might return 0.0 or any number up to but not including *max*.
`float llSqrt(float val)`	Returns a float that is the square root of *val*. Triggers a Math Error for imaginary results (*val* < 0.0).
`float llLog(float val)`	Returns a float that is the natural logarithm of *val*. If *val* <= 0 it returns 0.0 instead.
`float llLog10(float val)`	Returns a float that is the base-10 logarithm of *val*. If *val* <= 0 it returns zero instead.
`float llPow(float base, float exp)`	Returns a float that is *base* raised to the power *exp*.
`integer llModPow(integer base, integer exp, integer mod)`	Returns an integer that is *base* raised to the power *exp*, modulo *mod*: (*base*^{exp})% *mod*). Causes the script to sleep for 1.0 seconds.
`float llSin(float theta)`	Returns a float that is the sine of *theta* (in radians).
`float llAsin(float val)`	Returns a float (*theta*, in radians) that is the inverse sine in radians of *val*; that is, sin(*theta*)=*val*. *val* must fall in the range [−1.0, 1.0].
`float llCos(float theta)`	Returns a float that is the cosine of *theta* (in radians).
`float llAcos(float val)`	Returns a float (*theta*, in radians) that is the inverse cosine of *val*; that is, cos(*theta*)=*val*. *val* must fall in the range [−1.0, 1.0].
`float llTan(float theta)`	Returns a float that is the tangent of *theta* (in radians).
`float llAtan2(float y, float x)`	Returns a float (*theta*, in radians) that is the arctangent of *x*, *y*. Similar to tan(*theta*)=*y*/*x*, except it utilizes the signs of *x* and *y* to determine the quadrant. Returns zero if *x* and *y* are zero.

FUNCTIONS

A *function* is a portion of code that performs a specific task. LSL supports two kinds of functions: *built-in functions* that are provided by Linden Lab, and *user-defined functions* that exist inside your scripts.

LSL includes a large number of built-in functions that extend the language (such as the ones you've already seen for math and list-manipulation functions). Built-in functions are readily identifiable as they always begin with the letters `ll`. Thus, you can tell immediately that `llSetTexture()` and `llOwnerSay()` are not user-defined functions. This book describes most of these Linden Library functions along with examples of how to use many of them.

User-defined functions are blocks of code that help modularize your code and improve readability. If you need to do the same thing more than once in your script, there's a good chance that code should be put into a function. User-defined functions must be defined before the `default` state. Functions are global in scope, and are available to all states, event handlers, and other user-defined functions in the same script (but not other scripts in an object). An example of the general form a function takes is shown in Listing 1.7.

SCRIPTING
STRUCTURE 101

TYPES

VARIABLES

FLOW
CONTROL

OPERATORS

 FUNCTIONS

EVENTS
AND EVENT
HANDLERS

STATES

MANAGING
SCRIPTED
OBJECTS

AN LSL
STYLE GUIDE

SUMMARY

Listing 1.7: Function Form

COMMENTS   CONSTANTS   VARIABLES   TYPES   LIBRARY FUNCTIONS   KEYWORDS   FUNCTION NAMES

```
// say something a few times
// return how many times message is said
integer saySomeTimes (string message) {
    integer count = 1 + (integer) llFrand(5.0);  // up to 5 times
    integer i;
    for ( i=0; i<count; i++ ) {
        llOwnerSay(message);
    }
    return count;
}
```

This function prints the string passed into it, *message*, between one and five times to the owner's chat window.

A function has a name (`saySomeTimes` in Listing 1.7) and can have any number of parameters, each with a declared type (*message* is a `string`). A function with no parameters is just declared as its name with an open/close parenthesis pair, as in `foo()`. Only parameter values are passed into the function, and the original value (in the caller's scope) is guaranteed to be unchanged. There is no concept of pass-by-reference in LSL. If you have large data structures, it's probably best to keep them as global variables rather than passing them as parameters into functions, because the entire data structure will be copied—this process takes time and memory.

Variables defined inside the function (*count* and *i*) have scope only inside the function block: nothing outside the function can see the variables. Be careful about naming your variables, especially if you use similar names in different scopes. It is remarkably easy to get confused about which variable is which when you reuse names.

If a function has a return type, it can return a single value of that type using the `return` statement. Functions that don't return a value should simply not declare a return type. The function `saySomeTimes()` in Listing 1.7 returns an integer of the number of times it chatted the message.

If you look back at Listing 1.2, you'll see the definition of the `listen()` event handler follows exactly the same form. In fact, an event handler is just a special function that is called by *SL* when certain events occur. Event handlers must be one of the event names known to *SL*, must be declared to have the correct type parameters (but you may choose the names of the parameters!), and may not return values. The SYW website lists all the events, and there is more detail in the "Events" section of this chapter.

EVENTS AND EVENT HANDLERS

CHAPTER 1

CHAPTER 2
CHAPTER 3
CHAPTER 4
CHAPTER 5
CHAPTER 6
CHAPTER 7
CHAPTER 8
CHAPTER 9
CHAPTER 10
CHAPTER 11
CHAPTER 12
CHAPTER 13
CHAPTER 14
CHAPTER 15
APPENDICES

LSL is an *event-driven* language. This behavior is a major discriminating feature between LSL and many other languages. Essentially, the script's flow is determined by *events* such as receiving messages from other objects or avatars, or receiving sensor signals. Functionally, events are messages that are sent by a *Second Life* server to the scripts active in that sim. Event messages can be received by defining the matching *event handlers* in the state(s) of your scripts. *Nothing* happens in a script without event handlers: even the passing of time is marked by the delivery of timer events. Some events cannot happen without the matching event handler active somewhere in the object (in at least one of its prims). For instance, if an object doesn't have a script with a `money()` event handler, avatars cannot pay that object.

Many library functions have effects that take relatively long periods of time to accomplish. Rather than *blocking* (stopping execution), LSL uses *asynchronous* communications: your script fires off a request that something happen, and it is notified with an event when the request is satisfied. This pattern is used any time your script makes a call to a library function that cannot be handled locally by the host sim (for instance, the function `llHTTPRequest()` and the `http_response()` event handler), when physical simulation effects aren't going to be instantaneous (`llTarget()` and `at_target()`). You could also think of repeating events (`llSensorRepeat()` and `sensor()`) or even listeners (`llListen()` and `listen()`) as following the same model: make a request and get responses later. This model of asynchronous execution allows your script to keep functioning, handling other events and interactions without stopping to wait for long-term requests to happen.

As events occur, applicable ones (those that have handlers defined on the current state) are queued for execution by the script in the order they were raised. You should be aware of several important constraints on the delivery of event messages to handlers:

- By default, events are delivered to a script no more frequently than every 0.1 second. You can adjust this with `llMinEventDelay(float seconds)` but it can not be less than 0.05 second.

- A maximum of 64 events can be queued on a script—any additional events will be silently discarded!

- Queued events are silently discarded when a script transitions between states.

The combination of these factors means that if you have code that expects to get events rapidly and takes a relatively long time to execute (including artificial delays!), you may run the risk of missing events. As an example, sending an IM (which delays the script by 2 seconds) in response to collide events (which can happen as often as every 0.1 second) is probably asking for trouble.

Similarly, the LSL function `llSleep(float seconds)` pauses script execution for the specified number of seconds without leaving the current event handler, similar to the way that many LSL functions introduce artificial delays. In both cases, there is a potential problem if your script is likely to handle lots of events.

Some events are delivered to a script only if the script has made the appropriate request. For instance, a `listen()` event handler is never called unless another handler in the same state has called `llListen()`. The SYW website has a list of all the LSL event handlers, the functions required to enable the event, and the *Second Life* situation that results in that raised event. And, of course, there are lots of examples throughout the book.

25

STATES

SCRIPTING
STRUCTURE 101

TYPES

VARIABLES

FLOW
CONTROL

OPERATORS

FUNCTIONS

EVENTS
AND EVENT
HANDLERS

STATES

MANAGING
SCRIPTED
OBJECTS

AN LSL
STYLE GUIDE

SUMMARY

Second Life models scripts as ***event-driven finite state machines*** similar to paradigms often used to run hardware. Wikipedia defines an event-driven finite state machine as "a model of behavior composed of a finite number of states, transitions between those states, and actions"* where actions occur as a result of the observation of externally defined events. This sort of model is often used in real-world applications where entirely predictable behavior is required, especially when programs are interacting directly with hardware or external events (think automotive electronics, traffic signals, and avionics).

This model is certainly apt for **SL** because many LSL scripts control virtual simulations of real-world mechanisms. Perhaps more importantly, it is useful as a simulator language because of how gracefully such programs scale under simulator load: under conditions of high "simulator lag," slowed event delivery might hurt performance, but nothing ought to break outright.

LSL scripts must implement at least the `default` state: indeed, many only use the `default` state, either exhibiting behavior that requires simple event-driven programming, or using global variables in place of states. A script will always be in exactly one state. All script execution occurs in the context of the current state, and in the current event. States are defined in an LSL script as sets of event handlers, labeled with the key words `default` or `state` *statename*.

Second Life calls two special event handlers, `state_entry()` and `state_exit()`, when your script changes states.

 ## EVENT DEFINITION

`state_entry( ) { }`

This event handler is invoked on any state transition and in the default state when a script first runs or after it has been reset. This event is *not* triggered every time the object is rezzed. The SYW website provides additional documentation.

 ## EVENT DEFINITION

`state_exit( ) { }`

This event handler is invoked when the `state` command is used to transition to another state, before the new state is entered. It is *not* invoked by `llResetScript()`. The SYW website provides additional documentation.

* http://en.wikipedia.org/wiki/Finite_state_machine

A script transitions between states using a `state newStateName` statement. Note that transition statements are not allowed inside user functions. Listing 1.8 shows a complete script that does nothing until touched, and then transitions to the exploding state and back to the default state. Figure 1.2 shows how the script execution passes through the states and event handlers.

Listing 1.8: Example State Transitions

```
default {
    touch_end(integer count) {
        state exploding;
    }
    state_exit() {
        llOwnerSay("The fuse has been lit.");
    }
}
state exploding {
    state_entry() {
        llOwnerSay("Boom!");
        state default;
    }
    state_exit() {
        llOwnerSay("Ash is now falling.");
    }
}
```

CHAPTER 2
CHAPTER 3
CHAPTER 4
CHAPTER 5
CHAPTER 6
CHAPTER 7
CHAPTER 8
CHAPTER 9
CHAPTER 10
CHAPTER 11
CHAPTER 12
CHAPTER 13
CHAPTER 14
CHAPTER 15
APPENDICES

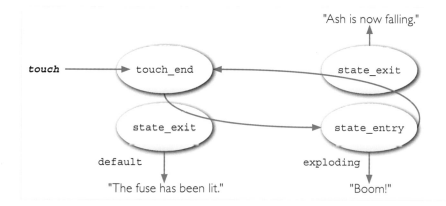

Figure 1.2: State transitions for Listing 1.9

A state transition will invoke the `state_exit()` event on the way out (still in the context of the origin state), allow it to run to completion, and then run the `state_entry()` event on the new state. In Listing 1.9 each state announces something as it is about to exit.

WARNING

Don't try state transitions from within a `state_exit()` event handler: it probably will not do what you hope for, and at the time of this writing it can result in some moderately bad (and varying) script behavior.

Additionally, avoid putting code after the command to transition states. It won't be executed, as shown in the following snippet:

```
touch_end( integer n ) {
    state exploding;
    llOwnerSay("I will never be executed!");
}
```

27

Any queued events, like touches or messages, that haven't been serviced yet are silently discarded during state transitions. Also, anything that was set up for delayed or repeated event handlers is invalidated: all in-progress listens, timers, sensors, and data server queries will need to be reopened. Global variable values survive state transitions, as well as granted permissions, taken controls, and XML-RPC channels.

SCRIPTING
STRUCTURE 101

TYPES

VARIABLES

FLOW
CONTROL

OPERATORS

FUNCTIONS

EVENTS
AND EVENT
HANDLERS

STATES

MANAGING
SCRIPTED
OBJECTS

AN LSL
STYLE GUIDE

SUMMARY

WHEN TO USE MULTIPLE STATES (OR NOT!)

Multiple states are good when you want to strongly separate different modes of a scripted object. Consider a highly configurable object like a vendor kiosk: you *really* don't want people making purchases from the vendor while you are reconfiguring it. Even simple objects like a door or an elevator might best be represented with multiple states (*open* versus *closed*, and *idle* versus *carrying* passengers versus *responding* to a call, respectively). On the other hand, if you have a script where two states have a great deal of repeated code (event handlers) that cannot be abstracted out to functions, it may be simpler to collapse those two states together with a global variable. For instance, the default state from the texture-flipping script in Listing 1.2 could have been split into two using `default` as the "off" state and `lit` as the "on" state and eliminating the *gOn* variable, as shown in Listing 1.9.

Listing 1.9: Neon Texture Flipper as Multiple States

```
// Insert variables and appropriate functions from Listing 1.2
default
{
    state_entry() {
        fliptexture(NEON_OFF_TEXTURE);
        llSetTimerEvent(TIMER_INTERVAL);
    }
    timer() {
        state lit;
    }
}
state lit
{
    state_entry() {
        fliptexture(NEON_ON_TEXTURE);
    }
    timer() {
        state default;
    }
}
```

This snippet only sets the timer in the `default` state. Timers are special in that they are the only event requests not discarded when a script changes state. It would do no harm to re-invoke `llSetTimerEvent()` in its `state_entry()`. The SYW website discusses this in detail.

MANAGING SCRIPTED OBJECTS

CHAPTER 1

CHAPTER 2
CHAPTER 3
CHAPTER 4
CHAPTER 5
CHAPTER 6
CHAPTER 7
CHAPTER 8
CHAPTER 9
CHAPTER 10
CHAPTER 11
CHAPTER 12
CHAPTER 13
CHAPTER 14
CHAPTER 15
APPENDICES

The mechanics of dealing with scripted objects can be challenging at times. Scripts, after all, lend behavior to inanimate objects—and if your scripts aren't exactly right, misbehavior! Not to worry, though: while *Second Life* doesn't offer the sorts of software development and debugging tools that professional programmers have come to expect for serious work, there are techniques and tools that can help. For instance, Chapter 14, "Dealing with Problems," is all about finding and fixing problems. The SYW website features a compendium of resources for getting (and offering!) scripting help, as well as a survey of external LSL scripting tools. Furthermore, there are a few specific tips you may find useful as you start writing more-complicated scripts. Just keep in mind that bugs happen to everyone—be prepared for them and you'll be just fine.

LOSING MOVING OBJECTS

Normally you edit a prim or an object, create a script, and then edit the script. You can stop editing the prim and keep editing the script (assuming you leave the script window open). If the selected prim goes flying out of range into the sky, you will not be able to save changes until it is back in range. This is a pain when you lose track of the object (say, by rotating it to somewhere completely unexpected). There are some easy fixes to this problem: copy and paste the text of the old script into a new one, keep a copy in an out-of-world editor, or create a `timer()` event that returns the object to its original position, as in Listing 1.10.

Listing 1.10: Using a Timer to Reset an Object's Position and Orientation

```
vector gInitialPosition;
rotation gInitialOrientation;

default
{
    state_entry() {
        gInitialPosition = llGetPos();
        gInitialOrientation = llGetRot();
        llOwnerSay("Pos:"+(string)gInitialPosition);
        llOwnerSay("Rot:"+(string)gInitialOrientation);
    }
    touch_start(integer n) {
        llOwnerSay("Doing experimental stuff");
        // add your experiment here
        llSetTimerEvent( 10 );
    }
    timer() {
        llSetPos(gInitialPosition);
        llSetRot(gInitialOrientation);
        llSetTimerEvent( 0 );
    }
}
```

When the script starts the `state_entry()` event handler, it uses the functions `llGetPos()` and `llGetRot()` to find the position and rotation of the object and cache them. (These functions are described in Chapter 4.) When the user touches the object, the `touch_start()` handler runs the experimental code, and, before exiting, sets up a timer event with `llSetTimerEvent()`. Magically, 10 seconds later when the `timer()` event triggers, the object is moved back to its original position using `llSetPos()` and `llSetRot()`. Note that `llSetPos()` is limited to moves of 10m or less; Chapter 2 shows how to move the object farther.

SCRIPTING
STRUCTURE 101

TYPES

VARIABLES

FLOW
CONTROL

OPERATORS

FUNCTIONS

EVENTS
AND EVENT
HANDLERS

STATES

 MANAGING
SCRIPTED
OBJECTS

AN LSL
STYLE GUIDE

SUMMARY

DEFINITION

$$llSetTimerEvent(float\ timerInterval)$$

Cause a `timer()` event to be triggered once every *timerInterval* seconds. A value of 0.0 stops further timer events.

> *timerInterval* — Any positive nonzero value.

EVENT DEFINITION

$$timer()\ \{\ \}$$

This event handler is invoked when triggered at periodic intervals specified by the parameter to `llSetTimerEvent(float interval)`. Only one timer can be active in the state at one time. The SYW website provides additional documentation.

A simple experiment to try would be to replace the commented line in the `touch_start()` event handler with the following snippet:

```
vector newPos = gInitialPosition + <1,1,1>;
llSetPos(newPos);
```

MULTIPLE SCRIPTS

A *Second Life* prim may contain any number of running scripts in its inventory and, of course, *SL* objects are often made from multiple prims. The result is that a complex scripted object can have many scripts cooperating to produce the object's behavior. Many scripters develop a suite of small, focused scripts to accomplish different tasks, rather like programmers in other languages often build libraries of utility functions. For example, you might develop a comfy pillow that has three scripts—one for sitting, one for changing textures, and one that is a sound trigger for some mood music if an avatar is sensed nearby. A suite of scripts like this can be combined to form new behaviors.

This modularity also makes it easier to debug, maintain, and reuse; store them in the Scripts section of your Inventory folder. Best of all, smaller scripts are more stable. Each script executes within its own block of memory, and **can not** accidentally write into the memory of other scripts or the protected simulator memory; this protection makes it much harder for your scripts to crash the simulator!

Multiple scripts on the same object run in parallel, as close to simultaneously as the sim server can manage, and are fired in no defined order. Each script can be in a different state, making for interesting possibilities. In Chapter 3 you'll see how to synchronize behavior among the scripts.

CHAPTER 1

CHAPTER 2
CHAPTER 3
CHAPTER 4
CHAPTER 5
CHAPTER 6
CHAPTER 7
CHAPTER 8
CHAPTER 9
CHAPTER 10
CHAPTER 11
CHAPTER 12
CHAPTER 13
CHAPTER 14
CHAPTER 15
APPENDICES

 ## RESETTING SCRIPTS

Scripts reset to default values when they are placed in another object. However, if a scripted object is in your possession and you rez it or transfer ownership, the script is *not* reset. Scripted objects do not "instinctively" reset when transferred, and thus either an explicit reset or careful handling of the change of ownership is often required. `llResetScript()` forces a reset of the script, restarting it from scratch. All global variables are set to their defaults, all pending events are cleared, the `default` state becomes active, and its `state_entry()` is triggered. When writing and debugging the script, you can achieve an identical effect by clicking Reset in the script editor.

 ## DEFINITION

`llResetScript()`

Resets the script completely, restarting it from scratch. This approach is a good way to catch ownership transfers. It does not correct persistent prim features such as sit text, a sit target, or floating text.

Certain persistent features of an object are *not* reset with `llResetScript()`, including floating text and sit targets; these must be explicitly deleted. Every script that maintains state must take care to reset when transferred, either by detecting transfers or resetting when rezzed. Our scripts do the latter by catching the `on_rez()` event, as shown in the following snippet. If you don't reset the script or double-check who the owner is, for example, a chatting script would still listen to the original owner.

```
default
{
    on_rez(integer start_param) {
        llResetScript();
    }
}
```

 ## EVENT DEFINITION

`on_rez(integer startParam) { }`

This event handler is invoked when an object is rezzed into the world from inventory or by another script. The SYW website provides additional documentation.

> *startParam* — The parameter the prim starts with; zero for an object rezzed from inventory, and any value if rezzed by another script.

You can also keep track of the expected owner in a global variable, and reset or adapt the script only when the owner changes:

```
key gOwner;
default
{
    state_entry() {
        gOwner = llGetOwner();
    }
    on_rez(integer p) {
        if (gOwner != llGetOwner()) {
            llResetScript();
        }
    }
}
```

WARNING

This book contains scripts that use `llResetScript()` in many different places depending on specific needs. It's usually needed in an `on_rez()` event handler; however, one place to *never* use it is in the `state_entry()` handler—it will result in infinite recursion.

Two LSL functions allow one script to control the state of another script in the same prim: `llSetScriptState(string statename, integer run)`, which causes a state transition in the current script to the named state, and `llResetOtherScript(string scriptname)`, which resets the named script.

AN LSL STYLE GUIDE

"Any fool can write code that a computer can understand. Good programmers write code that humans can understand."

—Martin Fowler et al, *Refactoring: Improving the Design of Existing Code*

Effective programming in LSL requires that developers use a disciplined practice for applying formatting and convention to their scripts. These guidelines are not as rigid as the rules required by the language compiler, but nonetheless are critical to creating maintainable code. The most critical aspect of a style is that you apply it consistently to the code you write. We are attempting to make a guideline, not a rigid coding style, and thus point out things that **must** be followed to make it compile and things that **should** be followed to make your scripts readable. The SYW website describes a variety of tools you can use outside of **SL** to help you script, but the principles are important no matter how you write your scripts.

SCRIPTING
STRUCTURE 101

TYPES

VARIABLES

FLOW
CONTROL

OPERATORS

FUNCTIONS

EVENTS
AND EVENT
HANDLERS

STATES

 MANAGING
SCRIPTED
OBJECTS

AN LSL
STYLE GUIDE

SUMMARY

CLEANLINESS

CHAPTER 1

CHAPTER 2
CHAPTER 3
CHAPTER 4
CHAPTER 5
CHAPTER 6
CHAPTER 7
CHAPTER 8
CHAPTER 9
CHAPTER 10
CHAPTER 11
CHAPTER 12
CHAPTER 13
CHAPTER 14
CHAPTER 15
APPENDICES

The most important practice in effective programming is to generate readable code. Readable code is easier to debug, understand, and maintain. A short snippet that is poorly formatted may be decipherable later, but a longer program will not be. If you pay attention to your coding style early on, it will quickly become second nature.

Here is a list of specific suggestions:

- **Bracketing**: You must always enclose blocks in curly braces. It is a good idea to always use braces, even for single statements. Opening braces for functions and states should start on the line after the declaration. Otherwise, place the brace on the same line as the control block.

- **Indentation**: On the line immediately following an open brace, you should add one indentation, usually four spaces. Remove an indentation on the line after a close brace.

NOTE

The two most important guidelines are indentation and bracketing. This code, for example, is not properly indented:

```
default{state_entry(){ llSay(0, "Hello, Avatar!"); } touch_
    start(integer total_number)  {  llSay(0, "Touched."); }}
```

If you look closely, you'll see that it's the same as Listing 1.1—which was much more readable!

- **Line wrap**: You should manually separate lines longer than 80 characters.

- **Coding styles**: In general, don't mix coding styles. When editing code you didn't create, keep the existing style (or change the style throughout).

- **Function length**: Try to keep functions short and focused. A good rule is that a function longer than a screen height should be refactored into multiple functions.

- **Comments**: Use comments to explain what you are doing; however, avoid excessive inline comments: well-written code should explain itself. Do, however, describe what each function does in a comment near the top of the definition.

- **Variable naming**:
  - Variable names must always start with a letter or underscore.
  - Don't abbreviate. Since case matters (**x** is not the same as **X**), longer names will cause significantly less confusion.
  - Global variables should begin with a lower case **g**; for example, ***gSelected***.
  - Variables used as constants should be in all caps, and words should be separated by underscores, like this: OWNER_KEY.
  - You should use camel case (lowercase first letter, and then capitalize each word) for variable names, such as this: ***myCountingVariable***.

SCRIPTING
STRUCTURE 101

TYPES

VARIABLES

FLOW
CONTROL

OPERATORS

FUNCTIONS

EVENTS
AND EVENT
HANDLERS

STATES

MANAGING
SCRIPTED
OBJECTS

AN LSL
STYLE GUIDE

SUMMARY

- *Function naming:*
  - Function names must also start with a letter, and usually are camel case, with each word capitalized similarly to the Linden Library functions like `doSomethingInteresting()`.
  - Linden Lab uses the prefix `ll` for built-in functions, such as `llGetScriptName()`, so don't use this syntax for your own code—it is considered very bad form. Look for `llPizza()` on the LSL wiki; it has a short discussion of user functions masquerading as Linden Library functions.
  - If you are creating functions that belong to a family, and you are likely to reuse them regularly, you should define a consistent naming convention across the family. LSL does not have an explicit "library" concept, but if you stick to one convention, you will find it easier to maintain a collection of reusable code for your projects.

NOTE

To conserve space, the scripts in this book don't follow all the rules all the time, especially for comments. The prose around the listings should be sufficient explanation.

MODULARITY

LSL doesn't offer any tools for writing and maintaining modular or especially reusable scripts, however, here are some tricks:

- Write and edit your code outside *Second Life*, only pulling it in for testing, integration into builds, and deployment. Not only does this approach allow you to use superior editors, but it gives you access to revision-control systems and code generators and transformers—see the SYW website for more.
- Package separable parts as different scripts in the same object. This can keep the individual pieces smaller if the parts don't require close coordination.
- Use *worker scripts* to do slow (artificially delayed) tasks, or jobs that require one script per avatar. This will usually require a "brain" script that instructs a set of subsidiary scripts what to do, so they can act in concert so that the brain isn't delayed while waiting for something to happen.

SUMMARY

CHAPTER 2
CHAPTER 3
CHAPTER 4
CHAPTER 5
CHAPTER 6
CHAPTER 7
CHAPTER 8
CHAPTER 9
CHAPTER 10
CHAPTER 11
CHAPTER 12
CHAPTER 13
CHAPTER 14
CHAPTER 15
APPENDICES

This chapter should have given you a good understanding of the LSL language and the basics of how to use it to manipulate *Second Life* functions. You should be aware that LSL is an evolving language; Linden Lab is fixing bugs and adding new capabilities all the time. That means you may run into something that isn't working the way you expect. Before it drives you up a tree, check the *Second Life* website of formal issues: `http://jira.secondlife.com`. The SYW website also has tips that can help get you out of a jam.

Most of the rest of this book is devoted to making effective use of LSL and the library to accomplish interesting things in *SL*. After you've absorbed some of the ideas elsewhere in the book, come back and re-read this chapter. Even for us, the authors, re-reading has been beneficial. We wrote this chapter, then spent several weeks doing heavy-duty scripting before the editors were ready for us to make a second pass on Chapter 1. Our re-read was enlightening, helping us understand certain things better or in a different way than we did when we first wrote the text. Take it from us: there are lots of things that will make much more sense on later perusal.

And now, on to the fun stuff!

CHAPTER 2

MAKING YOUR AVATAR STAND UP AND STAND OUT

Uniqueness is everything in *Second Life*. Appearance is part of that: clothing, gender, height, and species. So is action: nobody wants their avatar to look or act like anyone else's. Some of the major uses for *SL* scripting give avatars and content creators the mechanisms to control how avatars *behave*, and also to make radical alterations to avatar appearance that blend seamlessly with the basics *Second Life* provides to every user.

This chapter addresses some of the basics of making avatars look good in the world—from getting them to sit on objects so they don't look silly (with a side trip into teleportation), to letting avatars express themselves with controllable labels, to making them more visible in the dark. It also introduces some basic ways to add objects to your avatar that act like body parts that act in concert with whatever else the avatar is doing. Finally it introduces the basics of overriding *SL*'s standard avatar animations with those of your choosing.

▶ MOVING
YOUR AVATAR
AROUND THE
WORLD

ATTACHMENTS

ANIMATION

CONTROLLING
YOUR
ATTACHMENTS

SUMMARY

MOVING YOUR AVATAR AROUND THE WORLD

There are numerous options for helping your avatar move. Chapter 6, "Land Design and Management," has an example of a security screen that stops avatars from going where they are not wanted. You'll find vehicles and jet packs in Chapter 7, "Physics and Vehicles." On the SYW website, you'll find an in-depth project on controlling animations for dance. There are many, many options, but it all starts when an avatar sits down.

▶ SITTING

Sitting is one of several basic ways an avatar can interact with objects in **Second Life**. Apart from the obvious "sitting on a chair" sorts of actions, sitting is also how avatars can be moved (translated and rotated) directly under script control.

Sitting on a Dumb Plywood Box

What should the first script in a book on **Second Life** scripting be? The simplest one. But what is the simplest script? No script at all, of course. It may not be very interesting, but it is a great starting point.

Make a box. Sit on it. Exciting, isn't it? Turns out there **is** something interesting to say about it: you will always sit on an unscripted object on the upper edge of what was originally the eastern side of the object, as shown in Figure 2.1. Rotate the object around the z-axis, and the sit position will also rotate.

Figure 2.1: An unscripted box causes the avatar to sit oddly.

With some care, you can build an unscripted chair you look reasonable sitting on. The trick is to remember that the root prim's original rotation is what determines where and how an avatar sits on the object. You could, for example, use a very small prim to make the avatar appear to be sitting correctly. This approach, however, eats up your prim budget pretty quickly; especially given how easy it is to write a simple script, like the one in Listing 2.1, that controls where and how an avatar sits on a prim.

CHAPTER 1

CHAPTER 2

CHAPTER 3

CHAPTER 4

CHAPTER 5

CHAPTER 6

CHAPTER 7

CHAPTER 8

CHAPTER 9

CHAPTER 10

CHAPTER 11

CHAPTER 12

CHAPTER 13

CHAPTER 14

CHAPTER 15

APPENDICES

BUILD NOTE

Make a cube. Right-click on the cube, and notice that the pie menu offers a Sit Here option. Sit down, and notice where your avatar sits relative to the cube. Stand up.

Drop the code from Listing 2.1 into the object. (The prim that holds the code—in this case the cube—is called the *containing prim*.) In the object's Edit tab, open the Content folder, click New Script, double-click the new script that is created, and you will get the script you saw in the previous chapter in Listing 1.1. Delete all the text you see and replace it with the script in Listing 2.1. Click Save and wait until the compiler reports that the save has completed. If there are compiler errors, double-check that your script is *exactly* what is shown in Listing 2.1.

Right-click on the cube, and notice that the pie menu has changed. Sit down again, and notice how your avatar's position has changed. (If it didn't change, that's probably because you forgot to stand up.)

Listing 2.1: Simply Sitting

```
default {
    state_entry() {
        llSitTarget(<0,0,1>, ZERO_ROTATION);
        llSetSitText("Stay awhile");
    }
}
```

This script defines where the avatar should sit by specifying the location relative to the center of the prim holding the script, and the rotation to apply to the avatar. With this script's settings, the avatar will be seated unrotated and 1 meter above the center of the cube. All settings—location, rotation, and dynamics—are relative to the cube, meaning that if the cube rotates, the avatar also rotates and stays sitting in the same position, with orientation **relative to the cube**. Figure 2.2 illustrates this: Box 1 and the one behind it are plain unscripted boxes: a box like this looks fine if you are sitting squarely on it, but your avatar always sits somewhere on the top of the object. Box 2 is scripted with Listing 2.1. You can see that it gives you fine control of the avatar's location. Box 3 is spinning: since the position of the avatar stays constant relative to the orientation of the box, if the box changes then the avatar's position will change accordingly. Box 4's script specifies a different rotation for the sit target. Box 5 shows what happens if the sit position is really high: the avatar is about to hit the ground, having fallen 50 meters from box 5's sit target.

In addition, the script in Listing 2.1 changes the text displayed in the pie menu to be Stay Awhile instead of the default Sit Here.

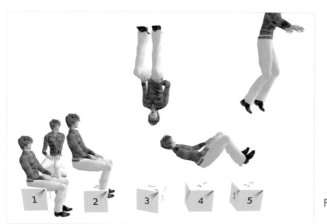

Figure 2.2: A seated progression

39

CHAPTER 2

Moving
Your Avatar
around the
World

Attachments

Animation

Controlling
Your
Attachments

Summary

DEFINITION

llSitTarget(vector *location*, rotation *rot*)

Sets the sit location relative to the containing prim. If the arguments passed are ZERO_VECTOR and ZERO_ROTATION, the sit target is canceled rather than set. A target must be set for the function llAvatarOnSitTarget() (discussed later in this chapter) to work correctly.

location — Offset of the sit target position from the center of the prim.

rot — Rotation of the avatar while seated at the location.

DEFINITION

llSetSitText(string *text*)

Sets the label on the sit action in the GUI pie chart.

text — Text used to label the sit action in the pie menu.

Both llSitTarget() and llSetSitText() are *persistent* features of the prim. That means that even if the script is deleted, the set text and target location remain in force until reset.

NOTE

You can use llSetTouchText(string *text*) in exactly the same way to change the label of the pie chart's touch action.

If an avatar is already sitting on the prim, the sit target doesn't do anything until the avatar stands up and sits again. The sit offset must be within 519m of the prim's center, with no axis more than 300m away. Also, an avatar must be close to the prim's location to sit directly; otherwise the avatar will attempt to walk or fly nearby before seating. When the avatar stands ("unsits"), they will do so from the current sit location, not from the prim center!

A small improvement to this script would be to use llGetPrimitiveParams() or llGetScale() to ask how big the prim is, and then calculate what the offset from the center needs to be, even if the prim is resized.

Sits and teleports are easy to build—you can pretty much drop these scripts into any sort of object you'd like. Sit scripts are very often put into "sit balls"—balls that are usually colored pink or blue to indicate that the seating is customized for female or male avatars.

CHAPTER 1

CHAPTER 2

CHAPTER 3
CHAPTER 4
CHAPTER 5
CHAPTER 6
CHAPTER 7
CHAPTER 8
CHAPTER 9
CHAPTER 10
CHAPTER 11
CHAPTER 12
CHAPTER 13
CHAPTER 14
CHAPTER 15
APPENDICES

◥ TELEPORTING

Teleporting is the act of moving from one place to another very quickly. It is the basis for many types of movement in **SL**, including movement of vehicles. Listing 2.2 is a simple teleport; you'll augment the script to go greater distances, improve the teleport speed, and, finally, turn one of **SL**'s limitations into a benefit, allowing you to cheat a little on the math!

Short-Distance Teleporter

In the previous section you saw that an avatar sits down relative to the center of the prim holding the script, and stands up at the sit target. You can use this same sit-displacement trick to teleport an avatar up to 519m away: you set the target position to your teleport location, then forcibly unsit the avatar at the destination.

You need to make two important changes to the basic sit script. The first is to figure out where the target position is relative to the prim's center. The second is to figure out when the avatar has arrived at the sit location so that you can unsit them.

Before testing this script, replace the DEST (destination) coordinates with something near the object so that you don't lose your avatar!

Listing 2.2: Teleport1—A Local Teleporter

```
vector DEST = <128,128,200>; // replace with nearby coordinates
default
{
    state_entry() {
        rotation primCurrentRotation = llGetRot();
        vector primCurrentPosn = llGetPos();
        vector targetOffsetPosn = DEST-primCurrentPosn;
        vector targetPosition = targetOffsetPosn/primCurrentRotation;
        rotation targetRotation = ZERO_ROTATION/primCurrentRotation;
        llSitTarget(targetPosition,targetRotation);
        llSetSitText("Teleport!");
    }
    changed(integer changebits) {
        if (changebits & CHANGED_LINK) {
            key av = llAvatarOnSitTarget();
            if (av != NULL_KEY) {
                llSleep(0.1);
                llUnSit(av);
            }
        }
    }
}
```

DEST is a destination target location that is relative to the sim, but sit targets must be relative to the prim. The first five lines of the `state_entry()` method convert DEST from sim-local to prim-local. `llGetRot()` calculates the rotation of the prim relative to the sim, while `llGetPos()` calculates the prim's location. The next line calculates the location of the target relative to the prim's current location:

```
vector targetOffsetPosn = DEST-primCurrentPosn;
```

Remember that it must be within 519m, with no one axis more than 300m away! The next two lines adjust for the fact that the prim might be rotated:

```
vector targetPosn = (DEST-targetOffsetPosn)/primCurrentRotation;
rotation targetRotation = ZERO_ROTATION/primCurrentRotation;
```

If you just moved the prim to *targetOffsetPosn* then the avatar could end up on any point on the sphere of that radius! Setting the target rotation to be the same as the prim's rotation is polite, but not strictly necessary. The underlying math is natively handled by quaternions: see the section called "Using Quaternions" in Chapter 4, "Making and Moving Objects," for more details.

 Moving
Your Avatar
around the
World

Attachments

Animation

Controlling
Your
Attachments

Summary

To figure out when the avatar has arrived at the sit location so that you can unsit them, the script relies on the changed() event. It is invoked under many conditions, including change of color, owner, or location. The argument *changebits* is a bit pattern that indicates exactly what has changed, but doesn't tell you *how* it changed; if you need to know the prior values, your script needs to get them from llGetPrimitiveParams() and cache those values. Because an avatar sitting on an object acts like an object being added to the linkset, we first check to see if the CHANGED_LINK bit is set in the pattern, using the bitwise "and" operator, &.

 EVENT DEFINITION

changed(integer *changebits*) { }

This event is invoked whenever the prim changes in one of several ways, including whether links have changed or an avatar has sat on the prim. Additional documentation about event handlers can be found at the SYW website.

changebits — The bit pattern describing what has changed in the prim.

The bits can be tested using the bitwise arithmetic, as shown in the following snippet:

```
if (changebits & CHANGED_LINK) {
    llOwnerSay("Object changed number of links");
}
```

The script then checks to see whether an avatar is actually sitting on the object using the function llAvatarOnSitTarget(), which returns the key of the avatar sitting on the prim, or NULL_KEY if nobody is sitting. Note that it will also return NULL_KEY if a sit-target position is not specified. If an avatar is seated, the script infers that it is the one that just sat. To finish the teleport, the script pauses for a moment using llSleep(float *time*) to make sure the sim has repositioned the agent, and then the script ejects the seated avatar.

 DEFINITION

key llAvatarOnSitTarget()

Returns a key that is the UUID of the user seated on the prim. If the prim lacks a sit target or there is no avatar sitting on the prim, then NULL_KEY is returned. If the sit target position has not been explicitly set or if the script called llSitTarget(ZERO_VECTOR, ZERO_ROTATION), then llAvatarOnSitTarget() will return NULL_KEY.

DEFINITION

`llUnSit(key id)`

If the agent identified by *id* is sitting on the object the script is attached to, or is over land owned by the object's owner, the agent is forced to stand up.

CHAPTER 1

CHAPTER 2

CHAPTER 3
CHAPTER 4
CHAPTER 5
CHAPTER 6
CHAPTER 7
CHAPTER 8
CHAPTER 9
CHAPTER 10
CHAPTER 11
CHAPTER 12
CHAPTER 13
CHAPTER 14
CHAPTER 15
APPENDICES

Medium-Distance Teleporter

But what if you want to teleport the sitter farther than 519m, or, more likely, more than 300m along one axis (say, straight up to your skybox)? The simplest option is to move the object while the avatar is seated, unseat the avatar at the destination, and return to the original location. The function `llSetPos()` will move the prim.

DEFINITION

`llSetPos(vector newLoc)`

Sets the position of the prim, up to a maximum of 10m away.

> *newLoc* — Target location. *newLoc* can be interpreted three ways, and is thus very confusing.

> Essentially, *newLoc* is interpreted relative to whatever the prim is attached to:

> - If the containing prim is attached to the sim (it is a root prim not attached to an avatar), *newLoc* is the region coordinates.
> - If the containing prim is attached to an avatar (it is a root prim attached to an avatar), *newLoc* is relative to the attachment point on the avatar.
> - If the prim is a child in a linked object, *newLoc* is relative to the root prim.

Unfortunately, it's not as straightforward as saying `llSetPos(`*destination*`)`: the complication is that an object may move a maximum of 10m at a time. Thus the script in Listing 2.3 takes the distance from the prim's original location to the target location, and divides it into 10m steps. However, repeated calls to `llSetPos()` reveal an unfortunate side effect: each call causes the script to pause (artificially) for 0.2 seconds, leading to a maximum effective "teleport speed" of 50 m/s. (Use `llSetPos()`, and a small value for *jumpdist*, if you want a slow teleport—for example, if you're making an elevator.)

The script in Listing 2.3 completes the teleport with a single 0.2-second delay by using the function `llSetPrimitiveParams()`. It takes advantage of the fact that you can supply a list of repeated `PRIM_POSITION` tuples (an ordered list of values); `llSetPrimitiveParams()` can move the prim to the destination in 0.2 seconds regardless of the distance.

CHAPTER 2

Moving
Your Avatar
around the
World

Attachments

Animation

Controlling
Your
Attachments

Summary

Listing 2.3: Teleport2—Intrasim Teleports

```
// this script must be in the root prim (or the only prim) to work

vector DEST = <128,128,200>; // the teleport will be to this location
vector SITPOS = <0,0,0.5>;

moveTo(vector origin, vector destination, float jumpdist) {
    vector relativeDestination = destination—origin;
    float dist = llVecMag(relativeDestination);
    if (jumpdist > 10.0) jumpdist = 10.0;
    integer steps = llCeil(dist / jumpdist) + 1;
    vector distanceVector = relativeDestination / steps;
    integer i;
    vector currPosition = origin;
    list params = [];
    for (i=0; i<steps; i++) {
        currPosition += distanceVector;
        params += [PRIM_POSITION, currPos];
    }
    llSetPrimitiveParams(params); // actually move the prim
}
teleport(key av) {
    vector origin = llGetPos();
    moveTo(origin, DEST, 10.0);
    // no need to sleep -- llSetPrimParams has 0.2s delay
    llUnSit(av);
    moveTo(DEST, origin, 10.0);
}
default
{
    state_entry() {
        llSitTarget(SITPOS, ZERO_ROTATION);
        llSetSitText("Teleport!");
    }
    changed(integer changebits) {
        if (changebits & CHANGED_LINK) {
            key av = llAvatarOnSitTarget();
            if (av != NULL_KEY) {
                teleport(av);
            }
        }
    }
}
```

Quicker Intrasim Teleport

A popular optimization of this technique makes use of the fact that if you try to move an object by more than 10m, the effect will be to move it exactly 10m toward the target. This means you can avoid computing all of the intermediate steps, and instead use the same [PRIM_POSITION, *dest*] expression for every tuple in the list. It also allows you to build up the list of teleportation steps much more quickly by doubling the list each time instead of inserting one element at a time, as shown in Listing 2.4.

Listing 2.4: Teleport3—Optimized Intrasim Teleport

```
moveTo(vector origin, vector destination ) { // removed jumpdist
    float dist = llVecDist(origin, destination);
    integer passes = llCeil( llLog(dist/10.0) / llLog(2.0) );
    integer i;
    list params = [PRIM_POSITION, destination];
    for (i=0; i<passes; i++) {
        params = (params=[]) + params + params;
    }
    llSetPrimitiveParams(params);
}
```

We construct the **params** list by doubling it each time through the loop. The local variable **passes** is set to the smallest whole number exponent of 2 that can be used to divide the distance to be covered into chunks of less than 10m; i.e., $2^{passes} > (dist \div 10.0)$.

NOTE

The odd-looking extra (params=[]) in Listing 2.4 is a trick to get the LSL compiler to save a significant amount of memory when manipulating large lists. The most robust version of this technique can be found on the LSL wiki as LibraryWarpPos.

Intersim Teleporter

As of the writing of this book, you cannot teleport across sim boundaries as easily as you can within a sim. One of your options is to have your object give the avatar a landmark to the destination point (as shown in Chapter 8, "Inventory"). While it isn't a teleport, it is simple to program. Another option is to expose a map of the destination point using `llMapDestination()` when your teleporter object is touched, as shown in Listing 2.5.

DEFINITION

`llMapDestination(string simname, vector position, vector lookat)`

Exposes a map showing the specified point. This works only within one of the three `touch()` events.

    simname — The name of the destination sim.

    position — The position of your destination in the named sim.

    lookat — A point within the sim that the map should indicate is being looked at; currently ignored.

Listing 2.5: Teleport4—Intersim Teleport Assistant

```
string SIM = "Hennepin";
vector LOC = <46,144,107>;  // LM for Scripting Your World
default {
    touch_start(integer n) {
        llMapDestination(SIM, LOC, ZERO_VECTOR); // 3rd param ignored
    }
}
```

CHAPTER 1
CHAPTER 2
CHAPTER 3
CHAPTER 4
CHAPTER 5
CHAPTER 6
CHAPTER 7
CHAPTER 8
CHAPTER 9
CHAPTER 10
CHAPTER 11
CHAPTER 12
CHAPTER 13
CHAPTER 14
CHAPTER 15
APPENDICES

☑ Moving
Your Avatar
around the
World

☑ Attachments

Animation

Controlling
Your
Attachments

Summary

It is possible to use the prim-movement techniques to cross sim boundaries if enough care is taken. However, sim crossings are perilous, and thus we suggest you wait to try it until you are an expert scripter.

ATTACHMENTS

An attachment is an object made from one or more prims that you wear on your avatar. Many clothes are attachments, as are most accessories, such as handbags, hats, and earrings. Even some body parts, like hair, can be attached to your avatar. Wherever you go, your attachments go with you. There are many places you can attach something—about 30 different places on your avatar's body, and also eight heads-up display (HUD) locations. A HUD is like a controller board that appears only to you—other residents won't see it. (The SYW website has a section on bowling; it presents a HUD that controls the fine-grained direction of the bowling ball.)

Every object in your inventory can be attached. Most people try to make sure the attachment location makes sense aesthetically: a skirt on the pelvis and a hat on the head, for example. (Note, however, that a hat might actually be attached to the chin or the nose, allowing something else, like hair, to be attached to the head.) Attachments can even be made invisible—really useful for attachments that do something but don't need to be seen, such as flip tags (discussed in the "Flip Tag" section of this chapter).

Full avatar building is beyond the scope of this book but we can give you a taste of what is possible. Human avatars generally have their shapes changed with a combination of basic appearance controls, the wearing of layers of clothing (including the skin layer), and prim-based add-ons like clothing or prim hair. Human prim clothing and body parts are rarely heavily scripted; normally they're limited to customization (for instance, coloring hair). Sexual body parts are the notable exception. For an example of a scripted item of clothing, see the "Dialogs" section of Chapter 3, "Communications."

You can also extend prim clothing to seemingly change the shape of avatar bodies, surrounding the "natural" body parts with differently shaped parts and adding totally new parts, as shown with the Frog Prince in Figure 2.3. This costume is available for free at enkythings, Orbiuna <200, 96, 351>.

Figure 2.3: The Frog Prince is constructed by creating body parts that surround the standard avatar body.

The rest of this section describes attachments that are fun to add to your avatar: a descriptive tag, a face light, and a key for a wind-up toy. (Additionally, the SYW website has a discussion of auto-deploying wings.) This section also shows how to figure out whether an object is attached, and how to automatically attach it where it belongs.

CHAPTER 2
CHAPTER 3
CHAPTER 4
CHAPTER 5
CHAPTER 6
CHAPTER 7
CHAPTER 8
CHAPTER 9
CHAPTER 10
CHAPTER 11
CHAPTER 12
CHAPTER 13
CHAPTER 14
CHAPTER 15
APPENDICES

❯ FLIP TAG

Flip tags are very common avatar attachments that allow you to express yourself more persistently than chat, but more dynamically than group membership. They are essentially invisible (or hidden) objects with a script that translates chatted commands so that they set the object's "floating text" property, as shown in Figure 2.4. Listing 2.6 shows a simple flip tag.

Figure 2.4: This avatar is wearing an object that announces he is fully scripted!

Listing 2.6: Flip Tag—Label Yourself

```
default
{
    on_rez(integer start_param) {
        llResetScript();
    }
    state_entry() {
        llListen(9, "", llGetOwner(), "");
    }
    listen(integer channel, string name, key id, string message) {
        llSetText(message, <1,1,1>, 1.0);
    }
}
```

BUILD NOTE

There are several places you can add the script from Listing 2.6. You can add it to an object you are already wearing, such as your hair or glasses. You can create an object to hold it, and then wear the object on an attachment point, such as your nose or ear, and then move it into the place you want. You probably will want to make the prim invisible using a full alpha texture once you like the position, as wearing a plywood box on your head isn't the most aesthetic of fashion statements. (Use Ctrl+Alt+T to keep seeing it.) You can also wear it on a HUD point, but as with all HUD objects, you'll be the only one who can see it.

Moving
Your Avatar
around the
World

 Attachments

Animation

Controlling
Your
Attachments

Summary

This script listens for commands typed by the owner and displays them as visible text. To use the script, chat **/9Hello World!** when wearing your flip tag. The **9** specifies which channel to chat on. `llListen()` sets up a listener event, `listen()`, that is called every time a chatted message passes the filters specified in `llListen()`. This script ensures that the listener pays attention to only channel number 9, and only when messages come from the owner of the containing object by specifying `llGetOwner()`. Chapter 3 describes the `llListen()` family of functions in more detail.

DEFINITION

> `key llGetOwner()`

Returns the key of the owner of the scripted object.

This script's `listen()` event handler sets the prim's floating text using `llSetText()`. Note that since the `llListen()` call listens only to the owner, there is no need to check whether the source of the chat is the right person. If the `llListen()` call specified `NULL_KEY` instead of `llGetOwner()`, the `listen()` event handler would accept changes from anyone chatting nearby on channel 9. Floating text is a persistent feature of the prim, in that it will stick even if the script is deleted or ownership is transferred. Just as for the sit target and sit text, it needs to be explicitly removed from the object.

DEFINITION

> `llSetText(string text, vector color, float alpha)`

Sets the floating text associated with the enclosing prim. This is a persistent feature of the prim.

> `text` — The text for the prim, or `" "` to turn it off. New lines are OK, but lines must contain at least one character (e.g., a space) and the total must be less than 256 characters.

> `color` — The color with which to display the text.

> `alpha` — The alpha for the displayed text (0.0 = transparent, 1.0 = opaque).

A common enhancement to the flip-text script is to allow the owner to change the text display color. You will find this augmented listing at SYW HQ; Listing 2.7 uses a similar mechanism to parse the user's command.

FACE LIGHT

Second Life environments can get very dark, and while darkness can be beautiful, scary, or romantic, it's often annoying when it is so dark that avatars cannot recognize each other's faces, as shown in Figure 2.5. A favorite remedy is a face light—a gadget you can have your avatar wear that illuminates their face with light from an invisible source. The required code is shown in Listing 2.7.

CHAPTER 1

CHAPTER 2

CHAPTER 3
CHAPTER 4
CHAPTER 5
CHAPTER 6
CHAPTER 7
CHAPTER 8
CHAPTER 9
CHAPTER 10
CHAPTER 11
CHAPTER 12
CHAPTER 13
CHAPTER 14
CHAPTER 15
APPENDICES

Figure 2.5: Face lighting makes it much easier to see avatars in the dark.

Listing 2.7: Face Light—Illuminate Me

```
vector gColor = <1,1,1>;
integer gLightOn = FALSE;

lightControl()
{
    llSetPrimitiveParams([PRIM_COLOR, ALL_SIDES, <0,0,0>, 0.0,
                          PRIM_POINT_LIGHT, gLightOn, gColor, 1.0, 10.0, 0.75]);
}

vector parseColor(string text) {
    list rgb = llParseString2List(text, [","," ","<",">"], []);
    vector color256 = <llList2Integer(rgb,0),
                       llList2Integer(rgb,1),
                       llList2Integer(rgb,2)>;
    return color256/255.0;
}

default
{
    on_rez(integer start_param) {
        llResetScript();
    }
    state_entry() {
        llListen(9, "", llGetOwner(), "");
        gLightOn = FALSE;
        lightControl();
    }
    listen(integer channel, string name, key id, string message) {
        if (llGetSubString(message, 0, 0)=="=") {
            gColor = parseColor(llGetSubString(message,1,-1));
        } else {
            if (message == "on") {
                gLightOn = TRUE;
            } else if (message == "off") {
                gLightOn = FALSE;
            }
        }
        lightControl();
    }
}
```

CHAPTER 2

MOVING
YOUR AVATAR
AROUND THE
WORLD

 ATTACHMENTS

ANIMATION

CONTROLLING
YOUR
ATTACHMENTS

SUMMARY

All the `listen()` components and color parsing are the same as in the flip-tag code. The script interprets the message as either a color (this time, to be used as the color of the projected light), or as an `"on"` or `"off"` command. If it sees a color specification it parses the color as in the flip tag; otherwise it updates the state. Then the script updates the light effect by invoking the new function `lightControl()`.

The `lightControl()` function invokes a new mechanism of the `llSetPrimitiveParams()` function, `PRIM_POINT_LIGHT`:

```
llSetPrimitiveParams([PRIM_POINT_LIGHT,
                gLightOn, // Boolean, TRUE means turn light on
                gColor,   // light color vector
                1.0,      // intensity (0.0-1.0)
                10.0,     // radius (0.1 - 10.0)
                0.75]);   // falloff (0.01 - 2.0)
```

`PRIM_POINT_LIGHT` is described in more detail in the "Lights" section of Chapter 9, "Special Effects." Appendix A, "Setting Primitive Parameters," describes all the prim properties you can set using `llSetPrimitiveParams()`. You will want to play with the intensity, radius, and falloff values to find the most pleasing effect for your situation.

 BUILD NOTE

 The simplest way to build a face light is to rez a plain box and drop in the code from Listing 2.7. Wear the box on the attachment point you'd like (such as the nose), then edit the box while you are wearing it, moving it to about a meter in front of your face. Change the size to be a 1cm cube. The script automatically makes the box transparent in `lightControl()` by setting the `PRIM_COLOR` attribute to a 0.0 alpha.

WIND ME UP!

Listing 2.8 animates a key that sticks out of the back of an avatar like a wind-up toy, as shown in Figure 2.6. This script has two pieces: it spins the key according to simple rules, and it allows other avatars to wind you up, altering the parameters of the spinning key to make it spin faster.

Figure 2.6: Wind me up and let me go.

Listing 2.8: Wind Me Up!

```
// rotate around (original) z axis (this is a direction!)
vector SPINAXIS = <0,0,1>;

float MAXRATE = 10.0;      // maximum spin rate—radians/sec
float DECAYTIME = 10.0;    // seconds to wake between slowing down
float DECAYLEVEL = 0.8;    // each decay cuts the speed by this much
float WINDLEVEL = 2.0;     // how much does each wind add

float gSpin = MAXRATE;     // how fast are we currently spinning?
float gMinSpin = 0.1;      // keep spinning a little when wound down

spin() {
    llTargetOmega(SPINAXIS, gSpin, 1.0);
}

default {
    // no on_rez—we want to maintain spins level across rezzes
    state_entry() {
        spin();
        llSetTimerEvent(DECAYTIME);
    }
    timer() {
        gSpin *= DECAYLEVEL;
        if (gSpin<gMinSpin) gSpin = gMinSpin;
        spin();
    }
    touch_end(integer count) {
        integer i;
        for (i=0; i<count; i++) {
            key winderKey = llDetectedKey(i);
            if (winderKey != llGetOwner()) {
                string winder = llDetectedName(i);
                llWhisper(0, winder+" has wound you");
                gSpin += WINDLEVEL;
            }
        }
        if (gSpin>MAXRATE) gSpin = MAXRATE;
        spin();
    }
}
```

BUILD NOTE

To use the script in Listing 2.8, the simplest thing to do is create a box sized x=0.01, y=1.0, z=1.0. Turn it into a triangle with a lot of y taper. Drop the script into the box's inventory, and then wear it on your spine. (You can attach items to the spine using the GUI, but, as noted later, you can't do it via scripting because there's no ATTACH_SPINE constant.) You can adjust the size and position while you're wearing it. If you've got a convenient key texture, make the (square) box transparent using a full-alpha texture (i.e., completely transparent), and then apply a texture that looks like a clock key to the large faces—the point that would enter the clock should be down and the handle should be up.

To actually spin the object, the script uses the llTargetOmega() function described in Chapter 4. It spins an object around the axis vector that runs through its center. This script specifies a vector that points straight up (<0, 0, 1>). Why, you ask, since it is going to be spinning around and pointing behind you (not upward)? Because when it is attached to your avatar's spine, its frame of reference will have been

CHAPTER 1
CHAPTER 2
CHAPTER 3
CHAPTER 4
CHAPTER 5
CHAPTER 6
CHAPTER 7
CHAPTER 8
CHAPTER 9
CHAPTER 10
CHAPTER 11
CHAPTER 12
CHAPTER 13
CHAPTER 14
CHAPTER 15
APPENDICES

CHAPTER 2

Moving
Your Avatar
around the
World

Attachments

Animation

Controlling
Your
Attachments

Summary

rotated so that its "local up" is sticking straight behind you. Perhaps a little confusing, but the important thing is consistency. This script never has to worry about which direction the avatar is facing—all it ever has to do is spin around the z-axis. Making sure the axis is normalized (that is, its length is 1.0) is good practice. If it is normalized, the rate parameter is how quickly the object will turn in radians per second. For now the important thing about the third parameter is that it not be 0; otherwise the rate at which the key spins won't ever change.

The script sets a maximum and minimum spin rate, and sets a timer to make the spin rate decay slowly. Each time the `timer()` event fires, the script updates the spin rate to the slow decay.

The last part of this script makes the attachment more fun and social: only a different avatar can wind your key. It uses the `touch_end()` event handler to capture when avatars finish touching the wind-up key. Note that `touch()` and `touch_start()` are similar event handlers.

EVENT DEFINITION

```
touch_start(integer numDetected) { }
```

```
touch(integer numDetected) { }
```

```
touch_end(integer numDetected) { }
```

These events are invoked when the user touches an object. `touch_start()` is used once at the start of a touch, `touch()` is called repeatedly during a touch, and `touch_end()` is called when the touch is over. The SYW website provides additional documentation on event handlers.

numDetected — The number of detected touch events.

The `touch_end()` event handler follows all sensor-event patterns: *any number* of similar events can be bundled into a single invocation of an event handler. This is indicated when the parameter *count* is greater than 1. To find the different event sources (in this case, who touched our key), you can call the `llDetectedKey()` function with the zero-based index of the object you are interested in. Table 2.1 shows a list of similar functions and their behaviors. Since this script cares both about *how many times* the key is wound and *who* is winding the key, it loops over the keys of all detected touchers, each time increasing the spin rate and telling anyone nearby about it. Finally, the script makes certain it hasn't been overwound and updates the spin rate.

TABLE 2.1: FUNCTIONS THAT DESCRIBE DETECTED OBJECTS

Function	Behavior
`key llDetectedKey(integer number)`	Returns the UUID of the detected object.
`string llDetectedName(integer number)`	Returns the name of the detected object.
`vector llDetectedPos(integer number)`	Returns the position of the detected object.
`rotation llDetectedRot(integer number)`	Returns the rotation of the detected object.
`vector llDetectedVel(integer number)`	Returns the velocity of the detected object.
`key llDetectedOwner(integer number)`	Returns the object owner's UUID.
`integer llDetectedGroup(integer number)`	Returns a Boolean value representing if the detected object or avatar is in the same group that the prim containing the script is set to.
`key llDetectedCreator(integer number)`	Returns the object creator's UUID.

Function	Behavior
vector llDetectedGrab(integer *number*)	Returns the grab offset of the user touching the object; that is, where the user is compared to the object.
integer llDetectedType(integer *number*)	Returns a bitmask that indicates the types of detected object: **AGENT** for an avatar, **ACTIVE**, **PASSIVE**, and/or **SCRIPTED** for objects. (See Chapter 10, "Scripting the Environment," for more details.)
integer llDetectedLinkNumber(integer *number*)	Returns the link number of the prim that triggered a touch or collision event. (See Chapters 3 and 10 for more details.)

CHAPTER 1

CHAPTER 2

CHAPTER 3
CHAPTER 4
CHAPTER 5
CHAPTER 6
CHAPTER 7
CHAPTER 8
CHAPTER 9
CHAPTER 10
CHAPTER 11
CHAPTER 12
CHAPTER 13
CHAPTER 14
CHAPTER 15
APPENDICES

DISCOVERING WHETHER OBJECTS ARE ATTACHED

You can find out whether an object is attached by using the function llGetAttached(). This function is very useful for changing the behavior of an object—for example, if the face light is attached the object becomes invisible, but when it is rezzed to the world it makes itself visible. The bowling project on the SYW website shows several additional examples.

 DEFINITION

integer llGetAttached()

Returns an integer identifying where the object is attached, or 0 if it is not attached. There are 36 possible values, including all the avatar body parts and HUD locations. (Values 29 and 30 correspond to the left and right pectorals, respectively, but their constants should not be used, see JIRA bug SVC-580. The is also no ATTACH_SPINE constant.) LSL is still evolving, and it's peppered with such small oddities.) The following table shows the constants and their associated values.

Constant	Value		Constant	Value
ATTACH_CHEST	1		ATTACH_RLARM	19
ATTACH_HEAD	2		ATTACH_LUARM	20
ATTACH_LSHOULDER	3		ATTACH_LLARM	21
ATTACH_RSHOULDER	4		ATTACH_RHIP	22
ATTACH_LHAND	5		ATTACH_RULEG	23
ATTACH_RHAND	6		ATTACH_RLLEG	24
ATTACH_LFOOT	7		ATTACH_LHIP	25
ATTACH_RFOOT	8		ATTACH_LULEG	26
ATTACH_BACK	9		ATTACH_LLLEG	27
ATTACH_PELVIS	10		ATTACH_BELLY	28
ATTACH_MOUTH	11		ATTACH_HUD_CENTER_2	31
ATTACH_CHIN	12		ATTACH_HUD_TOP_RIGHT	32
ATTACH_LEAR	13		ATTACH_HUD_TOP_CENTER	33
ATTACH_REAR	14		ATTACH_HUD_TOP_LEFT	34
ATTACH_LEYE	15		ATTACH_HUD_CENTER_1	35
ATTACH_REYE	16		ATTACH_HUD_BOTTOM_LEFT	36
ATTACH_NOSE	17		ATTACH_HUD_BOTTOM	37
ATTACH_RUARM	18		ATTACH_HUD_BOTTOM_RIGHT	38

CHAPTER 2

MOVING
YOUR AVATAR
AROUND THE
WORLD

 ATTACHMENTS

ANIMATION

CONTROLLING
YOUR
ATTACHMENTS

SUMMARY

Listing 2.9 uses `llGetAttached()` to detect whether the face light is attached, and if not, to attach the face light to the avatar's chin using `llAttachToAvatar()`.

Listing 2.9: Self-Attaching Face Light

```
// This script extends Listing 2.7 with the following code:
default
{
    state_entry() {
        llListen(9, "", llGetOwner(), "");
        gLightOn = FALSE;
        lightControl();
        if (llGetAttached() == 0) {
            llRequestPermissions(llGetOwner(), PERMISSION_ATTACH);
        }
    }
    run_time_permissions( integer perms ) {
        if (perms & PERMISSION_ATTACH) {
            llAttachToAvatar(ATTACH_CHIN);
        }
    }
}
```

DEFINITION

`llAttachToAvatar(integer attachPoint)`

Attaches the object to the owner after the owner has granted `PERMISSION_ATTACH` to the script. The object is taken into the user's inventory and attached to the specified attach point.

> `attachPoint` — Indicates the attachment point using one of the `ATTACH_*` constants or a valid integer value.

DEFINITION

`llDetachFromAvatar()`

Detaches the object from the avatar and places the object in inventory. There is no way to place the object down in-world, for example on the ground.

Knowing the value of a named constant can be useful. (The values for all LSL constants are shown on the SYW website.) For example, you can use the following test to have your script determine whether the object is attached as a HUD:

```
if (llGetAttached() >= 31) {
    // then the object is attached as a HUD
}
```

However, it is best not to rely heavily on the actual values because LSL may change—what might your code do if Linden Lab were to add another `ATTACH` constant, say `ATTACH_SPINE`, with a value of 39? Another consideration is that code using the *names* of constants is far easier to read than code using their *values*.

When an object attaches or detaches, the `attach()` event handler is triggered. The script will have very little time to execute after the user has detached the object. You can augment the script in Listing 2.9 with the following snippet:

```
attach( key id ) {
    if (id == NULL_KEY) {
        llOwnerSay("Detached; Returning to inventory.");
    } else {
        llOwnerSay("Successfully attached.");
    }
}
```

  EVENT DEFINITION

`attach(key id) { }`

This event is invoked when an object attaches or detaches from an avatar. The SYW website provides additional documentation.

> *id* — The UUID of the avatar the object was attached to. If *id* is NULL_KEY, the object was detached and the script will exit shortly because the object is being returned to inventory. *id* will be forgotten if `llResetScript()` is called.

Attaching and detaching objects requires the owner to grant `PERMISSION_ATTACH`. You request these permissions using the `llRequestPermissions()` function. The event `run_time_permissions()` is triggered when permissions are granted.

Once granted, a script retains permissions until they are released (when different permissions are requested or when the object is returned to inventory, for instance). If you ask for permissions that have already been granted to the script, the agent is not asked again and the `run_time_permissions()` event is triggered immediately. Also note that script permissions are not additive (additional requests replace any existing permissions granted) and a script may have permissions granted to only one avatar at a time.

 NOTE

Some permissions are implicitly granted (that is, without a dialog) when the avatar sits down or wears an attachment. If you know that permissions are implicit, you can take advantage of that fact to make your code slightly more efficient. Chapter 7 shows an example of this idea in Listing 7.6.

CHAPTER 1
CHAPTER 2
CHAPTER 3
CHAPTER 4
CHAPTER 5
CHAPTER 6
CHAPTER 7
CHAPTER 8
CHAPTER 9
CHAPTER 10
CHAPTER 11
CHAPTER 12
CHAPTER 13
CHAPTER 14
CHAPTER 15
APPENDICES

CHAPTER 2

MOVING
YOUR AVATAR
AROUND THE
WORLD

ATTACHMENTS

ANIMATION

CONTROLLING
YOUR
ATTACHMENTS

SUMMARY

DEFINITION

`llRequestPermissions(key avatarId, integer permissionsRequested)`

Asynchronously requests permissions. A `run_time_permissions()` event will be triggered when the permissions are granted. Nothing is generated if the user refuses to grant permissions.

  avatarId — The avatar to get permissions from.

  permissionsRequested — A bit pattern (also called a bitfield) indicating the permissions being requested. The following table shows the permissions that can be requested.

CONSTANT	VALUE	BEHAVIOR	GRANTED BY
PERMISSION_DEBIT	0x002	Take money from agent's account.	Owner
PERMISSION_TAKE_CONTROLS	0x004	Take avatar's controls.	Anyone
PERMISSION_TRIGGER_ANIMATION	0x010	Trigger animation on avatar.	Anyone
PERMISSION_ATTACH	0x020	Attach/detach from avatar.	Owner
PERMISSION_CHANGE_LINKS	0x080	Change links.	Owner
PERMISSION_TRACK_CAMERA	0x400	Track avatar's camera position and rotation.	Anyone
PERMISSION_CONTROL_CAMERA	0x800	Control avatar's camera.	Anyone

EVENT DEFINITION

`run_time_permissions(integer permissionsGranted)`

This event is invoked when the script is granted permissions. There is no event for when the avatar refuses to grant permissions. The SYW website provides additional documentation.

  permissionsGranted — A bitmask of the permissions that were granted.

Two other useful permissions functions are `llGetPermissions()`, which tells the script which permissions have been granted—identical to the parameter for `run_time_permissions()`—and `llGetPermissionsKey()`, which indicates who granted the permissions.

CHAPTER 1

CHAPTER 2

CHAPTER 3
CHAPTER 4
CHAPTER 5
CHAPTER 6
CHAPTER 7
CHAPTER 8
CHAPTER 9
CHAPTER 10
CHAPTER 11
CHAPTER 12
CHAPTER 13
CHAPTER 14
CHAPTER 15
APPENDICES

 DEFINITION

```
integer llGetPermissions()
```

Returns an integer bit pattern with the permissions the script has been granted. Permissions can be tested with a bitwise "and" operator (&), as shown in the following snippet:

```
integer grantedPerms = llGetPermissions();
if (grantedPerms & PERMISSION_TAKE_CONTROLS) {
    llOwnerSay("Script has permission to take controls.");
}
```

DEFINITION

```
key llGetPermissionsKey()
```

Returns the key of the avatar that granted permissions.

ANIMATION

An animation is a set of instructions that cause an avatar to engage in a sequence of motions. An animation describes the way your avatar walks, dances, waves hello, or even sits down. One of the first things that people notice when they start out in *Second Life* is how awkward and artificial the default avatar animations look. So early in an avatar's life, people want to upgrade by adding an animation override, or AO, that replaces the default settings with higher-quality, more realistic, or special-purpose animations.

 NOTE

You can create your own custom animations with tools such as Poser (http://graphics. smithmicro.com/go/poser) and Blender (www.blender.org), and then upload them into *SL*. Additionally, many high-quality animations are available in-world, many of them for free. Search for Animation in the All tab of the search window. Many people purchase a set of animators that have been packaged in a wearable attachment with an AO script, ready to go.

CHAPTER 2

MOVING
YOUR AVATAR
AROUND THE
WORLD

ATTACHMENTS

ANIMATION

CONTROLLING
YOUR
ATTACHMENTS

SUMMARY

ANIMATION OVERRIDES

The various AO scripts differ in relatively minor ways, but the basic idea is always the same: to watch what your avatar is doing, and override the default animation with one of your choice. Listing 2.10 replaces the default walking animation with a floating crossed-leg pose; this is possibly the simplest AO script. It may look pretty complicated, but we'll walk through the pieces slowly. Place the script in any attachment, such as a bracelet or a transparent hat. Most of the complexity comes from setting up permissions to animate the avatar—extending the methods shown in Listing 2.10—and that is functionality you will use in a lot of places.

Listing 2.10: WalkAO—Why Walk When You Can Float?

```
// the animation we're going to override
string AN_TRIGGER = "Walking";
// which animation are we overriding walking with?
string AN_OVERRIDE = "yoga_float";
integer gOverriding = FALSE;  // are we running the override right now?
integer gHasPermission = FALSE; // did we get permission yet?
integer gEnabled = TRUE;        // is the AO on?

animOverride() {
    if (gHasPermission) {
        string  curAnimState = llGetAnimation(llGetOwner());
        if (curAnimState == AN_TRIGGER && gEnabled) {
            if (!gOverriding) { // already overriding? skip
                gOverriding = TRUE;
                llStartAnimation(AN_OVERRIDE);
            }
        } else {
            if (gOverriding) {
                llStopAnimation(AN_OVERRIDE);
                gOverriding = FALSE;
            }
        }
    }
}

default {
    on_rez( integer _code ) {
        llResetScript();
    }
    state_entry() {
        gOverriding = FALSE;
        gHasPermission = FALSE;
        gEnabled = TRUE;
        if ( llGetAttached() ) {
            llRequestPermissions(llGetOwner(),
                        PERMISSION_TRIGGER_ANIMATION|
                        PERMISSION_TAKE_CONTROLS);
        }
        llSetTimerEvent(1.0);
```

```
    }
    run_time_permissions(integer parm) {
        if( parm == (PERMISSION_TRIGGER_ANIMATION|
                        PERMISSION_TAKE_CONTROLS) ) {
            llTakeControls(CONTROL_DOWN|CONTROL_UP|
                            CONTROL_FWD|CONTROL_BACK|
                            CONTROL_LEFT|CONTROL_RIGHT|
                            CONTROL_ROT_LEFT|CONTROL_ROT_RIGHT,
                        TRUE, TRUE);
            gHasPermission = TRUE;
        }
    }
    attach( key k ) {
        if ( k != NULL_KEY ) {
            llRequestPermissions(llGetOwner(),
                PERMISSION_TRIGGER_ANIMATION|PERMISSION_TAKE_CONTROLS);
        }
    }
    control( key _id, integer _level, integer _edge ) {
        animOverride();
    }

    timer() {
        animOverride();
    }
}
```

NOTE

Several of the scripts in this book have function or event handler parameters that begin with an underscore (_). This naming convention is sometimes used to indicate parameters that will not be used by the function.

AN_TRIGGER names the posture the script is going to animate: there are 21 standard *SL* postures that describe the sort of basic activity an avatar can be performing at a given time—examples include `"Walking"` (used in this script), `"Sitting"`, and `"Flying"`. The wiki page on llGetAnimation has a complete, current list.

AN_OVERRIDE names the animation the script will play when the avatar is detected to be in the chosen posture. This may be the name of a built-in animation or the name of an animation in the prim's inventory. For simplicity's sake, this script uses the built-in `"yoga_float"` animation (Figure 2.7). Note that some animations stop after they run and others loop and have to be stopped explicitly. For AO use, you probably want to use looping animations so that you don't have to guess when they naturally end.

Before you can control an avatar's animation, you need to request permissions to do so using `llRequestPermissions()`. This AO script begins by requesting two permissions: PERMISSION_TRIGGER_ANIMATION to let us control the animation of the owning avatar and PERMISSION_TAKE_CONTROLS to watch the keyboard controls of the user.

When the avatar responds to the permissions request, the script makes sure the required set was granted and then "takes controls" to watch the user interface (keys), using the `llTakeControls()` function. For each control the script is watching, a corresponding `control()` event is triggered every time the key is touched. Listing 7.6 in Chapter 7 describes `llTakeControls()` and `control()` in more detail; for now this script uses this mechanism to watch the "standard" six directions (up, down, left, right, forward and backward) brought together with bitwise "or" operators, indicated by the pipe symbol (|).

Moving
Your Avatar
around the
World

Attachments

 Animation

Controlling
Your
Attachments

Summary

This script doesn't actually use the information about which controls were pressed, but rather uses the *activation* of the controls to react more rapidly to avatar changes. However, avatars often do not change animations immediately on `control()` events, so the script also uses a relatively slow timer to poll for whether the avatar has changed animations.

When the script has either a `timer()` or a `control()` event, it calls the `animOverride()` function. There it asks the avatar what posture it is in using the `llGetAnimation()` function, which returns a string name of the current locomotion animation. If you want more options, use `llGetAnimationList()`, which returns a list of all animations that the avatar is currently playing.

Figure 2.7: Yoga float

If the avatar is in the posture the script wants to animate, the script will start the chosen animation with `llStartAnimation()` (if the avatar wasn't already doing that animation). If the avatar is no longer moving, the script will stop the animation using `llStopAnimation()`. The `llGetAnimation()`, `llGetAnimationList()`, `llStartAnimation()`, and `llStopAnimation()` functions are defined in Table 2.2.

TABLE 2.2: ANIMATION OVERRIDE FUNCTIONS

Function	Behavior
`string llGetAnimation(key avatarId)`	Returns the name of the locomotion animation posture the avatar is using.
`list llGetAnimationList(key avatarId)`	Returns a list of keys of all animations the avatar is currently running.
`llStartAnimation(string animation)`	Starts playing the animation on the avatar when permission `PERMISSION_TRIGGER_ANIMATION` has been granted.
`llStopAnimation(string animation)`	Stops playing the named animation.

AOs are complicated mainly because they need to get a number of permissions and controls to do their job. You could write an AO that associates an animation with each posture, or even a set of animations with each posture. Most of the AO scripts you will find in-world are able to cycle between multiple animations, even randomly, within the same posture to make the avatar look more natural. Add in a user interface with a HUD, and you have a complete AO solution for your avatar. See, for instance, the ZHAO-II scripts that are available at no charge in-world from many places, including SYW HQ.

 TYPING ANIMATOR

In your travels in-world, you may have already had the experience of chatting to a stranger and being surprised to see a keyboard (or something even more elaborate) appear as if by magic in front of the resident while they are typing, and then disappear just as quickly. Figure 2.8 shows a simple version of such a keyboard.

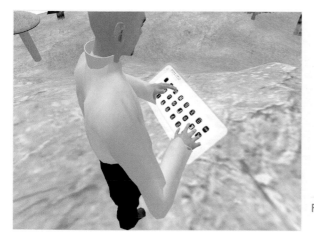

Figure 2.8: A basic keyboard animation.

In either case, how does this simple but effective effect work? Listing 2.11 shows a slight modification of a well-known implementation, attributed to Max Case (www.maxcase.info). It's simple, tight code but quite effective in carrying the illusion forward. A timer elapses every half second and tests whether the resident is typing. It's a narrow enough time frame to determine whether the keyboard user is typing, but not so narrow as to affect sim performance. Humans don't type at such a blindingly fast rate that a tiny bit of lag in initiating the animation at the onset of typing or halting it later will be noticed by others in the vicinity.

Listing 2.11: Max Case's Simple Keyboard Script

```
//Derived from Max Case's Free Keyboard Script 1.0 04/18/2005
key     owner;
integer status;
key kbtextureYellow = "eef62334-e85e-b8f5-0717-19056bdbafde";
initialize() {
        llSetTexture(kbtextureYellow, 2);
        llSetTextureAnim(ANIM_ON | LOOP, // mode
                        2,              // side
                        4, 1,           // rows, columns
                        0, 0,           // start and end frame
                        4);             // frame rate
        llSetAlpha(0.0, ALL_SIDES); // make completely transparent
        llSetTimerEvent(.5);
        owner = llGetOwner();
        status = 0;
}
```

CHAPTER 2

MOVING
YOUR AVATAR
AROUND THE
WORLD

ATTACHMENTS

ANIMATION

CONTROLLING
YOUR
ATTACHMENTS

SUMMARY

```
default {
    state_entry() {
        if (llGetOwner() != owner) {
            initialize();
        }
    }
    on_rez(integer total_number) {
        if(llGetOwner() != owner){
            initialize();
        }
    }
    timer() {
        integer temp = llGetAgentInfo(owner) & AGENT_TYPING;
        if (temp != status) { //status changed since last checked?
            llSetAlpha(!status, 2);  //flip the status only on face 2
            status = temp;  //save the current status.
        }
    }
}
```

The cleverness in the script and the illusion of animation comes from using a texture that is actually multiple rows and columns with small pictures in them, similar to multiple frames in a little movie. Figure 2.9 shows an object that has a one-row-by-four-column keyboard texture applied to it. Each frame has a slightly different set of keys that are brighter than the rest, thus making the keyboard appear to move. The number of rows and columns become arguments to the llSetTextureAnim() function. The animation moves through the animation cells one by one, like frames through a movie. The function is described in detail in Chapter 9.

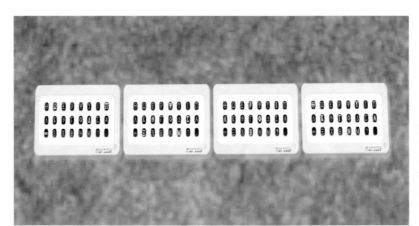

Figure 2.9: A texture containing four frames, laid out using one row of four columns. Different keys are highlighted in each frame.

DEFINITION

```
llSetTextureAnim(integer mode, integer side,
                 integer x_frames, integer y_frames,
                 float start, float length, float rate)
```

Animates the texture on one side of a prim. Only one animation can be run per prim, although all sides of a prim can be animated at the same time by setting side to ALL_SIDES. The "Texture Animation" section of Chapter 9 provides more details.

Note that the animation is *always* running—it's simply hidden because the keyboard is initially transparent from the call to `llSetAlpha(0.0, ALL_SIDES)`.

When the `timer()` event fires, it examines the avatar's state with

```
integer temp = llGetAgentInfo(owner) & AGENT_TYPING;
```

`llGetAgentInfo()` returns a bit pattern of 13 status items, including `AGENT_TYPING`, listed in Table 2.3. (If avatars are flying, both `AGENT_IN_AIR` and `AGENT_FLYING` will be true. Agents can be `AGENT_IN_AIR` but not `AGENT_FLYING` when they are jumping, falling, or kept away from the ground by means of a script.)

TABLE 2.3: CONSTANTS THAT DESCRIBE AGENT (AVATAR) STATUS

Constant	Value	Agent Status
AGENT_FLYING	0x0001	Is flying
AGENT_ATTACHMENTS	0x0002	Has attachments
AGENT_SCRIPTED	0x0004	Has scripted attachments
AGENT_MOUSELOOK	0x0008	Is in mouselook
AGENT_SITTING	0x0010	Is sitting
AGENT_ON_OBJECT	0x0020	Is sitting on an object
AGENT_AWAY	0x0040	Is in "away" mode
AGENT_WALKING	0x0080	Is walking
AGENT_IN_AIR	0x0100	Is in the air (hovering)
AGENT_TYPING	0x0200	Is typing
AGENT_CROUCHING	0x0400	Is crouching
AGENT_BUSY	0x0800	Is in "busy" mode
AGENT_ALWAYS_RUN	0x1000	Has Always Run enabled

DEFINITION

```
integer llGetAgentInfo(key id)
```

Returns a bitfield of information about the agent.

id — The agent's UUID.

Agent status can be tested using a bitwise "and" operator (&), as shown in the following snippet:

```
integer agentStatus = llGetAgentInfo( llGetOwner() );
if (agentStatus & AGENT_FLYING) {
    llOwnerSay("Agent is flying");
}
```

For this typing script, usually the *temp* variable will be **FALSE** because the avatar is not typing. That may seem like a waste of resources, but the test is short and yields a discrete result. When the result is **TRUE** the script changes the alpha (transparency) of the keyboard to make it visible.

CHAPTER 1
CHAPTER 2
CHAPTER 3
CHAPTER 4
CHAPTER 5
CHAPTER 6
CHAPTER 7
CHAPTER 8
CHAPTER 9
CHAPTER 10
CHAPTER 11
CHAPTER 12
CHAPTER 13
CHAPTER 14
CHAPTER 15
APPENDICES

Moving
Your Avatar
around the
World

Attachments

Animation

Controlling
Your
Attachments

Summary

CONTROLLING YOUR ATTACHMENTS

This chapter is full of neat toys...that could get extremely annoying in the wrong situations. Therefore, most good-quality builds provide a way to turn the effects on and off. One way to do this is with a simple HUD. HUDs are scripted objects that attach to "HUD points"—essentially the user's screen—instead of points on the avatar that are visible to others, as shown in Figure 2.10.

Figure 2.10: A floating avatar with a green HUD button showing that the **"yoga_float"** animation is enabled.

As you learned earlier, attachments are any objects your avatar wears, whether on the body or as a HUD and animation overrides (AOs) are sequences of internal commands that change the way your avatar moves. When you run an AO, the script asks your avatar permission to trigger the animation. While AOs do not need to be placed in attachments, they often are. In this case, the permissions are granted implicitly.

If you want to be able to control details of the attachment—for example to turn on the face light, to allow friends to wind up your key, or to float instead of walk—you can either create a chat interface for commands (as shown in Chapter 3) or create a HUD.

If you want to control an object that is not part of the HUD, you will probably want to add communication between the controller on the HUD (invisible to others) and the object you want to wear or otherwise have visible in the world. Chapter 3 talks about how to make this communication happen.

Listing 2.12 shows a modification to the WalkAO script from Listing 2.10. To make it work, put it in a box that you've sized to <0.2, 0.2, 0.2>. Instead of "wearing" it, attach it to your HUD at the bottom-left point. You'll see it on the lower-left corner of your *SL* screen, just above the communication buttons—other users will not be able to see it. It turns red when not enabled, and green when enabled. The bowling project on the SYW website demonstrates another example of a HUD.

Listing 2.12: WalkAO HUD—Adding a UI to Your AO

```
// This script is exactly the same as Listing 2.10 WalkAO except for
colorhud() { // new user-defined function
    if (gEnabled) {
        llSetColor(<0,1,0>, ALL_SIDES);
    } else {
        llSetColor(<1,0,0>, ALL_SIDES);
    }
}

default {
    // same on_rez, state_entry, timer and control event handlers
    attach( key k ) {
        if ( k != NULL_KEY ) {
            llRequestPermissions(llGetOwner(),
                PERMISSION_TRIGGER_ANIMATION|PERMISSION_TAKE_CONTROLS);
            colorhud();  // NEW LINE
        }
    }
    touch_end(integer count) {
        gEnabled = !gEnabled;
        colorhud();
        animOverride();
    }
}
```

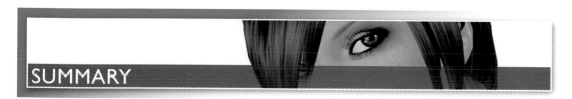

SUMMARY

This chapter has dealt mostly with getting avatars to look and act interesting by themselves. You can combine many of these techniques—for instance, mix the seating script with an animation override to have the avatar sit in a particular pose. We will revisit a few of these ideas later on—seating turns into vehicles in Chapter 7, animation overrides are the basis for coordinated animations in the dance project on the SYW website, and so on. The next chapter switches gears and looks into communications: how avatars and objects talk to each other (and to themselves!).

CHAPTER 1

CHAPTER 2

CHAPTER 3
CHAPTER 4
CHAPTER 5
CHAPTER 6
CHAPTER 7
CHAPTER 8
CHAPTER 9
CHAPTER 10
CHAPTER 11
CHAPTER 12
CHAPTER 13
CHAPTER 14
CHAPTER 15
APPENDICES

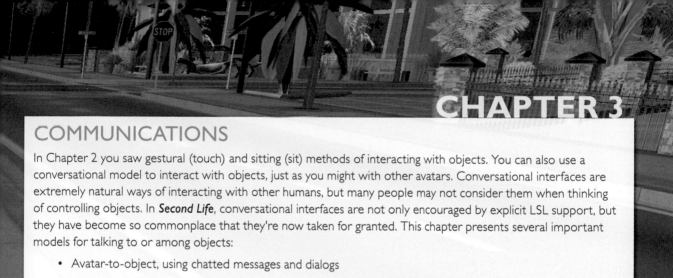

COMMUNICATIONS

In Chapter 2 you saw gestural (touch) and sitting (sit) methods of interacting with objects. You can also use a conversational model to interact with objects, just as you might with other avatars. Conversational interfaces are extremely natural ways of interacting with other humans, but many people may not consider them when thinking of controlling objects. In *Second Life*, conversational interfaces are not only encouraged by explicit LSL support, but they have become so commonplace that they're now taken for granted. This chapter presents several important models for talking to or among objects:

- Avatar-to-object, using chatted messages and dialogs
- Object-to-object, using chatted messages
- Prim-to-prim, within a single object, using link messages
- Long-distance communications, such as email, IM, and multi-object relays

TALKING TO AN OBJECT (AND HAVING IT LISTEN)

TALKING TO AN OBJECT (AND HAVING IT LISTEN)

DIALOGS

CREATING OBJECTS THAT COMMUNICATE WITH EACH OTHER

USING LINK MESSAGES FOR PRIM-TO-PRIM COMMUNICATION INSIDE AN OBJECT

EMAIL AND INSTANT MESSAGING

SUMMARY

Objects can talk to each other and talk back with the family of `llSay()` functions, shown in Table 3.1. Chapter 1, "Getting a Feel for the Linden Scripting Language," said to mostly use `llOwnerSay()`, and save `llSay()` for conscious use. In this chapter you'll learn why, how, and when to use `llSay()`.

TABLE 3.1: `llSay()` FAMILY OF FUNCTIONS

FUNCTION	BEHAVIOR
`llSay(integer channel, string text)`	Chat **text** on the specified chat **channel**. The range is a 20-meter-radius sphere, centered on the calling object.
`llWhisper(integer channel, string text)`	Chat **text** on the **channel**. Range is a 10-meter-radius sphere.
`llShout(integer channel, string text)`	Chat **text** on the **channel**. Range is a 100-meter-radius sphere.
`llOwnerSay(string msg)`	Chat **msg** to only the owner of the object running the script (if the owner is in the simulator).
`llRegionSay(integer channel, string msg)`	Chat **msg** on the **channel** to anything listening in the whole sim. Cannot be used with channel 0.

Chatting in **SL** uses channels. Messages can be chatted on any `integer` channel, from –2,147,483,648 to 2,147,483,647. Channel 0 is the public chat channel; anything typed in the chat window will be broadcast on channel 0. Avatars can also chat on other channels using the special prefix slash-number; for example typing **/9 hello world** means the string "hello world" will be broadcast on channel 9. Avatars cannot chat directly on negative channels; they can chat **indirectly** on negative channels when using dialogs (as shown in Listing 3.5 later in this chapter). You may also find the **DEBUG_CHANNEL** useful for printing debugging messages; errors in your script, such as dividing by 0, will also be shouted here.

You should avoid using channel 0 unless you want or need your interactions to be visible to anyone nearby—channel 0 is usually full of chat between avatars. Worse, most of the online tutorials have examples that use channel 0, so there is a proliferation of devices that use open chat for both control and feedback—annoying to everyone around you and creating lag in the sim. In general, avoid channels below 100 and **never** use a channel in the single digits if you care about channel cross-talk—it's far too easy for others to test and discover. Several examples in this chapter explain when and how to use randomly generated channels.

Objects can (and probably should) use a negative-number channel to talk with one another, as shown in the section "Creating Objects that Communicate with Each Other."

Note too that objects can react to other variants of the common `llSay()`, such as `llWhisper()` or `llShout()`, but they won't react to `llInstantMessage()`.

`llSay()` functions are good to use when objects want to **say** things. But how can you get objects to **listen** to you or to each other? LSL supports this capability through the `llListen()` family of methods. Generally, the simplest conversation you can have with an object is to talk with it through the normal chat capability. Try constructing an object and putting the code from Listing 3.1 in its Content folder.

Listing 3.1: The Simplest Conversation an Object Can Have

```
default
{
    state_entry() {
        llListen(0, "", NULL_KEY, "");
    }
    listen(integer channel, string name, key id, string message) {
        llSay(0, "I heard " + name + " say: " + message);
    }
}
```

CHAPTER 1
CHAPTER 2
CHAPTER 3
CHAPTER 4
CHAPTER 5
CHAPTER 6
CHAPTER 7
CHAPTER 8
CHAPTER 9
CHAPTER 10
CHAPTER 11
CHAPTER 12
CHAPTER 13
CHAPTER 14
CHAPTER 15
APPENDICES

The script sets up a listen event with `llListen()`, then responds to any listen events via `listen()`, the built-in event handler. The signature of `llListen()` specifies a set of filters that define when to trigger the `listen()` event: a **channel** to listen on, a **name** of an object or avatar to listen to, a **key** that identifies an object or an avatar, and a specific **message** string. The call to `llListen()` in Listing 3.1 listens to channel 0, but doesn't put any other restrictions on the event trigger—any user can say any message, and the `listen()` event will be triggered.

When the event is triggered, the actual values are sent to the handler; that is, the name and key of the object or avatar who chatted, and the specific message they said. Listing 3.1 deliberately uses channel 0 because it is going to repeat anything it hears on the public airwaves.

DEFINITION

```
integer llListen(integer channel,
                 string name, key speakerID, string message)
```

Creates a filtered listener on the specified chat `channel`. Returns the listener's handle. All listeners are canceled when control leaves the state they were defined in.

> `result` — An identifier to be used by `llListenControl()` or `llListenRemove()`.
>
> `channel` — Channel number to listen on.
>
> `name` — The name of the object that chatted (or the avatar's name) to use as a filter (wildcard is " ").
>
> `speakerId` — The key of the speaker to use as a filter (wildcard is NULL_KEY).
>
> `message` — The exact message being looked for (wildcard is " ").

EVENT DEFINITION

```
listen(integer channel, string name, key id, string message) {}
```

This event is invoked when a chatted message meets the filter constraints specified by an `llListen()`. Note that a script will never get chatted messages from scripts in the same prim; in these cases use `llMessageLinked()` instead. The SYW website documents event handlers in more detail.

> `channel` — The channel this message was received on.
>
> `name` — The name of the object or avatar that is the source of the message.
>
> `id` — The key of the object or avatar that is the source of the message.
>
> `message` — The actual message.

69

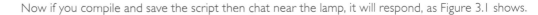

Now if you compile and save the script then chat near the lamp, it will respond, as Figure 3.1 shows.

CHAPTER 3

Talking to an Object (And Having it Listen)

Dialogs

Creating Objects that Communicate with Each Other

Using Link Messages for Prim-to-Prim Communication Inside an Object

Email and Instant Messaging

Summary

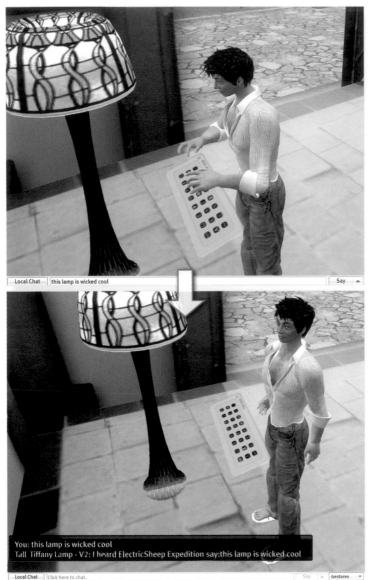

Figure 3.1: The lamp listens to nearby chat on channel 0 and repeats everything it has heard.

All of the parameters to `llListen()` filter when the sim triggers `listen()` events. Thus, if you want the script to listen to only messages chatted on channel 989, change the `llListen()` call to

```
llListen( 989, "", NULL_KEY, "" );
```

If you change Listing 3.1 so that it listens to only channel 989, you can use that focused channel to control the lamp. If you type **Hello, lamp** on the public chat channel (just as in Figure 3.1), the lamp will ignore you. If you type **/989 Hello, lamp**, the lamp will respond obediently.

Moving on to explore the other parameters, specifying a value for the second (string) parameter gives you an additional filter. You can say, for example,

```
llListen( 989, "Light Switch", NULL_KEY, "" );
```

and only messages from an object named Light Switch can be heard. The lamp will ignore all other objects, even when they chat on channel 989. Now you can see the power of a conversational interface such as this. Imagine, for example, having a light switch you can touch that controls every lamp in an entire room. (For more on this concept, see the section, "Creating Objects that Communicate with Each Other" later in this chapter.)

CHAPTER 4
CHAPTER 5
CHAPTER 6
CHAPTER 7
CHAPTER 8
CHAPTER 9
CHAPTER 10
CHAPTER 11
CHAPTER 12
CHAPTER 13
CHAPTER 14
CHAPTER 15
APPENDICES

 ## NOTE

 Listing 3.1 won't actually turn the light on or off—it just repeats what it has heard. If you want to augment this script, check out Listing 3.9, which shows the appropriate commands.

The script in Listing 3.2 shows a typical touch-sensitive script; when the user touches the object it chats a message on channel 989, and every nearby object whose `llListen()` filters are correct receives the message.

Listing 3.2: A Chatty Light Switch

```
default
{
    touch_start(integer total_number) {
        llSay(989, "Lights Out!");
    }
}
```

Incidentally, the second input parameter to `llListen()` can name an object or an avatar. Unfortunately, there is no way to logically "or" this parameter. To do that you would have to set up an `llListen()` for each resident or object that can control the target object, as shown here:

```
llListen(989, "Light Switch", NULL_KEY, "");
llListen(989, "ElectricSheep Expedition", NULL_KEY, "");
```

You can use the third parameter to specify the key (universal unique identifier, or UUID) of the chatting entity the object should respond to: the key can identify either an object or an avatar. A typical usage is to allow only an object's owner to talk to it, as shown in Listing 2.6 in the previous chapter. This means the object should listen only to its owner and ignore all other residents or objects. This construct is useful when an object's ownership transfers from one resident to another (as in a sale of goods).

```
gListenHandle = llListen(989, "", llGetOwner(), "");
```

Scripts that listen to their owners are *extremely* common command interfaces in **SL**. You'll find them in most "customizable" objects. The basic idea is that the script listens for specific commands from the owner, and then changes its behavior appropriately. A piece of jewelry might change how shiny it is, or an email script might change what address to send to. (In the previous chapter, Listing 2.6 set the text based on the owner's command while Listing 2.7 used this method to set the text's color.)

TALKING TO
AN OBJECT
(AND HAVING
IT LISTEN)

DIALOGS

CREATING
OBJECTS THAT
COMMUNICATE
WITH EACH
OTHER

USING LINK
MESSAGES FOR
PRIM-TO-PRIM
COMMUNICATION
INSIDE AN
OBJECT

EMAIL AND
INSTANT
MESSAGING

SUMMARY

WARNING

Be aware that listens persist unless explicitly canceled or until the script transitions into a different state, even if the filter criteria change! The filters on `llListen()` are not updated automatically if the values change—you need to update the listeners explicitly. If you use any construction like this, it is *absolutely critical* to have an `on_rez()` event handler in *every state that has listeners*; either call `llResetScript()` (thus starting the script over) or detect the change of owner (or other target key), name, or message, then close the old listeners (don't just deactivate them) and open new ones. Otherwise, you will end up with an object that will (for instance) only listen to the old owner—fun for gags, but highly embarrassing for serious scripts.

Note that both the object name and the key are used to filter event delivery if they are specified with nonwildcard values. Why? Objects can change their names, and names are certainly not unique. For instance, any of the `llListen()` calls discussed previously that specify an object name will respond to *any* object with the specified name, even if you intended to respond only to the avatar so named. That is,

```
llListen(47, "Vex Streeter", NULL_KEY, "")
```

will happily listen to messages from a mimic pretending to be Vex Streeter. It is pretty unlikely that you would actually want to use both **name** and **key**, because the key is always unique. (Imagine, though, wanting to listen to a particular key-identified object, but only when it has the right name—it's a stretch, but not impossible.)

NOTE

Set the filter parameters to `llListen()` as narrow as possible—this lowers the load on the simulators and avoids triggering your script's `listen()` event unnecessarily. Each wildcard value you use increases the number of listen events that are triggered. If you want the prim to jump when told to jump, set the **message** parameter to `"jump"`; *don't* listen to everything (with the wildcard `""`) and then test inside the event to see if the message matches the string `"jump"`.

Setting up multiple listeners is one of many situations in which you might want to have the script modify and control the listen. Fortunately, `llListen()` returns an integer value you can use later as a handle to the conversation. Create a global variable to cache the returned value, as shown here:

```
// global variables
integer gListenHandle;
integer gListenHandle2;

// in state_entry()
gListenHandle = llListen(989, "Light Switch", NULL_KEY, "");
gListenHandle2 = llListen(989, "Vex Streeter", NULL_KEY, "");
```

The `listen()` event handler can then process the events appropriately, depending on which listener triggered. Also, these handles allow the script to modify or remove a listener—particularly useful in situations where you need a temporary listener, such as for a dialog box (see the "Dialogs" section later in this chapter).

You can modify a listen using `llListenControl()`, passing it a handle (like *gListenHandle*) and a Boolean value, TRUE or FALSE. `llListenControl()` allows you to toggle a listen on or off without canceling it altogether, saving you the trouble (and the code) of reestablishing a previous listen. Additionally, there is of course an `llListenRemove()`, which takes a handle returned by a previous setup and deletes the listener.

CHAPTER 3

CHAPTER 4
CHAPTER 5
CHAPTER 6
CHAPTER 7
CHAPTER 8
CHAPTER 9
CHAPTER 10
CHAPTER 11
CHAPTER 12
CHAPTER 13
CHAPTER 14
CHAPTER 15
APPENDICES

 DEFINITION

```
llListenControl(integer handle, integer active)
```

Makes a `listen()` event callback active or inactive.

handle — The integer value returned by `llListen()`.

active — Boolean value; TRUE activates the listener, and FALSE turns it off.

 DEFINITION

```
llListenRemove(integer handle)
```

Removes the `listen()` event callback associated with the *handle*.

handle — The integer value returned by `llListen()`.

Making your filtering strategy as tight as possible to avoid potential griefers'* attempts to interfere with your build is always wise; however, given an enormous range of channels and conversational phrases, it may not be easy for the miscreant. You will find the tips on the LSL wiki at llListen useful as well.

In summary, using the `llListen()` family of methods enables an easy, convenient, asynchronous strategy for control and management, and of course can be linked to other control tactics as suggested in the light-switch example.

One downside to this approach is that complex interactions need a lot of support. For example, you may have to build a parser or force the user to remember the expected dialog or command set. Another alternative is to set up a large set of listeners. Note, however, that a given script may have no more than 64 active listeners at once; more will generate an error. You can, of course, set up a `usage()` function that prints all of the valid command options if the `listen()` event hears *help* or can't parse a message, as outlined in Listing 3.3.

---

* Wikipedia defines *griefer* as "a slang term used to describe a player in a multiplayer video game who plays the game simply to cause grief to other players through harassment" (`http://en.wikipedia.org/wiki/Griefer`). *Griefing* is a violation of the *Second Life* Terms of Service.

CHAPTER 3

TALKING TO
AN OBJECT
(AND HAVING
IT LISTEN)

DIALOGS

CREATING
OBJECTS THAT
COMMUNICATE
WITH EACH
OTHER

USING LINK
MESSAGES FOR
PRIM-TO-PRIM
COMMUNICATION
INSIDE AN
OBJECT

EMAIL AND
INSTANT
MESSAGING

SUMMARY

Listing 3.3: Giving Usage Hints

```
usage() {
    llOwnerSay("Use Channel 989. Example (typed into chat): /989 on");
    llOwnerSay("This object understands \"on\" or \"off\"");
}
default{
    state_entry() {
        llListen(989,"", NULL_KEY, "");
    }
    touch_start(integer n) {
        usage();
    }
    listen(integer ch, string name, key id, string msg) {
        string lowerMsg = llToLower(msg);
        if (lowerMsg=="help"){
            usage();
        } else if (lowerMsg == "on" | lowerMsg == "off") {
            // handle
        } else {
            usage();
        }
    }
}
```

 NOTE

Listing 3.3 shows a mechanism for having your script print quotes *inside* the string:

```
llOwnerSay("This object understands \"on\" or \"off\"");
```

This command prints the following:

```
This object understands "on" or "off"
```

The backslash (\) is used as an "escape" character, meaning the character immediately after it should be processed slightly differently. LSL supports four escape characters:

- \t prints four spaces.
- \n creates a new line.
- \" prints a double quote.
- \\ prints a backslash.

Using a randomly generated channel to listen or chat on is often a good idea. Create a variable to keep track of the channel and set it to a random number, as in

```
gChannel = llCeil( llFrand( 100000 ) ) + 100;
```

The +100 is an offset that ensures you aren't randomly generating a number that's too low. Your usage function can then correctly report which channel needs to be used.

CHAPTER 1
CHAPTER 2

CHAPTER 3

CHAPTER 4
CHAPTER 5
CHAPTER 6
CHAPTER 7
CHAPTER 8
CHAPTER 9
CHAPTER 10
CHAPTER 11
CHAPTER 12
CHAPTER 13
CHAPTER 14
CHAPTER 15
APPENDICES

A PRACTICAL JOKE: MIMIC!

Here's a fun prank you can play: create something you can attach to your avatar, then tell the object to mimic someone else. The object accepts the victim's name, and then everything you say on the control channel (selected randomly) is repeated on the open chat channel (0), but it's attributed to your mark. You only want to try this with your friends—it would be a rather rude thing to do to a stranger (unless the stranger were an exceptional lout), and in the wrong situation it could constitute a Terms of Service violation, getting you suspended from or kicked out of **SL**.

Figure 3.2 shows the effect. The prankster is wearing an innocuous (but ugly) bracelet on his left arm. He's instructed the object to mimic his friend, Danna. Then he tells the device to say, "I am such a nerd boy." How does it work?

MimicBracelet whispers: Pssst... Got it, boss. I am mimicking Danna Morane
Danna Morane: I am such a nerd boy

Figure 3.2: The bracelet, worn on the prankster, changes its name to mimic someone else.

The answer is pretty simple (but slick). In the `default` state of Listing 3.4, and in the `state_entry()` event handler, the owner's identity is established. The bracelet, when attached, is made invisible through the `llSetAlpha()` logic. (Here the lines are commented out so you could see the prop for the prank, but you'll likely want to make it invisible.) In `state_entry()`, the bracelet tells its owner what channel it's listening to and what commands it will accept, then it begins to listen on its command channel for inputs.

Listing 3.4: Mimic Someone

```
integer gCmdChannel;
string gMimic = "Someone";

sayAs(string name, string message) {
    string realname = llGetObjectName();
    llSetObjectName(name);
    llSay(0, message);
    llSetObjectName(realname);
}
```

75

CHAPTER 3

TALKING TO
AN OBJECT
(AND HAVING
IT LISTEN)

DIALOGS

CREATING
OBJECTS THAT
COMMUNICATE
WITH EACH
OTHER

USING LINK
MESSAGES FOR
PRIM-TO-PRIM
COMMUNICATION
INSIDE AN
OBJECT

EMAIL AND
INSTANT
MESSAGING

SUMMARY

```
default
{
    on_rez(integer x) {
        llResetScript();
    }
    state_entry()
    {
        // if (llGetAttached() > 0) {
        //      llSetAlpha(1.0, ALL_SIDES);
        // } else {
        //      llSetAlpha(0.0, ALL_SIDES);
        //}
        gCmdChannel = (integer)llFrand(10000) + 100;
        llOwnerSay("/"+(string)gCmdChannel +
                    "=name or /"+(string)gCmdChannel+"message");
        llListen(gCmdChannel, "", llGetOwner(), "");
    }
    listen(integer channel, string name, key id, string message) {
        if ("=" == llGetSubString(message, 0, 0)) {
            gMimic = llGetSubString(message,1,-1);
            llWhisper(0,
                    "Pssst... Got it, boss. I am mimicking "+gMimic);
        } else {
            sayAs(gMimic, message);
        }
    }

}
```

When the `listen()` event handler gets something on the command channel that starts with the equals sign (=), it sets a name for the resident to be mimicked. Otherwise, it takes the input and passes it to the `sayAs()` helper method.

Now here's the trick. The `sayAs()` method stores the real name of the object but sets the name of the bracelet to the resident name it was told to mimic, then it says the phrase and resets to its real name.

Later, our prankster tells the bracelet */987=Danna Morane*, and the prank is set. You can see the prankster innocently staring into a store window, and suddenly Danna Morane says, "I am such a nerd boy." Of course, you now know that it's really the bracelet saying this, but the rest of the world doesn't (provided no one looks very carefully).

Listing 3.4 is in the "just for fun" category, but please remember two things: use it only in your "play group" (don't grief), and be aware that it isn't difficult to identify who's using such tricks. The green text (shown in Figure 3.2), instead of the usual white, indicates that all isn't what it seems. *The moral is to never trust anything displayed in green!*

A few fine points are worth noting about the `llListen()` family of methods. Looking back at Listing 3.3, note the use of a string manipulator, `llToLower()`, to reduce the user's input to a common denominator casing before comparing it to some expected input. This is always a good practice. In Listing 3.4 note the use of a primitive parse, `llGetSubString()`, to pick apart the command input. Admittedly this is not a very flexible parser, but in a simple gadget for personal pranks it suffices.

DIALOGS

CHAPTER 4
CHAPTER 5
CHAPTER 6
CHAPTER 7
CHAPTER 8
CHAPTER 9
CHAPTER 10
CHAPTER 11
CHAPTER 12
CHAPTER 13
CHAPTER 14
CHAPTER 15
APPENDICES

Chatting with objects is flexible and easy to implement, but it is also easy for users to make errors and it can get annoyingly verbose when you want to issue more-complex commands. LSL offers an alternative bidirectional communication method with avatars, called *dialogs*.

Second Life dialogs are small, blue pop-up windows that give you a bit of text and as many as 12 small buttons (and the option to ignore the dialog altogether). Any interaction resulting from a dialog is chatted back to the object almost exactly as though the avatar had used the chat window. Listing 3.5 shows an example of using a dialog to control an object's color.

Listing 3.5: Dialog-Based Colorizer

```
list COLORS =
    ["white", <255,255,255>,    "black", <36,36,36>,
     "brown", <85,60,40>,       "olive", <67,71,44>,
     "violet", <72,40,89>,      "ivory", <216,204,151>,
     "denim", <43,46,85>,       "purple", <120,0,160>,
     "yellow", <255,255,0>];

integer gListenHandle;

default
{
    on_rez(integer param) {
        llResetScript();
    }
    touch_end(integer total_number) {
        key who = llDetectedKey(0);
        integer cmdChannel = (integer)llFrand(-200000) - 100;
        list choices = llList2ListStrided(COLORS, 0, -1, 2);
        llDialog(who, "Select a color", choices, cmdChannel);
        gListenHandle = llListen(cmdChannel, "", who, "");
    }
    listen(integer ch, string name, key id, string message) {
        integer choice = llListFindList(COLORS, [message]);
        vector color = llList2Vector(COLORS, choice+1)/255.0;
        llSetColor(color, ALL_SIDES);
        llListenRemove( gListenHandle );
    }
}
```

The script uses a randomly generated negative channel because you always want to use an uncrowded channel for conversation. The script sets up the `listen()` event handler using the correct chat channel, **cmdChannel**, and listens to the avatar who touched the object.

The central function of this example is `llDialog()`, which pops up an interactive dialog box with the specified avatar. The script puts a bit of explanatory text in the message portion of the dialog and supplies a list of buttons to display.

DEFINITION

TALKING TO
AN OBJECT
(AND HAVING
IT LISTEN)

 DIALOGS

CREATING
OBJECTS THAT
COMMUNICATE
WITH EACH
OTHER

USING LINK
MESSAGES FOR
PRIM-TO-PRIM
COMMUNICATION
INSIDE AN
OBJECT

EMAIL AND
INSTANT
MESSAGING

SUMMARY

```
llDialog(key avatarID, string message, list buttons,
         integer channel)
```

Displays a menu to the named avatar. If the avatar's user makes a choice, the text of the chosen button is chatted back on the specified `channel`; and the `listen()` event is triggered. If the avatar makes no choice, no message is sent.

> *avatarID* — The UUID of the avatar to send the dialog to.
>
> *message* — The explanatory text to appear above the buttons. Limited to 220 characters.
>
> *buttons* — A list of the buttons to display. At most 12 strings, each with at least one character and no more than 24 characters. The buttons are laid out left-to-right and bottom-to-top.
>
> *channel* — The channel on which to chat the chosen button.

Construction of the button list is the quirkiest part of the `llDialog()` process. You get at most 12 buttons (but you can have fewer). All buttons must be strings, and the strings must be non-empty but not too long. Worst of all, dialog buttons are drawn in a strange order: ***bottom up***, as shown in Figure 3.3. For this example it doesn't matter because the colors aren't in any particular order; however, in a more complex menu system, you'll want to show the buttons sorted in a more rational way. The LSL wiki entry for `llDialog()` has some examples of how to deal with this menu style. The buttons do not need to be unique: many dialogs use a single space as a "dead" button to make pleasing layouts. These dead buttons still appear, but with nothing visible; if selected, the buttons will still generate a chat message containing the single space.

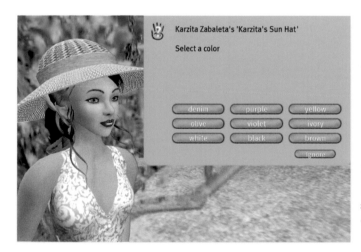

Figure 3.3: The dialog buttons from Listing 3.5 are drawn left-to-right and bottom-to-top; plan your layout carefully.

Listing 3.5 populates the buttons by taking just the names of the colors from the COLORS list, using `llList2ListStrided()` (which was described in more detail in Chapter 1). The script has initialized COLORS as a strided list of alternating color names and color values. The call to `llList2ListStrided(COLORS, 0, -1, 2)` searches through the list from element 0 to element -1 (the end), and returns the first element of each stride length, 2.

When the `listen()` event handler gets a response, the script "hears" the label of the chosen button, very much as though it had been chatted by the avatar, though it may be on a negative channel, and will never be out of range. (Recall that normal typing in the chat window must be within 20m of the object.) To retrieve the rest of the color name—color vector pair, the script uses the `llListFindList()` function, which searches the list for the message (the color name from the button). In this example, it will always find the string and retrieve the associated value that is sitting in the next index, which here is `llList2Vector(COLORS, choice+1)`. Finally, the script divides the vector *color* by 255 to normalize the color vector, and sets the color of the hat's band.

Be aware that the avatar may choose to ignore the menu—in which case the listener is never removed. You can remedy this problem by adding a `timer()` event that deletes the listener if enough time has passed. Add the following line to the `touch_end()` event handler (along with an appropriate definition of the `TIMEOUT` constant):

```
llSetTimerEvent( TIMEOUT );
```

Also add a `timer()` event handler that deletes the listener:

```
timer() {
    llOwnerSay("Assuming that the user clicked Ignore");
    llListenRemove( gListenHandle );
    llSetTimerEvent( 0 );
}
```

Because the *gListenHandle* caches only the most recent listener, these fixes will not work in the case of multiple clicks. When the dialog might be touched multiple times before completing, you'll need to store the listener handles in a `list`. Take care to remove only the right handle; Listing 3.10 later in this chapter shows how to manage this kind of list.

CREATING OBJECTS THAT COMMUNICATE WITH EACH OTHER

In the previous section we suggested that one light switch might communicate with a lot of nearby lights. Here we go into more detail about that concept. Consider, for example, a set of double doors you want to swing open or closed when you touch one of them. In this case, external communication using `llSay()` between the objects is a good strategy. The doors shown in Figure 3.4 are distinct objects, yet the user experience you most likely want to promote is that whenever one of them is touched, both spring open together (or close together).

When touched, the script in Listing 3.6 calls its `doorman()` function to rotate it. The doors take symmetrical actions: the left door opens by rotating `PI/2` radians and closes by rotating `-PI/2` radians; the right door does the opposite. Chapter 4's section on "Quaternions" explains these rotations in more detail.

TALKING TO
AN OBJECT
(AND HAVING
IT LISTEN)

DIALOGS

CREATING
OBJECTS THAT
COMMUNICATE
WITH EACH
OTHER

USING LINK
MESSAGES FOR
PRIM-TO-PRIM
COMMUNICATION
INSIDE AN
OBJECT

EMAIL AND
INSTANT
MESSAGING

SUMMARY

Figure 3.4: Both doors of the visitor's center spring open when either one is touched.

Listing 3.6: Automatic Left Door

```
integer gInboundCmdChannel =990; // SWITCH these for the right door.
integer gOutboundCmdChannel=991; // SWITCH
string  OPEN="open";
string  CLOSE="close";
string  gOpenClosed=OPEN;

doorman(string cmd){
    rotation delta;
    rotation rot = llGetRot();
    float desiredRot = PI/2;
    if (llGetObjectName() == "Left Door") {
        if (cmd==CLOSE)   desiredRot = -PI/2;
    } else {
        if (cmd==OPEN)    desiredRot = -PI/2;
    }
    delta = llEuler2Rot( <0,0,desiredRot> );
    rot = delta * rot;
    llSetRot(rot);
    gOpenClosed=cmd;
}
default
{
    state_entry() {
        llListen(gInboundCmdChannel, "", NULL_KEY, "");
    }
    touch_start(integer num) {
        llOwnerSay("Current ac ==>"+gOpenClosed);
        if (gOpenClosed==CLOSE) {
            doorman(OPEN);
            llSay(gOutboundCmdChannel, OPEN);
        } else {
            doorman(CLOSE);
            llSay(gOutboundCmdChannel, CLOSE);
        }
    }
```

CHAPTER 1
CHAPTER 2
CHAPTER 3
CHAPTER 4
CHAPTER 5
CHAPTER 6
CHAPTER 7
CHAPTER 8
CHAPTER 9
CHAPTER 10
CHAPTER 11
CHAPTER 12
CHAPTER 13
CHAPTER 14
CHAPTER 15
APPENDICES

```
listen(integer channel, string name, key id, string message) {
    llOwnerSay("Listen event handler. fired on channel "+
              (string) channel+message);
    if (channel==gInboundCmdChannel && message == OPEN) {
        doorman(OPEN);
        gOpenClosed = OPEN;
    } else if (channel==gInboundCmdChannel && message == CLOSE) {
        doorman(CLOSE);
        gOpenClosed = CLOSE;
    } else { // do nothing
    }
  }
}
```

Rotating one door 90 degrees in the vertical plane is only half the job. The other part of the job is to make the other door operate in concert. The controller has two communication channels, *inboundCmdChannel* (990) and *outboundCmdChannel* (991). The right door will listen on its *inboundCmdChannel* and speak on its *outboundCmdChannel*. Note that randomly generated channels won't work in this case because both doors need to know both values. The script shown is for the left door; the right door reverses the two channels, listening on 991 and speaking on 990. In either case, when the door script is activated, the door posts a listen event via

```
llListen(inboundCmdChannel, "", NULL_KEY, "");
```

After the `doorman()` function has completed, the script sends a command to the other door using `llSay()`. The `listen()` event handler on either door validates the message, making sure the message matches either the OPEN or CLOSE string. The other door then takes the appropriate and symmetrical action, and presto—your doors or gates swing open or snap shut in unison.

  ## BUILD NOTE

If you use simple rectangles for the doors with these scripts, they will swing at their centerlines rather than at their outer edges. The simplest fix for this problem is to make the doors from rectangles that are twice as wide as you want (the y coordinate) and then apply a path cut begin of 0.375 and end of 0.875. This leaves the rotation point halfway up the edge of the door instead of right in the middle. You can achieve a similar effect in a different way by linking each door to an invisible root prim for the script that will act as a hinge.

Note the redundant test for the command channel:

```
if (channel==gInboundCmdChannel && message ==OPEN) {
```

In this script there is only *one* `llListen()`; therefore the `listen()` event handler does not need to check whether the *channel* is *gInboundCmdChannel*. However, scripts that have multiple listens on multiple channels should *always* check which channel the message came from.

You may want to add additional effects, such as a creaking-door sound that you trigger with `llTriggerSound()` when the door is touched (see Chapter 11, "Multimedia"), or a locking system that lets only the doors' owner lock and unlock the gate (see Chapter 6, "Land Design and Management"). Come by SYW HQ to pick up a copy of that version.

TALKING TO
AN OBJECT
(AND HAVING
IT LISTEN)

DIALOGS

CREATING
OBJECTS THAT
COMMUNICATE
WITH EACH
OTHER

USING LINK
MESSAGES FOR
PRIM-TO-PRIM
COMMUNICATION
INSIDE AN
OBJECT

EMAIL AND
INSTANT
MESSAGING

SUMMARY

↘ CHAT RELAY

One of the issues you may encounter with interobject communication is that basic interobject conversations are limited to the ranges described in Table 3.1. Sometimes it can be useful to have a chat relay that allows chatted conversations to go farther than the 20m limit of `llSay()`. While `llShout()` goes up to 100m, how would you relay a chat over longer distances? `llRegionSay()` transmits a message to everyone (including `listen()` events) within a region, but won't cross sim boundaries. Listing 3.7 shows a script you can place into multiple objects to have the objects relay a chat across arbitrary distances (with an object placed every 75 or 100m apart). Make two prims, put them 75m apart, and have a friend chat into one box while you listen in the other. Because the script relies on `llShout()` to relay the messages, the maximum distance is 100m. Also, if the relays are less than 40m apart, an avatar standing in the middle will hear relays from both sides, and you probably want to avoid that.

Listing 3.7: Long-Distance Chat Relay

```
integer ECHOCHANNEL = 197583;  // Pick your own obscure value

string gMyName;

sayAs(string name, string message) {
    string realname = llGetObjectName();
    llSetObjectName(name);
    llSay(0, "(Relaying)"+message);
    llShout(ECHOCHANNEL, name+"|"+message);
    llSetObjectName(realname);
}

default
{
    on_rez(integer _x) {
        llResetScript();
    }
    state_entry() {
        gMyName = llGetObjectName();
        llListen(0, "", NULL_KEY, ""); // listen to open chat
        // listen to the ECHOCHANNEL for objects with the same name
        llListen(ECHOCHANNEL, gMyName, NULL_KEY, "");
    }
    listen(integer channel, string name, key id, string message) {
        if (channel == ECHOCHANNEL) {  // relay the message
            integer bar = llSubStringIndex(message, "|");
            string avName = llGetSubString(message, 0, bar - 1);
            string avMsg = llGetSubString(message, bar + 1, -1);
            sayAs(avName, avMsg);
        } else {                       // only repeat messages from avatars!
            key kowner = llList2Key(llGetObjectDetails(id,
                                        [OBJECT_OWNER]),0);

            if (kowner == id) {
                // if the speaker owns itself (== avatar!)
                llShout(ECHOCHANNEL, name+"|"+message);
            }
        }
    }
}
```

This script starts by setting up `listen()` events on both the public chat channel and on the ECHOCHANNEL. Chatting avatars (and possibly scripts) will chat on channel 0. If you've picked a really obscure ECHOCHANNEL, only your objects will chat on it. The `listen()` event handler checks first to see which channel the message was received on. If the channel was the ECHOCHANNEL, it parses the received message to pull out the avatar's name and the original chatted message, and calls the user-defined function sayAs() to repeat the message as if the original avatar had spoken. (Note the similarity to Listing 3.4.)

If the channel wasn't the ECHOCHANNEL, it double-checks that an avatar spoke the message, because you don't want this script to relay other objects. To determine if something is an object or an avatar, the script calls llGetObjectDetails() asking for the OBJECT_OWNER. (Chapter 5 describes this function in more detail.) The useful thing to note is that avatars always own themselves, and thus the key of the owner, *kowner*, will equal the key of the chatter, *id*. If in fact it was an avatar chatting on channel 0, the script repeats the message with the avatar's name by shouting on the ECHOCHANNEL for other relays to hear.

CHAPTER 1
CHAPTER 2

CHAPTER 3

CHAPTER 4
CHAPTER 5
CHAPTER 6
CHAPTER 7
CHAPTER 8
CHAPTER 9
CHAPTER 10
CHAPTER 11
CHAPTER 12
CHAPTER 13
CHAPTER 14
CHAPTER 15
APPENDICES

Note that the script calls llResetScript() in on_rez(): while open listeners don't care if the owner changed, the *name* of the object may have changed when it was sitting in the owner's inventory, thus breaking an un-reset listener!

You could easily set up a long-distance relay using this script. However, you'd have to augment it with checks to make sure a given message is repeated only once by each relay—you probably don't want a message to stay in the relays indefinitely.

The ECHOCHANNEL in Listing 3.7 is an example of one place you *can't* use a randomly generated value for the channel; *all* of the relay boxes need to use the same value. The script in Listing 4.4 in the following chapter shows how to have objects communicate with a randomly generated channel. If you were to do it here, the concept would be as follows:

- Have a script rez the relay boxes, telling them the communication channel (mechanism described in Listing 4.4).
- Have the relay script move the relay to its target location (using the moveTo() function from Listing 2.5), because the autorezzer can only make objects within 10m.

One other use for chat relays in *SL* is as *chat catchers*. Essentially, the idea is that chat catchers listen to the public channel and forward the conversation to either email or IM. Chat catchers have a long *Second Life* heritage. *Dr. Dobb's Journal* has a version in a Linux article at www.ddj.com/linux-open-source/198800545?pgno=4. You can also report the chat to a blog using the ideas presented in Chapter 12, "Reaching outside *Second Life*." Examples include blogHUD (http://www.bloghud.com/) and Twitterbox (http://ordinalmalaprop.com/twitter/).

USING LINK MESSAGES FOR PRIM-TO-PRIM COMMUNICATION INSIDE AN OBJECT

When prims in a single object need to talk to each other, you use the llMessageLinked() family. Why use link messages and not chat? It may seem that chat works for everything you need. However, link messages have the following advantages:

- Link messages are much more private (and hence more secure).
- Regular chat messages have a built-in delay of 0.2 seconds; link messages are *much* faster.
- Link messages don't have chat's limit of 255 characters. That's particularly useful if you're trying to pass data structures from prim to prim.

83

TALKING TO
AN OBJECT
(AND HAVING
IT LISTEN)

DIALOGS

CREATING
OBJECTS THAT
COMMUNICATE
WITH EACH
OTHER

 USING LINK
MESSAGES FOR
PRIM-TO-PRIM
COMMUNICATION
INSIDE AN
OBJECT

EMAIL AND
INSTANT
MESSAGING

SUMMARY

 NOTE

You can cast any structure into a string, and then on the receiving end, correctly cast it back, as in this example:

```
// Transmitter
    vector v = <1,2,3>;
    string s = (string)v;
// Receiver
    vector v2 = (vector)s;
```

If you are passing lists from prim to prim, you'll need the pair of functions `llDumpList2String()` and `llParseString2List()`:

```
// Transmitter
    list myList = [ "word", <1,2,3>, 0.25 ];
    string s = llDumpList2String( myList, "|" );
// Receiver
    list myList = llParseString2List( s, ["|"], []);
    vector v2 = (vector)llList2String( myList, 1 );
```

Now that you've been thoroughly convinced that link messages are the best thing to use whenever you can, recall that multiple objects attached to an avatar cannot be linked to each other—you'll need to use regular chat channels amongst them. Additionally, objects more than 10m apart can not be linked.

Recall that **objects** are composed of one or more **prims**: together, all the prims form the link set of the object, and one of the prims is the **root prim**. When building an object from components, the root prim is the very last prim to be selected. When highlighting a complex object, the root is selected in yellow rather than the blue of all the others. Additionally, every prim has an object-unique **link number** that isn't visible through the **Second Life** client. As every prim in a link set has physical properties, it also has its own inventory of interesting things: every prim in a link set may have running scripts. A prim's link number is the **only** way for a script to directly reference another specific prim in the object. You'll find more descriptions on the LSL wiki under Link. The key point is that linked prims can have names, keys, and link numbers that are visible to other prims in the link set, and all these pieces of information may be used to coordinate actions between the elements of a link set.

All LSL functions that operate on linked prims[*] take a link number as an argument to direct the control to that specific prim. There are some quirks, though. First, in an object made up of many objects, the root prim always has link number 1 (or the constant `LINK_ROOT`), but an object made from a single prim has link number 0. In addition, a few link-number constants have special meaning: `LINK_SET` indicates every prim in the set gets the same effect, `LINK_ALL_OTHERS` affects all prims except for the one holding the script, `LINK_ALL_CHILDREN` affects all prims except for the root, and `LINK_THIS` affects only the prim the script is in.

A common use for link messages is to allow any part of a linked prim to be touched and have the touched part send a message to the other linked parts. One of the parts is (generally) the actual target, although nothing precludes the existence of multiple targets.

---

[*] Chapter 4's section on "Making the flower petals into a flower" presents these functions and how to manipulate linked objects. This chapter focuses on the communication between the linked prims.

The scripts in Listings 3.8 and 3.9 illustrate how scripts inside one object can communicate, and you'll find that useful everywhere. When placed inside a lamp, Listing 3.8 sends a message to the root prim when the lamp is touched. Listing 3.9 receives the messages and turns the light on or off.

  BUILD NOTE

Insert the script of Listing 3.8 into each part of the lamp except the light bulb. Place the contents of Listing 3.9 into the bulb (which should be the root). If you've named each of the prims, the scripts will announce which prims received the initial touch.

Listing 3.8: Touch Relay in a Linked Set

```
default
{
    touch_start( integer numDetected ) {
        llOwnerSay("Touched the "+llGetObjectName());
        llMessageLinked(LINK_ROOT, 0, "Touched.", NULL_KEY);
    }
}
```

Listing 3.9: A Light Controlled by a Touch Relay Link Message

```
integer gLightState;

lamplighter()
{
    if ( gLightState == FALSE) {
        llSetPrimitiveParams([PRIM_FULLBRIGHT,ALL_SIDES,FALSE,
                              PRIM_COLOR,ALL_SIDES,<0.5,0.5,0.5>,1.0,
                              PRIM_POINT_LIGHT, FALSE,
                                  <0.0,0.0,0.0>, 0.0, 0.0, 0.5 ]);
    } else {
        llSetPrimitiveParams([PRIM_FULLBRIGHT,ALL_SIDES,TRUE,
                              PRIM_COLOR,ALL_SIDES,<1.0,1.0,0.4>,1.0,
                              PRIM_POINT_LIGHT,TRUE,
                                  <1.0,1.0,1.0>, 1.0, 10.0, 0.6 ]);
    }
}

default
{
    on_rez(integer num) {
        gLightState = FALSE;
        lamplighter();
    }
    state_entry() {
        gLightState = FALSE;
        lamplighter();
    }
    touch_start(integer total_number) {
        gLightState = !gLightState; // toggles between TRUE and FALSE
        lamplighter();
    }
    link_message(integer sender_num, integer num, string str, key id) {
        gLightState = !gLightState;
        lamplighter();
    }
}
```

TALKING TO
AN OBJECT
(AND HAVING
IT LISTEN)

DIALOGS

CREATING
OBJECTS THAT
COMMUNICATE
WITH EACH
OTHER

USING LINK
MESSAGES FOR
PRIM-TO-PRIM
COMMUNICATION
INSIDE AN
OBJECT

EMAIL AND
INSTANT
MESSAGING

SUMMARY

Listing 3.8 is wonderfully simple; it only sets up the relay messages using the function `llMessageLinked()`. You'll notice there is no corresponding event handler. That is because the handler, `link_message()`, needs to appear in the prims of the linked object that will hear the message (in this case the bulb). In `llMessageLinked()`, the first parameter is either a linked set constant or the specific link number of the prim that will be receiving the message. In this script we use `LINK_ROOT` to send a message to the root prim bulb; however, if you wanted, say, three light bulbs, then you'd probably use `LINK_SET` (or make three calls, each with the specific link number of one of the bulbs).

DEFINITION

```
llMessageLinked(integer linkNum,
                integer num, string message, key id)
```

Sends the *num*, *message*, and *id* to the prim specified by its *linkNum*.

linkNum — Linked-set constant describing which prim(s) to send the message to. One of `LINK_ROOT`, `LINK_SET`, `LINK_ALL_OTHERS`, `LINK_ALL_CHILDREN`, `LINK_THIS`, or the integer link number of the receiving prim.

num, message, id — Up to the scripter's discretion.

EVENT DEFINITION

```
link_message(integer senderNum,
             integer num, string message, key id) {}
```

This event is invoked in a script when the containing prim receives a message via `llMessageLinked()`. The SYW website provides additional documentation.

senderNum — The link number of the sending prim.

num, message, id — Up to the scripter's discretion.

The other three parameters of `llMessageLinked()` are passed directly to the `link_message()` event, and are up to the scripter's discretion, meaning any value can be passed. This can be really useful. For example, if you want your object to respond slightly differently depending on the parameters: you would set up the `link_message()` event handler to do different things depending on the input parameters.

When the root prim receives the link message, it toggles the lamp's state between the values of **TRUE** and **FALSE**. This trick can be a useful shortcut to the writing it out, like this:

```
if (gLightState == TRUE) {
    gLightState = FALSE;
} else {
    gLightState = TRUE;
}
```

Figure 3.5 shows the result of this set of linked scripts.

CHAPTER 1
CHAPTER 2

CHAPTER 3

CHAPTER 4
CHAPTER 5
CHAPTER 6
CHAPTER 7
CHAPTER 8
CHAPTER 9
CHAPTER 10
CHAPTER 11
CHAPTER 12
CHAPTER 13
CHAPTER 14
CHAPTER 15
APPENDICES

Figure 3.5: The avatar touched the shade to turn the light off, then touched it again to turn it back on.

Prims with no touch event handler will report the touch event to the root prim. Therefore, technically the script in Listing 3.8 is not needed, because this script does nothing except catch the touch event and report it. However, in a longer, more complex script, child prims may want to do something when touched, in addition to reporting the event to the root prim. You can accommodate this using `llPassTouches()`, which allows both the touched child prim and the root to react to touch events.

 DEFINITION

llPassTouches(integer *pass*)

When called with TRUE in a child prim, will allow touch events to be passed through to the root prim even when scripts in the child have touch event handlers. This function has no effect in a root prim or when the child has no touch event handlers.

pass — TRUE if you want touch events to be passed through to the root prim.

Another approach to making sure the target prim gets the message while avoiding the necessity of putting `llMessageLinked()` relays in all parts of the build is to place a transparent prim around the entire build and let *it* send the message to the `LINK_SET` or the target prim. Figure 3.6 shows an elongated sphere around a complicated build, highlighted so you can see it.

Figure 3.6: To simplify touch management, you can place a transparent prim around a complicated build.

87

A slight disadvantage with this approach is that if other residents enable Highlight Transparent in their client preferences, your object may appear strangely shaped. For most objects this is a nonissue, but for certain types of avatar attachments, wearing a huge bulbous prim may result in personal embarrassment.

TALKING TO
AN OBJECT
(AND HAVING
IT LISTEN)

DIALOGS

CREATING
OBJECTS THAT
COMMUNICATE
WITH EACH
OTHER

USING LINK
MESSAGES FOR
PRIM-TO-PRIM
COMMUNICATION
INSIDE AN
OBJECT

EMAIL AND
INSTANT
MESSAGING

SUMMARY

ASSOCIATING PRIMS WITH THEIR LINK NUMBERS

Scripts do not automatically know what link number is associated with what prim. Thus, if your script wants to talk to a specific prim, it needs to know what link number to use. Assuming you've named each of the prims in your object, the script in Listing 3.10 will create a strided list of pairs [*objectname*, *linknum*]. You could then use `llListFindList()` to look for the name (and then retrieve its link number) of the specific prim you want to send messages to. An observant reader will notice that the strided list happens to be constructed in order of link numbers; however, because you may not always want to cache the entire list, it is useful to remember the link numbers explicitly.

Listing 3.10: Matching Link Numbers to Prim Names

```
list gLinkInfo;
default
{
    state_entry() {
        gLinkInfo = [];
        integer n = llGetNumberOfPrims();
        if (n==1) {
            llOwnerSay("This is a prim, not a linked object");
        } else {
            integer i;
            for (i = 1; i<=n; i++) {
                gLinkInfo += llGetLinkName(i);
                gLinkInfo += i;
            }
            llOwnerSay("Prims in this object are: "+
                    llDumpList2String(gLinkInfo,", "));
        }
    }
}
```

The function `llGetNumberOfPrims()` returns the number of prims in the object. In a multiprim object, the root is number 1, and other prims follow. A single-prim object has the link number 0. The function `llGetLinkNumber()` returns the link number of the prim containing the script. The key and the name of specific prims can be retrieved with the functions `llGetLinkKey()` and `llGetLinkName()`.

 DEFINITION

key llGetLinkKey(integer *linkNum*)

Returns the key of the prim with the associated *linkNum*. Do not provide a *linkNum* that may refer to multiple prims, such as LINK_SET. Do not use LINK_THIS as the *linkNum*; use llGetKey() instead.

linkNum — The link number of the prim for which the key is requested.

DEFINITION

string llGetLinkName(integer linkNum)
```

Returns `string`, which contains the name of the prim with the associated `linkNum`. Do not provide a `linkNum` that may refer to multiple prims, such as `LINK_SET`. Do not use `LINK_THIS` as the `linkNum`; use `llGetObjectName()` instead. The name will be truncated to 266 characters.

> `linkNum` — The link number of the prim for which the name is requested.

# EMAIL AND INSTANT MESSAGING

Thus far, this chapter has presented ways for controlling in-world objects by talking with them, for objects to talk to each other, and for objects to talk to themselves. Your creations can usefully employ other important conversations—for example, those between in-world artifacts and the 2D Web. You can also write handler methods capable of sending and receiving email-message traffic. Common uses for this include sending an instant message or an email to an object's owner, as shown in this section.

Chapter 12 expands this theme, showing how *Second Life* supports HTTP requests—for example, to get content from the Web or to accept RSS-style news feeds.

## SEND ME SOME EMAIL

You may have received email from other residents on your contacts roster when you were not in-world (assuming you provided a real email account when you created your avatar). Thus, you may already know that email somehow manages to get from *Second Life* to the "rest of life." This section explains the "somehow," giving you a script for using email in conjunction with *Second Life*.

In Listing 3.11 you create an email-enabled service bell that customers can ring to summon you in-world if you're offline. It's the kind of thing you see in "rest-of-life" boutique hotels or at service counters. A customer walks up to the counter and taps a little bell, summoning help. That's what you're going to construct, and you'll put the code from Listing 3.11 into it. You can see an example of its use in Figure 3.7, where a customer walks into the shop, taps the service bell, hears a reassuring "ding," then is asked to make a single-line comment, which will be sent via instant message to the shop owner. If the shop owner is offline an email will be sent.
```

TALKING TO
AN OBJECT
(AND HAVING
IT LISTEN)

DIALOGS

CREATING
OBJECTS THAT
COMMUNICATE
WITH EACH
OTHER

USING LINK
MESSAGES FOR
PRIM-TO-PRIM
COMMUNICATION
INSIDE AN
OBJECT

EMAIL AND
INSTANT
MESSAGING

SUMMARY

Listing 3.11: Customer Bell—Service Please!

```
key      gOnlineRequest;
key      gNameRequest;
integer gIsOnline = FALSE;
integer gLandOwner = FALSE;
key      gKey = NULL_KEY;
string  gMailAddr = "noone@somewhere.com"; // replace with yours
integer gEmail = FALSE;
string  gName = "";
list     gAgents = [];
list     gHandles = [];
list     gMessages = [];
float    UPDATE_INTERVAL = 5.0;

key getAnOwner() {
    if (gKey == NULL_KEY) {
        if (gLandOwner) {
            return llGetLandOwnerAt(llGetPos());
        } else {
            return llGetOwner();
        }
    } else {
        return gKey;
    }
}
init() {
    llSetTimerEvent(UPDATE_INTERVAL);
    updateName();
    updateOnlineStatus();
    llSetTimerEvent(1);
}
updateOnlineStatus() {
    gOnlineRequest = llRequestAgentData(getAnOwner(),DATA_ONLINE);
}
updateName() {
    gNameRequest = llRequestAgentData(getAnOwner(),DATA_NAME);
}
updateStatus(string s) {
    key k = getAnOwner();
    if (s=="1")   gIsOnline = TRUE;
    else          gIsOnline = FALSE;
}
repeatStoredMessages() {
    integer i;
    for (i=0; i<llGetListLength(gMessages); i++) {
        llInstantMessage(getAnOwner(), llList2String(gMessages, i));
    }
    gMessages = [];
}
```

CHAPTER 1
CHAPTER 2
CHAPTER 3
CHAPTER 4
CHAPTER 5
CHAPTER 6
CHAPTER 7
CHAPTER 8
CHAPTER 9
CHAPTER 10
CHAPTER 11
CHAPTER 12
CHAPTER 13
CHAPTER 14
CHAPTER 15
APPENDICES

```
default {
    state_entry() {
        init();
    }
    on_rez(integer n) {
        init();
    }
    timer() {
        updateOnlineStatus();
        if (gIsOnline) {
            llSetText(gName + " is online.\n"+
                    "Click here to send a message.", <0,1,0>, 1);
            repeatStoredMessages();
        } else {
            llSetText(gName+
                    " is offline.\nClick here to send a message.",
                <1,0,0>, 1);
        }
    }
    dataserver(key request, string data) {
        if (data == "1" || data == "0"){
            updateStatus(data);
        } else {
            gName = data;
            llSetText("Getting online status for "+gName,<1,1,1>,1);
            llSetTimerEvent(UPDATE_INTERVAL);
        }
    }

    touch_start(integer touch_num) {
        integer i;
        llTriggerSound("a4f16ad0-4471-ddbb-ad5e-d7b2d0df5d21", 1.0);
        for (i=0; i<touch_num; i++) {
            gAgents += llDetectedKey(i);
            gHandles += llListen(0, "", llDetectedKey(i), "");
            llSay(0, llDetectedName(i) +
                    ", please say your message (one line only) "+
                    "and it will be recorded or sent.");
        }
    }
    listen(integer number, string name, key id, string message) {
        integer agent_index = llListFindList(gAgents, [id]);
        if (agent_index != -1) {
            llListenRemove(llList2Integer(gHandles, agent_index));
            gHandles = llDeleteSubList(gHandles, agent_index, agent_index);
            gAgents = llDeleteSubList(gAgents, agent_index, agent_index);
            if (gIsOnline) {
                llInstantMessage(getAnOwner(), name+": "+message);
            } else {
                llEmail(gMailAddr, "SL Listening", message);
            }
            llSay(0, "Thank you, " + name +", your message has been sent.");
        }
    }
}
```

TALKING TO
AN OBJECT
(AND HAVING
IT LISTEN)

DIALOGS

CREATING
OBJECTS THAT
COMMUNICATE
WITH EACH
OTHER

USING LINK
MESSAGES FOR
PRIM-TO-PRIM
COMMUNICATION
INSIDE AN
OBJECT

 EMAIL AND
INSTANT
MESSAGING

SUMMARY

Figure 3.7: The visitor interacts with the bell to have a message sent to the owner.

The script in Listing 3.11 is longer than most of the others in this chapter, but bears inclusion because of its utility. This script owes its inspiration, and parts of its code, to Online Status Indicator v1.6 (author unknown), and other parts attributed to Online Tracker/Message Keeper by Guzar Fonzarelli.

The script has a number of helper functions. The `getAnOwner()` function gets either the shop owner or the bell's owner. While you could just use `llGetOwner()`, checking who owns the land can be useful. For example, the location may be up for rent, and you want to contact the store's owner to negotiate a rental agreement.

The `init()` function gets the name of the bell's owner and does a periodic check to see whether the owner is online. Both `state_entry()` and `on_rez()` call `init()`. The bell finds its owner by first determining the UUID of the owner, and then getting the owner's name through this request:

```
gNameRequest = llRequestAgentData(getAnOwner(), DATA_NAME);
```

It knows the owner's online state through the following call:

```
gOnlineRequest = llRequestAgentData(getAnOwner(), DATA_ONLINE);
```

Note that `llRequestAgentData()` sets up an asynchronous request whose results are handled by the `dataserver()` event handler in the `default` state. `dataserver()` receives the direct responses to these requests and sets the global variable *gName* to cache the name of the correct owner. The first call to `llRequestAgentData()` asks for the agent's name, using `DATA_NAME`. When the name is returned in the `dataserver()` event, the script makes the second call to `llRequestAgentData()`—this time for the agent's status, using `DATA_ONLINE`.

 DEFINITION

> ### `key llRequestAgentData(key id, integer data)`
>
> Requests data about the agent specified by `id`. When the data is ready, the `dataserver()` event is triggered. Returns the handle that identifies this request.
>
> `id` — The UUID of an avatar. IDs of objects or groups will not trigger events.
>
> `data` — Bitwise flag; a combination of `DATA_ONLINE`, `DATA_NAME`, `DATA_BORN`, `DATA_RATING`, and `DATA_PAYINFO`.

EVENT DEFINITION

```
dataserver(key queryHandle, string data) {}
```

This event is invoked when the script receives asynchronous data originally requested by one of several different functions. The SYW website provides additional documentation.

queryHandle — The handle returned by the requesting function.

data — The requested data.

CHAPTER 4
CHAPTER 5
CHAPTER 6
CHAPTER 7
CHAPTER 8
CHAPTER 9
CHAPTER 10
CHAPTER 11
CHAPTER 12
CHAPTER 13
CHAPTER 14
CHAPTER 15
APPENDICES

The `timer()` event handler does a periodic update to see if the owner is online using `updateOnlineStatus()`. If she is, the script forwards all stored messages. Otherwise, it sets the float text of the bell to say the owner is offline, but a message can still be sent.

The `touch_start()` handler responds to someone touching the bell. It finds the key of the avatar who touched it, and then sends that avatar a message (on the public channel 0) to ask them to type a message. It also sets up a `listen()` event handler to catch the response.

Notice how this script manages the `llListen()` handles, *gHandles*. In the `touch_start()` event handler, it creates a new `llListen()` event filter, which returns a handle. The script adds that handle to the `list` variable *gHandles*:

```
gHandles += llListen(0, "", llDetectedKey(i), "");
```

Note that while this listen is on channel 0, it will only listen to the specified avatar. Also, as soon as the avatar chats a message, the script removes the handle from the *gHandles* list:

```
llListenRemove(llList2Integer(gHandles, agent_index));
```

This script does not have an error-checking step that removes the listener if the avatar decides not to send the message. Because `llListen()` on channel 0 is so expensive, a griefer could potentially cause serious problems to the sim. To solve this problem, you could add a timer that removes the listen (for that particular avatar) after a certain timeout interval has passed, in a similar manner as for dialogs.

The `listen()` event handler loops through the list of residents who have dinged the bell. You may ask, Why not simply dispose of each bell ring? Why stack requests into the list *gAgents*? The answer is that owing to the long delay that can result from sending an email, additional residents may have rung up the shopkeeper. Creating and working through a cache (in this case, the list of residents who have rung the bell) is an excellent way of dealing with the asynchronous nature of event handling. When the owner is online, the script sends the owner an IM; otherwise it sends an email. In an attempt to reduce the amount of spam in **SL**, both functions delay the script after sending their messages. Spam relies on being able to send millions of messages in no time flat. Any significant delay—especially 20 seconds caused by `llEmail()`—means that much less spam can be generated.

TALKING TO
AN OBJECT
(AND HAVING
IT LISTEN)

DIALOGS

CREATING
OBJECTS THAT
COMMUNICATE
WITH EACH
OTHER

USING LINK
MESSAGES FOR
PRIM-TO-PRIM
COMMUNICATION
INSIDE AN
OBJECT

EMAIL AND
INSTANT
MESSAGING

SUMMARY

DEFINITION

llEmail(string *address*, string *subject*, string *message*)

Sends an email to the *address* with the specified *subject* and with the *message* in the body. Pauses the script for 20 seconds. These emails will always have the sender [key]@lsl. secondlife.com where [key] is the UUID of the prim containing the script sending the email. The length of the entire email is limited to 4,096 characters, including the *subject*, *message*, and other headers (such as the address).

    address — A valid email address.

    subject — A string for the subject line of the email.

    message — A string containing the body of the message.

DEFINITION

llInstantMessage(key *userID*, string *message*)

Sends the user an IM to containing the *message*. Delays the script for 2.0 seconds.

    userID — A valid avatar UUID.

    message — A string containing the body of the message.

OBJECT-TO-OBJECT EMAIL

Objects can send each other email using the address [key]@lsl.secondlife.com. A script calls the function llGetNextEmail() to request the next waiting email, and if an email is waiting it will be returned in the event email().

DEFINITION

llGetNextEmail(string *address*, string *subject*)

Gets the next waiting email with the appropriate address and/or subject. *address* and *subject* act like filters, just as for llListen(). If a matching email is found, it will trigger an email() event. If no matching email is found, this function has no effect.

    address — The address of the sender. Wildcard is "".

    subject — The subject of the email. Wildcard is "".

EVENT DEFINITION

CHAPTER 1
CHAPTER 2

CHAPTER 3

CHAPTER 4
CHAPTER 5
CHAPTER 6
CHAPTER 7
CHAPTER 8
CHAPTER 9
CHAPTER 10
CHAPTER 11
CHAPTER 12
CHAPTER 13
CHAPTER 14
CHAPTER 15
APPENDICES

```
email(string time, string address, string subject,
      string message, integer numRemaining) {}
```

This event is triggered when a request by `llGetNextEmail()` is answered. The SYW website provides additional documentation.

> *time* — Timestamp of the email, in number of seconds elapsed since midnight, January 1, 1970.
>
> *address* — The sender's email address.
>
> *subject* — The subject line.
>
> *message* — The body of the message.
>
> *numRemaining* — The number of emails left to process.

Listing 3.12 shows a simple script that announces the key of its containing prim and then waits to be touched. When touched, it calls `llGetNextEmail()` to retrieve any waiting email.

Listing 3.12: Retrieving Email

```
default
{
    state_entry() {
        llOwnerSay("My key is "+(string)llGetKey());
    }
    touch_start(integer _n) {
        llGetNextEmail("", "");
    }
    email( string time, string address, string subject, string message,➥
            integer numRemaining ) {
        llOwnerSay("Message from "+address+" received at time "+time);
        llOwnerSay("Subject: "+subject);
        llOwnerSay(message);
        llOwnerSay("There are "+(string)numRemaining+" remaining");
    }
}
```

Listing 3.13 shows the simple script that sends the email to the key that Listing 3.12 announced.

Listing 3.13: Object-to-Object Email

```
default
{
    state_entry() {
        string target = "30e0c7e0-55d9-cd8e-c477-6bb4e9e99a2f";
        target += "@lsl.secondlife.com";
        llEmail(target, "Testing", "Hello!");
    }
}
```

The results of this interaction are shown below; you can see that the email headers include some additional information. The `Local-Position` is the location of the sending object, rounded *down* to the nearest integer (the actual position was `<65.999, 143.056, 106.862>`).

TALKING TO
AN OBJECT
(AND HAVING
IT LISTEN)

DIALOGS

CREATING
OBJECTS THAT
COMMUNICATE
WITH EACH
OTHER

USING LINK
MESSAGES FOR
PRIM-TO-PRIM
COMMUNICATION
INSIDE AN
OBJECT

EMAIL AND
INSTANT
MESSAGING

SUMMARY

```
[20:13]   Receiving Object: Message from e86b6322-e573-fafd-4360-1c57152b680b@
             lsl.secondlife.com received at time 1209266020
[20:13]   Receiving Object: Subject: Testing Email!
[20:13]   Receiving Object: Object-Name: Sending Object
Region: Hennepin (263168, 254208)
Local-Position: (65, 143, 106)

Hello!
[20:13]   Receiving Object: There are 0 remaining
```

The headers are separated from the body with two newlines, so the "real" message can be retrieved with this snippet:

```
integer startMsg = llSubStringIndex(message, "\n\n");
message = llDeleteSubString(message, 0, startMsg + 1);
```

SUMMARY

Thinking in terms of conversations has become natural for commanding and controlling objects and applications. It is becoming an accepted design model, even outside the context of *Second Life*. Many applications, for example, are using the Jabber (XMPP) protocol to create intelligent, responsive applications. Many more are using AJAX for rich Internet applications. If you understand and embrace this model, you're on your way to creating unique applications, especially in *Second Life*.

MAKING AND MOVING OBJECTS

Much of the excitement of *Second Life* is built upon active objects—objects that suddenly appear or disappear, objects that change their location, objects that carry avatars, objects that can create other prims, and objects that convey animation. This chapter presents the basics of making, controlling, and moving objects. Here you will encounter a flower that creates its own petals, an animated sculpture, whirling dust devils, and all manner of things that rotate merrily.

THE PRESTO, ABRACADABRA OF REZZING

THE PRESTO, ABRACADABRA OF REZZING

CONTROLLING MOTION OF NONPHYSICAL OBJECTS

SUMMARY

Rezzing is the creation of a new object in-world. You are already familiar with manual creation of objects; scripting this process gives you additional flexibility and power in any situation where you have build privileges. This section presents a few examples of how to automatically rez and control objects—including how to cheat on your prim budget.

A few caveats do apply. For example, a rezzed object must already exist in the inventory of the rezzing object. That is, you can rez a basic object that you have in inventory and mutate it, but unlike the build tool in-world, a script needs to start from *something*. The rezzing object must have full modify permissions on the rezzed object. Additionally, LSL does not allow you to create new LSL scripts automatically.

LOOP REZZERS

One thing we all know from firsthand experience is that making large numbers of repetitive objects is a huge pain. Anyone who has ever made skirts or hair or any other artifacts with large numbers of prims has certainly experienced the pain. Fortunately, a class of scripts generically known as *loop rezzers* has evolved to handle the creation of a large number of similar objects, such as skirts, flower petals, spiral staircases, and sculptures. You can find some excellent examples of loop rezzers in-world, including a very nice one offered freely at Vint's primskirtbuilder sandbox, Mindulle <231, 152, 125>.

Loop rezzers can be used as the basis of your own projects. Often, loop rezzers delete themselves after they have rezzed the more complex object. Other rezzers can play a more active part in the life cycle of their rezzed items. The next few examples illustrate how to use these automatic loop rezzers.

Making a Flower with a Loop Rezzer

Listing 4.1 illustrates a loop rezzer that creates a flower complete with petals. Put it inside the root prim. For this flower, that would probably mean the "eye" of the flower head. Note that this script doesn't actually **link** the prims together, so you could always delete the "generator" prim after the autogeneration has completed. This kind of script is extremely useful in place of finicky builds that need prims to line up exactly: you can do all the math in the script, rather than manually.

Listing 4.1: Flower Loop Rezzer

```
integer gNumPetals = 8;                    // how many objects
list    gPetals = [];
integer gCmdChannel = 990;
integer gCmdPetalChannel = 991;

makePetals() {
    integer petal;
    float basicAngle = (360.0 / gNumPetals) * DEG_TO_RAD;
    float deltaRot = 0.0;
    vector   currPos = llGetLocalPos();
    rotation rootRot = llGetRootRotation();
```

CHAPTER 1
CHAPTER 2
CHAPTER 3

CHAPTER 4

CHAPTER 5
CHAPTER 6
CHAPTER 7
CHAPTER 8
CHAPTER 9
CHAPTER 10
CHAPTER 11
CHAPTER 12
CHAPTER 13
CHAPTER 14
CHAPTER 15
APPENDIX

```
    for (petal=0; petal<gNumPetals; petal++) {
        rotation newRotation = llEuler2Rot(<deltaRot+0,0,0>);
        newRotation = newRotation * rootRot;
        vector newOffset = <0,0,0.2> * newRotation + currPos;
        llRezObject(llGetInventoryName(INVENTORY_OBJECT, 0),
                    newOffset, ZERO_VECTOR, newRotation, gCmdPetalChannel);
        deltaRot += basicAngle;
    }
}
unLoop() {
    integer i = 0;
    for (; i < llGetListLength(gPetals); i++){
        key k = llList2Key(gPetals, i);
        llSay(gCmdPetalChannel, (string)k); // tell it to go away
    }
    gPetals = [];
}

default
{
    state_entry() {
        llListen(gCmdChannel,"", llGetOwner(), "");
    }
    listen(integer channel, string name, key id, string message) {
        llOwnerSay("Message received: "+message);
        if (llToLower(message) == "rez") {
            makePetals();
        } else if (llToLower(message) == "vanish"){
            llOwnerSay("cleaning up ...");
            unLoop();
        } else {
            llOwnerSay("psst! Say either \"rez\" or \"vanish\"");
        }
    }
    object_rez(key id) {
        list details =llGetObjectDetails(id, [OBJECT_NAME, OBJECT_POS, OBJECT_ROT]);
        gPetals += [id];
    }
}
```

When the user types **rez** on the command channel, the script calls the function makePetals(). That function calculates how many petals to make and where to put them. The math of the quaternions is covered in the "Using Quaternions" section of this chapter, but basically the plan is to put a circle of petals around the root prim. The key line is

```
llRezObject(llGetInventoryName(INVENTORY_OBJECT, 0),
            newOffset, ZERO_VECTOR, newRotation, gCmdPetalChannel);
```

The llRezObject() call creates the named object at a given offset, velocity, and rotation. The last parameter is a "start" parameter for the rezzed object, and in this case the petal will use it to listen to commands from the controller. The function llRezAtRoot() is a useful alternative: it allows you to control the position of the new object based on its root prim.

The other important activity this script does is maintain a list of all the objects it has rezzed. You can then use the list to send messages to the new objects, to link them together, and to otherwise coordinate. The object_rez() event handler is raised for all objects rezzed by this prim. Conveniently, this event is raised for all scripts inside the controller prim, allowing one script to do the actual rezzing while another script manages the newly rezzed objects. This script uses the list of petals to send each petal a message;

CHAPTER 4

THE PRESTO,
ABRACADABRA
OF REZZING

CONTROLLING
MOTION OF
NONPHYSICAL
OBJECTS

SUMMARY

for this demonstration, the petals will kill themselves to clean up the extra prims, but of course you can use that communication channel for any instruction. It also calls `llGetObjectDetails()`, described in Chapter 5, "Sensing the World," to find some useful facts about the object it just rezzed.

 DEFINITION

```
llRezObject(string inventory,
            vector pos, vector vel, rotation rot,
            integer param)
```

```
llRezAtRoot(string inventory,
            vector pos, vector vel, rotation rot,
            integer param)
```

`llRezObject()` rezzes inventory so that its geometric center is at *pos*, whereas `llRezAtRoot()` positions *inventory*'s root prim centered at *pos*. Silently fails to rez if *pos* is more than 10m away or you do not have build permissions.

> *inventory* — The name of an object in inventory (best stored in the prim's Content folder, along with the script).

> *pos* — Position to rez the object (in region coordinates).

> *vel* — Velocity (max. is 250).

> *rot* — Rotation (circular; no max.).

> *param* — Start parameter of the new object; it will be passed to the new object in the parameter for `on_rez()`, and also returned by `llGetStartParameter()`. The value 0 should be reserved for objects rezzed from inventory.

 EVENT DEFINITION

```
object_rez(key id) {}
```

This event is invoked when the script has successfully rezzed an object. The SYW website provides additional documentation.

> *id* — The key of the newly rezzed object.

Listing 4.2 shows the script in the petal. This script uses the ***start_param*** parameter in the `on_rez()` event handler as the listen channel for controller commands. When a `listen()` event arrives, it double-checks to make sure the received message is specifically for it, and then calls `llDie()` to self-delete. If the controller has other interesting activities to coordinate, the script can manage them appropriately. If the script needs to find the start parameter outside the `on_rez()` event, it can also call `llGetStartParameter()`.

DEFINITION

```
integer llGetStartParameter()
```

Returns an integer that represents what the script was started or rezzed with. If rezzed from inventory, the value is zero.

DEFINITION

```
llDie()
```

Deletes the object when called in any prim in a link set. The object does not go to the owner's Inventory:Trash. Will not delete attachments.

Listing 4.2: Flower Petal

```
integer gCmdChannel;
string gMyKey;
default{
    on_rez(integer start_param) {
        gCmdChannel = start_param;
        gMyKey = (string) llGetKey(); // get my own key
        llListen(gCmdChannel, "", NULL_KEY,"");
    }
    listen(integer channel, string name, key id, string message) {
        if (message == gMyKey){
            llDie();
        }
    }
}
```

Figure 4.1 shows the flower pots. With only one tiny change to the code you can make the flowers multilayered. After you've read the section on quaternions, come back to this script and see if you can figure it out. (The script is at SYW HQ if you want to check the answer.)

WARNING

These rez functions will silently fail to rez an object if the target position is more than 10 meters away. If your script is mysteriously failing to rez things, make sure you haven't (for example) written `pos = <0,0,1>` rather than `pos = llGetPos() + <0,0,1>`.

CHAPTER 1
CHAPTER 2
CHAPTER 3

CHAPTER 4

CHAPTER 5
CHAPTER 6
CHAPTER 7
CHAPTER 8
CHAPTER 9
CHAPTER 10
CHAPTER 11
CHAPTER 12
CHAPTER 13
CHAPTER 14
CHAPTER 15
APPENDICES

CHAPTER 4

THE PRESTO,
ABRACADABRA
OF REZZING

CONTROLLING
MOTION OF
NONPHYSICAL
OBJECTS

SUMMARY

Figure 4.1: Three flower pots autogenerate their petals. The flowers generate many petals with only a tiny change to the script.

Making the Flower Petals into a Flower

If you want to connect the new objects together you can use `llCreateLink()` to link them. This script must have permission to modify links, which it can do with a call to `llRequestPermissions()`, as shown in Listing 4.3. There are also two functions that break links: `llBreakLink(integer linkNum)` and `llBreakAllLinks()`. Each time a link changes a `changed()` event is triggered. `llCreateLink()` doesn't return the *linkNum* because link numbers can change a lot—not only the new parent and its new child, but also any other prims in the linkset.

 DEFINITION

`llCreateLink(key target, integer parent)`

Links the target object to the calling object (the one containing the script).

target — The UUID of the object to link into the set.

parent — Boolean: if *parent*==TRUE, the caller is the parent; if *parent*==FALSE, the target is the parent.

Listing 4.3: Linking Objects

```
string gObjectName;
default
{
    state_entry() {
        gObjectName = llGetInventoryName(INVENTORY_OBJECT, 0);
        llRequestPermissions(llGetOwner(), PERMISSION_CHANGE_LINKS);
    }
    touch_start(integer n) {
        vector pos = llGetPos();
        llRezObject( gObjectName, <pos.x+1,pos.y+1,pos.z>,
                        ZERO_VECTOR, ZERO_ROTATION, 0);
    }
    object_rez(key id) {
        if (llGetPermissions() & PERMISSION_CHANGE_LINKS)  {
            llCreateLink(id,TRUE); // caller will be the root
        }
    }
    changed(integer change) {
        if (change & CHANGED_LINK) {
            llOwnerSay("NewLink "+(string)llGetLinkNumber());
        }
    }
}
```

When you have created the linkset, you can use a master script to set many of the properties of the linked prims using `llSetLinkPrimitiveParams()`, which is described in Appendix A, "Setting Primitive Parameters." Table 4.1 also shows a small handful of functions for specific properties. The function `llGetNumberOfPrims()` tells you how many prims are in the object. Some of these functions were demonstrated in Listing 3.10.

TABLE 4.1: FUNCTIONS THAT GET AND SET LINK PROPERTIES

FUNCTION	BEHAVIOR
integer llGetLinkNumber()	Returns an integer that tells the script what number is assigned to the prim containing the script.
key llGetLinkKey(integer *linkNum*)	Returns a key that is the UUID of the prim that is link number *linkNum* in the current link set.
string llGetLinkName(integer *linkNum*)	Returns a string that is the name of *linkNum* in link set.
llSetLinkAlpha(integer *linkNumber*, float *alpha*, integer *face*)	Sets *face* of *linkNum* to *alpha*.
llSetLinkColor(integer *linkNumber*, vector *color*, integer *face*)	Sets *face* of *linkNum* to *color*.
llSetLinkTexture(integer *linkNumber*, string *texture*, integer *face*)	Sets *face* of *linkNum* to *texture*.
llSetLinkPrimitiveParams(integer *linkNum*, list *properties*)	Sets a variety of *properties* for *linkNum*. Details are provided in Appendix A.

DEFINITION

```
integer llGetNumberOfPrims()
```

Returns an integer that represents the number of prims in the link set, including any avatars sitting on the object. `llGetObjectPrimCount(key *id*)` gets the number of prims in another object.

CHAPTER 4

THE PRESTO,
ABRACADABRA
OF REZZING

CONTROLLING
MOTION OF
NONPHYSICAL
OBJECTS

SUMMARY

↘ A TEMPORARY REZZER

As you perhaps already know, it's possible to make an object or a set of linked objects persist in-world temporarily simply by checking the object's Temporary check box. Temporary objects automatically die after approximately 60 seconds and do not count against a parcel's prim limit. You might use this to create a little rain shower, to make flowers bloom, or to produce a small school of flying fish on cue.

Essentially, the temporary object springs into existence, creates its transient effect on the environment or other avatars, and approximately 60 seconds later is removed by *SL*'s garbage-collection system. The hopping ball, illustrated in Figure 4.2 and described in Listing 4.4, is an example of a just-for-fun visual effect you might use to attract attention to your shop or herald an event. The key thing this script does when rezzing the set of objects is to **set up communication channels** between the objects so you can control them. This script shows temporary rezzing, communication between the items, and basic prim animation.

Listing 4.4: A Chain of Temporary Hopping Balls

```
string  COMM_MESSAGE = "bounceYou";
integer MAX_BALLS = 5;
integer NUMBER_HOPS = 3;
integer gListenChannel;
integer gSpeakChannel;
integer gCountHops=0;
string  gObjectName;

hop_ball(){
    gCountHops++;
    vector pos = llGetPos();
    llSetPrimitiveParams([PRIM_POSITION, <pos.x,pos.y,pos.z+1>]);
    llSleep(0.5);
    // tell the next ball to bounce
    string msg = "Ball #"+(string)gSpeakChannel+" "+COMM_MESSAGE;
    llSay(gSpeakChannel,msg);
    // go back to original position
    llSetPrimitiveParams([PRIM_POSITION, <pos.x,pos.y,pos.z>]);
}

setUpListens(){
    key myKey = llGetKey();
    gObjectName = llKey2Name(myKey);
    gListenChannel = llGetStartParameter();
    if (gListenChannel == 0) {
        llSetText("Touch me for ball sculpture!",<1.0,1.0,1.0>,1.0);
        gSpeakChannel = llCeil( llFrand( 100000 ) );
    } else {
        llSetText("",<0.0,0.0,0.0>,0.0);
        gSpeakChannel = gListenChannel+1;
        llListen(gListenChannel,gObjectName,NULL_KEY,"");
        llSetPrimitiveParams([PRIM_TEMP_ON_REZ, TRUE]);
    }
    vector color= < llCeil(llFrand(255.0)),
                    llCeil(llFrand(255.0)),
                    llCeil(llFrand(255.0))> / 255.0;
    llSetColor( color, ALL_SIDES);
}
```

CHAPTER 1
CHAPTER 2
CHAPTER 3

CHAPTER 4

CHAPTER 5
CHAPTER 6
CHAPTER 7
CHAPTER 8
CHAPTER 9
CHAPTER 10
CHAPTER 11
CHAPTER 12
CHAPTER 13
CHAPTER 14
CHAPTER 15
APPENDICES

```
default {
    on_rez(integer n) {
        setUpListens();
    }
    state_entry() {
        setUpListens();
    }
    listen(integer channel, string name, key k, string msg) {
        string checkString = "Ball #"+(string)gListenChannel+" "+COMM_MESSAGE;
        if (msg == checkString) {
            hop_ball();
        }
    }
    touch_start(integer n){
        if (gListenChannel == 0) { // first object
            vector pos = llGetPos();
            integer i;
            for (i=0; i<MAX_BALLS; i++) {
                llRezObject(gObjectName, <pos.x+i+1,pos.y,pos.z>,
                            ZERO_VECTOR, ZERO_ROTATION, gSpeakChannel+i);
            }
            llSleep(0.2);
            hop_ball();
            gCountHops = 0;
            llSetTimerEvent(10.0);
        }
    }
    timer(){
        hop_ball();
        if (gCountHops > NUMBER_HOPS) llSetTimerEvent(0.0);
    }
}
```

Figure 4.2: Temporary balls self-generate and then hop on command.

The action begins in the main ball (the brown one with the floating text), which is the controller for the other five balls in the chain of hopping balls. The main ball's Content folder contains the script and an identical copy of itself that will be used for the automatic rez. When the main ball is touched, it rezzes a set of five balls, each of which sets up a communication channel to listen to the ball immediately before it in the chain.

The first thing the script does is call setUpListens(), which sets up prim properties depending on whether the ball was rezzed from inventory or from the main ball. It uses the line

```
gListenChannel = llGetStartParameter();
```

to find out how the object was rezzed: if the parameter is zero, it was rezzed from inventory. Throughout the code, the test if (gListenChannel == 0) checks whether the ball is the main ball or one of the children.

CHAPTER 4

THE PRESTO,
ABRACADABRA
OF REZZING

CONTROLLING
MOTION OF
NONPHYSICAL
OBJECTS

SUMMARY

In the function `setUpListens()`, the first thing the balls do is get their start parameters. The main ball sets up the floating text with `llSetText()` and selects a random number to use as a communication channel for the next ball—*gSpeakChannel*. The main ball speaks to the first ball in the chain, the channel *gSpeakChannel*, and rezzes it with the value *gSpeakChannel* as its start parameter; the first ball then caches that value in *gListenChannel* and sets up an `llListen()` on it. Each ball gets a unique communication channel for passing messages along the chain; each ball except the main one selects the channel to speak on using the following line:

```
gSpeakChannel = gListenChannel + 1;
```

`setUpListens()` takes care of a few other initialization things. All balls except the main one set themselves to Temporary with a call to `llSetPrimitiveParams()`, using the property `PRIM_TEMP_ON_REZ`. Because floating text is a persistent feature of the prim, the script must explicitly set the text to be empty; otherwise the balls will all have a message. Finally, all balls select a random color.

When the main ball is touched, its `touch_start()` event handler fires. (Avatars can of course touch other balls, but the script ignores it.) The handler generates all the children with a sequence of calls to `llRezObject()`, selects an appropriate position for the new object, and sets zero velocity and rotation. Most importantly, the event handler passes in a parameter that the new object will start with so the object knows it was rezzed by a script and can set up an appropriate `llListen()`. The script then sleeps for a moment to give the rezzed balls time to set themselves up before calling the function `hop_ball()` and setting up a timer event that will hop the ball a few more times. `hop_ball()` moves the ball, waits a moment, tells the next ball in the chain to hop, and moves back to its original position.

Meanwhile, the `listen()` event handlers for the balls down the chain are waiting to be told to hop. When the right message comes in, the ball hops and tells the next one to hop, creating a nice, wavy, hopping pattern.

Because this script sets off the communication channels only once, touching the ball more than once produces some interesting effects. Interesting modifications to this script include selecting a new *gSpeakChannel* every time the ball is touched, or moving the main ball slightly.

 ## A LESS-TEMPORARY TEMPORARY REZZER

As you may know by now, land owners in *Second Life* are limited in the number of prims allowed on a parcel of a given size. You can build anything you can dream up on a common 512m² parcel as long as you don't use more than 117 primitives. You can find your land's limits by selecting "About Land..." on the World menu. If this limit cramps your style or your vision, then read on; perhaps the "permanent" temporary rezzer can help.

The five garden objects shown in Figure 4.3 use 38 prims: the pink flamingo is 14 prims, the decorative jack-o'-lantern is 3 prims, the Japanese lamp is 6 prims, the wind chime is 12 prims, and the prairie flowers are 3 prims. Of course, if you rez these objects and set their Temporary attributes, they won't count against your prim count on the basis that they will soon be garbage-collected by the simulator engine. Alas, that won't do you much good, because somewhere in about 60 seconds your lovely lawn adornments will be as gone as an April snowfall...unless you can devise a way to make your temporary creations less temporary. Listing 4.5 reveals the solution.

CHAPTER 1
CHAPTER 2
CHAPTER 3

CHAPTER 4

CHAPTER 5
CHAPTER 6
CHAPTER 7
CHAPTER 8
CHAPTER 9
CHAPTER 10
CHAPTER 11
CHAPTER 12
CHAPTER 13
CHAPTER 14
CHAPTER 15
APPENDICES

Figure 4.3: These five permanent garden ornaments use 38 available prims. Temporary objects do not count against the limits.

Listing 4.5: The Perpetual Temp Rezzer

```
integer gListenChannel = 989;
float   gExpiration = 75.0;
list    gPositions = [<0, 0, 1.0>,   // Chimes
                      <1, 0, -0.4>,  // Jackolantern
                      <0, 1, -0.1>,  // Japanese lamp
                      <1, 1, 0.35>]; // Pink Flamingo
list    gRotations = [<0,0,225>,
                      <0,0,66>,
                      <0,0,0>,
                      <275,0,0>];

rotation simpleEuler2Rot(vector eul) {
    eul *= DEG_TO_RAD; //convert to radians rotation
    return llEuler2Rot( eul ); //convert to quaternion
}

default
{
    state_entry() {
        llListen(gListenChannel, "", llGetOwner(),"");
    }
    listen(integer channel, string name, key id, string message) {
        if (llToLower(message) == "presto"){
            llSetTimerEvent(2.0);
        } else if (llToLower(message) == "vanish"){
            llOwnerSay("Objects will be cleaned up shortly");
            llSetTimerEvent(0.0);
        } else {
            llOwnerSay("psst! Say either \"presto\" or \"vanish\"");
        }
    }
    timer() {
        integer nItems = llGetInventoryNumber(INVENTORY_OBJECT);
        integer i = 0;
        vector controlPos = llGetPos();
        rotation controlRot = llGetRot();
        vector tempObjPos;
        rotation tempObjRot;
        for (; i < nItems; i++){
            string name = llGetInventoryName(INVENTORY_OBJECT, i);
            tempObjPos = controlPos + llList2Vector(gPositions,i);
            tempObjRot = simpleEuler2Rot(llList2Vector(gRotations,i));
            llRezObject(name, tempObjPos, ZERO_VECTOR, tempObjRot, 1);
        }
        llSetTimerEvent(gExpiration);
    }
}
```

CHAPTER 4

THE PRESTO,
ABRACADABRA
OF REZZING

CONTROLLING
MOTION OF
NONPHYSICAL
OBJECTS

SUMMARY

Because the prairie-flowers object has the lowest prim count of these five objects, it will become the core controller using Listing 4.5; that is, it will be a permanent object. Its `state_entry()` posts an `llListen()`, awaiting a conversational command on its listen channel (*gListenChannel*). If its owner utters **presto**, a timer is set. When the `timer()` event fires, the script reads the items in its inventory. In our example, the flower's inventory has been stocked with the pink flamingo, the jack-o'-lantern, the Japanese lamp, and the wind chimes. Those items were already marked as Temporary objects prior to being added to the flower's inventory. This is an alternative approach to the one used in Listing 4.4, in which a script sets the object's prim parameters to `PRIM_TEMP_ON_REZ=TRUE`.

When reading an item from inventory, the control loop reads entries from a pair of lists, *gPositions* and *gRotations*, and the object is rezzed from inventory at the specified position relative to the flower, and at the specified rotation. Notice that the list *gRotations* is expressed in degrees, but `llRezObject()` needs the rotation expressed as a quaternion. The `simpleEuler2Rot()` function does that, using the `llEuler2Rot()` method to convert the vector of `x`, `y`, and `z` degree values.

Unlike the hopping ball, the rezzed objects need not contain scripts to control the terms of their existence. They simply spring into existence at the appropriate places and disappear as dictated by the garbage collector. Just before they vanish, the script rezzes a new set of identical objects in the identical locations. It's a bit like the comedian Steven Wright who quipped that one night a burglar broke into his apartment and stole all of his furniture and replaced it with exact duplicates.

You'll probably need to experiment with the value of *gExpiration*, because garbage collection is dependent on object complexity, and rez timing is dependent on the virtual "mass" of the object being rezzed. You need to provide enough overlap so the illusion of continuity is maintained. Finally, while positions relative to the controlling object could be worked out algorithmically, positions are usually best calculated manually.

If your script is managing many objects, you may find it difficult to keep track of which rotation matches which position for which object. You may find it easier to create a single strided list with all the object names, positions, and rotations.

As with any "free lunch" proposition, there are some practical limits. The total number of prims that can be contained in inventory is 255—the same as the limit on linked objects—regardless of whether this is 255 single-prim objects, or a single object of 255 parts. Also, the rezzing object's owner must have full permission for the temporary rezzed objects.

Despite all this talk of limitations, the take-away point is that this approach works, and it works extremely well. You can place several temporary rezzers about and multiply the number of prims your parcel supports to a very high degree: those 38 prims for the garden are now only 3.

 NOTE

 One potential use of temporary rezzers in parcels that allow building is to proliferate large numbers of objects—usually temporary, but potentially permanent—sometimes for the purpose of "griefing" other residents or disrupting public order in *Second Life*. Linden Lab does not take kindly to antisocial behavior (neither do other residents, including your humble authors). In an attempt to combat malevolent scripts, a strategy known as the "grey goo fence" exists and is documented on the wiki at GreyGooFence. Essentially, the grey goo fence says that if you attempt to rez too many objects in too short a time, *SL* will slow or stop you.

OTHER OBJECT-MANIPULATION FUNCTIONS

CHAPTER 1
CHAPTER 2
CHAPTER 3

CHAPTER 4

CHAPTER 5
CHAPTER 6
CHAPTER 7
CHAPTER 8
CHAPTER 9
CHAPTER 10
CHAPTER 11
CHAPTER 12
CHAPTER 13
CHAPTER 14
CHAPTER 15
APPENDICES

You have already seen most of the functions that get (or set) your object's properties, including `llGetAlpha()`, `llGetColor()`, `llGetScale()`, and the master controller `llGetPrimitiveParams()`. You will see many others elsewhere in this book. A few properties can't be retrieved or set with `llGetPrimitiveParams()` or `llSetPrimitiveParams()`; the ones that aren't covered elsewhere are outlined in Table 4.2.

TABLE 4.2: PRIMITIVE PROPERTIES THAT CAN'T BE MANAGED WITH THE `llGetPrimitiveParams()` FUNCTIONS

FUNCTION	BEHAVIOR
integer llGetNumberOfSides()	Returns an integer that represents the prim's number of sides (or faces).
string llGetObjectName()	Gets the prim's *name*.
llSetObjectName()	Sets the prim's *name*.
string llGetObjectDesc()	Returns a string that contains the description of the prim the script is attached to.
llSetObjectDesc(string *desc*)	Sets the prim's description.

NOTE

It is also possible for a scripted object to load scripts into a different object. The function `llRemoteLoadScriptPin()` copies the script *name* into the *target* object, and if *running* is TRUE, starts it with the *start_param*, as follows.

```
llRemoteLoadScriptPin(key target, string name, integer pin,
                      integer running, integer start_param)
```

Before you can call `llRemoteLoadScriptPin()`, the *target* object must be modifiable by the owner and the *target* object must grant the permission to load scripts using `llSetRemoteScriptAccessPin()`.

```
llSetRemoteScriptAccessPin(integer pin)
```

The *pin* value in both `llRemoteLoadScriptPin()` and `llSetRemoteScriptAccessPin()` must be the same:

The following script-management functions are also useful:

- `string llGetScriptName()` returns a string that is the name of the script that called this function.

- `integer llGetScriptState(string name)` returns TRUE if the script *name* is running.

- `llSetScriptState(string name, integer run)` sets the running state of the script name.

CONTROLLING MOTION OF NONPHYSICAL OBJECTS

THE PRESTO,
ABRACADABRA
OF REZZING

CONTROLLING
MOTION OF
NONPHYSICAL
OBJECTS

SUMMARY

Nonphysical objects are moved by carefully manipulating position and rotation. You've already seen both in this book. The fun stuff, and what this chapter really focuses on, is motion. Position is relatively straightforward. Controlling rotation is done with Target Omega or quaternions. Target Omega sets a continuous rotation on an object. LSL uses quaternions to calculate orientation; any time you set the rotation of a nonphysical object (as you did, for example, in Chapter 3's Listing 3.6), you have used quaternions, possibly unknowingly.

Two events—`moving_start()` and `moving_end()`—can be triggered when a nonphysical object moves; (they are triggered under the same conditions for physical objects).

EVENT DEFINITION

```
moving_start() {}
```

```
moving_end() {}
```

For nonphysical objects, these events are invoked when an avatar moves an object. Both `moving_start()` and `moving_end()` are triggered when the mouse is *released,* or, if the object is attached, constantly when the avatar is moving. The SYW website provides additional documentation and Chapter 7 describes these events for physical objects.

CONTROLLING POSITION

You've seen `llSetPos()` in several previous scripts. The way it works is pretty straightforward: you calculate a position and tell the prim to go there. You can use the `llGetLocalPos()` and `llGetPos()` functions to get a prim's local and global positions. There is, however, only one function to set the position—`llSetPos()`—and it uses regional, avatar, or local coordinates depending on whether it is an unlinked prim, attached to an avatar, or linked in an object as a child prim. Table 4.3 shows basic (nonphysical) position-setting functions and related events. You can also use physics to set object positions, as explained in Chapter 7, "Physics and Vehicles."

WARNING

Because `llSetPos()` uses different coordinates depending on the object, double-check all your calculations to make sure you haven't (for example) written `pos = <0,0,1>` rather than `pos = llGetPos() + <0,0,1>`. Also recall from Chapter 2 that `llSetPos()` won't set a position farther away than 10 meters.

CHAPTER 1
CHAPTER 2
CHAPTER 3
CHAPTER 4
CHAPTER 5
CHAPTER 6
CHAPTER 7
CHAPTER 8
CHAPTER 9
CHAPTER 10
CHAPTER 11
CHAPTER 12
CHAPTER 13
CHAPTER 14
CHAPTER 15
APPENDICES

TABLE 4.3: FUNCTIONS THAT SET THE POSITION OF OBJECTS

Function	Behavior
`vector llGetPos()`	Returns the position of the prim, relative to the region.
`vector llGetLocalPos()`	Returns the position of the prim, relative to its attachment point (region, avatar, root).
`vector llGetRootPosition()`	Returns the position of the root prim in a linkset, relative to region.
`llSetPos(vector pos)`	Sets the position of the prim, relative to its attachment point, parent prim position, or region.
`list llGetPrimitiveParams(list properties)`	Returns a list of requested property values.
`llSetPrimitiveParams(list properties)`	Sets the prim's properties.
`llSetLinkPrimitiveParams(integer linkNum, list properties)`	Sets the properties of the prim that has the specified `linkNum`.

ROTATION WITH TARGET OMEGA

The simplest prim movement, and one often seen in-world, is to continuously rotate a prim on one or more of its axes, relative to world coordinates. This continuous rotation is called an **omega**. You may have seen this type of prim movement in one of those "For Sale" signs that hover obnoxiously (usually on your neighbor's parcel, right in the sight line of your beautifully worked-out Japanese-temple build). Moving a prim this way can accomplish some really interesting effects that add vitality to the local landscape. Figure 4.4 shows a mélange of trash whirling in a local dust devil, whipped up by wind currents in a building's corner alcove.

The technique used here is relatively simple; it's implemented as a rotation relative to the region's axial orientation and created by a single call to `llTargetOmega()`. As Figure 4.4 shows, the prim is a simple hollowed cylinder wrapped by a (mostly) transparent texture on the outside and the texture's color complement on the inside.

Figure 4.4: The whirlwind is made from a hollow cylinder.

Thus, all you need to create the effect is a bit of GIMP or Photoshop skills, and a single call to `llTargetOmega()`, as shown in Listing 4.6. In the little whirlwind viewable at SYW HQ, the single rotating prim is **phantom**, so you can walk through it without getting your hair mussed. Unless the prim or object is created as **physical**, this type of rotation is purely a client-side effect (meaning that two residents observing the same effect, each using their own viewer, may observe slight differences in the effect).

Listing 4.6: Whirling Trash Using Target Omega

```
float spinrate = TWO_PI;

default
{
    state_entry() {
        llSetPrimitiveParams([PRIM_PHANTOM, TRUE]);
        llTargetOmega(<0.0,0.0,0.5>,spinrate,1.0);
    }
    touch_start(integer total_number) {
        if (spinrate == TWO_PI){
            spinrate = PI;
        } else {
            spinrate = TWO_PI;
        }
        llTargetOmega(<0.0,0.0,0.5>,spinrate,1.0);
    }
}
```

 # DEFINITION

---

llTargetOmega(vector *axis*, float *spinrate*, float *gain*)

Specify a smooth, client-rendered spin for the containing prim or object.

axis — The axis around which the rotation will occur. For instance, <0, 0, I> specifies the rotation should be around the prim's z-axis.

spinrate — How fast the rotation should be, counterclockwise, about the axis of rotation, in radians per second when the axis is normalized.

gain — The strength of the spin. Must always be nonzero for a spin to occur.

When the script begins, the script calls `llTargetOmega()`, which starts the rotation. The first argument is the axis of rotation, namely the axis the object will rotate around. In this script, the axis is <0, 0, 0.5>, so the leaves and newspaper rotate only about the z-axis. The direction of spin is controlled by the positive or negative sign of the term in the vector: a positive value is counterclockwise, while a negative value is clockwise.

This means the prim completes a tour around the vertical axis once every two seconds. You get the same perceived rotation rate by changing the z term's axial rate to 1.0 and the spin rate to π; the rotation is the product of the spin rate and the axial rate.

If you want something to rotate around the end of a long arm, you create a small prim located at the center of the rotation, and link the objects together so that the central prim is the root. Listing 4.6 goes into the root. The Earth described in the section "Sun, Earth, and Moon" uses this idea.

Side navigation

THE PRESTO, ABRACADABRA OF REZZING

CONTROLLING MOTION OF NONPHYSICAL OBJECTS

SUMMARY

CHAPTER 4

114

CHAPTER 1
CHAPTER 2
CHAPTER 3

CHAPTER 4

CHAPTER 5
CHAPTER 6
CHAPTER 7
CHAPTER 8
CHAPTER 9
CHAPTER 10
CHAPTER 11
CHAPTER 12
CHAPTER 13
CHAPTER 14
CHAPTER 15
APPENDICES

 USING QUATERNIONS

Up until now we've managed to avoid getting into the details of how rotations work. Target Omega is one way, but for more-complex rotations you need to understand the gory details of how to set prim rotations. All rotations in LSL are represented with a variable type internally called **quaternions**. (You can use the terms **rotation** and **quaternion** interchangeably.) Table 4.4 shows the key functions that set an object's orientation. Quaternions are four-valued vectors whose internals you will rarely want to access because they don't make much sense to a human.

TABLE 4.4: FUNCTIONS THAT SET THE ROTATION OF A NONPHYSICAL OBJECT

FUNCTION NAME	BEHAVIOR
`rotation llGetRot()`	Relative to region (or avatar if attached).
`rotation llGetLocalRot()`	Relative to attachment (difference between region/avatar/root and self).
`rotation llGetRootRotation()`	Root prim relative to region.
`llSetRot(rotation rot)`	Relative to region or avatar; awkward for child prims.
`llSetLocalRot(rotation rot)`	Relative to attachment (root, region, avatar).
`list llGetPrimitiveParams(list properties)`	Returns a list of the property values requested.
`llSetPrimitiveParams(list properties)`	Sets the prim's properties.
`llSetLinkPrimitiveParams(integer linkNum, list properties)`	Sets the properties of the prim with the specified *linkNum*.

Four-dimensional quaternions aren't the easiest way to visualize a rotation in three dimensions. The *Euler* representation is a three-part vector that describes rotations around the **x**-, **y**-, and **z**-axis (or roll, pitch, and yaw respectively). You can do a lot with rotations in your scripts just using the Euler notation because LSL provides translation capabilities: `llEuler2Rot()` and `llRot2Euler()`. Rather than using degrees, both functions use radians, which range from 0 to 2π. Thus 180 degrees is π radians. Fortunately, LSL gives us the two constants `DEG_TO_RAD` and `RAD_TO_DEG` for converting from degrees to radians and back. For example, if you have a prim oriented at <0.0, 0.0, 0.0>, the following code will rotate it by 45 degrees around the **z**-axis:

```
vector rotZ = <0.0, 0.0, 45.0> * DEG_TO_RAD;
llSetRot( llEuler2Rot( rotZ ) );
```

You can see the returned values like this:

```
rotation currentRotationQ = llGetRot();
llOwnerSay( (string)( llRot2Euler( currentRotationQ ) * RAD_TO_DEG ));
```

 DEFINITION

`rotation llEuler2Rot(vector vec)`

Returns a quaternion representation of the Euler vector represented by *vec*.

THE PRESTO,
ABRACADABRA
OF REZZING

▸ CONTROLLING
MOTION OF
NONPHYSICAL
OBJECTS

SUMMARY

DEFINITION

---

vector llRot2Euler(rotation _quat_)

Returns a vector that is the Euler representation (roll, pitch, yaw) of _quat_.

To set a prim's rotation around the x-, y-, or z-axis, you simply add the appropriate value to the appropriate axis. The following snippet rotates the prim by 80 degrees around the z-axis, as illustrated in Figure 4.5:

```
vector currentRotation = llRot2Euler( llGetRot() );
currentRotation.z += 80.0 * DEG_TO_RAD;
llSetRot( llEuler2Rot( currentRotation ) );
```

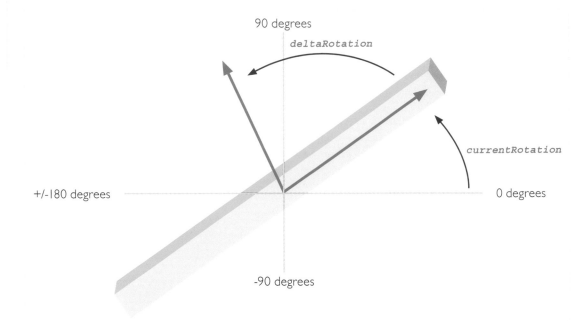

Figure 4.5: The object is rotated by 80 degrees (or 1.39 radians) counterclockwise.

However, Euler representation has limits. While it's easy to understand, it's hard to manipulate. What if, for example, your original prim has an orientation that isn't zero or your rotation isn't just around one axis? What would you do if the prim you're rotating is offset from the point you are trying to rotate around?

Calculating Offsets after Rotating

LSL performs all rotations around the center of the object. Figure 4.6 shows a simple signpost made of two prims. The post is the root prim, and you want to rotate the sign relative to the post. As you can see, simply rotating the sign by 45 degrees is not enough; you also have to adjust the offset of the flag. Without quaternions you would have to manage a lot of trigonometry to calculate the correct new offset, taking care about the quadrants of the rotations and so forth. As your rotation scripts become more complex, for example combining rotations, the complexity grows beyond reason.

Figure 4.6: If you compensate for the offset, the sign stays attached to the post, but rotating the sign around its center causes it to detach.

CHAPTER 1
CHAPTER 2
CHAPTER 3
CHAPTER 4
CHAPTER 5
CHAPTER 6
CHAPTER 7
CHAPTER 8
CHAPTER 9
CHAPTER 10
CHAPTER 11
CHAPTER 12
CHAPTER 13
CHAPTER 14
CHAPTER 15
APPENDICES

You can perform several useful operations on quaternions:

- You can add two quaternions (using the * operator).
- You can subtract one quaternion from another (using the / operator).
- You can apply (* or /) a quaternion to a vector, and compute a new offset.

Note that addition and subtraction are * and /, and not + and -. While + and - are mathematically *legal*, they won't give you the geometric behavior you probably want. When using quaternions you also have to remember that evaluations are done in left-to-right order (except for parenthesized expressions). If you compose a sequence of rotations incorrectly, you can get into trouble. Writing a timer-based reset (described in Chapter 1) that puts your prim back in its original location can be very useful.

If you convert the signpost example to quaternions you get a short script, shown in Listing 4.7, which has no trigonometry and correctly rotates the sign around the post by 45 degrees every time it is touched.

Listing 4.7: Rotating a Sign around a Post

```
default
{
    touch_start(integer total_number) {
        rotation deltaRot = llEuler2Rot( <0.,0.,45.> * DEG_TO_RAD);
        rotation currentRot = llGetLocalRot();
        rotation newRot = currentRot * deltaRot;
        vector currentOffset = llGetLocalPos();
        vector newOffset = currentOffset * deltaRot;
        llSetLocalRot(newRot);
        llSetPos( newOffset );
    }
}
```

The script firsts calculate a "delta" rotation, *deltaRot*, which captures the amount of change you want to apply to the current rotation. In this script, *deltaRot* changes the prim's current orientation by 45 degrees around the z-axis. It then uses llGetLocalRot() to find the orientation of the sign *relative to the post*. The sign's new orientation, *newRot*, is then the sum of the current orientation plus (*) the delta. The script uses llSetLocalRot() to set the new orientation, relative to the root prim. Figure 4.7 shows how the three angles work together. Note that the "zero" axis in the figure is the *root's* zero.

THE PRESTO,
ABRACADABRA
OF REZZING

CONTROLLING
MOTION OF
NONPHYSICAL
OBJECTS

SUMMARY

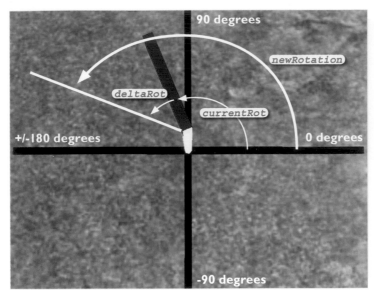

Figure 4.7: The new rotation is the current rotation plus the change.

For the new offset, the script takes the prim's current offset and multiplies it by the delta rotation, which yields the *newOffset* position, as illustrated in Figures 4.8 and 4.9. Finally, the script uses `llSetPos()` to set the new offset—also relative to the root prim because there isn't an `llSetLocalPos()` function in LSL, and `llSetPos()` acts locally when attached.

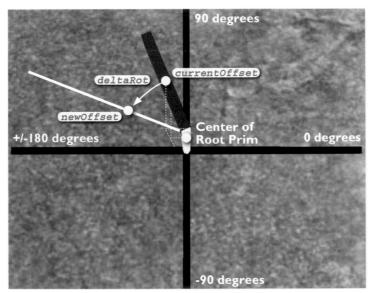

Figure 4.8: The new offset of the sign is calculated by rotating the vector *currentOffset* by the rotation, *deltaRot*.

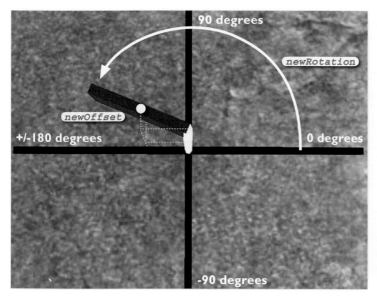

Figure 4.9: Careful management of the rotation ensures that the sign correctly moves to its new position and offset.

CHAPTER 1
CHAPTER 2
CHAPTER 3

CHAPTER 4
CHAPTER 5
CHAPTER 6
CHAPTER 7
CHAPTER 8
CHAPTER 9
CHAPTER 10
CHAPTER 11
CHAPTER 12
CHAPTER 13
CHAPTER 14
CHAPTER 15
APPENDICES

One of the benefits of these calculations is that everything is local to the root. That way, if the root prim's orientation changes, the sign stays attached to the post.

NOTE

You will note pretty quickly that the rotation and offsets are handled separately, which looks kind of odd. You may therefore be tempted to use `llSetPrimitiveParams()` with both the rotation and offset values in the hopes it will make a nice smooth rotation. Unfortunately, that won't help; it still does them separately. Using physics-based rotations (described in Chapter 7) can improve matters, but it's still fiddly, and even the ways in which it's fiddly are not perfectly consistent

Rotating around an Arbitrary Point

With our signpost, the sign was rotated only on the z-axis, around the center of the pole. But what if we want a different rotation point? An object can be rotated around an arbitrary point by first calculating the offset from the object to the center of the rotation, and then multiplying the vector by the desired rotation. The final step is to calculate the correct offset location using the following process:

rotationOffset = currentOffset − centerOfRotation

newOffset = rotationOffset × desiredRotation

newPosition = centerOfRotation + newOffset

CHAPTER 4

THE PRESTO,
ABRACADABRA
OF REZZING

CONTROLLING
MOTION OF
NONPHYSICAL
OBJECTS

SUMMARY

Markers of a Clock Face

Listing 4.8 rotates a prim around a fixed point. When the script is reset, the center of rotation is calculated to be <1, 1, 0> meters away—if you imagine a clock face, the prim starts sitting at the 7:30 position. On state_entry() and on_rez(), the script calculates the new center of the rotation (the center of the clock). Then every time it is touched, it calculates rotationOffset, which is the offset of the prim relative to the center of rotation. It rotates the offset point to get **newOffset**, and finally adds it back to the center of rotation to get **newPosition**. The correct behavior rotates nicely around the center of rotation, as shown in Figure 4.13.

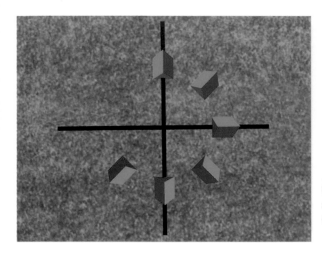

Figure 4.10: This object caches the center of rotation appropriately, and correctly places itself.

Listing 4.8: Rotate around a Point

```
vector gCenterOfRotation;
calcCenterOfRotation()
{
    vector currPos = llGetPos();
    gCenterOfRotation = <currPos.x + 1.0, currPos.y + 1.0, currPos.z>;
}

default
{
    on_rez(integer n) {
        calcCenterOfRotation();
    }
    state_entry() {
        calcCenterOfRotation();
    }
    touch_start(integer total_number) {
        rotation deltaRot = llEuler2Rot( <0.,0.,45.> * DEG_TO_RAD);
        rotation currentRot = llGetLocalRot();
        vector currentOffset = llGetPos(); // rel to region

        rotation newRotation = deltaRot * currentRot;
        llSetLocalRot( newRotation );

        vector rotationOffset = currentOffset - gCenterOfRotation;
        vector newOffset = rotationOffset * deltaRot;
        vector newPosition = gCenterOfRotation + newOffset;
        llSetPos( newPosition );
    }
}
```

NOTE

This code will work oddly if your prim is linked to something else. The call to `llSetPos()` sets the *local* position of the prim. If you're tempted to try rotating a child prim around a point that has nothing to with the root, it's not as easy as using `llGetLocalPos()`. Try it, and *then* read about articulation on the SYW website.

So now you should be asking, "Why didn't we explicitly handle the center of rotation for the sign post?" The reason is because the center of rotation is conveniently equal to the rotational offset (because we're ignoring the z-axis).

NOTE

Slerp, or spherical linear interpolation, is a technique for interpolating along a curve. If you want to carefully place an object at regular intervals, you use slerp math to figure out the locations. `http://en.wikipedia.org/wiki/Slerp` describes the concept in more detail.

CHAPTER 5
CHAPTER 6
CHAPTER 7
CHAPTER 8
CHAPTER 9
CHAPTER 10
CHAPTER 11
CHAPTER 12
CHAPTER 13
CHAPTER 14
CHAPTER 15
APPENDICES

Rotational Shortcuts

Table 4.5 provides a few functions that can be convenient shortcuts for common rotation calculations. These functions are particularly useful for deciding where to aim projectiles!

TABLE 4.5: FUNCTIONS THAT PROVIDE SHORTCUTS TO COMMON ROTATION CALCULATIONS

Function	Behavior
`rotation llAxes2Rot(vector fwd, vector left, vector up)`	Returns a rotation that is defined by the three coordinate axes *fwd*, *left*, and *up*.
`rotation llAxisAngle2Rot(vector axis, float angle)`	Returns a rotation that is a generated *angle* about *axis*. *axis* should be normalized.
`float llAngleBetween(rotation a, rotation b)`	Returns a float that is the angle between rotation *a* and *b*. Equivalent to `llRot2Angle(a/b)`.
`float llRot2Angle(rotation rot)`	Returns a float that is the rotation angle represented by *rot*.
`vector llRot2Axis(rotation rot)`	Returns a vector that is the rotation axis represented by *rot*.
`vector llRot2Fwd(rotation q)`	Returns a unit vector that is the forward vector after rotating by *q*.
`vector llRot2Left(rotation q)`	Returns a unit vector that is the left vector after rotating by *q*.
`vector llRot2Up(rotation q)`	Returns a unit vector that is the up vector after rotating by *q*.
`rotation llRotBetween(vector start, vector end)`	Returns a rotation that is the rotation between the direction *start* and the direction *end*.

Listing 4.9 shows an example where a script is used to rez the 12 markers of a clock face. When touched, the object initializes *delta* to be the number of degrees between markers, and *orient* to be the orientation of the first marker. It then uses the shortcut `llRot2Fwd()` to calculate the unit vector (i.e. length 1.0) of where the marker should be placed—*unitpos*. It then multiplies *unitpos* by `DISTANCE`, adds the current location of the object, and rezzes the marker. It loops around 12 times, each time adding *delta* to *orient*. Try modifying Listing 4.1 in a similar manner.

CHAPTER 4

THE PRESTO,
ABRACADABRA
OF REZZING

CONTROLLING
MOTION OF
NONPHYSICAL
OBJECTS

SUMMARY

LISTING 4.9: MAKING A CLOCK FACE USING A ROTATION SHORTCUT FUNCTION

```
float DISTANCE = 2.0;
default
{
    touch_start(integer total_number) {
        rotation delta = llEuler2Rot(<0,0,30>*DEG_TO_RAD);
        rotation orient = ZERO_ROTATION;
        integer i;
        for (i=0; i<12 ; i++) {
            vector unitpos = llRot2Fwd( orient );
            vector pos = llGetPos() + unitpos * DISTANCE;
            llRezObject("marker", pos, ZERO_VECTOR, orient, 1);
            orient = orient * delta;
        }
    }
}
```

SUN, EARTH, AND MOON (COMBINING TARGET OMEGA AND QUATERNIONS)

You can use (almost) exactly the same code as in Listing 4.8 to make an Earth that rotates around the sun, as shown in Figure 4.14. The moon uses Target Omega to rotate around its own axis. The Earth uses Target Omega to rotate on its own axis, and since it is linked to the moon, the moon rotates in geosynchronous orbit around the Earth. The Earth uses quaternions to rotate around the sun.

Figure 4.11: The moon rotates around the Earth using linked prims and Target Omega, while the Earth rotates around the sun by calculating its position using a modification of Listing 4.9.

BUILD NOTE

Make three prims: a big sun, a small Earth, and a tiny moon. Link the moon to the Earth, *but do not link them to the sun.* If you link them to the sun, the moon won't rotate around the Earth correctly. Place the code from Listing 4.10 in the moon. Then place the modified version of Listing 4.8 in the Earth.

Listing 4.10 causes the moon to rotate on its own axis once every 29.5 days.

Listing 4.10: The Moon's Rotation

```
default {
    state_entry() {
        llTargetOmega(llVecNorm(<0,0,1>), 1.0/29.5, 1);
    }
}
```

Listing 4.8 is almost ready to place in the Earth. Make the following changes:

- Double-check that your **gCenterOfRotation** is correct for where you put the Earth's position relative to the sun.

- Add two lines of code to `calcCenterOfRotation()`, causing the Earth to spin on its own axis and invoking a timer that calculates the rotation around the sun:

  ```
  llTargetOmega(llVecNorm(<0,0,1>), 1, 1);
  llSetTimerEvent(1.0);
  ```

- Change the `touch_start()` event handler to be a `timer()` event handler.

- Comment out the call to `llSetLocalRot()`. The Earth's rotation is automatically managed by the Target Omega.

Almost like magic, the Earth will start to spin, *and the moon will correctly spin around the Earth*, because its local offset always remains the same, relative to the Earth. Because the Earth's orbit around the sun is *not* tied to the sun's internal rotation, you can easily add other planets and have each one rotate at its own rate.

Wouldn't it be nice if we could simply set the Earth-moon pair to be a single child of the sun in a nice hierarchical fashion? If we could, we could set the sun to rotate with a Target Omega, and the Earth would magically stay at the same relative location, with a sum total of 15 lines of code (5 in each prim). Unfortunately it is not so easy: there is no such thing as hierarchical linking of prims in LSL. Articulation, in the sense of an articulated arm or leg, is therefore quite challenging in *SL*; you will find a description of how to do articulation on the SYW website.

SUMMARY

This chapter focused largely on controlling objects—bringing them into existence and moving them around. Mastering these techniques may give you the keys to the most important fundamental aspects of scripting in *Second Life*. In succeeding chapters, you'll learn a number of advanced techniques for bringing these creations to life and using the physics model of *Second Life*. You can combine and extend these scripts in many ways to gain even greater power over your virtual environment.

SENSING THE WORLD

The ability to sense avatars and objects is a very important technique in creating interesting interactions. Sensors allow you to monitor who is visiting your land, to cause lights to turn on automatically and doors to open, and to create attention-grabbing animations as objects interact with each other. In a forest you need bees that pollinate flowers and deer that startle and run away. In a city slum you need rats that run out of dark alleys and police cars that drive past on patrol. In a store you need greeters that say hello, lights that turn on, and doors that open.

BUILDING SENSORS

BUILDING
SENSORS

DETECTION
WITH
COLLISIONS

USING
GREETERS TO
WELCOME
VISITORS

SUMMARY

Sensing in LSL is governed by a trio of sensor functions: `llSensor()`, `llSensorRepeat()`, and `llSensorRemove()`. A script can have only one sensor at a time. You can remove a repeating sensor by calling one of these functions again. The sensing functions trigger `sensor(numDetected)` and `no_sensor()` events.

`llSensorRepeat()` is a very costly LSL activity, in terms of server effort, and also has problems if there's a lot of lag. Consider using a collision detector (covered later in this chapter) instead of a sensor when you can—it's significantly cheaper than a repeating sensor.

 DEFINITION

```
llSensor(string name, key id, integer type,
         float range, float arc)
```

Performs a single scan for *name* and *id* with *type* within *range* meters and *arc* radians of the forward vector, within the same region.

```
llSensorRepeat(string name, key id, integer type,
               float range, float arc, float rate)
```

Performs a scan for *name* and *id* with *type* within *range* meters and *arc* radians of the forward vector, similar to `llSensor()`, but repeating every *rate* seconds, and sensing even across sim boundaries.

> *name* — Object or avatar in the same region. Wildcard is `""`.
>
> *id* — Object or avatar UUID that is in the same region. Wildcard is `NULL_KEY`.
>
> *type* — Bitmask; `AGENT` for avatars, `ACTIVE` for moving objects or active scripts, `SCRIPTED` for active scripts, and `PASSIVE` for nonmoving, nonscripted objects or scripts that aren't consuming any sim resources.
>
> *range* — Radius of the sensing action. Maximum range 96m, within the same region.
>
> *arc* — The maximum angle, in radians, between the local x-axis of the prim and detectable objects. `PI` is a sphere.
>
> *rate* — Seconds between scans (`llSensorRepeat()` only).

 DEFINITION

```
llSensorRemove()
```

Removes the sensor set up by `llSensorRepeat()`. Also removes all of the sensor data that triggered the event!

EVENT DEFINITION

CHAPTER 1
CHAPTER 2
CHAPTER 3
CHAPTER 4

CHAPTER 5

CHAPTER 6
CHAPTER 7
CHAPTER 8
CHAPTER 9
CHAPTER 10
CHAPTER 11
CHAPTER 12
CHAPTER 13
CHAPTER 14
CHAPTER 15
APPENDICES

```
sensor(integer numDetected) {}
```

```
no_sensor() {}
```

Events in the sensor family are invoked after a sensor scan is created with `llSensor()` or `llSensorRepeat()`. `sensor()` is triggered when something is sensed; `no_sensor()` is triggered if nothing matches the sensing criteria. Additional documentation can be found on the SYW website.

> *numDetected* — The number of items detected that match the sensing criteria. A maximum of 16 items will be detected; they are sorted so that the closest item is first.

The values for the *type* mask can be combined with a bitwise "or" (|), but it's not always intuitive what is detected (it's buggy, too), so plan to spend a little time experimenting. For the sensor event, *active* means that the script is consuming sim resources or it's a moving physical object; a *passive* object is a script not consuming resources, or a nonmoving object. Once inside the `sensor()` and `no_sensor()` event handlers, you can use `llDetectedType()` to discern the whether the detected object is active or passive; be aware, however, that the semantics of the type are slightly different than for the sensor—the type from `llDetectedType()` refers only to whether the object is physical (and makes no reference to the script inside it).

The sensing functions will never detect the object that contains them or the avatar they're attached to. Sensors cannot detect objects attached to any other avatar either. `llGetAgentInfo()` tells you if an avatar has attachments, but not how many or what they are. `llSensor()` detects only objects within the same sim as the script, but you can use `llSensorRepeat()` to detect across sim boundaries.

OPEN UP! A SIMPLE AUTOMATED DOOR SLIDER

A common use for sensing is to open doors for visitors. Adding operating doors adds realism and a sense of place to a building, and doors can be scripted to respond only to the building's owner or a select set of visitors. Listing 5.1 and Figure 5.1 show a simple door slider. A sensor is used to detect the approach of an avatar near the door. Note that the doors do not need to communicate with each other, because they both sense approaching avatars.

Listing 5.1: Sliding Doors

```
float SENSOR_INTERVAL = 10.0;
//float doorXOffset = 3.4; // for the right door
float doorXOffset = -3.4; // for the left door
vector gPosOffset = <doorXOffset, 0.0, 0.0>;

doorman(float closingtime) {
    llSetPos( llGetPos() + gPosOffset * llGetRot() );
    gPosOffset *= -1; // negate, to move back
    llSetTimerEvent(closingtime);
}
default {
    state_entry() {
        llSensorRepeat("", NULL_KEY, AGENT, 0.5, PI, SENSOR_INTERVAL);
    }
```

```
    sensor(integer total_number) {
        doorman(3.0);
    }
    timer() {
        doorman(0.0);
    }
}
```

 BUILDING
SENSORS

DETECTION
WITH
COLLISIONS

USING
GREETERS TO
WELCOME
VISITORS

SUMMARY

Figure 5.1: The door senses an avatar and opens, giving the avatar enough time to cross the threshold.

The sensor sweep is set to `PI` in the call to `llSensorRepeat()` because you want sensing on both sides of the door—the avatar will want to exit automatically as well as enter! Every time the `sensor()` event triggers, it calls the `doorman()` function to move the door back and forth. Using `llSetPos()`, the door slides from one position to the other on alternate sensed events. *gPosOffset* moves along the prim's x-axis; the rotation by `llGetRot()` compensates for world rotations.

To make the door close automatically, the script uses `llSetTimerEvent(3.0)`. When the `timer()` event is handled, the door reverses track and closes. You want to make the time interval broad enough (here it is 3 seconds) to allow an avatar to get through the door, even accounting for lag.

If you wanted your sensor to react to different sorts of things, you could combine the *type* bits with the | operator. For instance, to detect the approach of an avatar or a robot, you could use the following:

```
    llSensorRepeat("", NULL_KEY, AGENT|ACTIVE, 2.0, TWO_PI, 2.5);
```

OUTDOORS: THE BIRDS AND THE BEES

Birds, bees, and all manner of wildlife can add interest to an outdoor scene. The hummingbird, flitting from flower to flower to avatars (Figure 5.2), makes a wonderful greeter at Surfline Aloha Rezzable <40, 151, 22>. Cats can search for warm sunny spots to sleep in. Dogs can chase cats, cats can chase mice, and mice can search for cheese.

CHAPTER 5

CHAPTER 6
CHAPTER 7
CHAPTER 8
CHAPTER 9
CHAPTER 10
CHAPTER 11
CHAPTER 12
CHAPTER 13
CHAPTER 14
CHAPTER 15
APPENDICES

Figure 5.2: This hummingbird, (sold by Animania at Synkx <88, 71, 24>), makes a wonderful greeter.

Listing 5.2 shows how to sense objects with a simple example of a bee that flies from the hive to the flowers it senses, and then flies back to the hive, as shown in Figure 5.3.

Listing 5.2: Bee

```
string FLOWER_NAME = "Flower"; // Names of objects the bee looks for
string HIVE_NAME = "Beehive";

default
{
    state_entry() {
        llSetTimerEvent(1);
    }
    on_rez(integer n) {
        llSetTimerEvent(1);
    }
    timer() {
        llSensor(FLOWER_NAME, NULL_KEY, ACTIVE | PASSIVE, 10.0, PI);
        llSetTimerEvent(0);
    }
    sensor(integer numDetected) {
        integer i;
        string name = llDetectedName(0);
        if (name == FLOWER_NAME) {
            for (i=0; i<numDetected; i++) {
                llSetPos(llDetectedPos(i));
                llSetRot(llDetectedRot(i));
                llSleep(2);
            }
            llSensor(HIVE_NAME, NULL_KEY, ACTIVE | PASSIVE, 10.0, PI);
        } else { // hive
            llSetPos(llDetectedPos(0));
            llSetRot(llDetectedRot(0));
            llSetTimerEvent(10);
        }
    }
    no_sensor() {
        llSetTimerEvent(30);
    }
}
```

Building
Sensors

Detection
with
Collisions

Using
Greeters to
Welcome
Visitors

Summary

Figure 5.3: The script neatly has the bee check out all the flowers in the area.

The script starts by initiating one sensing event, looking for all objects named Flower within 10 meters. When the **sensor()** event is triggered, the bee loops through all the sensed flowers, visiting each one for two seconds. It then sets up a sensing event for the beehive, and returns there when the hive is found. It uses the functions `llDetectedName()`, `llDetectedPos()`, and `llDetectedRot()` to find the name, position, and rotation of the items that were sensed.

If you look closely, you'll notice that the `timer()` event is not a regularly scheduled every-*n*-second timer. When the script starts, the timer fires *once*, sets up the single sensing event, then turns itself off. Then, after all the flowers have been visited, the timer is reactivated. It's more intuitive to use an `llSleep()` after visiting the flowers, but the `timer()` mechanism is a cheaper way to cause the script to pause. The script also has a **no_sensor()** handler that will schedule another timer event in case the bee cannot find any objects by name it is looking for. Without this, the bee would be lost forever (or at least until rerezzed) if it couldn't find its hive; it would never bother to look again.

This script has a few caveats, most notably that it doesn't handle situations when the flowers (or the hive) are out of the 10m maximum range for `llSetPos()`. You can use one of Chapter 2's `moveTo()` functions to fix that problem. Longer distances will also look more realistic if you use the physics `llMoveToTarget()` functions described in Chapter 7, "Physics and Vehicles." You could also augment this script with interesting random "walk" patterns to make the bee appear to search for the flowers, or add buzzing sounds if the bee happens to pass near an avatar as it's flying along.

INDOORS: ROOMBA

A lot of folks seem to think that the outdoors is the only place that needs interesting scripted behavior. That's unfortunate, as indoor locations seem rather flat and boring without something interesting to capture visitors' attention. Be creative!

At SYW HQ we have a plant that regularly loses its leaves. It's become so regular, in fact, that we got tired of cleaning up after it and made a Roomba to vacuum up the fallen leaves. To set up this scene (Figure 5.4), you need four things: a leaf that will fall off (called Dead Leaf), a plant that contains the leaf in its inventory, a home location for the Roomba (Recharging Station), and the Roomba itself (Roomba). This build relies on the physics engine, described in Chapter 7.

CHAPTER 1
CHAPTER 2
CHAPTER 3
CHAPTER 4

CHAPTER 5

CHAPTER 6
CHAPTER 7
CHAPTER 8
CHAPTER 9
CHAPTER 10
CHAPTER 11
CHAPTER 12
CHAPTER 13
CHAPTER 14
CHAPTER 15
APPENDICES

Figure 5.4: The robotic vacuum cleans up the dead leaf every time it falls.

Listing 5.3 shows the short script for the plant that rezzes the Dead Leaf. The newly rezzed leaf turns on physics so it can fall, and then sets up a sensor repeat looking for the Roomba (Listing 5.4). Because the leaf lives only a short time, the repeating sensor won't hurt the sim. In case there are problems with the triggering of the sensor events or the physics engine, the script has a backup mechanism to self-delete: it sets the TEMP_ON_REZ property to TRUE. (A timer would also work if you want it to stay around a little longer.) If you want your Roomba to stay on the ground (rather than having flying capabilities), make sure your build is set up so that when the Dead Leaf falls, it lands on the floor.

Listing 5.3: Leaf Rezzer

```
string  LEAF_NAME = "Dead Leaf"; // what object will be rezzed?
integer TIMER_INTERVAL = 120;

default
{
    state_entry() {
        llSetTimerEvent(TIMER_INTERVAL);
    }
    on_rez(integer n) {
        llSetTimerEvent(TIMER_INTERVAL);
    }
    timer() {
        vector pos = llGetPos(); // same position as original
        rotation rot = llGetRot();
        llRezObject(LEAF_NAME,pos,ZERO_VECTOR,rot,0);
    }
}
```

Listing 5.4: Dying Leaf

```
string VACUUM_NAME = "Roomba";  // what is going to vacuum us up?
init()
{
    llSetStatus(STATUS_PHYSICS, TRUE); // causes leaf to fall
    llSetStatus(STATUS_DIE_AT_EDGE, TRUE);
    // don't expect to be around a long time, so repeat sensor is OK
    llSensorRepeat(VACUUM_NAME, NULL_KEY, ACTIVE, 1.0, PI, 3);
    llSetPrimitiveParams([ PRIM_TEMP_ON_REZ, TRUE ]); // just in case
}
```

CHAPTER 5

BUILDING SENSORS

DETECTION
WITH
COLLISIONS

USING
GREETERS TO
WELCOME
VISITORS

SUMMARY

```
default
{
    state_entry() {
        init();
    }
    on_rez(integer n) {
        init();
    }
    sensor(integer numDetected) {
        llDie(); // as soon as Roomba is nearby, vanish
    }
}
```

Most of the work happens in the vacuum. The script in Listing 5.5 sets up a `timer()` event to watch for dead leaves every `TIMER_INTERVAL` seconds. When the `sensor()` event triggers, it turns off the timer and uses the physics engine to tell the Roomba to `llMoveToTarget()`, at a speed of 0.5 meters per second. The script controls the orientation of the robot using `llRotLookAt()`, which makes sure the robot doesn't spin at random. The script also sets up a target monitor with `llTarget()` that watches for when the vacuum arrives at the target location.

Listing 5.5: Roomba

```
integer TIMER_INTERVAL   = 5;    // s
float   DETECTION_RADIUS = 10.0; // m
float   SPEED = 0.5;             // m/s
string  LEAF_NAME = "Dead Leaf"; // vacuum up objects with this name
string  RECHARGER_NAME = "Recharging Station"; // recharge at this object

integer gTargetID;
string  gTargetName;
vector  gTargetPos;

default
{
    state_entry() {
        llSetTimerEvent(TIMER_INTERVAL);
    }
    state_entry() {
        llSetTimerEvent(TIMER_INTERVAL);
    }
    timer() {
        llSensor(LEAF_NAME, NULL_KEY, ACTIVE | PASSIVE, DETECTION_RADIUS, PI);
    }
    sensor(integer numDetected) {
        llSetTimerEvent(0);
        list details = llGetObjectDetails(llDetectedKey(0),
                                    [OBJECT_NAME, OBJECT_POS, OBJECT_ROT]);
        gTargetName = llList2String(details,0);
        gTargetPos = (vector)llList2String(details,1);
        rotation targetRot = (rotation)llList2String(details,2);
        vector currPos = llGetPos();
        float dist = llVecMag(gTargetPos - currPos);
        if (gTargetName == LEAF_NAME) {
            llSetStatus(STATUS_PHYSICS, TRUE);
            llSleep(0.2); // give time for physics to kick in
        }
        targetRot.x = 0;
        targetRot.y = 0;
        llRotLookAt(targetRot, 0.2, 0.2);
        llMoveToTarget( gTargetPos, dist / SPEED );
        gTargetID = llTarget(gTargetPos, 0.1);
    }
```

```
    at_target(integer targetNum, vector targetPos, vector currPos) {
        if (targetNum == gTargetID) {  // arrived at goal
            llTargetRemove(gTargetID);
            llStopMoveToTarget();
            if (gTargetName == LEAF_NAME) { // arrived at leaf
                llSleep(2); // give time for leaf to self-delete
                llSensor(RECHARGER_NAME, NULL_KEY,
                        ACTIVE | PASSIVE, DETECTION_RADIUS, PI);
            } else { // arrived at recharger
                llSetStatus(STATUS_PHYSICS, FALSE);
                llSetTimerEvent(TIMER_INTERVAL);
            }
        }
    }
    not_at_target() {
        vector currPos = llGetPos();
        float dist = llVecMag(gTargetPos - currPos);
        llMoveToTarget( gTargetPos, dist / SPEED );
    }
}
```

When the robot reaches its target location, the robot sets up a sensing event for its home location, the Recharging Station. When it finds the recharger, it uses another `llMoveToTarget()` to head home. When it reaches the recharger it turns the physics engine off and sets up another timer to watch for the next falling leaf.

Because we're using physics, the robot sometimes overshoots or undershoots its target. Here the `llTarget()` function uses an error of 0.1m, given that the two targets were about 0.5m in their longest dimension. It's not enough to just make sure that the target error is large enough; the robot can still over- or undershoot. Two fixes are necessary to ensure that the whole system works. First, make sure that both the Recharging Station and the Dead Leaf are *phantom* objects, which allow the robot to travel right "into" them and actually come closer to the goal location. Second, set up a `not_at_target()` event handler that keeps trying to get the robot to its goal. You may also want to add a dead-man counter that turns off the physics engine and sends you an email if enough sensor events or physically managed movement efforts have failed.

Note that this script doesn't use the `llDetected*()` functions shown in Listing 5.2. You have two options—the suite of `llDetected*()` functions or the `llGetObjectDetails()` function, as sketched in Table 5.1.

DEFINITION

list llGetObjectDetails(key *id*, list *query*)

Returns a list of the details specified in *query* for the object with key *id* as an alternative to using the `llDetected*()` and similar functions. This function works on any object or avatar currently in the sim, even if it wasn't detected via sensor. Returns `OBJECT_UNKNOWN_DETAIL` or empty lists when passed invalid parameters.

    id — Object or avatar UUID that is in the same region as the script.

    query — A list of the details you want about *id* as OBJECT_* flags, shown in the left column of Table 5.1.

CHAPTER 5

BUILDING
SENSORS

DETECTION
WITH
COLLISIONS

USING
GREETERS TO
WELCOME
VISITORS

SUMMARY

TABLE 5.1: QUERY PARAMETERS FOR `llGetObjectDetails()`

FLAG	DESCRIPTION	ALTERNATIVE FUNCTION
OBJECT_NAME	Gets the object's name as a **string** up to 63 characters long.	`llKey2Name()` `llDetectedName()`
OBJECT_DESC	Gets the object's description (empty if avatar) as a **string** up to 127 characters long.	—
OBJECT_POS	Gets the object's position as a **vector** in region coordinates.	`llDetectedPos()`
OBJECT_ROT	Gets the object's rotation as a **rotation**.	`llDetectedRot()`
OBJECT_VELOCITY	Gets the object's velocity as a **vector**.	`llDetectedVel()`
OBJECT_OWNER	Gets an object's owner's UUID as a **key**. If group-owned or avatar, a **NULL_KEY** is returned.	`llDetectedOwner()` `llGetOwnerKey()`
OBJECT_GROUP	Gets the prims's group UUID as a **key**. If avatar, a **NULL_KEY** is returned.	`llDetectedGroup()`
OBJECT_CREATOR	Gets the object's creator UUID as a **key**. If avatar, a **NULL_KEY** is returned.	`llGetCreator()`

DETECTION WITH COLLISIONS

In many situations a collision sensor is a cheaper way to detect things. You can place filters on the collision events with `llCollisionFilter()`, which sets the name and/or key of the item to detect and indicates whether to ignore or accept the collision. You can play sounds on collision via `llCollisionSound()`, and use `llPassCollisions()` to control whether child prims tell the root prim about collisions. The details are sketched in Table 5.2.

TABLE 5.2: COLLISION FUNCTIONS

FUNCTION	BEHAVIOR
`llCollisionFilter(string name, key id, integer accept)`	Filter collision events. Boolean **accept**; FALSE means reject collisions from **name**, and TRUE means accept them.
`llCollisionSound(string sound, float volume)`	Play **sound** on collisions instead of the default. The **sound** parameter may be the name of a sound in inventory, a built-in sound, or the UUID of a sound anywhere. If **sound** is an empty string ("") no sound is played. **volume** ranges from 0.0 to 1.0.
`llPassCollisions(integer pass)`	Pass collisions to parents. If the parent is using a phantom volume detect, then the child prim will not receive collision events and the child will also become phantom.

Three events can be triggered—`collision()`, `collision_start()`, and `collision_end()`—each taking the single parameter **numDetected**. Avatars and physical objects will trigger collisions. Attachments and nonphysical objects won't.

EVENT DEFINITION

$$\texttt{collision\_start(integer numDetected) \{\}}$$

$$\texttt{collision(integer numDetected) \{\}}$$

$$\texttt{collision\_end(integer numDetected) \{\}}$$

Events in the collision family are invoked in an object after an avatar or physical object collides with it. `collision_start()` is triggered when the collision starts; `collision()` is triggered periodically while the objects are colliding; `collision_end()` is triggered when the collision ends. Compare to the `touch()` and `land_collision()` families of events in Chapters 2 and 7, respectively. Additional documentation can be found on the SYW website.

> `numDetected` — The number of objects or avatars that have collided.

Collisions are a nice, simple way to detect whether there's an avatar nearby, but the avatar will collide with the object, and that may not be the effect you are after. However, because you can't simply make the objects phantom so that avatars can walk through them without colliding (phantom objects don't trigger collisions), another useful function is `llVolumeDetect()`, which can make the object phantom but still trigger collision events when something enters the object.

DEFINITION

$$\texttt{llVolumeDetect(integer detect)}$$

If `detect` is TRUE, the object becomes phantom but triggers `collision_start()` and `collision_end()` events when other objects enter or leave the object. It will not trigger `collision()` events. When FALSE, the object does not become phantom and thus can trigger all three event types: `collision()`, `collision_start()`, and `collision_end()`*. This function must appear in the root prim.

> `detect` — Enables or disables phantom collision detection.

---

* The FALSE case makes nonphysical objects react to collisions as if they were physical. While useful, this is undocumented behavior, so be careful if you use this feature.

In comparison to `llSensorRepeat()`, the volume detector is a lot less expensive in terms of computational resources, and you don't need to worry about delay. (The sensor may not catch an object if it moves too quickly through the sensor zone.) You can use any arbitrary object (any shape, size, etc) to hold the volume detector. That's cool because `llSensorRepeat()` will sense only in conical slices from spheres.

Whether the sensor or the volume detector is better for your situation depends on a variety of factors. Table 5.3 summarizes the most common situations.

BUILDING
SENSORS

DETECTION
WITH
COLLISIONS

USING
GREETERS TO
WELCOME
VISITORS

SUMMARY

TABLE 5.3: `llSensorRepeat()` VERSUS `llVolumeDetect()`

LLSENSORREPEAT()	LLVOLUMEDETECT()
Sensing distance up to 96m.	Sensing distance in one prim of 10m; larger areas require multiple prims.
Sensing across sim boundaries.	Objects shouldn't "drift" into the neighbors.
Periodic sensing (depending on timer).	Immediate sensing (with `collision_start()`).
Heavier computational burden.	Significantly lighter computational burden.
Shape of sensing is spherical cone.	Shape of the sensor is arbitrary—whatever shape the object is.
No additional burden on prim count.	Extra prims may be needed (to be the sensor around the original object).
When you absolutely do not want anyone to know you're sensing.	Transparent object can be seen with Highlight Transparent; objects may interpenetrate.
Each prim in the object can handle its own collisions.	`llVolumeDetect()` must appear in the root prim. The root prim overrides any child-prim collision handlers.

Listing 5.6 shows a very simple example of the phantom-object collision detector. Note that we use the `collision_start()` event handler; `collision()` doesn't work, possibly due to a bug. Figure 5.5 shows the ghost that floats around SYW HQ. It uses this mechanism to say "Boo!" when it collides with you.

Listing 5.6: Collisions

```
default
{
    state_entry() {
        llVolumeDetect(TRUE); // automatically makes object phantom
    }
    collision_start(integer total_number) {
        llWhisper(0, "Boo!");
    }
}
```

Figure 5.5: The highlighted sphere is transparent normally. The ghost says "Boo!" when avatars pass into the phantom sphere.

USING GREETERS TO WELCOME VISITORS

Chapter 4, "Prims and Objects," was primarily about using objects to create and manipulate other physical objects, but objects can have other important artifacts in their inventory to cajole into existence. Some of the most important of these artifacts have to do with making visitors feel welcome to your *pied à terre* in *Second Life*.

A simple greeter should detect patrons coming into an area and generate a message to acknowledge them. You can rig a simple sensor to notice when a resident comes into range and then use `llSay()` or `llWhisper()` to utter a greeting to the resident, as shown in Listing 5.7.

Listing 5.7: Simple Greeter—Using Sensing

```
default {
    state_entry(){
        llSensorRepeat("", NULL_KEY, AGENT,6.0, PI, 5.0);
    }
    sensor(integer total_number) {
        llWhisper(0, "Welcome to SYW Old Town");
    }
}
```

If you embed Listing 5.7 in something at your parcel, it will detect passing avatars and greet them. Placing a greeter like this into a portal or beside a fence will have the effect you want. The result of this listing is illustrated in Figure 5.6, where an avatar is shown passing under a gateway arch.

Figure 5.6: As a visitor passes under the city portal, a simple welcome is whispered.

As an alternative to a sensing-based greeter, you can use `llVolumeDetect()` by simply changing the chatted greeting in Listing 5.6. Make a thin, transparent, rectangular prim, and place it under the archway where an avatar will walk through it. It will greet visitors passing under the arch (but not those who fly over).

A PERSONALIZED MEMORY GREETER

One problem that limits the utility of the most basic greeter is that it's a bit flat. It would be nice if the greeter addressed visitors by name, and noted the *Second Life* time of day. Additionally, you may notice in Figure 5.6 that when visitors loiter near the greeter, it keeps sensing and greeting them until the end of time (or at least until the sim reboots). Every time a visitor passes, including leaving the building, the same greeting is uttered, which will certainly make your patrons roll their eyes. You may laugh, but a number of stores in *Second Life* (including some well-known ones) don't remember you in any way. (The volume detector in Listing 5.2 doesn't have memory, but won't be *quite* so annoyingly repetitive.) One solution to this annoying lack of attention is to track visitors and tailor the greeting based on whether they've been greeted recently.

Listing 5.8 adds both personalization and memory to the basic greeter. The function `llDetectedName()` determines the visitor's identity. A list of the 25 most recent visitors is kept in *gRecentVisitors*. (There's nothing sacred about 25; it's cached in the constant MEMORY_LENGTH.) Now when a visitor who is not on the list is detected, he is added and a first-time greeting is whispered. Notice that the script checks whether the visitor has been seen before:

BUILDING
SENSORS

DETECTION
WITH
COLLISIONS

USING
GREETERS TO
WELCOME
VISITORS

SUMMARY

```
integer index = llListFindList(gRecentVisitors, [visitor]);
```

You can adjust the chattiness level with the Boolean *gBeChatty* to decide whether to welcome the visitor back or not.

Listing 5.8: Personalized Memory Greeter

```
integer MEMORY_LENGTH = 25;
integer gAfternoon = 43200;    // i.e., 3600 seconds * 12h
integer gEvening   = 64800;    // i.e., 3600 seconds * 18h
list    gRecentVisitors;
string  gGreetingFirst = " Welcome to SYW, Old Town ";
string  gGreetingReturn = " Welcome Back to SYW, Old Town ";
integer gBeChatty = TRUE;

string sayTimeOfDay() {
        float timeOfDay = llGetWallclock();
        if(timeOfDay < gAfternoon) return "Good Morning!";
        else if (timeOfDay < gEvening) return "Good Afternoon!";
        else return "Good Evening!";
}
default {
    state_entry() {
        gRecentVisitors = [];
        llSensorRepeat("", NULL_KEY, AGENT, 6.0, PI, 5.0);
    }
    sensor(integer total_number) {
        string visitor = llDetectedName(0);
        integer index = llListFindList(gRecentVisitors, [visitor]);
        if ( index != -1 ){ //we saw this avatar recently
            if (gBeChatty) {
                llWhisper(0,sayTimeOfDay() + gGreetingReturn + visitor +".");
            }
        } else {
            llWhisper(0,sayTimeOfDay()+ gGreetingFirst + visitor + ".");
            gRecentVisitors += visitor;
        }
        if (llGetListLength(gRecentVisitors) > MEMORY_LENGTH) {
            // make a little room
            llDeleteSubList(gRecentVisitors, 0, 1);
        }
    }
}
```

The greeter recognizes three divisions in the day: *morning*, from 00:00:00 to 11:59:59; *afternoon*, from 12:00:00 to 17:59:59; and *evening*, from 18:00:00 to 23:59:59. The function `sayTimeOfDay()` uses the `llGetWallclock()` function to determine the *Second Life* time of day.

A worthwhile refinement to this script reports who has recently visited. When the greeter's owner touches it, the greeter shown in Listing 5.9 reports the most recent visitors and optionally clears the list. You can see the report of recent visitors in Figure 5.7. An additional refinement (not shown) would be to record the visit time using `llGetTimestamp()`, and record both the name and time in a strided list.

Listing 5.9: Reporting Greeter

```
// Add the following code to Listing 5.4
integer gClearList = TRUE;

    touch_start(integer total_number) {
        if (llDetectedKey(0) == llGetOwner()){
            llOwnerSay("Visitors since last time:");
            integer i =0;
            integer len = llGetListLength(gRecentVisitors);
            for (; i < len; i++) {
                llOwnerSay(llList2String(gRecentVisitors,i));
            }
            if (gClearList) gRecentVisitors = [];
        }
    }
```

City Column whispers: Good Evening! Welcome to SYW, Old Town Minimal Ballyhoo
City Column: Vistors since last time:
City Column: Vex Streeter
City Column: ElectricSheep Expedition
City Column: Maryce Wozniak
City Column: Karzita Zabaleta

Figure 5.7: An enhanced greeter takes note of the time of day and identity of the visitor, and remembers whether the visitor has been greeted recently.

NOTE

The problem with keeping the visitor list in a global variable is that script memory is somewhat limited: a busy detector will run out of space pretty quickly if it tries to remember everyone it sees, breaking it or missing visitors. While it would be really useful to employ a simple persistent method such as adding to a text file, it's not possible to create or write into a notecard (in the inventory of the fountain, for example). Chapter 12: "Reaching outside *Second Life*" will revisit this example to demonstrate how to achieve information persistence by talking to an external data store.

SUMMARY

This chapter focused largely on using sensing to perform some interesting interactions. Mastering these techniques may give you the keys to the most important fundamental aspects of scripting in *Second Life*. Automation is often based on sensing; remember that automation exists in a specific context, and that badly done automation almost always adds more annoyance than effect.

In succeeding chapters you'll learn a number of advanced techniques for bringing these creations to life and using the physics model of *Second Life*. You can combine and extend these scripts in many ways to gain even greater power over your virtual environment.

CHAPTER 1
CHAPTER 2
CHAPTER 3
CHAPTER 4

CHAPTER 5

CHAPTER 6
CHAPTER 7
CHAPTER 8
CHAPTER 9
CHAPTER 10
CHAPTER 11
CHAPTER 12
CHAPTER 13
CHAPTER 14
CHAPTER 15
APPENDICES

LAND DESIGN AND MANAGEMENT

Landscape design is an important aspect of creating the environment you live in. In *SL*, you can make mountains, canyons, and water falls. Making mountains and canyons is a form of **terraforming**. Water is a particularly interesting aspect of terraforming, because *SL* water isn't real and you have to create it from a plywood box.

The other important aspect of managing your land is setting up your security system. This chapter will show you how to limit access to your property and eject intruders.

A WATERFALL

 A WATERFALL

SHAPING THE
LAND BY
TERRAFORMING

LAND
SECURITY—
ARE YOU ON
THE LIST?

LAND
INFORMATION
FUNCTIONS

SUMMARY

New scripters may not realize that water (pools, rivers, rainstorms, waves) is not "real" in the sense of being interactive or reactive to its surrounding environment. Thus, if you want water, you have two options:

- Terraforming to make the official **SL** water level higher than the ground level. Terraforming is covered in the "Shaping the Land by Terraforming" section of this chapter.
- Creating objects that act as waves or water cascades, and applying texture animation and particle effects to them. This approach is used in this section.

At SYW HQ, we have a water mill that is powered by the waterfall falling from the cliff behind. Figure 6.1 shows the completed mill from a long view.

Figure 6.1: A water mill with working wheel, gears, and turbulent waters

You have probably seen fountains galore in **Second Life**, and the technical approach is simple and consistent. You simply choose an appropriate water texture (Linden Lab supplies an excellent assortment in your free Library folder), then animate it with a recipe such as the one in Listing 6.1. This script provides the animation in the pool below the waterfall, and is sufficiently convincing for the human eye to perceive what appears to be real water.

Listing 6.1: Water Animation

```
default {
    state_entry(){
        llSetTextureAnim(ANIM_ON | SMOOTH | LOOP, ALL_SIDES, 1, 1, 1.0, 1.0, 0.05);
    }
}
```

`llSetTextureAnim()` is intended to use textures with multiple frames embedded; it usually plays them as frames like in a movie. This function is described in detail in the "Texture Animation" section of Chapter 9, "Special Effects." This listing combines SMOOTH and LOOP in the first parameter (**mode**) so the water appears to flow continually in the **x** direction. LOOP makes the animation play over and over, while SMOOTH slides from one frame to the next. The number of **rows** and **columns** is set to 1 because there's only a single logical frame to this texture, and likewise for the length.

This is sufficient for the catch pool, but the parts of the waterfall itself are slightly more complex (and visually interesting as a result). Note in Figure 6.2 that the waterfall consists of three nearly hollow vertical cylinders tapered toward their tops. These are joined to a horizontal cylinder at the top of the falls.

CHAPTER 1
CHAPTER 2
CHAPTER 3
CHAPTER 4
CHAPTER 5
CHAPTER 6
CHAPTER 7
CHAPTER 8
CHAPTER 9
CHAPTER 10
CHAPTER 11
CHAPTER 12
CHAPTER 13
CHAPTER 14
CHAPTER 15
APPENDICES

Figure 6.2: Multipart waterfall composed of tapered flexiprim cylinders

Using the animation described in Listing 6.2 would be visually interesting enough, and, given the fact that the individual cylinders are flexible (**flexiprims**), could be visually convincing. Real waterfalls hardly ever drop at constant rates, however, so Listing 6.2 attempts to add further realism by varying the animation rate for each of the three cylinders over time.

Listing 6.2: Improved Water Animation

```
float randBetween(float min, float max) {
    return llFrand(max - min) + min;
}
default {
    state_entry() {
        float rand = llFrand(10.0);
        llSetTimerEvent(rand);
    }
    timer() {
        state fallingWater;
    }
}

state fallingWater {
    state_entry() {
        float rate = randBetween(0.05, 0.35);
        llSetTextureAnim(ANIM_ON | SMOOTH | LOOP, ALL_SIDES, 1, 1, 1.0, 0.0, rate);
        llSleep(1.5);
        state default;
    }
}
```

The `default` state sets a random timer event using the `llFrand()` function to return a random floating-point number between 0.0 and 10.0. When the timer elapses, control transitions immediately to the `fallingWater` state, the `state_entry()` event handler chooses a random number to approximate a reasonable flow rate in harmony with the rotational rate of the water wheel. It selects the random number and then initiates the animation with its new variable rate.

143

▶ A Waterfall

▶ Shaping the Land by Terraforming

Land Security— Are You on the List?

Land Information Functions

Summary

There's an additional twist to the waterfall: if you impart horizontal motion into the root-prim cascade at the top of the waterfall, the flexiprims will wave gently from side to side. By slowly moving the root prim between two horizontal positions using `llSetPos()`, the cascade appears to move slowly from side to side, and more importantly, drags the three parts of the sheeting waterfall with it. The sheets of the waterfall have been set to react to Drag and Wind*, so the effect is visually quite arresting and creates a strong illusion of random motion.

The particular waterfall has a strict east-west orientation, so the values shown are appropriate for the precise world coordinates in which this specific waterfall exists. We reached these coordinates by moving the waterfall between its easternmost and westernmost extent and then recording the values. The `move_on()` function of Listing 6.3 makes the cascade move in steps of 10 centimeters per increment, so any jerkiness of motion would be only slightly perceptible at worst. Combined with the texture animation of the cascade (it too has a texture-animation script), the motion appears absolutely smooth.

Listing 6.3: Waving Waters

```
vector gFullWest = <98.500, 188.700, 113.00>; // substitute your coordinates here
vector gFullEast = <99.325, 188.700, 113.00>; // substitute your own coordinates
vector gCurrentPos; // will vary between full west and full east
float gAdjuster;

move_on()
{
    if (gCurrentPos.x <= gFullWest.x){ gAdjuster = 0.01; }
    if (gCurrentPos.x >= gFullEast.x){ gAdjuster = -0.01; }
    gCurrentPos.x += gAdjuster;
    llSetPos(gCurrentPos);
}

default
{
    state_entry() {
        gCurrentPos = gFullWest;
        llSetTextureAnim(ANIM_ON | SMOOTH | LOOP, ALL_SIDES, 1, 1, 1.0, 1.0, 0.05);
        llSetTimerEvent(1.0);
    }
    timer() {
        move_on();
    }
}
```

To complete the effect of the waterfall, you need to add particle effects and sound; on the SYW website you can find the complete suite of scripts we used.

---

* Drag and Wind are properties of flexible prims, allowing builders to indicate that flexible objects should drag against the wind (should they flop around or sway), and how much they are affected by the ambient wind strength. See `http://secondlife.com/app/help/new/flexy.php` for more details. These properties can also be set using `llSetPrimitiveParams()`, as described in Appendix A, "Setting Primitive Parameters."

SHAPING THE LAND BY TERRAFORMING

You can certainly be your own landscape contractor in *Second Life*, as this next series of scripts reveals. Most people terraform their land manually, using the *SL* GUI. You can raise and lower the land to create mountains or pools. You can also use a scripted approach to terraforming, which might allow you to, for example, quickly create a mountain range or a sequence of tidal pools. The script shown in Listing 6.4 lowers the land and rezzes a pool of water into the depression. (The ground at SYW HQ is at such a high altitude that only a very deep well would reach the real *SL* water.) You can extend this idea to have each mountain rez its own forest, snow-capped peaks, and ski lodges.

 ## BUILD NOTE

 Create a cylinder, name it Pool, apply a watery texture to it, and place the code from Listings 6.2 and 6.5 in its Content folder. Create another object and call it Digger; place Listing 6.4's code and the Pool in its Content folder.

Listing 6.4: Terraforming Pool Digger

```
integer OB_CHANNEL = -654321; // or use a random value

integer gRadius = 4;  // how far to scan around starting point
integer gBrush = 0;   // brush size 0=2m, 1=4m, 2=8m: see wiki
integer gDig = TRUE;  // should we dig on the next touch?

scan(vector center, integer operation) {
    float step = llPow(2.0, (float) gBrush);
    float x;
    for (x = -gRadius; x <= gRadius; x += step) {
        float y;
        for (y = -gRadius; y <= gRadius; y += step) {
            vector p = <center.x + x, center.y + y, center.z>;
            float dist = llVecDist(p, center);
            if (dist <= gRadius) {
                llSetPos(p);
                integer z;
                integer c = (integer) (((float) gRadius - dist) / 2);
                for (z = 0; z <= c; z++) {
                    llModifyLand(operation, gBrush);
                }
            }
        }
    }
}
```

A Waterfall

▶ Shaping the
Land by
Terraforming

▶ Land
Security—
Are You on
the List?

Land
Information
Functions

Summary

```
default
{
    touch_start(integer total_number) {
        vector home = llGetPos();
        if (gDig) {
            scan(home, LAND_LOWER);
        } else {
            llSay(OB_CHANNEL, "die");
            scan(home, LAND_RAISE);
        }
        llSetPos(home);

        if (gDig) {
            llRezObject("Pool", <home.x, home.y, home.z - 1.0>,
                                <0,0,0>, ZERO_ROTATION, OB_CHANNEL);
            llSay(OB_CHANNEL, "size=" + (string)(2 * (gRadius + 1)));
        }
        gDig = !gDig;
    }
}
```

When the Digger is touched, if the state of *gDig* is TRUE, it lowers the land; that is, it digs a pool *gRadius* meters wide and rezzes the Pool (a cylinder with a water texture) to fill it. The digger object must also have the Pool in inventory, as `llRezObject()` will be used to generate it. Figure 6.3 shows the digger at work and the finished pool.

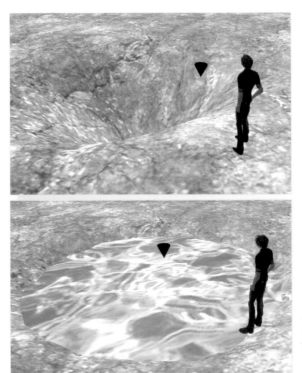

Figure 6.3: Terraforming **Digger** at work before the **Pool** is rezzed, and the completed **Pool**

The basic function call, used in a loop, is `llModifyLand()`. The loop control moves around the starting point from east to west in the **y** direction and north to south in the **x** direction. The *brush* argument pushes the land beneath the object in which it exists in the direction specified by the *action* argument. On alternate touches, the Digger lowers the land and raises it back.

DEFINITION

---

llModifyLand(integer *action*, integer *brush*)

Modifies land with *action* using *brush*.

action — Integer constant, either LAND_LEVEL, LAND_RAISE, LAND_LOWER, LAND_SMOOTH, LAND_NOISE, or LAND_REVERT. Actions are with respect to the prim center; for example LAND_LEVEL levels to the prim center.

brush — Integer constant. 0 is 2m×2m, 1 is 4m×4m, and 2 is 8m×8m. *You may notice references to named constants for this parameter* (LAND_SMALL_BRUSH, LAND_MEDIUM_BRUSH, *and* LAND_LARGE_BRUSH). *Do not use these constants; due to an outstanding LSL bug they do not have the effect that the names imply. Use 0, 1, or 2 instead.* See https://wiki.secondlife.com/wiki/LlModifyLand *for information and discussion. (Wiki entries at other locations do not contain this specific information.)*

CHAPTER 6

CHAPTER 7
CHAPTER 8
CHAPTER 9
CHAPTER 10
CHAPTER 11
CHAPTER 12
CHAPTER 13
CHAPTER 14
CHAPTER 15
APPENDICES

Listing 6.5 enables the pool digger to automatically set the size of the pool and to delete the pool when the land is being raised. When the pool object is rezzed, Listing 6.4 sends a message on the OB_CHANNEL with the size information; Listing 6.5 sets the pool's scale via the llSetScale() function to the size of the land depression created. When the digger is touched again, Listing 6.4 sends a message on the OB_CHANNEL telling the pool to die, and Listing 6.5 destroys the pool.

Listing 6.5: Watery Pool Controller

```
default
{
    on_rez(integer channel) {
        llListen(channel, "", NULL_KEY, "");
    }
    listen(integer ch, string n, key id, string m) {
        if (m == "die") {
            llDie();
        } else {
            list pl = llParseString2List(m, ["="], []);
            string com = llList2String(pl, 0);
            if (com == "size") {
                float r = llList2Float(pl, 1);
                llSetScale(<r,r,0.5>);
            }
        }
    }
}
```

LAND SECURITY—ARE YOU ON THE LIST?

Security can be an important part of land management. The two examples in this section describe how to create an access list of avatars allowed to use an object, and how to monitor your land for members of a specified group.

ACCESS-CONTROLLED TELEPORTS

A WATERFALL

SHAPING THE
LAND BY
TERRAFORMING

 LAND
SECURITY—
ARE YOU ON
THE LIST?

LAND
INFORMATION
FUNCTIONS

SUMMARY

Listing 6.6 shows an elementary access controller for an in-home port key. Port keys are an excellent way to go from floor to floor in a store or house as they provide you an alternative means to get residents from one location or level to another without using precious prims on staircases or elevators. Port keys are a form of teleporting, covered extensively in Chapter 2. The port key can be any object.

The script's behavior is triggered by a left mouse click: if a resident touching the object is on an access list read each time the script is reset, the object holding the script will complete a teleport; otherwise it will deny the individual entry. Access control can be very useful in a variety of circumstances, such as separating public and private areas in your home.

The port key access system is based on a name lookup of an in-memory list. The preparation of the access list itself is completely manual. You need to create a notecard with the list of names of avatars who may enter, and place this notecard in the inventory of the port key object. Each time you want to change the list (by adding or deleting a name), you edit the notecard and reset the script shown in Listing 6.6; resetting the script forces a reread of the notecard's data.

Listing 6.6: Access-Controlled Teleport

```
// Read the access List on entry / reset.
// Whenever you add a new name to the access list,
// manually reset the script to force a full re-read
string gAccessCard;     // name of a notecard in the object's inventory
integer gLine = 0;      // current line number
key gQueryID;           // id used to identify dataserver queries
list gAccessList = [];

vector targetPos = <12.5, 250.0, 120.50>; //The x, y, z coordinates to teleport.
string fltText = "1st Floor"; //label that floats above Teleport

integer onTheList(string name) {
    return (llListFindList(gAccessList, [name]) > -1);
}

reset() {
    vector target;
    target = (targetPos- llGetPos()) * (ZERO_ROTATION / llGetRot());
    llSitTarget(target, ZERO_ROTATION);
}

default {
    state_entry() {
        llSetText(fltText, <1.0, 1.0, 1.0>,1.0);
        llSetSitText(fltText);
        // select the first notecard in the object's inventory
        gAccessCard = llGetInventoryName(INVENTORY_NOTECARD, 0);
        // force full read by asking for first line
        gQueryID = llGetNotecardLine(gAccessCard, gLine);
    }
    dataserver(key query_id, string data) {
        if (query_id == gQueryID) {
            if (data != EOF) {     // not at the end of the notecard
                gAccessList += data;
                ++gLine;           // increase line count
                gQueryID = llGetNotecardLine(gAccessCard, gLine);  // get next line
```

```
        } else {
            llOwnerSay("Access List: " +(string)llGetListLength(gAccessList));
        }
    }
}
changed(integer change) {
    key avatarKey = llAvatarOnSitTarget();
    if ((avatarKey != NULL_KEY) && (change & CHANGED_LINK)) {
        if (onTheList(llKey2Name(avatarKey))){
            llSleep(0.15);
            llUnSit(avatarKey); // will be at destination
            reset();
        } else {
            llWhisper(0, "Access denied. Ejecting you!");
            // more polite script would add a delay
            llTeleportAgentHome(avatarKey);
        }
    }
}
}
```

The `state_entry()` event handler is invoked on script reset and initiates the read by grabbing the first notecard it finds in inventory:

```
gAccessCard = llGetInventoryName(INVENTORY_NOTECARD, 0);
```

It then sets off a `dataserver()` event by requesting the first line on the notecard:

```
gQueryID = llGetNotecardLine(gAccessCard, gLine);
```

 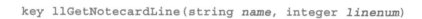

DEFINITION

key llGetNotecardLine(string *name*, integer *linenum*)

Requests the line number *linenum* of the notecard *name* from the dataserver. Returns a key that is the handle for a `dataserver()` event response. `dataserver()` is described in Chapter 3.

> *name* — A notecard in inventory or UUID.
>
> *line* — Line number on a notecard. The first line is number zero. If the *linenum* is past the end of the notecard, EOF is returned by the dataserver.

If the notecard contains embedded inventory items (such as textures and landmarks), EOF will be returned, regardless of the line requested. Only the first 255 characters of the line will be returned.

DEFINITION

key llGetNumberOfNotecardLines(string *name*)

Requests from the dataserver a count of the number of lines of text in notecard *name*. Returns a key that is the handle for a `dataserver()` event response.

> *name* — A notecard in inventory or a UUID.

CHAPTER 1
CHAPTER 2
CHAPTER 3
CHAPTER 4
CHAPTER 5

CHAPTER 6

CHAPTER 7
CHAPTER 8
CHAPTER 9
CHAPTER 10
CHAPTER 11
CHAPTER 12
CHAPTER 13
CHAPTER 14
CHAPTER 15
APPENDICES

A WATERFALL

SHAPING THE
LAND BY
TERRAFORMING

 LAND
SECURITY—
ARE YOU ON
THE LIST?

LAND
INFORMATION
FUNCTIONS

SUMMARY

When `dataserver()` is invoked it reads exactly one line from the card and adds it to the growing list of names. It then forces the next invocation of `dataserver()` by requesting a line from the notecard. As long as the line is not the EOF (end of file) marker, the read continues. This may seem rather roundabout, but it's consistent with a system where events dominate the landscape. You could instead use `llGetNumberOfNotecardLines()` to see how many lines you need to read, but doing so wouldn't make the script any simpler or faster. The list is read only once but is consulted each time the port key is touched via a function call to `onTheList()`, which returns TRUE or FALSE. If `onTheList()` returns TRUE, the avatar is teleported and stood up in the destination location.

This script uses the function `llTeleportAgentHome()` to eject the avatar. It could alternatively use `llEjectFromLand()`, which does not specify the final location. *Take care ejecting people from land; sometimes people innocently fly over it, often at high altitude, and ejecting people under this circumstance is griefing and is against the terms of service.* Build in some kind of warning and delay to your system, or something that doesn't send people home just because they accidentally flew over your land for a few moments.

If you have specific avatars whose access you want to enable or restrict, it is usually better to add them to a specific land ban list. This technique also allows time-limited restrictions. As an example, you could replace the call to `llTeleportAgentHome()` from Listing 6.6 with the following line to ban them from your land for a week:

```
llAddToLandBanList(avatarKey, 7*24);
```

Table 6.1 shows the complete set of land-access functions.

TABLE 6.1: LAND ACCESS FUNCTIONS

FUNCTION	DESCRIPTION
`llAddToLandBanList(key avatar, float hours)`	Adds *avatar* to the land ban list for a time equal to *hours*. Causes the script to sleep for 0.1 second.
`llAddToLandPassList(key avatar, float hours)`	Adds *avatar* to the land pass list for *hours*. Causes the script to sleep for 0.1 second.
`llRemoveFromLandBanList(key avatar)`	Removes *avatar* from the land ban list. Causes the script to sleep for 0.1 second.
`llRemoveFromLandPassList(key avatar)`	Removes *avatar* from the land pass list. Causes the script to sleep for 0.1 second.
`llResetLandBanList()`	Removes all residents from the land ban list. Causes the script to sleep for 0.1 second.
`llResetLandPassList()`	Removes all residents from the land access/pass list.
`llEjectFromLand(key avatar)`	Ejects from the parcel any avatar identified by key. If the land is deeded to a group the object must be deeded to the same group.
`llTeleportAgentHome(key avatar)`	Teleports *avatar* on owner's land to the ejected avatar's home location without any warning. The object owner must also be the land owner.

A LAND MONITOR AND EJECTOR

Listing 6.6 used `llTeleportAgentHome()` to boot an unwelcome guest from a premises. Listing 6.7 uses a variation on both the access criteria and ejection function to achieve a similar level of land protection. This script adds a warning and delay before ejecting the avatar.

Listing 6.7: Land Monitor and Ejector

```
float EJECT_DELAY = 10.0;    // seconds
float SENSOR_REPEAT = 30.0;  // seconds
list  gIntruders;
default {
    state_entry() {
        llSensorRepeat( "", NULL_KEY, AGENT, 20, PI, SENSOR_REPEAT );
    }
    sensor( integer vIntFound ){
        integer vIntCounter = 0;
        do {
            string vStrName = llDetectedName( vIntCounter );
            if (llOverMyLand( llDetectedKey( vIntCounter ) )) {
                //if (llSameGroup( llDetectedKey( vIntCounter )))
                if (llDetectedGroup( vIntCounter )) {
                    //llWhisper(0, vStrName + " is in the same group");
                } else {
                    llSay(0, vStrName+", this is a private estate. Please leave.");
                    llSetTimerEvent(EJECT_DELAY);
                    gIntruders += llDetectedKey( vIntCounter );
                }
            }
        } while (++vIntCounter < vIntFound);
    }
    timer() {
        integer i;
        integer len = llGetListLength( gIntruders );
        for (i=0; i<len; i++) {
            key intruder = llList2Key( gIntruders, i );
            if (llOverMyLand( intruder )) llEjectFromLand(intruder);
        }
        gIntruders = [];
        llSetTimerEvent(0);
    }
}
```

CHAPTER 1
CHAPTER 2
CHAPTER 3
CHAPTER 4
CHAPTER 5
CHAPTER 6
CHAPTER 7
CHAPTER 8
CHAPTER 9
CHAPTER 10
CHAPTER 11
CHAPTER 12
CHAPTER 13
CHAPTER 14
CHAPTER 15
APPENDICES

Instead of using an explicit access list, the script sets up a slow-polling radar that detects avatars using `llSensorRepeat()` with a 30-second cycle time. (Chapter 5 discusses the use of `llSensorRepeat()` versus `llVolumeDetect()`.) When an avatar is sensed, the `sensor()` event handler fires. `llSensorRepeat()` guarantees the detection is an avatar, as its third argument specifies `AGENT` and nothing else. Note that if `EJECT_DELAY` is greater than `SENSOR_REPEAT`, the script should more carefully manage duplicate keys in the *gIntruders* list. The `sensor()` event checks to make certain the detected avatar is on land owned by the object's owner via `llOverMyLand()`, passing it the avatar's UUID.

DEFINITION

integer llOverMyLand(key *avatar*)

Returns TRUE if *avatar* is over land owned by the script owner; returns FALSE otherwise. This function works on group land only if the object holding the script is group-deeded.

CHAPTER 6

A Waterfall

Shaping the
Land by
Terraforming

Land
Security—
Are You on
the List?

Land
Information
Functions

Summary

Next the script determines whether the avatar is in the same **SL** group as the owner; `llSameGroup()` or, equivalently, `llDetectedGroup()` will return TRUE when the detected avatar has the same *active* group (and is currently in the same simulator) as the object containing the script. Whether you use `llSameGroup()` or `llDetectedGroup()` depends on whether you have access to the avatar's key; Listing 6.7 shows how both functions can be used.

DEFINITION

integer llSameGroup(key *agent*)

Returns TRUE if *agent* has the same active group as the object containing the script; otherwise returns FALSE.

agent — The UUID of an avatar. The avatar must be in the same sim as the script.

DEFINITION

integer llDetectedGroup(integer *number*)

Returns TRUE if the detected object or avatar has the same active group as the object containing the script; otherwise returns FALSE.

number — The index of the detected object or avatar.

If the avatar is *not* in the same group, it sends a warning message and sets up a timer. When the `timer()` event fires, it ejects any avatars that are still over the land.

For this script to work, the group permissions on the object device should match the criterion you intend to filter on. Thus, if you want only members of the **Scripting Your World** group to be admitted, make that tag active when you create the security device, and make certain group privileges are set.

Turning this land monitor into an avatar-radar device is a trivial matter: instead of ejecting the avatars, report them to the owner of the radar. Radar devices are commonly worn as HUD devices.

LAND INFORMATION FUNCTIONS

Table 6.2 shows the list of functions that describe a piece of land, including how many prims are on it, who owns it, and what activities are permitted. The functions `llGetParcelFlags()` and `llGetRegionFlags()` are useful for determining what your objects are permitted to do. Table 6.3 shows the list of parcel flags and Table 6.4 shows the list of region flags.

TABLE 6.2: LAND INFORMATION FUNCTIONS

CHAPTER 1
CHAPTER 2
CHAPTER 3
CHAPTER 4
CHAPTER 5
CHAPTER 6
CHAPTER 7
CHAPTER 8
CHAPTER 9
CHAPTER 10
CHAPTER 11
CHAPTER 12
CHAPTER 13
CHAPTER 14
CHAPTER 15
APPENDICES

FUNCTION	DESCRIPTION
`integer llGetParcelPrimCount (vector position, integer category, integer sim_wide)`	Returns the number of prims of the given category on the parcel at the specified *position* (in region coordinates). If *sim_wide* is TRUE it returns the count for the entire sim; if *sim_wide* is FALSE it returns the count for the current parcel. The precise number returned depends on the argument *category*; if *category* is PARCEL_COUNT_TOTAL, it counts all prims on the parcel except PRIM_TEMP_ON_REZ objects PARCEL_COUNT_OWNER, it counts prims owned by the parcel owner PARCEL_COUNT_GROUP, it counts prims owned by a group PARCEL_COUNT_OTHER, it counts prims not owned by the owner or a group PARCEL_COUNT_SELECTED, it counts prims all prims selected or sat on PARCEL_COUNT_TEMP, it counts all PRIM_TEMP_ON_REZ objects
`integer llGetParcelFlags (vector pos)`	Returns an integer bitmask of parcel flags (PARCEL_FLAG_*) for the parcel that includes the point *pos*, specified in region coordinates. Table 6.3 shows the list of parcel flags.
`integer llGetParcelMaxPrims (vector pos, integer sim_wide)`	Returns an integer that is the maximum number of prims allowed on the parcel at *pos*, in region coordinates. If *sim_wide* is TRUE it returns the count for the entire sim; if *sim_wide* is FALSE it returns the count for the current parcel.
`list llGetParcelDetails (vector pos, list params)`	Returns a list that is the parcel details specified in *params* (in the same order) for the parcel at *pos*, in region coordinates. *params* can contain any or all of the following: PARCEL_DETAILS_NAME: The name of the parcel returned as a 63-character string PARCEL_DETAILS_DESC: The description of the parcel returned as a (maximum) 127-character string PARCEL_DETAILS_OWNER: The parcel owner's key returned as key PARCEL_DETAILS_GROUP: The parcel group's key returned as key PARCEL_DETAILS_AREA: The parcel's area, in square meters, returned as integer
`list llGetParcelPrimOwners (vector pos)`	Returns a list of keys of all residents who own objects on the parcel at *pos* and with individual prim counts. You can get avatar names by using llKey2Name(). The list is strided and formatted as [key *agent*, integer *count*]. 100 entries maximum.
`vector llGetRegionCorner ()`	Returns a vector in meters that is the global location of the southwest corner of the region the object is in. The **z** component is 0.0.
`float llGetRegionFPS ()`	Returns a float that is the average region frames per second (FPS).
`integer llGetRegionFlags ()`	Returns an integer that is a bitmask with the region flags (REGION_FLAG_*) for the region the object is in. Table 6.4 shows the list of region flags; several other values (without named constants) can be returned—see the wiki for more details.
`string llGetRegionName ()`	Returns a string that is the current region name.
`key llGetLandOwnerAt (vector pos)`	Returns a key of the land owner at *pos*. Find the owner's name by using llKey2Name() of the returned key.
`integer llEdgeOfWorld (vector pos, vector dir)`	Returns a Boolean, TRUE if the border hit by *dir* from *pos* is the edge of the world (i.e., has no neighboring simulator).

CHAPTER 6

A WATERFALL

SHAPING THE
LAND BY
TERRAFORMING

LAND
SECURITY—
ARE YOU ON
THE LIST?

▶ LAND
INFORMATION
FUNCTIONS

▶ SUMMARY

TABLE 6.3: PARCEL FLAGS RETURNED BY `llGetParcelFlags()`

Flag	Value	Description
PARCEL_FLAG_ALLOW_FLY	0x00000001	Parcel allows flying.
PARCEL_FLAG_ALLOW_SCRIPTS	0x00000002	Parcel allows outside scripts.
PARCEL_FLAG_ALLOW_LANDMARK	0x00000008	Parcel allows landmarks to be created.
PARCEL_FLAG_ALLOW_TERRAFORM	0x00000010	Parcel allows anyone to terraform the land.
PARCEL_FLAG_ALLOW_DAMAGE	0x00000020	Parcel allows damage.
PARCEL_FLAG_ALLOW_CREATE_OBJECTS	0x00000040	Parcel allows anyone to create objects.
PARCEL_FLAG_USE_ACCESS_GROUP	0x00000100	Parcel limits access to a group.
PARCEL_FLAG_USE_ACCESS_LIST	0x00000200	Parcel limits access to a list of residents.
PARCEL_FLAG_USE_BAN_LIST	0x00000400	Parcel uses a ban list, including restricting access based on payment info.
PARCEL_FLAG_USE_LAND_PASS_LIST	0x00000800	Parcel allows passes to be purchased.
PARCEL_FLAG_LOCAL_SOUND_ONLY	0x00008000	Parcel restricts spatialized sound to the parcel.
PARCEL_FLAG_RESTRICT_PUSHOBJECT	0x00200000	Parcel restricts `llPushObject()` calls.
PARCEL_FLAG_ALLOW_GROUP_SCRIPTS	0x02000000	Parcel allows scripts owned by group.
PARCEL_FLAG_ALLOW_CREATE_GROUP_OBJECTS	0x04000000	Parcel allows object creation by group members or objects.
PARCEL_FLAG_ALLOW_ALL_OBJECT_ENTRY	0x08000000	Parcel allows all objects to enter a parcel.
PARCEL_FLAG_ALLOW_GROUP_OBJECT_ENTRY	0x10000000	Parcel only allows group (and owner) objects to enter the parcel.

TABLE 6.4: REGION FLAGS RETURNED BY `llGetRegionFlags()`*

Flag	Value	Description
REGION_FLAG_ALLOW_DAMAGE	0x00000001	Region is damage-enabled.
REGION_FLAG_FIXED_SUN	0x00000010	Region has a fixed sun position.
REGION_FLAG_BLOCK_TERRAFORM	0x00000040	Region's terraforming is disabled.
REGION_FLAG_SANDBOX	0x00000100	Region is a sandbox.
REGION_FLAG_DISABLE_COLLISIONS	0x00001000	Region has disabled collisions.
REGION_FLAG_DISABLE_PHYSICS	0x00004000	Region has disabled physics.
REGION_FLAG_BLOCK_FLY	0x00080000	Region blocks flying.
REGION_FLAG_ALLOW_DIRECT_TELEPORT	0x00100000	Region allows direct teleports.
REGION_FLAG_RESTRICT_PUSHOBJECT	0x00400000	Region restricts `llPushObject()` calls.

---

* `llGetRegionFlags()` can also return several values that do not have named constants—see the wiki for more details.

SUMMARY

This chapter focused largely on making your land "operational"; that is, giving your land natural and human-created elements with attributes that closely rival their real-world counterparts. High correlation with how things move or operate in reality is not always necessary, desirable, or in many cases even possible—we don't know with certainty what starships might look like if some day humans invent them. However, when you do want to emulate things found in real life, it's important to consider how they actually operate there, and to make your designs reflect that.

CHAPTER 1
CHAPTER 2
CHAPTER 3
CHAPTER 4
CHAPTER 5

CHAPTER 6

CHAPTER 7
CHAPTER 8
CHAPTER 9
CHAPTER 10
CHAPTER 11
CHAPTER 12
CHAPTER 13
CHAPTER 14
CHAPTER 15
APPENDICES

CHAPTER 7

PHYSICS AND VEHICLES

You can use *Second Life's* built-in physics model to manipulate physical objects (those that move according to the laws of *SL* physics). Most of Chapter 4, "Making and Moving Objects," dealt with nonphysical objects and presented the various functions that manipulate them. *SL* provides a set of kinetic functions that operate on forces and torques of physical objects; the resulting motion depends on the object's mass and available energy. Physics makes *SL* seem much more real, and because it isn't *exactly* like the real world, it can be a lot more fun!

WARNING

Linden Lab recently transitioned from the Havok1 to the Havok4 physics engine. Havok4 is generally more stable, but many problems still exist and more are being found regularly. The key thing you should be aware of is that the physics engine is changing *very* frequently; if you find apparent errors in this chapter, it may be due to a change in *SL*.

PHYSICAL OBJECTS

PHYSICAL OBJECTS

VEHICLES

SUMMARY

Physical objects are created either by checking the Physical check box in the object editor, or with scripts. Physical objects will roll down hills, collide with other objects, and float away. If you kick a physical object (or otherwise apply an impulse), it will eventually come to a rest. Physical objects can also exist at a much higher altitude than regular objects before the sim returns them to inventory.

Phantom objects (objects that don't collide with anything) can be physical, but will only collide with terrain; avatars and other objects can pass right through them. *Flexible* prims (*flexiprims*) are client-side effects that are automatically phantom and nonphysical. You can link them to physical objects, although doing so is buggy. For example, objects can't become physical when they have flexible prims!

A physical object may have no more than 31 prims. *SL* considers an interaction closer than 10cm together to be a collision. If physics is enabled on an object within 10cm of another object (or is interpenetrating another object), your object will work its way upward until the objects have separated by at least 10cm. This behavior can cause problems; for example, bowling pins might fall over.

Most of the functions described in this chapter require physics to be TRUE. An object's physics flag, STATUS_PHYSICS, can be changed using llSetStatus() or llSetPrimitiveParams() and read back with llGetStatus() and llGetPrimitiveParams(). It usually takes a moment for the status to become active, so it's a good idea to either put an llSleep(0.2) after turning physics on or off, or include some other (nonphysics) code.

DEFINITION

llSetStatus(integer *status*, integer *value*)

Sets the object status attributes indicated in the *status* mask to *value*.

status — Bitmask over 10 STATUS_* flags, shown in the following table.

value — TRUE or FALSE.

CONSTANT	VALUE	DEFAULT
STATUS_PHYSICS	0x1	FALSE
STATUS_ROTATE_X	0x2	TRUE
STATUS_ROTATE_Y	0x4	TRUE
STATUS_ROTATE_Z	0x8	TRUE
STATUS_PHANTOM	0x10	FALSE
STATUS_SANDBOX	0x20	FALSE
STATUS_BLOCK_GRAB	0x40	FALSE
STATUS_DIE_AT_EDGE	0x80	FALSE
STATUS_RETURN_AT_EDGE	0x100	FALSE
STATUS_CAST_SHADOWS	0x200	TRUE

CHAPTER 1
CHAPTER 2
CHAPTER 3
CHAPTER 4
CHAPTER 5
CHAPTER 6

CHAPTER 7

CHAPTER 8
CHAPTER 9
CHAPTER 10
CHAPTER 11
CHAPTER 12
CHAPTER 13
CHAPTER 14
CHAPTER 15
APPENDICES

DEFINITION

---

integer llGetStatus(integer *status*)

Returns an integer that contains the current TRUE or FALSE value of *status*.

status — One of the STATUS_* flags.

SL's primary physical properties are *Friction* and *Gravity*. Just as in the real world, friction is the effect of objects colliding with each other. The script can control an object's friction value by changing its material type or its buoyancy. Glass, for example, has a lower friction value than most of the other materials. Gravity in *SL* is also like gravity in the real world, operating at an acceleration of 9.8 m/s². That means if you drop an object, it will fall at a force of *object mass* × 9.8 m/s². There is no concept of terminal velocity.

The *Mass*, *Energy*, *Buoyancy*, and *Hover* properties modulate how forces work on the object, and are less like their real-world counterparts than friction and gravity are. Mass, reported by llGetMass() for a prim or llGetObjectMass() for a complete object, depends only on the object's size and shape, not on its material. A hollow object is lighter than a solid object.

Energy, reported by llGetEnergy(), acts as a throttle on how much a script can move a physical object. If an object's energy is 1.0, LSL functions that attempt to change the object's motion have full effect. If the energy is 0.0, the same functions have no effect. An object's mass determines the amount of energy a function uses. For small objects, energy isn't usually an issue. The "Energy Drain" section later in this chapter goes into more detail about the relationship between function, mass, and energy.

Buoyancy has nothing to do with water, but rather works to offset gravity. (Yes, it's antigravity.) The default value—0.0—makes the object act normally in gravity. A value of 1.0 makes it float as if no gravity exists, while values greater than 1.0 make it float up and away. (Note that wind and other forces can still apply, so an object with a buoyancy of exactly 1.0 may still rise or fall due to ambient wind or contact with avatars and other objects.) Values between 0.0 and 1.0 make the object tend to sink and a negative value acts like a downward force (such as strong gravity).

Hover and its partner *Ground Repel* also let you counteract gravity. You can set a physical object to hover at a certain height over water or ground, or inversely for the ground to push the object up.

Force, *Torque*, *Impulse*, *Velocity*, *Omega*, and *Acceleration* behave very much like those same properties in the real world. Force is a push applied to an object and torque is a rotational force. Impulse is an instantaneous force. Velocity is a vector indicating speed along each of the three axes, and omega is the rotational speed. Acceleration is the acceleration of the object that can be predicted from constant forces (but not the rate of change of the object's velocity over time, since impulses are ignored). Note that impulse drains the energy of an object while force does not.

Table 7.1 shows the functions that allow you to access this data.

PHYSICAL
OBJECTS

VEHICLES

SUMMARY

TABLE 7.1: ACCESSING THE PHYSICAL PROPERTIES OF OBJECTS

FUNCTION	BEHAVIOR
vector llGetAgentSize(key *id*)	Returns a vector that is the size of the requested avatar with the UUID *id*.
list llGetBoundingBox(key *object*)	Returns a list containing two vectors, [vector *min_corner*, vector *max_corner*], that describe the bounding box of the entire linkset.
vector llGetGeometricCenter()	Returns the geometric center of the object, relative to the root prim's location.
float llGetMass()	Returns the mass of the object containing the script, including the mass of an avatar sitting on the prim.
float llGetObjectMass(key *id*)	Returns the mass of the object with the key *id*. It includes the mass of any avatar sitting on the prim, but not, for example, the total mass of a stack of unlinked objects.
vector llGetCenterOfMass()	Returns the location of the center of mass, in region coordinates.
float llGetEnergy()	Gets the energy of the object (ranges between 0.0 and 1.0).
vector llGetForce()	Returns the force.
vector llGetTorque()	Returns the torque, or rotational force.
vector llGetVel()	Returns the velocity, in regional coordinates.
vector llGetOmega()	Returns the rotational speed around the axes, in radians per second.
vector llGetAccel()	Returns the acceleration being applied to the object by constant forces (not impulses). To get the object's net acceleration, you need to keep track of velocity and measure its changes, as shown in Listing 7.1.

WORKING WITH ACCELERATION

Acceleration works in **SL** roughly as you'd expect; however, the function llGetAccel() doesn't. This function returns the acceleration that can be derived from constant forces such as gravity, wind, and functions like llSetForce(). It does **not** include any acceleration caused by impulses. Essentially, it is the instantaneous acceleration of the object, approximately derivable from the function *acceleration = force ÷ mass*.

To get the object's net acceleration (including impulses), you need to keep track of velocity and measure its changes using the function *acceleration = change in velocity ÷ change in time* ($a = dv ÷ dt$). Listing 7.1 shows how to do this. The touch_start() event handler moves the object up to 1,000m, then turns on physics with the call to llSetStatus(). A moment later the object starts to fall. Every two seconds the timer() event calculates the object's acceleration. When the object collides with something, the script calls the returnHome() function, which turns off physics and moves the object back to the original position, *gHomePosition* and *gHomeRotation*. The collision() event handler is described in Chapter 5, "Sensing the World."

Listing 7.1: Calculating Acceleration Accurately

```
vector gHomePosition;
vector gHomeRotation;
vector oldVel;
float oldTime;
integer count = 0;

// insert listing 2.6 moveTo(origin, destination)
```

```
returnHome()
{
    llSetStatus(STATUS_PHYSICS, FALSE);
    moveTo(llGetPos(),gHomePosition);
    llSetTimerEvent(0);
    llSetRot(gHomeRotation);
}
calculate_acceleration()
{
    vector currPos = llGetPos();
    float currTime = llGetTime();
    vector currVel = llGetVel();
    vector accel = (currVel-oldVel) / (currTime - oldTime);
    llOwnerSay("a=dv/dt    :"+(string)accel);
    llOwnerSay("llGetAccel:"+(string)llGetAccel());
    oldTime = currTime;
    oldVel = currVel;
}
default
{
    state_entry() {
        gHomePosition = llGetPos();
        gHomeRotation = llGetRot();
    }
    on_rez(integer _n) {
        llResetScript();
    }
    touch_start(integer n) {
        moveTo(gHomePosition,gHomePosition+<0,0,1000>);
        llSetStatus(STATUS_PHYSICS,TRUE); // drop from 1000m
        llSetTimerEvent(2.0);
        oldTime = llGetTime();
        oldVel = <0,0,0>;
    }
    timer() {
        calculate_acceleration();
        count++;
        if (count>20) { // just in case landed on non-ground
            returnHome();
        }
    }
    collision(integer n) {
        calculate_acceleration();
        returnHome();
    }
}
```

The function `calculate_acceleration()` contains the math to calculate *a = dv ÷ dt*. (To get elapsed time, the script uses `llGetTime()`, described in Chapter 10's "Time" section.) We used this math in a vehicle to show the difference between `llGetAccel()` and `calculate_acceleration()`. You can easily see where the vehicle was traveling up, then to the side, and then down.

```
[9:04:00]  Vehicle: At rest
[9:04:00]  Vehicle:    a=dv/dt   :< 0.00000,  0.00000,  0.00000>
[9:04:00]  Vehicle:    llGetAccel:< 0.00000,  0.00000,  0.00000>
[9:04:07]  Vehicle: Going up
[9:04:07]  Vehicle:    a=dv/dt   :< 0.00003,  0.00197,  3.81528>
[9:04:07]  Vehicle:    llGetAccel:< 0.00000,  0.00000, -9.80000>
[9:05:09]  Vehicle:    a=dv/dt   :<-0.00002, -0.00051,  2.09604>
[9:05:09]  Vehicle:    llGetAccel:< 0.00000,  0.00000, -9.80000>
[9:05:11]  Vehicle:    a=dv/dt   :<-0.00001, -0.00048,  0.65188>
[9:05:11]  Vehicle:    llGetAccel:< 0.00000,  0.00000, -9.80000>
```

CHAPTER 1
CHAPTER 2
CHAPTER 3
CHAPTER 4
CHAPTER 5
CHAPTER 6
CHAPTER 7
CHAPTER 8
CHAPTER 9
CHAPTER 10
CHAPTER 11
CHAPTER 12
CHAPTER 13
CHAPTER 14
CHAPTER 15
APPENDICES

```
[9:05:12]   Vehicle: Going west
[9:05:13]   Vehicle:    a=dv/dt    :<  0.00007, -0.00022, -3.31292>
[9:05:13]   Vehicle:    llGetAccel:<-0.03063, -0.02828, -9.76271>
[9:05:15]   Vehicle:    a=dv/dt    :<-0.00002, -0.00005, -0.97607>
[9:05:15]   Vehicle:    llGetAccel:< 0.01289, -0.07607, -9.79540>
[9:05:17]   Vehicle:    a=dv/dt    :<-0.00002, -0.00003, -0.31171>
[9:05:17]   Vehicle:    llGetAccel:< 0.06252, -0.02654, -9.78832>
[9:05:18]   Vehicle: Going down
[9:05:19]   Vehicle:    a=dv/dt    :<-0.51556, -0.37274, -4.47548>
[9:05:19]   Vehicle:    llGetAccel:< 0.00089, -0.00050, -9.79502>
[9:05:21]   Vehicle:    a=dv/dt    :< 0.37280,  0.19362, -1.37771>
[9:05:21]   Vehicle:    llGetAccel:< 0.00001, -0.00001, -9.79985>
[9:05:23]   Vehicle:    a=dv/dt    :< 0.19378,  0.11658, -0.41832>
[9:05:23]   Vehicle:    llGetAccel:< 0.00000, -0.00000, -9.80000>
```

PHYSICAL FUNCTIONS

A large suite of functions cause physical objects to move. This chapter has several small examples of how to use these functions (more physical objects are described in future chapters).

The functions in Table 7.2 set various physical properties (essentially the opposite of the "get" functions in Table 7.1). In the functions that have a *local* parameter, *local* indicates whether the push is relative to the prim's orientation (TRUE) or to the region (FALSE).

TABLE 7.2: FUNCTIONS THAT SET FORCES AND PROPERTIES OF PHYSICAL OBJECTS

FUNCTION	BEHAVIOR
llApplyImpulse(vector *force*, integer *local*)	Instantaneous push.
llSetForce(vector *force*, integer *local*)	Continuous push.
llApplyRotationalImpulse(vector *force*, integer *local*)	Instantaneous rotational impulse (spin).
llSetTorque(vector *torque*, integer *local*)	Continuous rotational force.
llSetForceAndTorque(vector *force*, vector *torque*, integer *local*)	Continuous force and torque.
llSetBuoyancy(float *buoyancy*)	Sets a physical object's buoyancy.
llSetHoverHeight(float *height*, integer *water*, float *time*)	Causes the object to hover at a specified *height*. If *water* is TRUE it will hover above water too. The object will move smoothly to the new *height* over *time* seconds.
llStopHover()	Stops hovering. Object will fall until collision and probably bounce.
llGroundRepel(float *height*, integer *water*, float *time*)	Similar to llSetHoverHeight() but takes more energy. If *water* is TRUE it will hover above water too. The object will move smoothly to the new *height* over time *seconds*.
llPushObject(key *target*, vector *impulse*, vector *ang_impulse*, integer *local*)	Pushes another physical object.
llTargetOmega(vector *axis*, float *spinrate*, float *gain*)	Sets spin rate. In a physical object the position is updated at the server. (In a nonphysical object it is a client-side effect only.)

The force functions `llSetForce()`, `llSetTorque()`, and `llSetForceAndTorque()` push until the force is explicitly removed. In contrast, the impulse functions `llApplyImpulse()` and `llApplyRotationalImpulse()` apply the force to the object and then stop pushing. Despite its name, `llPushObject()` is an instantaneous impulse function. To illustrate this difference, if you apply a force to a cube, it will start moving; if it trips and falls over, it will try to continue moving. If, on the other hand, you apply an impulse to that same object, a trip will almost definitely cause it to stop.

`llPushObject()` is the only function in Table 7.2 that allows a script to move another object. Just as for regular forces, a heavier object needs more force applied to move it. You can use `llGetObjectMass()` to get the mass of the other object. The farther the object holding the script is away from the object being pushed, the weaker the push will be. It's also important to know that many sims do not allow objects to push each other.

Table 7.3 describes functions that are related to making physical objects move toward (or stop moving toward) a target. There is no guarantee the object will reach the target—something may be in the way or it might over- or undershoot.

TABLE 7.3: FUNCTIONS THAT CAUSE PHYSICAL OBJECTS TO MOVE TOWARD TARGETS

Function	Behavior
`llMoveToTarget(vector targetPos, float time)`	Moves to the position *targetPos* in *time* seconds. Only one target can be in force at a time.
`llStopMoveToTarget()`	Stops trying to move to the target position.
`llLookAt(vector targetPos, float viscosity, float time)`	Rotates to have the z-axis (the "top") orient to face *targetPos*. Only one target can be specified at a time. *viscosity* (resistance to change) must be at least 0.05 to have any effect.
`llRotLookAt(rotation targetRot, float viscosity, float time)`	Orients to *targetRot*. (Similar to `llSetRot()`.) Only one target can be specified at a time. *viscosity* must be at least 0.05.
`llStopLookAt()`	Removes targets set by `llLookAt()` and `llRotLookAt()`.

If you want to know for sure whether your object has reached the target position or rotation you specified, you need to set up appropriate event triggers. The functions in Table 7.4 set up or remove the monitoring, which will trigger the events as noted in the table.

Multiple targets are permitted; if the *range* or *error* values overlap, both events will trigger (approximately) simultaneously. Make sure to double-check which target *handle* fired.

TABLE 7.4: FUNCTIONS THAT MONITOR WHETHER A PHYSICAL OBJECT HAS REACHED A TARGET LOCATION OR ROTATION

Function	Behavior
`integer llTarget(vector targetPos, float range)`	Sets up event handlers for the `at_target()` and `not_at_target()` events that are triggered when the object arrives within *range* meters of *targetPos*. Returns the *handle*. Can have more than one target.
`llTargetRemove(integer handle)`	Removes the target specified by the *handle*.
`integer llRotTarget(rotation targetRot, float error)`	Sets up event handlers for the `rot_target()` and `not_at_rot_target()` events that are triggered when the object arrives within *error* radians of *targetRot*. Returns the *handle*. Can have more than one target.
`llRotTargetRemove(integer handle)`	Removes the rotation target specified by the *handle*.

CHAPTER 1
CHAPTER 2
CHAPTER 3
CHAPTER 4
CHAPTER 5
CHAPTER 6

CHAPTER 7

CHAPTER 8
CHAPTER 9
CHAPTER 10
CHAPTER 11
CHAPTER 12
CHAPTER 13
CHAPTER 14
CHAPTER 15
APPENDICES

PHYSICAL
OBJECTS

VEHICLES

SUMMARY

 EVENT DEFINITION

```
at_target(integer targetHandle,
          vector targetPos, vector currPos) {}
```

```
not_at_target() {}
```

These events are triggered when an object reaches (or does not reach) a positional target specified by *targetPos*. `llTarget()` sets up the monitor and `llTargetRemove()` removes the monitor. The SYW website provides more details.

 EVENT DEFINITION

```
at_rot_target(integer targetHandle, rotation targetRot,
              rotation currRot) {}
```

```
not_at_rot_target() {}
```

These events are triggered when an object reaches (or does not reach) a rotational target specified by *targetRot*. `llRotTarget()` sets up the monitor and `llRotTargetRemove()` removes the monitor. The SYW website provides more detail.

One last set of events you need to know about is the pair `moving_start()` and `moving_end()`. (Unlike the `*at_*target()` events, these do not need functions to set them up.)

 EVENT DEFINITION

```
moving_start() {}
```

```
moving_end() {}
```

For *physical* objects, these events are invoked when the object is moving. If the object is moving due to physics (such as rolling down a hill), both events trigger constantly while it is moving; be aware that most physics objects tend to move a lot more than you expect. If the object is attached, both events trigger constantly when the avatar is moving. If the object is being moved through mouse clicks, `moving_start()` is triggered when the mouse is *clicked*, and `moving_end()` is triggered when the mouse is *released*. Additional documentation can be found on the SYW website, and Chapter 4 describes these events for nonphysical objects.

↘ OPTICAL ILLUSIONS

Listing 7.2 contains a basic script for spinning a wheel. Every time an avatar touches the object, it applies a rotational impulse that starts the object spinning. If you apply a spiral texture onto a cylinder you'll have a great optical illusion, as shown in Figure 7.1.

Listing 7.2: Optical Illusion

```
init()
{
    llSetStatus(STATUS_PHYSICS, FALSE);
}
default
{
    state_entry() {
        init();
    }
    on_rez(integer _n) {
        llResetScript();
    }
    touch_start(integer total_number) {
        vector currPos = llGetPos();
        llSetStatus(STATUS_PHYSICS, TRUE);
        llSleep(0.2); // give time for physics to kick in.
        vector force = <0,0,1>;
        llApplyRotationalImpulse( force*llGetMass(), TRUE);
        llMoveToTarget(currPos,0.1); // stay in place
    }
}
```

CHAPTER 1
CHAPTER 2
CHAPTER 3
CHAPTER 4
CHAPTER 5
CHAPTER 6

CHAPTER 8
CHAPTER 9
CHAPTER 10
CHAPTER 11
CHAPTER 12
CHAPTER 13
CHAPTER 14
CHAPTER 15
CHAPTER 16

Figure 7.1: A spinning spiral makes a great optical effect.

The core physics activity of this script is shown in these lines:

```
llSetStatus(STATUS_PHYSICS, TRUE);
llSleep(0.2); // give time for physics to kick in.
vector force = <0,0,1>;
llApplyRotationalImpulse( force*llGetMass(), TRUE);
llMoveToTarget(currPos,0.1); // stay in place
```

The first line starts the physics engine. It takes a moment for physics to kick in, so if you immediately call the physics function, it will have no effect. In this script, a pause is provided with a call to `llSleep()`, but you can use any other code that allows enough time for physics to start. The rotational impulse is given by `llApplyRotationalImpulse()`, which is just like giving an instantaneous spin to an object. Because the power of the impulse (and hence the speed at which the object spins) depends mostly on the object's mass, the script scales the **force** vector with `llGetMass()`. Try increasing the values in **force** to increase the total power of the impulse, and see how much faster it spins. Also try nonzero values in the vector's `x` and `y` slots to see the effect of different axes of rotation.

`llApplyRotationalImpulse()` takes a second parameter (Boolean) that determines whether the axis of the impulse is local to the wheel (`TRUE`), or regional (`FALSE`). In this object the texture is applied to the flat `xy` surface of the cylinder; therefore you will apply the rotation around the z-axis. Because the impulse is local, you can orient the wheel however you want and still get the spin to appear the same. A Buddhist prayer wheel or a child's spinning top would work the same way, with the texture applied to the rounded, vertical surface instead.

If you were to use `llSetTorque()` instead of `llApplyRotationalImpulse()`, your wheel would spin forever, getting faster and faster over time:

```
llSetTorque(<0,0,llGetMass()>, TRUE);
```

Because *SL* has no concept of a single object that has both a moving part *and* a stationary part by which you can build an "axle," you also have to manage the location of the wheel. When you enable physics, gravity starts operating, and you don't want the wheel to fall. The line `llMoveToTarget()` keeps the wheel in place.

 NOTE

You can create an axle with a moving wheel around it in *SL* as long as they are separate parts, as shown in the following image. The wheel needs to be a ring, tube, or torus. After you line up the wheel and the axle, the rotational impulse will be around the wheel's x axis, `<1, 0, 0>`. Because of the 10cm collision rule, the wheel won't spin very easily unless it's *much* bigger than the axle. The stronger the impulse, the more likely the physics engine won't be able to keep them together.

A HUMAN CANNON BALL

Have you ever wanted to be a human cannon ball? In **SL** you can be! Say you write a script for the cannon ball, sit your avatar on the ball, and get it to work. Now you start building your cannon around the cannon ball. Then you discover that if you want the avatar to sit on the cannon ball, you have to link the ball to the rest of the cannon. But then the whole cannon tries to fly with you (because you're sitting on the cannon, not the ball), **and** you can't break the link between the cannon and the ball. When an object is attached or an avatar is sitting on something, you can't change the links or have the avatar try to sit on the cannon but "redirect" so they actually sit on the ball.

There are lots of workarounds, none of them elegant. The bowling glove in the online chapter on bowling is one approach; the script in Listing 7.3 is another—it uses a transparent shell around the cannon ball and leaves the cannon and the ball-with-shell as two separate objects. The avatar sits on the transparent shell and fires the cannon with a touch. The desired visual effect is for the avatar and the ball to fly in a parabola, as shown in Figure 7.2, landing (roughly) in the same place every time if nothing gets in the way. After the flight, the ball returns home, reloading the cannon.

CHAPTER 1
CHAPTER 2
CHAPTER 3
CHAPTER 4
CHAPTER 5
CHAPTER 6
CHAPTER 7
CHAPTER 8
CHAPTER 9
CHAPTER 10
CHAPTER 11
CHAPTER 12
CHAPTER 13
CHAPTER 14
CHAPTER 15
APPENDICES

Figure 7.2: The avatar and the ball fly through the air in a parabola.

BUILD NOTE

Make an unscripted cannon-shaped object. Create a sphere, color it, and place it in the muzzle of the cannon. Create a transparent shell that surrounds the cannon; the cannon at SYW HQ uses a rectangle `<1.3, 0.5, 1.5>` with x taper = 0.7. The z-axis is aligned with the barrel of the cannon. Link the ball and the shell together with the shell as the root prim. Insert the code from Listing 7.3 into the shell.

Listing 7.3: The Cannon Ball's Transparent Shell

```
integer   SCALING_FACTOR = 22;
float     RETURN_DIST = 0.5; // meters of movement
vector    gPrevPos;
vector    gHomePosition;
rotation  gHomeRotation;

init()
{
    gHomePosition = llGetPos();
    gHomeRotation = llGetRot();
    llSetStatus(STATUS_PHANTOM,TRUE);
    llSetPrimitiveParams([ PRIM_COLOR, ALL_SIDES, <1,1,1>, 0 ]);
    vector size = llGetScale();
    rotation sitRot = llEuler2Rot(<0,0,90>*DEG_TO_RAD);
    llSitTarget(<0,size.y/2,size.z/2+0.3>, sitRot);
    llSetSitText("Load!");
    llSetTouchText("Fire!");
}
```

167

```
// insert listing 2.6 moveTo( origin, destination )

// insert returnHome() from Listing 7.1

default
{
    on_rez(integer n) {
        llResetScript();
    }
    state_entry() {
        init();
    }
    touch_start(integer total_number) {
        key avatar = llAvatarOnSitTarget();
        if (avatar != NULL_KEY) {
            float mass = llGetMass();
            gPrevPos = llGetPos();
            llSetStatus(STATUS_PHYSICS, TRUE);
            llSleep(0.2);
            llApplyImpulse( <0,0,SCALING_FACTOR*mass>, TRUE );
            llUnSit(avatar);
            llSetTimerEvent(1.0);
        } else {
            llWhisper(0, "I launch when someone's sitting on me.");
        }
    }
    land_collision(vector pos) {
        returnHome();
    }
    timer() {
        vector currPos = llGetPos();
        if (llVecMag(currPos-gPrevPos) < RETURN_DIST) {
            returnHome();
        }
        gPrevPos = currPos;
    }
}
```

This script uses two mechanisms to determine when to reload. Since the ball (not the transparent shell) should be the thing that bounces on the ground, the script sets the status of the transparent shell to phantom—that means the shell will not collide with anything except the ground. Therefore the first detector for reloading uses the `land_collision()` event. The second is based on a timer that starts when the ball is launched, and returns home if the ball hasn't moved more than `RETURN_DIST` meters. (Alternatively, you could put a `collision()` detector into the ball.)

Notice that this script doesn't tweak the impulse direction based on the orientation of the transparent shell: its shape is structured so that the z-axis is along the barrel.

As you work with this script, you'll quickly see that the physics means you get similar (but not always identical) results from shot to shot. You should also explore how changing impulse force, ball mass, and barrel angle change the results.

If you use `llSetForce()` instead of `llApplyImpulse()` as shown in the script, with exactly the same parameters, your cannon ball won't fly the way you'd expect. It might fly off into space, never returning; it might bump into your avatar on the way up; or it might just go nowhere. Perhaps most importantly, though, your avatar certainly won't fly in a lovely parabola that you'd expect from a human cannon ball.

```
llSetForce(<0,0,SCALING_FACTOR*mass>, TRUE);
```

There are several ways you can change the script to use `llPushObject()`. One way is to use `llPushObject()` to have the cannonball push itself:

```
key k = llGetKey();
llPushObject(k, <0,0,SCALING_FACTOR*mass>, ZERO_VECTOR, TRUE);
```

CHAPTER 1
CHAPTER 2
CHAPTER 3
CHAPTER 4
CHAPTER 5
CHAPTER 6

DEFINITION

---

land_collision_start(vector *pos*) {}

---

land_collision(vector *pos*) {}

---

land_collision_end(vector *pos*) {}

Land-collision-family events are invoked when a physical object collides with land. land_collision_start() triggers when the collision starts, land_collision() triggers periodically during a collision, and land_collision_end() triggers when the collision ends. The SYW website offers more details.

> *pos* — The position, in region coordinates, where the collision occurred.

CHAPTER 8
CHAPTER 9
CHAPTER 10
CHAPTER 11
CHAPTER 12
CHAPTER 13
CHAPTER 14
CHAPTER 15
CHAPTER 16

Scripts generally use this function to apply impulses to other objects, so it is a little strange to use it in this way. Less strange would be for the cannon body to be scripted to use llPushObject() to push the ball. Another possibility would be to do away with the ball entirely, have the avatar sit on the cannon, and push the avatar directly after unsitting her.

In all cases with llPushObject(), you will also need to adjust the SCALING_FACTOR, for example to 2200, since not only is the effect of llPushObject() weaker than that of llApplyImpulse(), but it is affected by the pushing object's mass and the distance between the pushing and pushed objects. Don't forget that regions may be marked as limited push areas, dramatically reducing the strength of the impulse.

If you decide to augment your cannon with the ability to rotate the barrel or the entire cannon, you must make sure that both the cannon and the ball are aware of the change. The impulse vector of the launch will not need to change, just the *gHomePosition* and *gHomeRotation*.

DAMAGE

There is a simple combat model built into *Second Life* that directly supports concepts such as injury and damage. It integrates well into the world, relying on land settings to enable the system, and relatively simple scripting support to let you build weapons that will interact with avatars. The most important consideration is that only physical objects can damage avatars, and then only if they collide. The only additional call is llSetDamage(), which allows you to set how much injury the physical object will cause when it collides with an avatar.

The only additional call is llSetDamage(float *injury*), which allows you to set how much injury the physical object will cause when it collides with an avatar. The normal valid range for injury is 0.0 to 100.0, but energy depletion can reduce the effect. A value of 100.0 should be assumed to kill an avatar, and 0.0 to have no effect.

SL's damage model was designed to support projectile weaponry, and thus creating swords or other non-projectile weapons is harder: attached objects cannot be physical and are always phantom! The workaround to this problem is to have the visible weapon emit invisible bullet-like damager objects to cause damage on its behalf.

There are several things you should do to avoid littering the area with stray bullets. Detect collisions with both land and avatars and call `llDie()` to delete the bullet. On setup, make them temporary objects by setting their `TEMP_ON_REZ` property and having them die at the edge of the sim. A typical `on_rez()` event for a bullet might look like this:

```
on_rez(integer param) {
    if (param) {  // fired? Zero means rez from inventory
        llSetStatus(STATUS_DIE_AT_EDGE, TRUE);
        llSetPrimitiveParams([PRIM_TEMP_ON_REZ, TRUE]);
        llSetTimerEvent(TIMEOUT); // about 10 seconds fizzle
        llSetDamage(llFrand(100.0));
    }
}
```

For a deeper discussion, the Scripting Your World website has a bonus chapter entitled "Violence." You can also find discussions of combat and weapons on the *SL* wiki.

HOW LAND SETTINGS AFFECT DAMAGE

Damage-enabled land: Land may be *damage-enabled* or not. While this property must be *set* manually, it can be queried using `llGetRegionFlags()` and `llGetParcelFlags(vector pos)`. See Chapter 6, "Land Design and Management," for more details. The important thing here is that an avatar can suffer damage only on damage-enabled land.

Push-limited land: Land may be marked as *push-limited*, attenuating the effect of calls to `llPushObject()`. This feature is less important to realistic simulation of combat, but heavy pushing can be used to simulate the effects of explosions, magical weapons, and of course to annoy other people.

Avatar health and death: Avatars have a health parameter, visible when on damage-enabled land (a little heart with a number from 0 to 100). Health is recovered automatically. If your health drops to 0 you are teleported home, similarly to `llTeleportAgentHome(key avatar)`.

Damage and collisions: Objects may set how much damage they will cause on collision with an agent (avatar). Objects with nonzero damage will die when colliding with another object. Damage is a simple value that will be subtracted from the target's health on collision. Values above 100 will kill the avatar. Collision with a very large or fast object can cause damage. Collision with the ground (falling from high up) also can cause damage.

PUSHING OBJECTS: FLIGHT ASSIST

You've probably noticed that you can't fly very high—only about 300m in altitude. `llPushObject()` makes a great "flight assist" box, kind of like a jet pack. Worn as an attachment, even as a HUD, it can push your avatar essentially as high as you want to go (but beware that above 4,096m, objects not attached to avatars are considered "off-world" and will be returned to your inventory).

Listing 7.4 has two states: the `default` state when the avatar is not flying, and the `flying` state when she is. When the jet pack is attached to the avatar, the `attach()` event handler in the `default` state resets the script—this causes the `state_entry()` event handler to trigger, and a timer to be set when the object is attached. The timer uses `llGetAgentInfo()` to detect whether the agent is flying, and if so, transitions to the `flying` state.

WARNING

An alternative way to figure out if the object has been attached is to use the key *id* that is passed into `attach()`. However, take care in situations when both `attach()` and `on_rez()` may be triggered, such as when something is "worn" from Inventory; the key sent to `attach()` may be erased by a call to `llResetScript()` used in `on_rez()`. Also be aware that if you're editing the script while it is attached, the `attach()` event won't fire at all! `llGetAttached()`, in the `state_entry()` event, is much more reliable.

CHAPTER 1
CHAPTER 2
CHAPTER 3
CHAPTER 4
CHAPTER 5
CHAPTER 6

CHAPTER 7

CHAPTER 8
CHAPTER 9
CHAPTER 10
CHAPTER 11
CHAPTER 12
CHAPTER 13
CHAPTER 14
CHAPTER 15
APPENDICES

Listing 7.4: Basic Flight Assist

```
vector  VERTICAL_PUSH = <0,0,5>;
integer gPermissions;
default
{
    state_entry() {
        gPermissions = CONTROL_UP|CONTROL_DOWN|
                        CONTROL_LEFT | CONTROL_RIGHT |
                        CONTROL_ROT_LEFT | CONTROL_ROT_RIGHT |
                        CONTROL_FWD | CONTROL_BACK;
        if (llGetAttached() > 0) {
            llSetTimerEvent(1);
        } else {
            llSetTimerEvent(0);
        }
    }
    on_rez(integer n) {
        llResetScript();
    }
    attach(key k) {
        llResetScript();
    }
    timer() {
        if (llGetAgentInfo(llGetOwner()) & AGENT_FLYING) {
            state flying;
        }
    }
}

state flying
{
    state_entry() {
        llRequestPermissions(llGetOwner(), PERMISSION_TAKE_CONTROLS);
        // perms implicitly granted. take them.
        llTakeControls(gPermissions, TRUE, TRUE);
        // DON'T HAVE TO SET TIMER -- IT's CARRIED OVER
        // But just in case it's actually a bug...
        llSetTimerEvent(2);
    }
    timer() {
        integer nowFlying = llGetAgentInfo(llGetOwner()) & AGENT_FLYING;
        if (!nowFlying) {
            state default;
        }
    }
```

```
        attach(key k) { // detach
            if (k == NULL_KEY) {
                state default;
            }
        }
        control(key id, integer held, integer change) {
            if (held & CONTROL_UP) {
                llPushObject(id, VERTICAL_PUSH, ZERO_VECTOR, FALSE);
            } else if (held & CONTROL_DOWN) {
                llPushObject(id, -VERTICAL_PUSH, ZERO_VECTOR, FALSE);
            }
            // other keys controlled by avatar directly
        }
        state_exit() {
            llReleaseControls();
        }
    }
```

The `state_entry()` event handler for the `flying` state requests `PERMISSION_TAKE_` `CONTROLS`. The "Animation Overrides" section of Chapter 2, "Making Your Avatar Stand Up and Stand Out," has more details on `llRequestPermissions()`. Because the jet pack is attached, permissions are implicitly granted, so the script can immediately call `llTakeControls()` to grab the flying-control commands. Note that the third parameter is `TRUE`, which allows the avatar to receive the commands too. The `state_entry()` handler also sets a timer to watch for when the avatar stops flying.

NOTE

The call to `llSetTimerEvent()` in the `flying` state is redundant. `timer()` events carry across state transitions! But just in case it's a bug that Linden Lab will correct, the script sets the timer event on `state_entry()` anyway.

DEFINITION

`llTakeControls(integer controls, integer accept, integer giveToAvatar)`

Takes controls from the agent task if `PERMISSION_TAKE_CONTROLS` has been granted. The `control()` event handler receives the keystrokes.

controls — Bitmask of control fields, `CONTROL_FWD`, `CONTROL_BACK`, `CONTROL_LEFT`, `CONTROL_RIGHT`, `CONTROL_ROT_LEFT`, `CONTROL_ROT_RIGHT`, `CONTROL_UP`, `CONTROL_DOWN`, `CONTROL_LBUTTON`, `CONTROL_ML_LBUTTON`.

accept — Boolean for whether controls are wanted (`TRUE`) or should be ignored (`FALSE`).

giveToAvatar — Boolean for whether to also send the signals to the avatar.

The `control()` event handler receives the user's keystrokes for each of the items that were grabbed, but it only acts on `CONTROL_UP` and `CONTROL_DOWN`. (Listing 7.5 will act on all of the user's keystrokes that match the list of controls in *gPermissions*.) This script sets the push based on which controls are currently in effect (*held*). The amount of vertical push is controlled by the value

VERTICAL_PUSH. It would be an interesting extension to change the value to give more push at higher altitudes or to increase push slowly the longer keys are held down.

EVENT DEFINITION

```
control(key id, integer held, integer recentChange) {}
```

Triggered when one or more of the keyboard or mouse controls "taken" previously by `llTakeControls()` are pressed, held, or released.

id — The UUID identity of the avatar using the controls.

held — The bitfield of the keys being held down.

recentChange — The bitfield of the keys changed since the last control event.

You can work out whether a button has been held or touched by combining the *held* and *recentChange* parameters, as in the following example:

```
if (held & recentChange & CONTROL_FWD)
    llOwnerSay("forward just pressed");
if (~held & recentChange & CONTROL_FWD)
    llOwnerSay("forward just released");
if (held & ~recentChange & CONTROL_FWD)
    llOwnerSay("forward held down; saw on previous call to control");
if (~held & ~recentChange & CONTROL_FWD)
    llOwnerSay("forward untouched");
```

The `state_exit()` event handler allows the script to do some cleanup before transitioning out of the `default` state. Here, it just releases the controls that it has grabbed.

DEFINITION

```
llReleaseControls()
```

Stops taking inputs that were taken with `llTakeControls()`. Removes remaining control events from the queue.

A simple but useful extension to Listing 7.4 is to add an altimeter. The `timer()` handlers are a great place to make this function call:

```
altimeter()
{
    vector pos = llGetPos();
    llSetText("Altitude is " + (string)((integer)pos.z), <0,0,0>, 1 );
}
```

Flight Assist with Hover

While the flight assist from Listing 7.4 allows you to go as high as you'd like, it won't **keep** you there. When you release the keys you'll slowly drift back to somewhere near 160m altitude. That's rather annoying

PHYSICAL
OBJECTS

VEHICLES

SUMMARY

if you're trying to build a high-altitude project such as a mountain getaway or a sky platform, and you don't want to stand on it as shown in Figure 7.3. To solve this problem, the additions in Listing 7.5 use key releases to add an `llMoveToTarget()` that keeps the avatar at the most recent location. Then, when keys are pressed again, it calls `llStopMoveToTarget()` to allow the avatar to move around. Note that if Listing 7.4 had grabbed only the `CONTROL_UP` and `CONTROL_DOWN` keys, the hover assist would not work except for those two controls.

Figure 7.3: A jet pack with hover control makes it easer to work with a sky platform at high altitudes.

Listing 7.5: Flight Assist with Hover

```
// Replace the control() handler from Listing 7.4
    control(key id, integer held, integer change) {
        if (held & change & gPermissions) { // just touched
            llStopMoveToTarget();
        }
        if (held & CONTROL_UP) {
            llPushObject(id, VERTICAL, ZERO_VECTOR, FALSE);
        } else if (held & CONTROL_DOWN) {
            llPushObject(id, -VERTICAL, ZERO_VECTOR, FALSE);
        } else if (~held & change & gPermissions) { // released
            llMoveToTarget(llGetPos(), 1.0);
        }
        // other keys controlled by avatar directly
    }
// Replace the state_exit() handler from Listing 7.4
    state_exit() {
        llReleaseControls();
        llStopMoveToTarget();
    }
```

A fun extension to this script would be to use the jet pack to get to high altitude, and then stop flying. You can then have a parachute or paraglider automatically deploy as you fall.

174

CHAPTER 1
CHAPTER 2
CHAPTER 3
CHAPTER 4
CHAPTER 5
CHAPTER 6

◥ ENERGY DRAIN

Most of the physics functions in LSL drain energy from the object. If an object runs out of energy, it ceases to be able to cause physical effects. For small objects, you generally don't have to worry: they replenish energy faster than they expend it.

Most of the physical motion functions reduce the amount of energy available to the script. The SYW website has a table showing the available energy immediately after a physical function call for an object of mass 640.0, and every second thereafter until either energy restabilizes at 1.0, or a continuous drain is evident. Results will vary depending on a variety of factors, including sim load, but the trend will hold. `11PushObject()`, `11ApplyImpulse()`, and `11ApplyRotImpulse()` have the same instantaneous drain. On the day of the tests, `11SetForce()` had no measurable effect and `11SetTorque()` had a small effect, but the combined `11SetForceAndTorque()` had much more drain than either component independently. `11MoveToTarget()` showed a continuous drain. Although `11SetHoverHeight()` and `11GroundRepel()` have similar effects on the objects, `11GroundRepel()` drains less energy from the script.

The amount of energy used depends on the object's mass. However, by simply staying in-world, objects can earn energy at a rate of 200 ÷ *mass* units per second. So, for example, an object with a mass of 270 would earn energy at a rate of about 0.741 units per second. The more massive the object, the longer it takes to earn energy. Table 7.5 shows the correlation between an object's mass, its energy expenditure, and its energy re-acquisition.

CHAPTER 7

CHAPTER 8
CHAPTER 9
CHAPTER 10
CHAPTER 11
CHAPTER 12
CHAPTER 13
CHAPTER 14
CHAPTER 15
APPENDICES

TABLE 7.5: ENERGY EXPENDITURE AND REACQUISITION AFTER CALLING
`11ApplyImpulse(<0,0,1>*11GetMass())`

Object Mass	Available Energy Immediately Following Call to `11ApplyImpulse()`	Seconds to Return to Energy = 1.0
1.25	0.99875	0.0
270.00	0.98650	0.0
640.00	0.96800	0.1
1,250.00	0.93750	0.4
2,160.00	0.89200	1.2
3,430.00	0.82850	2.9
5,120.00	0.74400	6.6
7,290.00	0.63550	13.3
10,000.00	0.50000	25.0

It can also be useful to know that energy is *earned* and *owned* by an object and *spent* by scripts, so multiple scripts in one object can observe each other's expenditure.

NOTE

If an object doesn't have enough energy to move, look for any prims in the object that can be hollowed. That will significantly reduce the weight and make it both easier to move and faster to earn energy.

CHAPTER 7

VEHICLES

PHYSICAL
OBJECTS
 VEHICLES
SUMMARY

You've seen several methods for making objects move. LSL also provides extensive support for custom vehicles. With relatively natural physics you can make a vehicle that flies, floats, or glides. Your avatar sits on or in the vehicle, and pilots using the arrow keys and Page Up/Page Down. Your vehicle will bank, turn, hover, dive, and respond to gravity and friction. The LSL wiki has a good vehicle tutorial that goes into much more detail.

A vehicle is created with `llSetVehicleType()`; you can make sleds, cars, boats, airplanes, and balloons. Each comes with a default model of what physics makes sense for that vehicle. An airplane uses linear deflection for lift, doesn't hover, and banks when it turns. The full set of default settings is described on the wiki, one page for each type of vehicle.

 DEFINITION

`llSetVehicleType(integer type)`

Defines an object as a vehicle.

type — **One of** VEHICLE_TYPE_NONE, VEHICLE_TYPE_AIRPLANE, VEHICLE_TYPE_BALLOON, VEHICLE_TYPE_BOAT, VEHICLE_TYPE_CAR, VEHICLE_TYPE_SLED.

Listing 7.6 shows a very basic flying vehicle. The `state_entry()` event handler sets up some basic object properties. When the avatar sits down or stands up, the vehicle enables. The `control()` event handler deals with the details of what happens while flying.

Listing 7.6: Basic Vehicle

```
float X_THRUST = 20;      // forward/back
float Y_THRUST = TWO_PI;  // turning
float Z_THRUST = 15;      // up/down

set_airplane_properties()
{
    llSetVehicleType( VEHICLE_TYPE_AIRPLANE );
    llSetVehicleFloatParam( VEHICLE_ANGULAR_MOTOR_TIMESCALE, 0 );
    llSetVehicleFloatParam( VEHICLE_BUOYANCY, 0.997 );
    llSetVehicleFloatParam( VEHICLE_BANKING_TIMESCALE, 0.01);
    llRemoveVehicleFlags( VEHICLE_FLAG_LIMIT_ROLL_ONLY );
}

default {
    state_entry() {
        llSetStatus(STATUS_PHYSICS, FALSE);
        llSetSitText("Fly");
        vector size = llGetScale();
        llSitTarget(<-(size.x/2), 0.0, size.z/2+0.7>, ZERO_ROTATION);
        set_airplane_properties();
    }
```

CHAPTER 1
CHAPTER 2
CHAPTER 3
CHAPTER 4
CHAPTER 5
CHAPTER 6

CHAPTER 8
CHAPTER 9
CHAPTER 10
CHAPTER 11
CHAPTER 12
CHAPTER 13
CHAPTER 14
CHAPTER 15
APPENDICES

```
    on_rez(integer num) {
        llResetScript();
    }
    changed(integer change) {
        key agent = llAvatarOnSitTarget();
        if (change & CHANGED_LINK) {
            if (agent == NULL_KEY) {
                vector currPos = llGetPos();
                llReleaseControls();
                llSetStatus(STATUS_PHYSICS, FALSE);
                llSetPos(currPos); // to deal with drift
            } else if (agent == llGetOwner()) {
                key pilot = llAvatarOnSitTarget();
                llRequestPermissions(pilot,
                    PERMISSION_TAKE_CONTROLS | PERMISSION_TRIGGER_ANIMATION);
            }
        }
    }
    run_time_permissions(integer perm) {
        if (perm & (PERMISSION_TAKE_CONTROLS)){
            llTakeControls(CONTROL_UP | CONTROL_DOWN |
                           CONTROL_FWD | CONTROL_BACK |
                           CONTROL_RIGHT | CONTROL_LEFT |
                           CONTROL_ROT_RIGHT | CONTROL_ROT_LEFT,
                    TRUE, FALSE);
            llSetStatus(STATUS_PHYSICS, TRUE);
        }
        if (perm & PERMISSION_TRIGGER_ANIMATION) {
            llStartAnimation("sit_ground");
            llStopAnimation("sit");
        }
    }
    control(key id, integer held, integer diff) {
        vector linearMotor;
        if (held & CONTROL_FWD)       linearMotor.x =  X_THRUST;
        else if (held & CONTROL_BACK) linearMotor.x = -X_THRUST;

        if (held & CONTROL_UP)        linearMotor.z =  Z_THRUST;
        else if (held & CONTROL_DOWN) linearMotor.z = -Z_THRUST;

        llSetVehicleVectorParam(VEHICLE_LINEAR_MOTOR_DIRECTION, linearMotor);

        vector angularMotor;
        if (held & (CONTROL_RIGHT|CONTROL_ROT_RIGHT)) {
            angularMotor.x = Y_THRUST;
        }
        if (held & (CONTROL_LEFT|CONTROL_ROT_LEFT)) {
            angularMotor.x = -Y_THRUST;
        }
        llSetVehicleVectorParam(VEHICLE_ANGULAR_MOTOR_DIRECTION, angularMotor);
    }
}
```

The function set_airplane_properties() causes the vehicle to become an airplane using llSetVehicleType(), and overrides a couple of the default values using llSetVehicle<type>Param(). Each vehicle type has a set of default values, so this script only overrides a few to get the desired behavior. A full description of the 28 available vehicle properties and their behavior is coming in the next section, "Vehicle Properties." Details on the 10 vehicle flags follow in the section "Vehicle Flags." This script's properties make it act reasonably well as a magic carpet, like the one in Figure 7.4.

Figure 7.4: Magic carpets are an extremely popular *SL* vehicle.

When the avatar sits down, the `changed()` event handler requests permissions to take controls and trigger animations. When permissions are granted in `run_time_permissions()`, the script grabs control of the appropriate motion-control keys using `llTakeControls()`, turns on the vehicle by setting `STATUS_PHYSICS` to `TRUE`, and finally changes the sitting animation to be `sit_ground` rather than a plain `sit`. When the avatar stands up, it releases controls using `llReleaseControls()` then uses `llSetStatus()` to set physics status to `FALSE`. Due to timing issues when setting status, turning off physics sometimes doesn't take effect; the call to the nonphysical function `llSetPos()` helps ensure physics gets turned off correctly.

Just as in Listing 7.4, permissions are implicitly granted in Listing 7.6 because the avatar sat on the vehicle. A small optimization, therefore, would be to move the action from `run_time_permissions()` into `changed()`.

The `control()` event handler receives the user's keystrokes for each of the items that was grabbed. This script doesn't care whether keys are still being held—it just sets the motors based on which controls are currently in effect. The linear motor moves the vehicle in a straight line, while the angular motor turns it. This script only sets the `x` and `z` values of the linear motor (forward/back and up/down); setting the `y` value would allow the vehicle to slide left and right. The left/right control keys affect only the `y` value of the angular motor.

VEHICLE PROPERTIES

In general, the default settings for a particular vehicle are not exactly what you want. Moreover, default settings may change, so it can be a good idea to set all properties manually. You'll usually start with a basic vehicle type and change some of its default parameter settings. Unlike the functions `llSetPrimitiveParams()` and `llParticleSystem()`, which take a list of concatenated parameters, there are three function calls you need (one for each type of parameter):

- `llSetVehicleRotationParam()`
- `llSetVehicleVectorParam()`
- `llSetVehicleFloatParam()`

They each take two parameters: the name of the vehicle property and its value.

You can set the linear direction and speed of your vehicle with

```
llSetVehicleVectorParam(VEHICLE_LINEAR_MOTOR_DIRECTION, <x,y,z>);
```

The **x** direction is forward and back, **y** is left and right, and **z** is up and down. **Note that these are local to the vehicle, not the world.** If you don't want your car to fly, you should never set the **z** motor; you should, however, set the vehicle flag `VEHICLE_FLAG_LIMIT_MOTOR_UP`. Most vehicles prefer going forward or backward (the preferred axis of motion), so the **y** value, which slides left and right, will often be 0. A skateboard whose wheels can turn would have a linear **y** motor. A shopping cart with really rotten steering might pick a random value for its **y** vector.

The linear motor can change the direction the vehicle **moves**, but will not change the direction the vehicle is **facing**. For that, you need an angular motor:

```
llSetVehicleVectorParam(VEHICLE_ANGULAR_MOTOR_DIRECTION, <x,y,z>);
```

If you want to tip the avatar sitting on the vehicle in Listing 7.4 in the direction of acceleration, use the forward and backward controls to adjust the angular motor:

```
if (held & CONTROL_FWD)  angularMotor.y =  3;
if (held & CONTROL_BACK) angularMotor.y = -3;
```

Similarly, if you want the vehicle to turn much faster than what the **x** value of angular motor yields, you could add a little push around the z-axis.

Normally, a vehicle's "zero" orientation is that of its root prim. If you plan carefully, every vehicle's **x**, **y**, and **z** should make sense when it moves. Sometimes it may make sense to pick a root prim with a different orientation than the overall vehicle. Maybe, for example, you build a row boat whose root prim is the seat, set up so the avatar sits backward. In these cases, you'll need to use `llSetVehicleRotationParam()` with a new `VEHICLE_REFERENCE_FRAME` rotated appropriately.

Table 7.6 summarizes these motor direction and rotation properties.

TABLE 7.6: VEHICLE PROPERTIES: DIRECTION AND ROTATION

Constant	Description
`VEHICLE_ANGULAR_MOTOR_DIRECTION` vector	Angular velocity the vehicle will try to achieve (turning).
`VEHICLE_LINEAR_MOTOR_DIRECTION` vector	Linear velocity the vehicle will try to achieve (range = 0 to 30 m/s).
`VEHICLE_LINEAR_MOTOR_OFFSET` vector	Offset from the vehicle's center of mass where the linear motor is applied (range = 0 to 100m).
`VEHICLE_REFERENCE_FRAME` rotation	Rotation of vehicle axes relative to the local frame.

Many of the parameters are of the form `VEHICLE_<BEHAVIOR>_TIMESCALE`, measured in seconds. Shown in Table 7.7, the timescale properties control how rapidly the behavior occurs. A small value means you'll see the behavior very quickly, while a large value means it will take longer to see the behavior's full effect. The valid range is from 0.07 seconds to practical infinity. One pair of useful parameters is the motor timescale, `VEHICLE_LINEAR_MOTOR_TIMESCALE`, and the motor decay timescale, `VEHICLE_LINEAR_MOTOR_DECAY_TIMESCALE`, both measured in seconds. The **motor** timescale indicates how quickly the motors cause the effect. The **motor decay** timescale is the exact opposite: after you apply a motor push, its effectiveness decays. For example, a large heavy cement truck with great brakes would have a large timescale value for getting up to speed and a small timescale value for stopping. A boat might have a pair of larger values so you can see the boat slowly accelerating, and then it

CHAPTER 1
CHAPTER 2
CHAPTER 3
CHAPTER 4
CHAPTER 5
CHAPTER 6

CHAPTER 7

CHAPTER 8
CHAPTER 9
CHAPTER 10
CHAPTER 11
CHAPTER 12
CHAPTER 13
CHAPTER 14
CHAPTER 15
APPENDICES

quietly keeps sailing after you turn off the engine. Another useful timescale is for vertical attraction, which helps keep vehicles rightside up.

There are also timescales for banking and hover behavior. *Banking* means leaning into the turn, and is what airplanes and motorcycles do when they turn—if they turn left, they lean left. Since physics isn't real in *SL*, you can lean out of the turn too, and maybe create some interesting vehicles. *Hover* indicates the height at which your vehicle tries to hover above the ground (or water).

TABLE 7.7: VEHICLE PROPERTIES: TIMESCALE

CONSTANT	DESCRIPTION
VEHICLE_LINEAR_MOTOR_TIMESCALE float	Exponential timescale for the vehicle to achieve its full linear motor velocity.
VEHICLE_LINEAR_MOTOR_DECAY_TIMESCALE float	Exponential timescale for the linear motor's effectiveness to decay toward zero.
VEHICLE_LINEAR_FRICTION_TIMESCALE vector	Vector of timescales for exponential decay of linear velocity along the three vehicle axes.
VEHICLE_LINEAR_DEFLECTION_TIMESCALE float	Exponential timescale for the vehicle to redirect its velocity to be along its x-axis (preferring to travel forward).
VEHICLE_ANGULAR_MOTOR_TIMESCALE float	Exponential timescale for the vehicle to achieve its full angular motor velocity.
VEHICLE_ANGULAR_MOTOR_DECAY_TIMESCALE float	Exponential timescale for the angular motor's effectiveness to decay toward zero.
VEHICLE_ANGULAR_FRICTION_TIMESCALE vector	Vector of timescales for exponential decay of angular velocity along the three vehicle axes.
VEHICLE_ANGULAR_DEFLECTION_TIMESCALE float	Exponential timescale for the vehicle to achieve full angular deflection.
VEHICLE_BANKING_TIMESCALE float	Exponential timescale for the banking behavior to take full effect.
VEHICLE_HOVER_TIMESCALE float	Period of time for the vehicle to achieve its hover height.
VEHICLE_VERTICAL_ATTRACTION_TIMESCALE float	Exponential timescale for the vehicle to make itself upright.

Another set of parameters, shown in Table 7.8, are of the form VEHICLE_<BEHAVIOR>_ EFFICIENCY, measured from 0.0 to 1.0, indicating the range of none to a lot. VEHICLE_HOVER_ EFFICIENCY, for example, can be thought of as a slider between bouncy (0.0) and smoothed (1.0). The DEFLECTION efficiency parameters have slightly different semantics, more similar to the TIMESCALEs, in that they range from zero to maximum deflection.

TABLE 7.8: VEHICLE PROPERTIES: EFFICIENCY

CONSTANT	DESCRIPTION
VEHICLE_ANGULAR_DEFLECTION_EFFICIENCY float	Slider between 0 (no deflection) and 1 (maximum strength).
VEHICLE_BANKING_EFFICIENCY float	Slider between −1 (leans out of turns), 0 (no banking), and +1 (leans into turns).
VEHICLE_HOVER_EFFICIENCY float	Slider between 0 (bouncy) and 1 (critically damped) hover behavior.
VEHICLE_LINEAR_DEFLECTION_EFFICIENCY float	Slider between 0 (no deflection) and 1 (maximum strength).
VEHICLE_VERTICAL_ATTRACTION_EFFICIENCY float	Slider between 0 (bouncy) and 1 (firm) to keep vehicle vertical.

The last set of useful parameters provides more control over the realism (or nonrealism) of your vehicle. You're already familiar with **Banking** and **Hover**. **Buoyancy** indicates how much gravity affects your vehicle. **SL** has complete antigravity. While buoyancy and hover height are independent, you may need to set a high buoyancy if hover height is low. In addition to appropriate `TIMESCALE` and `EFFICIENCY` parameters, banking, buoyancy, and hover properties can be controlled with the values shown in Table 7.9.

TABLE 7.9: VEHICLE PROPERTIES: BANKING, HOVER, AND BUOYANCY

Constant	Description
`VEHICLE_BANKING_MIX` `float`	Slider between 0 (banking allowed when stopped) and 1 (banking only when moving forward).
`VEHICLE_BUOYANCY` `float`	Slider between −1 (double-gravity) and 1 (full antigravity).
`VEHICLE_HOVER_HEIGHT` `float`	Desired height for the vehicle's center of mass to hover (ground-, water-, or global-relative); maximum 100m.

CHAPTER 1
CHAPTER 2
CHAPTER 3
CHAPTER 4
CHAPTER 5
CHAPTER 6
CHAPTER 7
CHAPTER 8
CHAPTER 9
CHAPTER 10
CHAPTER 11
CHAPTER 12
CHAPTER 13
CHAPTER 14
CHAPTER 15
APPENDICES

WARNING

You may notice that you can also set many vehicle parameters with other LSL calls that push your objects around, such as `llSetBuoyancy()` and `llSetTorque()`. *Don't mix and match.* You'll get very unpredictable behavior.

VEHICLE FLAGS

In addition to a set of properties, vehicles have a set of flags (detailed in Table 7.10) that can be added with `llSetVehicleFlags()` and removed with `llRemoveVehicleFlags()`. These flags control things like whether ground-based vehicles can fly, whether airplanes can bank, and what to consider when hovering.

TABLE 7.10: VEHICLE FLAGS

Constant	Description
`VEHICLE_FLAG_NO_DEFLECTION_UP`	No linear deflection up. (No flying cars.)
`VEHICLE_FLAG_LIMIT_ROLL_ONLY`	For vehicles with a vertical attractor that want to be able to climb/dive; for instance, airplanes that want to use the banking feature.
`VEHICLE_FLAG_LIMIT_MOTOR_UP`	Prevents ground vehicles from motoring into the sky.
`VEHICLE_FLAG_HOVER_WATER_ONLY`	Ignore terrain height when hovering.
`VEHICLE_FLAG_HOVER_TERRAIN_ONLY`	Ignore water height when hovering.
`VEHICLE_FLAG_HOVER_GLOBAL_HEIGHT`	Hover at global height instead of height above ground or water.
`VEHICLE_FLAG_HOVER_UP_ONLY`	Hover doesn't push down.
`VEHICLE_FLAG_MOUSELOOK_STEER`	Steer the vehicle using mouselook (first-person view). Use this flag to make the angular motor try to make the vehicle turn such that its local x-axis points in the same direction as the client-side camera.
`VEHICLE_FLAG_MOUSELOOK_BANK`	Same as above but relies on banking. It remaps left-right motions of the client camera to rotations about the vehicle's local x-axis.
`VEHICLE_FLAG_CAMERA_DECOUPLED`	Makes mouselook camera rotate independently of the vehicle. By default the client mouselook camera will rotate about with the vehicle, but when this flag is set the camera direction is independent of the vehicle's rotation.

DEFINITION

llSetVehicleFlags(integer *flags*)

Sets each flag specified in *flags* to TRUE

    flags — Bitmask of VEHICLE_FLAG_* flags shown in Table 7.10.

DEFINITION

llRemoveVehicleFlags(integer *flags*)

Sets each flag specified in *flags* to FALSE

    flags — Bitmask of VEHICLE_FLAG_* flags shown in Table 7.10.

NOTE

There are many interesting ways you can augment the script in Listing 7.4. Many of the magic carpets in *SL* are controlled by a script originally developed by Cubey Terra because it is freely distributed. Cubey Terra's script is much more complete and complex than Listing 7.4; you can get a copy of it in many places around *SL*, including at SYW HQ. A complete suite of scripts for a sailboat is described at http://rpgstats.com/wiki/index.php?title=LibrarySailboat. Also, you can get a working Flying Tako Sailboat, with modifiable scripts, at Grey <29, 158, 23>.

You can allow other avatars (not the owner) to drive your vehicle by removing the condition if(agent == llGetOwner()) in the changed() event handler. If you do this, add a "Lo-Jack" beacon to tell the owner where the vehicle was abandoned. Email works nicely.

Another nice touch is particle scripts for exhaust on a car, magic fairy dust on a carpet, flames on a rocket, or a contrail on an airplane. Since the particles won't be emitted from the root prim, you'll need to add a set of linked messages to turn the particles on and off at appropriate times. You can pass information such as the state of the vehicle (in the message) and the name of the pilot (in the key).

CAMERAS AND MOUSELOOK

You should probably set your camera position and angle to make it easier to drive the vehicle. A good position is slightly above and behind your avatar. Camera offsets are persistent features of the object, and need to be changed explicitly:

```
vector offset = <-5.0, 0, 1.0>;
llSetCameraEyeOffset(offset);
vector angle = <0.0, 0.0, 0.5>;
llSetCameraAtOffset(angle);
```

You can also use mouselook to drive the vehicle (type **m** to enter mouselook), using the MOUSELOOK vehicle flags. It's hard to get it right, but when you do you can achieve a "driver's-eye view." By default the mouselook direction **will change** when the vehicle you are sitting on moves: since this is likely to cause motion sickness, disconnect the mouselook camera from the vehicle's rotation by setting the VEHICLE_FLAG_CAMERA_DECOUPLED flag. To modify Listing 7.4 for a working mouselook vehicle—albeit in need of other work—first comment out the last line in `control()` that sets the **angularMotor**, and then add the following lines to `set_airplane_properties()`:

```
llSetVehicleFlags(VEHICLE_FLAG_MOUSELOOK_BANK | VEHICLE_FLAG_CAMERA_DECOUPLED);
llSetVehicleVectorParam(VEHICLE_ANGULAR_MOTOR_DIRECTION, <5,0,0>);
```

There are seven camera control functions in LSL, listed in Table 7.11. They can be used for objects other than vehicles, but there aren't many real examples. Table 7.12 shows a list of camera-related constants that support the function `llSetCameraParams()`.

CHAPTER 1
CHAPTER 2
CHAPTER 3
CHAPTER 4
CHAPTER 5
CHAPTER 6

CHAPTER 7

CHAPTER 8
CHAPTER 9
CHAPTER 10
CHAPTER 11
CHAPTER 12
CHAPTER 13
CHAPTER 14
CHAPTER 15
APPENDICES

TABLE 7.11: CAMERA-CONTROL FUNCTIONS AND THE PERMISSIONS THAT MUST BE REQUESTED

FUNCTION	DESCRIPTION	PERMISSION REQUIRED
`llClearCameraParams()`	Resets all camera parameters to default values and turns off scripted camera control.	PERMISSION_CONTROL_CAMERA
`vector llGetCameraPos()`	Returns a `vector` that is the current camera position for the agent the task has permissions for.	PERMISSION_TRACK_CAMERA
`rotation llGetCameraRot()`	Returns a `rotation` that is the current camera orientation for the agent the task has permissions for.	PERMISSION_TRACK_CAMERA
`llForceMouselook(integer mouselook)`	Sets whether a sitting avatar should be forced into mouselook when they sit on this prim. If `mouselook` is TRUE, the avatar is forced into mouselook mode when they sit.	—
`llSetCameraAtOffset(vector offset)`	Sets the camera at `offset` from the object's center when an avatar sits on it.	—
`llSetCameraEyeOffset(vector offset)`	Sets the camera eye `offset` from the object's center when an avatar sits on it.	—
`llSetCameraParams(list properties)`	Sets multiple camera parameters at once. `properties` is a strided list of stride 2 with the format `[property_1, data_1, property_2, data_2, ..., property_n, data_n]`. Each property is a named constant, as shown in Table 7.12.	PERMISSION_CONTROL_CAMERA

TABLE 7.12: CAMERA-PROPERTY CONSTANTS FOR `llSetCameraParams()`

PROPERTY	DEFAULT VALUE	VALUE RANGE	DESCRIPTION
CAMERA_ACTIVE integer *isActive*	FALSE	TRUE or FALSE	Sets scripted control of the camera on or off.
CAMERA_BEHINDNESS_ANGLE float *degrees*	10.0	0 to 180	Sets the angle in degrees within which the camera is not constrained by changes in target rotation.
CAMERA_BEHINDNESS_LAG float *seconds*	0.0	0 to 3	Sets how strongly the camera is forced to stay behind the target if outside of the "behindness" angle.
CAMERA_DISTANCE float *meters*	3.0	0.5 to 10	Sets how far away the camera should be from its target.
CAMERA_FOCUS vector *position*	—	—	Sets camera focus (target position) in region coordinates.
CAMERA_FOCUS_LAG float *seconds*	0.1	0 to 3	Sets how much the camera lags as it tries to aim toward the target.
CAMERA_FOCUS_LOCKED integer *isLocked*	FALSE	TRUE or FALSE	Locks the camera focus so it will not move.
CAMERA_FOCUS_OFFSET vector *meters*	<0.0, 0.0, 0.0>	<−10, −10, −10> to <10 ,10, 10>	Adjusts the camera focus position relative to the target.
CAMERA_FOCUS_THRESHOLD float *meters*	1.0	0 to 4	Sets the radius of a sphere around the camera's target position within which its focus is not affected by target motion.
CAMERA_PITCH float *degrees*	0.0	−45 to 80	Adjusts the angular amount the camera aims straight ahead versus straight down, maintaining the same distance; analogous to "incidence."
CAMERA_POSITION vector *position*	—	—	Sets camera position in region coordinates.
CAMERA_POSITION_LAG float *seconds*	0.1	0 to 3	Sets how much the camera lags as it tries to move toward its "ideal" position.
CAMERA_POSITION_LOCKED integer *isLocked*	FALSE	TRUE or FALSE	Locks the camera position so it will not move.
CAMERA_POSITION_THRESHOLD float *meters*	1.0	0 to 4	Sets the radius of a sphere around the camera's ideal position, within which it is not affected by target motion.

CHAPTER 1
CHAPTER 2
CHAPTER 3
CHAPTER 4
CHAPTER 5
CHAPTER 6

CHAPTER 7

CHAPTER 8
CHAPTER 9
CHAPTER 10
CHAPTER 11
CHAPTER 12
CHAPTER 13
CHAPTER 14
CHAPTER 15
APPENDICES

If you've played with a magic carpet, you may have noticed that the tassels are not flexible. You may have even tried to make them flexible (as in the graphic here) and found that the vehicle no longer works. You can't add a flexiflag for your favorite sports team, you can't add streamers for newlyweds, and you can't add a banner behind your airplane— at least, not without some work. The difficulty is probably a bug: it seems you can't use `llSetStatus(STATUS_PHYSICS, TRUE)` when the linkset contains a flexiprim.

The workaround, therefore, is to enable physics when there are no flexiprims, then add the flexiprims to the linkset. However, you can't change links when the avatar is seated, so you have to do it before they sit down. The basic approach is as follows:

1. Have the avatar touch or say something to "turn on" the engines.
2. Break all links to flexiprims.
3. Enable physics.
4. Relink the flexiprims.
5. Allow the avatar to sit down.

You'll have several challenges to deal with, including these:

- Making sure you recognize the difference between linking prims and the avatar sitting.
- Making sure the vehicle doesn't drift away from the flexiprims (physics may be on just long enough).
- Dealing with the fact that linking takes a while and the avatar needs to know when they can sit; they shouldn't be allowed to sit unless the vehicle is *completely* ready to fly.
- Correctly handling permissions requests—just remember that permissions do not accumulate.

The full script is available at SYW HQ. It's a hack, but it works.

SUMMARY

Figuring out the way the physics engine works and how to manipulate it allows you to create all kinds of interesting objects. The effort is well worth it! Be aware, though, that the *SL* physics engine is probably the buggiest part of the system, despite the transition from the Havok1 to the Havok4 engine. If you find yourself frustrated about something not working the way you expect it to, browse the JIRA pages (`https://jira.secondlife.com/secure/Dashboard.jspa`) to see if any bug reports have been made.

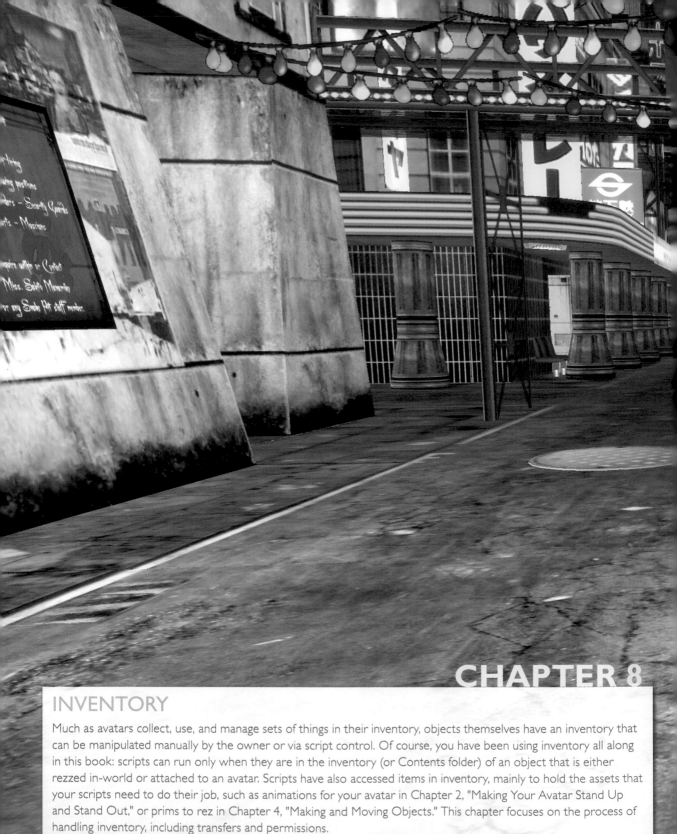

CHAPTER 8

INVENTORY

Much as avatars collect, use, and manage sets of things in their inventory, objects themselves have an inventory that can be manipulated manually by the owner or via script control. Of course, you have been using inventory all along in this book: scripts can run only when they are in the inventory (or Contents folder) of an object that is either rezzed in-world or attached to an avatar. Scripts have also accessed items in inventory, mainly to hold the assets that your scripts need to do their job, such as animations for your avatar in Chapter 2, "Making Your Avatar Stand Up and Stand Out," or prims to rez in Chapter 4, "Making and Moving Objects." This chapter focuses on the process of handling inventory, including transfers and permissions.

INVENTORY PROPERTIES

 INVENTORY
PROPERTIES

 GIVING
INVENTORY

TAKING
INVENTORY

PERMISSIONS

SUMMARY

A prim's inventory folder can contain every kind of **SL** inventory except calling cards. Table 8.1 shows the supported set of items. The descriptions should be self-evident from the names of the constants. Note that these values are not bit flags: you cannot combine these values in a single call to the inventory functions to select, for instance, notecards and objects. Because the inventory functions do not distinguish between textures and snapshots, you will always use `INVENTORY_TEXTURE` for snapshots as well. Finally, because object inventories cannot currently hold calling cards, there is no constant defined for them.

TABLE 8.1: INVENTORY TYPES

CONSTANT NAME	VALUE
INVENTORY_NONE	−1
INVENTORY_ALL	−1
INVENTORY_TEXTURE	0
INVENTORY_SOUND	1
INVENTORY_LANDMARK	3
INVENTORY_CLOTHING	5
INVENTORY_OBJECT	6
INVENTORY_NOTECARD	7
INVENTORY_SCRIPT	10
INVENTORY_BODYPART	13
INVENTORY_ANIMATION	20
INVENTORY_GESTURE	21

Listing 8.1 shows how to find the number of items in inventory and several properties about each item. The functions used here are described in Table 8.2. The function `llRequestInventoryData()` goes to the **SL** dataserver to find more information about the inventory item. Currently, it is used only for landmark objects, and will return the landmark's region coordinates.

Listing 8.1: Getting Properties of Inventory Items

```
default
{
    state_entry() {
        integer i;
        integer n = llGetInventoryNumber(INVENTORY_ALL);
        for (i=0; i<n; i++) {
            string  name = llGetInventoryName( INVENTORY_ALL, i );
            key     creatorID = llGetInventoryCreator( name );
            integer type = llGetInventoryType( name );
            key     id = llGetInventoryKey(name);
            if (type == INVENTORY_LANDMARK) {
                llRequestInventoryData( name );
            }
            // use the information
        }
    }
}
```

```
    dataserver(key requestID, string data) {
        vector regionCoords = (vector)data;
        llOwnerSay("Landmark is at " + (string)regionCoords );
    }
}
```

TABLE 8.2: INVENTORY INFORMATION FUNCTIONS

Function	Behavior
`integer llGetInventoryNumber(integer type)`	Returns an integer that is the number of items of a given *type* in the prim's inventory.
`string llGetInventoryName(integer type, integer number)`	Returns a string that is the name of the inventory item *number* of *type*. Returns an empty string if nothing is found.
`integer llGetInventoryType(string name)`	Returns an integer that is the *type* of the inventory item *name*. Using the item's key will not work.
`key llGetInventoryCreator(string name)`	Returns a key of the creator of the inventory *name*. Using the item's key will not work.
`key llGetInventoryKey(string name)`	Returns a key that is the UUID of the inventory *name*. If you do not have full permissions on the inventory object, this returns `NULL_KEY`.
`key llRequestInventoryData(string name)`	Returns to the dataserver query a key that is a unique identifier. A `dataserver()` event will be triggered when the data is ready. Currently valid only for landmarks.

CHAPTER 1
CHAPTER 2
CHAPTER 3
CHAPTER 4
CHAPTER 5
CHAPTER 6
CHAPTER 7

CHAPTER 8

CHAPTER 9
CHAPTER 10
CHAPTER 11
CHAPTER 12
CHAPTER 13
CHAPTER 14
CHAPTER 15
APPENDIX

GIVING INVENTORY

Containers are objects that hold on to things until they are needed in the environment or in interactions with residents. Containers that give out landmarks and notecards are prime examples of interaction tools you will find necessary every day in *Second Life*. When you've given away singleton objects a couple of times, you will realize how convenient it is to give a long list of items at one time.

 PLEASE TAKE A NOTE(CARD)

Listing 8.2 shows a simple notecard giver. At SYW HQ, it is embodied in a fountain that offers each sensed avatar a notecard containing a horoscope. The core is a simple one-liner that offers each detected avatar the first (i.e., zeroth) notecard item found in inventory:

```
    llGiveInventory(llDetectedKey(i), llGetInventoryName(INVENTORY_NOTECARD, 0));
```

Listing 8.2: Notecard Giver

```
integer MEMORY_LENGTH = 25;
list gAvatars;
add_avatar(string name) {
    gAvatars += name;
    if (llGetListLength(gAvatars) > MEMORY_LENGTH) {
        gAvatars = llDeleteSubList(gAvatars,0,0);
    }
}
```

189

INVENTORY
PROPERTIES

GIVING
INVENTORY

TAKING
INVENTORY

PERMISSIONS

SUMMARY

```
default {
    state_entry() {
        llVolumeDetect(TRUE);
    }
    touch_start(integer num) { // report who received notecard
        if (llDetectedKey(0) == llGetOwner()){
            integer i;
            integer numAvs = llGetListLength(gAvatars);
            for (i=0; i<numAvs; i++){
                llOwnerSay("Gave a note to " + llList2String(gAvatars, i));
            }
            gAvatars = [];
        }
    }
    collision_start(integer total_number) {
        integer i;
        for (i=0; i<total_number; i++) {
            if (llListFindList(gAvatars,[llDetectedName(i)]) == -1) {
                // Pick out the first NOTECARD and offer it
                llGiveInventory(llDetectedKey(i),
                        llGetInventoryName(INVENTORY_NOTECARD,0));
                add_avatar(llDetectedName(i));
            }
        }
    }
}
```

Figure 8.1 shows a resident walking up to the fountain, and the subsequent interaction. Note that, as with the memory greeter from Listing 5.8 in Chapter 5, "Sensing the World," the fountain keeps a list of the latest 25 residents who have received a notecard, and rolls off the oldest whenever it adds the newest avatar in the `add_avatar()` function.

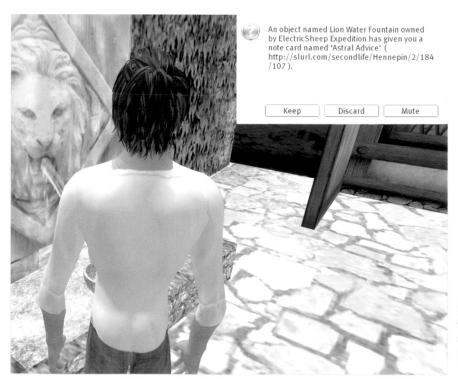

Figure 8.1: A fountain offers a notecard to passersby.

Whenever the owner touches the fountain, it reports the latest residents to have approached, and then (optionally) clears the list altogether, just like the reporting greeter of Listing 5.9 in Chapter 5. You may or may not want to determine whether a resident has previously seen a notecard, but you can test for the name in the **gAvatars** list. You may also want to offer the avatar the notecard when they touch the fountain, just in case they accidentally clicked Ignore on the first menu.

DEFINITION

llGiveInventory(key *recipient*, string *inventory*)

Offers an item from an object's inventory. There is no way to tell if an offer is accepted, refused, or silently failed. An offer to an avatar delays the script by three seconds; an offer to another object is not delayed at all.

> *recipient* — The key of a potential recipient (an avatar or another object). Avatars have the opportunity to refuse the offer. Offers to objects not in the same sim will fail silently.

> *inventory* — The name of an item from the object's inventory.

Looking at Figure 8.2, you can see the kind of prescient, insightful advice this particular notecard giver dispenses. Some residents will find value in receiving fresh astrological guidance in-world every day. However, remember that the notecard giver's advice is static, and this makes it weak for a usage where data freshness might be important for drawing repeat visitors. This too can be remedied by talking to an external web server that creates a custom notecard, as covered in Chapter 12, "Reaching outside *Second Life*."

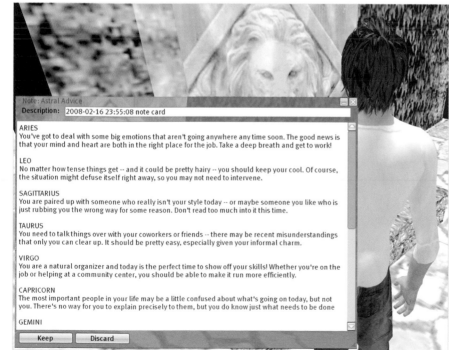

Figure 8.2: Your fortune in a notecard!

INVENTORY LIST: GIVING FOLDERS

After you've clicked Accept for a few items given individually, you will quickly want to give collections in a single dose. A good approach is to create a container with all the items in it and govern it with a script such as Listing 8.3.

INVENTORY
PROPERTIES

GIVING
INVENTORY

TAKING
INVENTORY

PERMISSIONS

SUMMARY

Listing 8.3: Giving a List of Inventory

```
integer gNumItems;
init() {
    gNumItems = llGetInventoryNumber(INVENTORY_TEXTURE);
    llSetText((string)gNumItems+"\nfree SYW textures.", <1.0,0.0,0.0>, 1.0);
}
default
{
    on_rez(integer param) {
        init();
    }
    state_entry() {
        init();
    }
    touch_start(integer total_number) {
        list      inventory;
        string    name;
        string    folder = llGetObjectName();
        integer   i;
        key       user = llDetectedKey(0);
        for (i = 0; i < gNumItems; i++) {
            name = llGetInventoryName(INVENTORY_ALL, i);
            if (llGetScriptName() != name) {
                inventory += name;
            }
        }
        if (llGetListLength(inventory) < 1) {
            llSay(0, "No items to offer.");
        } else {
            llGiveInventoryList(user, folder, inventory);
            llInstantMessage(user, "Accept the inventory offer to copy "
                                + folder + " to your inventory");
        }
    }
}
```

The listing initializes the container's floating text string by counting the number of texture items in the collection and setting the text appropriately. When touched, the container collects the names of the items in inventory and places them into a list called *inventory*. Note that you don't want to give the **script** to the user; thus the script adds only objects that don't have the same name as the script itself.

The script then offers up the texture collection using `llGiveInventoryList()`, as shown in Figure 8.3. When the user accepts the offer, the textures are copied into the user's inventory.

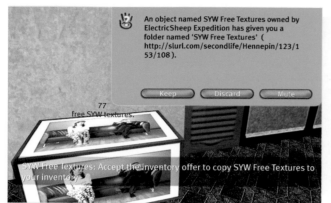

An object named SYW Free Textures owned by ElectricSheep Expedition has given you a folder named 'SYW Free Textures' (http://slurl.com/secondlife/Hennepin/123/153/108).

Keep   Discard   Mute

77 free SYW textures.

SYW Free textures: Accept the inventory offer to copy SYW Free Textures to your inventory.

Figure 8.3: The container offers a folder of textures.

CHAPTER 1
CHAPTER 2
CHAPTER 3
CHAPTER 4
CHAPTER 5
CHAPTER 6
CHAPTER 7

CHAPTER 8

CHAPTER 9
CHAPTER 10
CHAPTER 11
CHAPTER 12
CHAPTER 13
CHAPTER 14
CHAPTER 15

DEFINITION

```
llGiveInventoryList(key recipient,
              string category, list inventory)
```

Gives a set of items from the container's inventory to the *recipient*. If the *recipient* accepts the items, they will appear in the recipient's inventory as a folder named *category*.

recipient — The key of the avatar or object to receive the objects.

category — Recipient's inventory folder that will hold the given items.

inventory — A list of the names of the inventory items to be given.

Instead of giving a folder directly, you can also give a single object that unpacks itself and then gives the folder. While this may sound complicated, it can be much simpler to manage inventory this way. Since object inventory doesn't allow nested folders, it can be difficult to manage complicated inventory that you give only parts of. Vending machines are a good example—you might want to sell the same basic outfit in different colors or different variations for men, women, and quadrupeds, or two dozen different varieties of Coke. It is much simpler for the vending system to manage only one inventory object at a time instead of collecting the correct parts for each sale.

TAKING INVENTORY

Slavishly aping the workings of real-life counterparts doesn't always make sense, but at times metaphors are so compelling and familiar that it's irresistible. The mailbox shown in Figure 8.4 might be such a case. It works much like its real-world analog; to figure out how it should work, consider how such fixtures of everyday life are used. Someone prepares a package or a letter (in *Second Life*, a notecard is a suitable metaphor), walks up to a mailbox, then drops the mail in. That's the model you'll use in this build—an old-fashioned mailbox you'll be able to use as an in-world, local note-delivery system or as a model for a suggestion box.

INVENTORY
PROPERTIES

GIVING
INVENTORY

 TAKING
INVENTORY

PERMISSIONS

SUMMARY

Figure 8.4: A typical street-corner mailbox from Anytown, USA

The basic operation is just the opposite of the notecard givers built earlier in this chapter. You could think of this as a sort of inventory taker, in the sense that it responds to something being dropped into it. The examples so far have used the changed() event handler only to detect changes in the object's link structure; reacting when an avatar sits (in Chapter 2) and noticing when new prims are linked into the object (in Chapter 4). Here the script is taking action when the contents of the object change, so it bears a bit of additional explanation.

The changed() event handler is triggered when some aspect of an object has been changed by an external action. The SYW website's coverage of event handlers shows the comprehensive list of potential detectable changes. Changes in texture color and transparency, ownership, size, and inventory are all eligible for detection. In the mailbox implemented in Listing 8.4, you're interested only in discovering when someone drops something into the mailbox's inventory.

Listing 8.4: A Basic Mailbox

```
default
{
    state_entry() {
        llAllowInventoryDrop(TRUE);
    }
    touch_start(integer total_number) {
        llSay(0,"Create a notecard and drop it into the mailbox");
    }
    changed(integer mask) {
        if (mask & (CHANGED_INVENTORY | CHANGED_ALLOWED_DROP)){
            llSay(0, "Thanks for the mail!");
        }
    }
}
```

To allow something to be dropped into inventory, the script calls llAllowInventoryDrop(). When the object is touched, the script gives the resident a simple instruction. If the resident leaves a note, changed() is fired. When an item is dropped, the value of *mask* will have one of elements of the CHANGED_INVENTORY bit set or the CHANGED_ALLOWED_DROP bit set. The CHANGED_INVENTORY bit is set when the owner changes the contents, while the CHANGED_ALLOWED_DROP bit is set when someone other than the owner adds an object to inventory (allowed only because of the call to llAllowInventoryDrop(TRUE)). The expression

```
if (mask & (CHANGED_INVENTORY | CHANGED_ALLOWED_DROP))
```

means "if *mask* has any bits set that are also set in CHANGED_INVENTORY or CHANGED_ALLOWED_DROP." Notice that these are the bitwise operations & and |, not the true/false operations && and ||.

CHAPTER 1
CHAPTER 2
CHAPTER 3
CHAPTER 4
CHAPTER 5
CHAPTER 6
CHAPTER 7

 ## DEFINITION

11AllowInventoryDrop(integer *add*)

Allows users without Modify permissions to add inventory items to a prim. Ownership of the dropped item changes to prim's owner. Scripts can not be dropped onto a prim. When a user *with* Modify permissions drops the item, then the changed() event handler is triggered with CHANGED_INVENTORY. When a user *without* Modify permissions drops the item, then the changed() event handler is triggered with CHANGED_ALLOW_DROP.

> *add* — Boolean. If TRUE allows anyone to drop inventory on prim; FALSE revokes the permission.

CHAPTER 8

CHAPTER 9
CHAPTER 10
CHAPTER 11
CHAPTER 12
CHAPTER 13
CHAPTER 14
CHAPTER 15
APPENDICES

So what's to prevent a griefer from dropping some nefarious script in the mailbox? There are some smart built-in exceptions to guard against this sort of occurrence. Calling cards cannot be dropped by anyone, under any circumstances. Scripts can be dropped only by the object's owner (and group members, if the object is group-editable). If a nonowner attempts to drop a script into an object, they receive a stern, "Not permitted to edit this!" message. (11RemoteLoadScriptPin(), described in Chapter 4, is the only way to get a script to transfer and run in another object.) Notecards can be dragged from inventory and dropped into the box, and other assets, including textures and objects, can be dropped by dragging while holding the Control key; the target object will be highlighted in red to indicate where the dropped inventory will go.

Even an owner should be careful. For example, the gesture of an owner dropping a texture onto an object **without holding the Control key** is indistinguishable from dropping a texture onto an object face in edit mode. You may inadvertently retexture your postal box with fluffy bunnies. Another quirk is that if you enable inventory drop in the root prim of a complex object, dropped inventory will go into the root's inventory even if dropped onto a child prim—except for textures, which will go into whichever prim they are dropped into!

PERMISSIONS

You may sometimes need to know what permissions you have on an object. There are four permissions you can grant to an **object**: Transfer, Modify, Copy, and Move. A **script** can have Transfer, Modify, and Copy permissions. Objects are usually given away with either **Trans/NoCopy/NoMod** permissions, or **NoTrans/Copy/Mod**. If you want to retain control over distribution of an object, avoid giving it away with **Trans/Copy** permissions, which allows the recipient to copy the original and sell as many of the copies as they like. Table 8.3 shows the list of constants related to permissions.

INVENTORY
PROPERTIES

GIVING
INVENTORY

TAKING
INVENTORY

 PERMISSIONS

 SUMMARY

TABLE 8.3: PERMISSIONS CONSTANTS

CONSTANT	VALUE	DESCRIPTION
PERM_TRANSFER	0x2000	Allowed to transfer to another owner.
PERM_MODIFY	0x4000	Allowed to modify.
PERM_COPY	0x8000	Allowed to make copies.
PERM_MOVE	0x80000	Allowed to move while rezzed.
PERM_ALL	0x7FFFFFFF	All permissions (Transfer, Modify, Copy, and Move, plus any that are added in the future).

The function `llGetObjectPermMask()` will ask for the current permissions mask for the object containing the script, and `llGetInventoryPermMask()` will do the same for objects held in the object's inventory. Some activities require appropriate permissions. For example, getting a prim's key requires full permissions, giving something away requires Transfer permissions, and changing the color of a prim requires Modify permissions.

Here's an example of when you might want to check permissions: You could implement a clothing swap box by combining the functions of the notecard giver of Listing 8.2 and the mailbox of Listing 8.4. Extend the mailbox with code that checks to make sure the donated item can be transferred but not copied. This makes it slightly more likely that the donated objects are valuable and not just full-permission freebies:

```
integer i;
for (i=0; i<llGetInventoryNumber(INVENTORY_ALL); i++) {
    string name = llGetInventoryName(INVENTORY_ALL, i);
    integer type = llGetInventoryType(name);
    if (type != INVENTORY_SCRIPT) {
        integer perms = llGetInventoryPermMask(name, MASK_OWNER);
        if ((perms & PERM_TRANSFER) == PERM_TRANSFER &&
            (perms & PERM_COPY) == 0) {
            llSay(0, "Thanks for the "+name);
            // keep track so you don't keep receiving same object
        } else {
            llSay(0, "Sorry, "+name+" isn't nocopy, trans");
            // probably delete using llRemoveInventory(name)
        }
    }
}
```

The expression `(perms&PERM_TRANSFER) == PERM_TRANSFER` will be true if the object has the transfer bit set. The expression `(perms&PERM_COPY) == 0` will be true only if the copy bit is not set. A common use for this permissions check is to accept only full-permission textures from others, since that is the only way a script can get the UUID of the texture or display it on a child prim. If the item doesn't have enough permissions, you can use `llRemoveInventory()` to delete it. Another good use for a check like this is in a vendor script (see Chapter 13, "Money Makes the Word Go Round") to be sure that your vendor can actually give the object to the purchaser.

DEFINITION

`llRemoveInventory(string item)`

Removes the `item` from the prim's inventory.

`item` — The name of the item in inventory.

DEFINITION

```
integer llGetObjectPermMask(integer whichClass)
```

```
integer llGetInventoryPermMask(string item, integer whichClass)
```

`llGetObjectPermMask()` returns the permissions that a class of users, indicated by `whichClass`, has to manipulate the object containing the script. `llGetInventoryPermMask()` does the same for items in inventory. The returned integer is a bit pattern of any combination of the constants in Table 8.3.

> `whichClass` — One of five constant values, shown in the table below, indicating which class of user to get the permissions for. Note that `whichClass` is not itself a bit pattern.

> `item` — The name of the inventory item to check.

Mask Constant	Value	Description
MASK_BASE	0	The base permissions of the object
MASK_OWNER	1	Current owner permissions
MASK_GROUP	2	Active group permissions
MASK_EVERYONE	3	Permissions everyone has
MASK_NEXT	4	Permissions the next owner will have

WARNING

Scripted objects that have been transferred, or *deeded*, to a group can be difficult to work with. There is no way for a group-deeded object to acquire permissions. Group objects cannot pay anyone. Any money these objects are paid is distributed evenly among the group members who have the Pay Group Liabilities and Receive Group Dividends option enabled. The owner of such an object is the group itself, so `llGetOwner()` returns the group key, and `llOwnerSay()` has no effect. Finally, on group-owned land the only way to get land-control LSL functions like `llSetParcelMusicURL()` and `llEjectFromLand()` to work is for the scripted objects themselves to be group-deeded.

SUMMARY

The most important other use for scripted inventory management in *Second Life* is, of course, vendor systems. If you are interested in taking the next step, turn to Chapter 13 for detail and examples. You can also find additional detail on rezzing objects from inventory on the SYW website in the bonus chapter called "Violence," which describes the *SL* combat model.

CHAPTER 1
CHAPTER 2
CHAPTER 3
CHAPTER 4
CHAPTER 5
CHAPTER 6
CHAPTER 7
CHAPTER 8
CHAPTER 9
CHAPTER 10
CHAPTER 11
CHAPTER 12
CHAPTER 13
CHAPTER 14
CHAPTER 15
APPENDICES

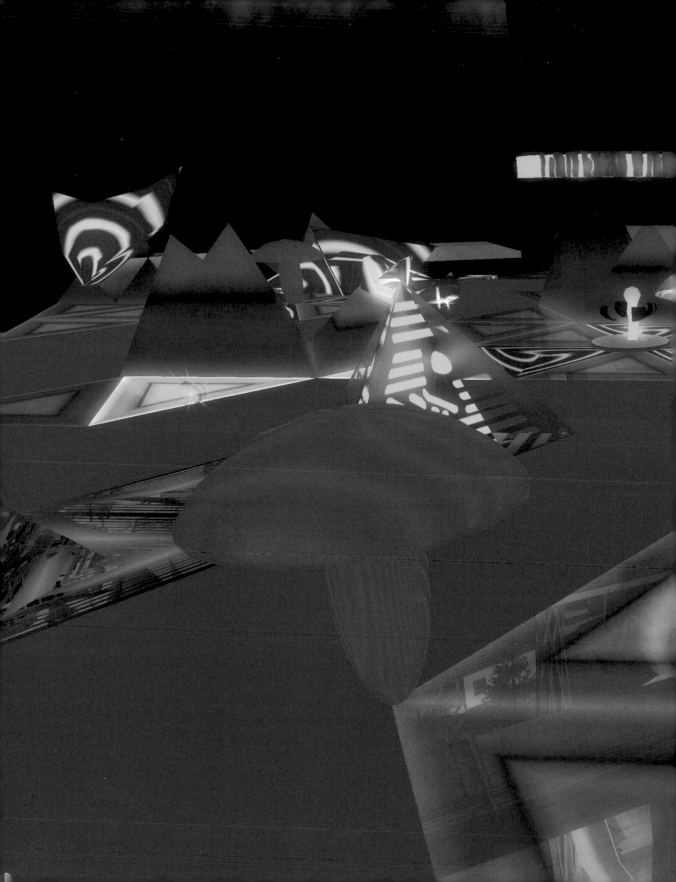

CHAPTER 9

SPECIAL EFFECTS

Half the fun of going into a virtual world is watching for the special effects. A nicely placed explosion or funky lighting attracts interest. Moving water and flickering flames add realism. There are many different ways you can combine the ideas in this book to create highly realistic and surreal experiences, but even a few simple things will add fun!

To create special effects of all stripes, you'll need to have a good grasp of particle effects, texture animation, and lighting. All three topics are presented in this chapter.

PARTICLE EFFECTS

 PARTICLE
EFFECTS

TEXTURE
ANIMATION

LIGHT

SUMMARY

Particles are probably the most popular form of special effects in **SL**, and you'll encounter particles in various places in the standard **SL** environment. For instance, when you create an object, a thin line of particles extends from your avatar's arm to the object. And when an object chats, it is surrounded by a swirl of particles.

Particles are simply floating images emitted from a particular location, the **emitter**. By controlling their number, speed, size, color, texture, and so forth, you can create a wide variety of effects, including shiny jewelry (**bling**); flame and smoke; water splashes and bubbles; falling leaves and petals; and weather effects like rain, snow, fog, and lightning. Stretch it further and make butterflies, rainbows, or kite strings. By combining many particle effects, you can create surprisingly realistic effects, as shown in Figure 9.1.

Figure 9.1: This inactive volcano, Volcán Tenorio <174, 37, 23>, shows a mix of waterfalls, lightning, and rain particles to create a fabulous natural effect.

You can create particles with the Linden Lab function `llParticleSystem()`. Chapter 10, "Scripting the Environment," shows an example of how to make a snow storm. Appendix B, "The Particle System," describes the `llParticleSystem()` function, including each of the function's properties, a number of very short examples, and a template script.

DEFINITION

`llParticleSystem(list rules)`

Defines a particle system for the containing prim based on a list of `rules`. Turns the emitter off using `llParticleSystem([])`. Appendix B describes the properties in more detail.

`rules` — Particle system rules; a strided list with a stride of length 2 in the format
`[property_1, data_1, property_2, data_2, ...,`
`property_n, data_n]`.

Particles are properties of **prims**, not scripts or objects. Each prim can have only one particle system in effect. The particle system is a persistent property of the prim, meaning you have to explicitly turn off the particles; simply deleting the script does not stop the emitter.

In this section you'll see how to combine various particle-system parameters and be guided through creating fireworks with a fairly standard particle script. The sections on rainbows and kite strings take the idea in different directions.

CHAPTER 1
CHAPTER 2
CHAPTER 3
CHAPTER 4
CHAPTER 5
CHAPTER 6
CHAPTER 7
CHAPTER 8

NOTE

CHAPTER 9

CHAPTER 10
CHAPTER 11
CHAPTER 12
CHAPTER 13
CHAPTER 14
CHAPTER 15
APPENDICES

Particles are client-side effects, so the idea of particles being "laggy" is a misconception. Be aware of two problems. First, particle scripts often have server-side lag in *other* parts of the script. Bling, for example, frequently uses an `llListen()` on channel 0 (ouch!); either change the channel or use a touch interface. The second thing to keep in mind is that *viewers* can be overloaded trying to manage too many particles. Linden Lab offers a simple user control to limit the number of particles (go to the Edit menu ▶ Preferences ▶ Graphics tab, click the check box for *Custom*, and set the value for *Max Particle Count*).

⊾ FIREWORKS

Fireworks are a fun way to learn how to put together a complete particle system. You can explore most of the parameters in interesting ways and end up with creative, fun-to-watch displays. Of course you'll also need to make sure the little balls of fire are pleasantly launched into the air, that they wait just the right amount of time before they explode, and that they don't litter the neighbor's yard.

Listing 9.1 shows a sample fireworks script that creates an explosion of long, thin, red particles that move very quickly and turn blue just before they vanish. The PSYS_PART_INTERP_COLOR_MASK does two things. First, it allows the particles to change from red to blue (PSYS_PART_START COLOR to PSYS_PART_END_COLOR). Second, it allows the particles to fade a bit during their lifetime (from PSYS_PART_START_ALPHA to PSYS_PART_END_ALPHA).

Listing 9.1: Fireworks—An Explosion of Red Shooters

```
fireworks() {
    // Based on Listing B.1 in App. B. Unchanged values removed to save trees
    // Default values indicated with //
    llParticleSystem( [
        PSYS_PART_FLAGS,    PSYS_PART_INTERP_COLOR_MASK |
                            PSYS_PART_EMISSIVE_MASK |
                            PSYS_PART_FOLLOW_VELOCITY_MASK,
    //Appearance
        PSYS_PART_START_SCALE,    < 0.1, 1.0, 0.0 >, // <1,1,1>
        PSYS_PART_END_SCALE,      < 1.0, 1.0, 0.0 >,
        PSYS_PART_START_COLOR,    < 1.0, 0.0, 0.0 >, // <1,1,1>
        PSYS_PART_END_COLOR,      < 0.0, 0.0, 1.0 >, // <1,1,1>
        PSYS_PART_START_ALPHA,    1.00,
        PSYS_PART_END_ALPHA,      0.25,  // 1.0
    //Flow
        PSYS_PART_MAX_AGE,           3.00, // 10.0
        PSYS_SRC_BURST_RATE,         0.50, // 0.1
        PSYS_SRC_BURST_PART_COUNT, 100,  // 1
```

CHAPTER 9

PARTICLE
EFFECTS

TEXTURE
ANIMATION

LIGHT

SUMMARY

```
    //Placement
        PSYS_SRC_PATTERN,         PSYS_SRC_PATTERN_EXPLODE, // DROP
    //Movement
        PSYS_SRC_BURST_SPEED_MIN,  5.00,  // 1.0
        PSYS_SRC_BURST_SPEED_MAX, 10.00,  // 1.0
        PSYS_SRC_ACCEL,            < 0.0, 0.0, -1.0 > // 0,0,0
    ]);
    llSleep(0.3);
}

init(integer delay)
{
    llSetStatus(STATUS_PHYSICS, TRUE );
    llSetStatus(STATUS_PHANTOM, TRUE );
    float d = (float)( (float)delay / 10.0 );
    llSetTimerEvent( d );
}
default {
    state_entry() {
        init(5);
    }
    on_rez(integer t) {
        init(t);
    }
    timer() {
        fireworks();
        llSetTimerEvent(0);
        if (llGetStartParameter() > 0) {
            llDie();
        } else {
            llParticleSystem([]);
        }
    }
}
```

The `PSYS_PART_EMISSIVE_MASK` makes the particles glow—absolutely mandatory for a nighttime display.

The third mask, `PSYS_PART_FOLLOW_VELOCITY_MASK`, makes the particles turn toward the direction of travel—very useful for these long thin particles.

The emitter uses a `PSYS_SRC_PATTERN_EXPLODE` pattern, which causes particles to shoot out in all directions. This pattern is extremely common for fireworks. It releases 50 particles on its first (and only) burst, each of which will live 3.0 seconds. The particles move pretty quickly, between 5.0 and 10.0 meters per second, and have a light gravity pull from `PSYS_SRC_ACCEL`. If you want the particles to respond to wind, add the `PSYS_PART_WIND_MASK` to the `PSYS_PART_FLAGS`.

The burst rate, however, is almost irrelevant: there is a 0.3 second delay after initializing the particle system, and then the particle system stops. The script is set up to allow you to edit and play with the particles, but to work correctly (without littering) when you're ready to put on your show. It checks the start parameter using `llGetStartParameter()`, and when it's nonzero, causes the prim to die using `llDie()`. If the start parameter is zero (meaning you rezzed it directly), it simply turns the particle system off.

When the fireworks prim is rezzed (or the script is saved or reset), `state_entry()` calls the `init()` function with a *delay* parameter. `init()` turns on physics and makes the prim phantom so it won't hit anything—for example your avatar waiting to catch the fireworks. (Isn't *SL* fun?) It then sets a timer based on the *delay* parameter to wait before starting the particle system. *delay* is 5 (for 0.5 seconds) when the fireworks are rezzed by an avatar, and *delay* is based on the start parameter when the fireworks are rezzed by the fireworks cannon.

Did you notice the one deliberately planted "bug"? The `PSYS_PART_END_SCALE` isn't the same size as the `PSYS_PART_START_SCALE`. However, if you run this script as is, the particles won't change size. This bug is the kind of thing that can trip you up frequently—Appendix B suggests some of the things to look for. In this case, the `PSYS_PART_INTERP_SCALE_MASK` was not set, so the particle system won't change the size of the particles.

As a second example, Listing 9.2 shows a fireworks ball materializing in a huge sphere. The most significant difference between Listings 9.1 and 9.2 is that the pattern is `PSYS_SRC_PATTERN_ANGLE_CONE`. The cone pattern allows you to control the `PSYS_SRC_BURST_RADIUS` of where the particles materialize; in comparison, the explode pattern from Listing 9.1 ignores radius.

Listing 9.2: Fireworks—A Big Ball of Small, Slow-Moving Particles

```
fireworks()
{
    // Based on Listing B.1 in App. B. Unchanged values removed to save trees
    // Default values indicated with //
    llParticleSystem( [
        PSYS_PART_FLAGS, PSYS_PART_INTERP_COLOR_MASK | PSYS_PART_EMISSIVE_MASK,
    //Appearance
        PSYS_PART_START_SCALE,    <0.25, 0.25, 0.0>, // <1,1,0>
        PSYS_PART_START_COLOR,    <0.0, 0.8, 0.0>,   // <1,1,1>
        PSYS_PART_END_COLOR,      <1.0, 0.0, 0.0>,   // <1,1,1>
    //Flow
        PSYS_PART_MAX_AGE,          5.0,  // 10.00,
        PSYS_SRC_BURST_RATE,        1.0,  // 0.10,
        PSYS_SRC_BURST_PART_COUNT, 4000, // 1,
    //Placement
        PSYS_SRC_PATTERN,         PSYS_SRC_PATTERN_ANGLE_CONE, // DROP,
        PSYS_SRC_BURST_RADIUS, 5.0,                  // 0.00,
        PSYS_SRC_ANGLE_BEGIN,  0.00,
        PSYS_SRC_ANGLE_END,    PI,                   // 0.00,
    //Movement
        PSYS_SRC_BURST_SPEED_MIN, 1.75, // 1.00,
        PSYS_SRC_BURST_SPEED_MAX, 2.0,  // 1.00,
        PSYS_SRC_ACCEL,          < 0.00, 0.00, -0.25 > // <0,0,0>
    ]);
    llSleep(0.2);
}
// the rest of script is the same as Listing 9.1
```

Because this script aims to create a complete sphere of particles, it specifies the `PSYS_SRC_ANGLE_BEGIN` at its minimum value of 0.0, and `PSYS_SRC_ANGLE_END` at its maximum value of π (`PI`). Figure B.2 in Appendix B explains how these angles affect where particles are emitted.

You might notice this particle system appears to try to manage 20,000 particles (age × part count ÷ rate = 5.0 × 4,000 ÷ 1.0). However, because the particle system is killed after its first (and only) emission, only 4,000 particles are created. If other particles are in view, this value still might be too much: *Second Life* viewers are usually configured to draw at most 4,096 particles, so some users might not see all the particles that are emitted. If you want a big barrage of different fireworks to be visible, you might want to limit this value even further.

Pulling together a suite of different fireworks is fun, but then you have to display them. Borrow the cannon you built for Chapter 7, "Physics and Vehicles," and place the code from Listing 9.3 in it, along with an object containing each of the fireworks scripts you wrote.

CHAPTER 1
CHAPTER 2
CHAPTER 3
CHAPTER 4
CHAPTER 5
CHAPTER 6
CHAPTER 7
CHAPTER 8

CHAPTER 9

CHAPTER 10
CHAPTER 11
CHAPTER 12
CHAPTER 13
CHAPTER 14
CHAPTER 15
APPENDICES

PARTICLE
EFFECTS

TEXTURE
ANIMATION

LIGHT

SUMMARY

Listing 9.3: Fireworks Cannon

```
default
{
    touch_start(integer total_number) {
        vector rootRot = llRot2Euler(llGetRootRotation());
        vector mod = <llFrand(-0.2), llFrand(0.2), 0> + <0, -0.1, 0>;
        rotation rot = llEuler2Rot( rootRot + mod );

        integer n = llGetInventoryNumber( INVENTORY_OBJECT );
        integer choice = llFloor( llFrand(n) );
        string name = llGetInventoryName(INVENTORY_OBJECT,choice);
        llRezObject(name, llGetPos(), <0,0,15>*rot, ZERO_ROTATION, 12);
    }
}
```

👁 NOTE

When you make changes to a particle script, be sure the emitter is managing no more than 4,096 particles at any one time (age × burst count ÷ rate). If you want to make sure you're under the limit, add this code to the script:

```
integer numParticles = 1000;
float age = 10.0;           // you can also use these vars in the
float burstRate = 0.1;      // call to llParticleSystem()
integer total = (age * numParticles) / burstRate;
llOwnerSay("This emitter manages "+(string)total+" particles");
```

Each time someone touches the cannon, it shoots one ball of fireworks. The cannon first selects a direction: the current rotation plus a little randomness (just in case the physics engine was too stable for your taste). The root prim of the cannon at SYW HQ is the barrel (a cylinder), oriented so the y value corresponds to left/right, and the x value corresponds to up. The randomness vector, *mod*, allows an additional 0.2 radians in vertical lift, and ±0.1 radians left or right.

Then the script selects a ball of fireworks to shoot: it checks how many objects are in its inventory (n) then picks a random number less than n. It uses `llRezObject()` to rez the object using a velocity of `<0,0,15>` times the desired direction, *rot*. (The "Using Quaternions" section of Chapter 4, "Making and Moving Objects," explains the concept of rotations thoroughly.)

Figure 9.2 shows a fireworks display over SYW HQ.

Figure 9.2: Try out the fireworks display on the roof of SYW HQ. You can contribute your own scripts by dropping notecards in the mailbox at the front door.

A RAINBOW

Rainbows have been a symbol of promise, hope, and life for thousands of years. Particles are a fabulous way to re-create the ephemeral, glowing nature of a rainbow.

Color interpolation in particle scripts goes approximately around the color wheel: red to orange to yellow to green to blue to purple and back to red (or vice versa). You can't, therefore, create a rainbow with only one emitter: if you make the start color purple and the final color red, you'll get a rainbow that goes from red to reddish-purple to purple. The full official rainbow sequence of red, orange, yellow, green, blue, indigo, and violet needs two particle emitters: one for the reds, oranges and yellows (ROY), and one for the greens, blues, indigos, and violets (GBIV), yielding the rainbow shown in Figure 9.3.

CHAPTER 1
CHAPTER 2
CHAPTER 3
CHAPTER 4
CHAPTER 5
CHAPTER 6
CHAPTER 7
CHAPTER 8

CHAPTER 9

CHAPTER 10
CHAPTER 11
CHAPTER 12
CHAPTER 13
CHAPTER 14
CHAPTER 15
APPENDICES

Figure 9.3: This rainbow uses two particle emitters: one for the ROY colors and one for the GBIV colors.

 BUILD NOTE

Create a sphere and copy it. Make the second one slightly smaller than the first. Place the code from Listing 9.4 in one sphere, and the code from Listing 9.4 modified for the reds and yellows in the other. Place both spheres at exactly the same location and link them.

Listing 9.4 shows the particle emitter for the GBIV spectrum in a small rainbow. The `PSYS_SRC_PATTERN_ANGLE` ensures they're emitted in a flat plane, while the rainbow's arc is a half sphere above the emitter.

Listing 9.4: Rainbow—Green, Blue, Indigo, and Violet

```
integer NUM_PARTICLES_PER_RADIAN = 50;
float RAINBOW_ARC = PI_BY_TWO;

startRainbowGBIV()
{
    integer numParticles = (integer)(RAINBOW_ARC * NUM_PARTICLES_PER_RADIAN);
    // Based on Listing B.1. Unchanged values removed to save trees
    // Default values indicated with //
    llParticleSystem( [
        PSYS_PART_FLAGS, PSYS_PART_INTERP_COLOR_MASK | // change color
                         PSYS_PART_INTERP_SCALE_MASK | // let it grow
                         PSYS_PART_FOLLOW_VELOCITY_MASK, // x direction
```

PARTICLE
EFFECTS

TEXTURE
ANIMATION

LIGHT

SUMMARY

```
    //Appearance
        PSYS_PART_START_SCALE, <0.75, 0.3, 0.0>,    // <1,1,0>,
        PSYS_PART_END_SCALE,   <1.00, 0.3, 0.0>,    // <1,1,0>,
        PSYS_PART_START_COLOR, <1.0, 0.0, 1.0>,     // <1,1,1>,
        PSYS_PART_END_COLOR,   <0.0, 1.0, 0.0>,     // <1,1,1>,
        PSYS_PART_START_ALPHA, 0.8,  // 1.00,
        PSYS_PART_END_ALPHA,   0.8,  // 1.00,
    //Flow
        PSYS_PART_MAX_AGE,          10.0,           // 10.00,
        PSYS_SRC_BURST_RATE,        0.2,            // 0.10,
        PSYS_SRC_BURST_PART_COUNT, numParticles, // 1,
    //Placement
        PSYS_SRC_PATTERN, PSYS_SRC_PATTERN_ANGLE, // DROP,
        PSYS_SRC_BURST_RADIUS, 1.0,                 // 0.00,
        PSYS_SRC_ANGLE_BEGIN,  0.0,                 // 0.00,
        PSYS_SRC_ANGLE_END,  RAINBOW_ARC,           // 0.00,
    //Movement
        PSYS_SRC_BURST_SPEED_MIN, 0.1,  // 1.00,
        PSYS_SRC_BURST_SPEED_MAX, 0.1   // 1.00,
    ]);
}

default {
    state_entry() {
        llSetAlpha(ALL_SIDES,0);
        startRainbowGBIV();
    }
}
```

The inside of the arc is 1.0m from the center of the emitter and the initial color is purple. By the time the particles' lifespan is over (10 seconds), they will be green and will have moved 1.0 meter (10 seconds × 0.1 m/s) farther from the emitter. If they had no velocity you wouldn't get the nice banding of color in the rainbow.

Notice the particle shape. The particles are wide in the **x** direction and narrow in the **y** direction. The width helps reduce the number of particles while still appearing connected, while the narrowness controls the width of the band of color. Notice also that the particles get a bit larger the farther away they are from the emitter, because longer straight lines won't cross over into other colors. The **PSYS_PART_ FOLLOW_VELOCITY_MASK** ensures the particles will orient correctly.

You will sometimes see particles described as **2D sprites**: you don't need to specify the **z** component of particle scale because the particles have no visual depth. To see for yourself what this means, create your rainbow and view it from one end. You'll get a result something like what's shown in Figure 9.4.

 NOTE

A *sprite* is an axis-aligned textured polygon, meaning it always points its x-axis to face the camera.

Figure 9.4: Particles are 2D sprites that turn to face the viewer. This behavior is obvious when looking at a rainbow from the side.

CHAPTER 1
CHAPTER 2
CHAPTER 3
CHAPTER 4
CHAPTER 5
CHAPTER 6
CHAPTER 7
CHAPTER 8

CHAPTER 9

CHAPTER 10
CHAPTER 11
CHAPTER 12
CHAPTER 13
CHAPTER 14
CHAPTER 15
APPENDICES

The particle emitter for the rainbow's yellows and reds is almost identical to Listing 9.4. The innermost color is yellow and the outermost color is red. The radius is a bit farther out than the GBIV emitter—just far enough to look like it is one smooth movement from purple all the way to red. The parameters that you need to change are as follows:

```
PSYS_PART_START_SCALE, <1.0, 0.3, 0.0>,
PSYS_PART_END_SCALE,   <1.5, 0.3, 0.0>,
PSYS_PART_START_COLOR, <1.0, 1.0, 0.0>,
PSYS_PART_END_COLOR,   <1.0, 0.2, 0.0>,
PSYS_SRC_BURST_RADIUS, 2.0,
```

The maximum value for `PSYS_SRC_BURST_RADIUS` is 50 meters, which is a nice, big rainbow. The rainbow in Figure 9.3 has a radius of 15 meters. The script uses 2 meters. As you increase the radius you also need to increase particle size (but you do not need to change burst part count).

An interesting observation in Listing 9.4 is that you don't need an `on_rez`() event handler. Because particles are a persistent feature of the prim, when the particle system starts the particles stay until turned off. Even if you delete the script and put them in inventory they will emit particles when you take them out of inventory later.

 ## KITE STRING

If you've ever wanted to build a kite in **SL** you may have realized it would be hard to build the string using prims. Prims have a maximum length of 10m, and flexiprims can be attached at only one end. The trick to making string (and many other things that appear flexible but are attached at both ends) is using particles with a target location.

The kite in Figure 9.5 uses two scripts in the same prim: one to generate the particles and one to manage the physics of flying. This modularity is a good way to create and manage scripts, to help with efficiency and parallel execution, and to make multiple things seem to happen at once.

CHAPTER 9

PARTICLE
EFFECTS

TEXTURE
ANIMATION

LIGHT

SUMMARY

Figure 9.5: Particles make a realistic-looking string.

BUILD NOTE

The kite in Figure 9.5 needs four prims: one for the spool and three for the kite (the tail, the kite body, and the cross stick). The tail here is a torus: *size* = <2.0, 0.5, 0.25>, *holesize* = <0.05, 0.05, 0.0>, *radiusoffset* = 0.947, *revolutions* = 4.0, and *skew* = 0.8. The kite body is a cube: *size* = <0.5, 0.01, 0.46> and *topshear* = <0.5, 0, 0>. The cross stick is a cube to which the string "ties." When you link these three prims, the cross stick should be the root; make sure it is oriented so that its x-axis orients down toward the spool. Place the code from Listings 9.5 and 9.6 in the inventory of the cross stick.

The fourth prim is a completely unscripted object of any shape, named KiteSpool, that you place in the inventory of the cross stick along with the two scripts.

If you want to create a flexiprim tail, see the "Physics and Flexiprims" sidebar in Chapter 7.

Listing 9.5 contains the script for the kite's string. When it hears a SPOOL_REZZED link message it initiates the particle system. Any other message turns off the particles. The link_message() handler contains the spool's key in the *id* parameter and passes it as a parameter to makeString(). This key is then used as a parameter to the llParticleSystem() call, defining the PSYS_SRC_TARGET_KEY.

Listing 9.5: The Kite String

```
string SPOOL_REZZED = "SpoolRezzed";

makeString(key targetID) {
    // Based on Listing B.1. Unchanged values removed to save trees
    integer FollowSrcMask      = TRUE; // move with emitter
    integer FollowVelocityMask = TRUE; // turn to face
    integer WindMask           = TRUE; // let wind blow string
    integer TargetPosMask      = TRUE; // head to the spool
    integer ScaleMask          = TRUE; // grow
    llParticleSystem([
      PSYS_PART_FLAGS, (
          (            WindMask * PSYS_PART_WIND_MASK ) |
          (      FollowSrcMask * PSYS_PART_FOLLOW_SRC_MASK ) |
          ( FollowVelocityMask * PSYS_PART_FOLLOW_VELOCITY_MASK ) |
          (          ScaleMask * PSYS_PART_INTERP_SCALE_MASK ) |
          (      TargetPosMask * PSYS_PART_TARGET_POS_MASK ) ),
```

```
        //Appearance
        PSYS_PART_START_SCALE,   < 0.04, 0.2, 0.0>,   // <1,1,0>
        PSYS_PART_END_SCALE,     < 0.04, 1.00, 0.0>,  // <1,1,0>
        PSYS_PART_END_ALPHA,     1.0,                 // 0.0
        //Flow
        PSYS_PART_MAX_AGE,           5.00,    // 10.0
        PSYS_SRC_BURST_RATE,         0.05,    // 0.10
        PSYS_SRC_BURST_PART_COUNT, 1,         // 1
        //Placement
        PSYS_SRC_PATTERN,        PSYS_SRC_PATTERN_ANGLE, // DROP
        //Movement
        PSYS_SRC_BURST_SPEED_MIN, 1.00,       // 1.0
        PSYS_SRC_BURST_SPEED_MAX, 1.00,       // 10.0
        PSYS_SRC_TARGET_KEY,        targetID   // llGetKey()
    ]);
}
default
{
    state_entry() {
        llParticleSystem([]);
    }
    on_rez(integer param) {
        llResetScript();
    }
    link_message(integer sender,integer num, string str, key id) {
        if (str==SPOOL_REZZED) {
            makeString( id );
        } else {
            llParticleSystem([]);
        }
    }
}
```

CHAPTER 1
CHAPTER 2
CHAPTER 3
CHAPTER 4
CHAPTER 5
CHAPTER 6
CHAPTER 7
CHAPTER 8
CHAPTER 9
CHAPTER 10
CHAPTER 11
CHAPTER 12
CHAPTER 13
CHAPTER 14
CHAPTER 15
APPENDICES

Similar to the rainbow, these string particles are long and skinny. However, in the kite string the skinny dimension is in the x-axis, so the `PSYS_PART_FOLLOW_VELOCITY_MASK` makes the string appear to drop out of the cross stick and travel to the `PSYS_SRC_TARGET_KEY`. The `PSYS_PART_WIND_MASK` makes the string appear to blow a bit in the wind. The `PSYS_PART_FOLLOW_SRC_MASK` adds a little more realism, in that the particles move relative to the kite, thereby appearing to stay connected.

The script that manages the kite's movement is shown in Listing 9.6. The `state_entry()` handler turns on physics and tells the kite to start floating with a call to `llMoveToTarget()`. This script also sets up an `at_target()` event handler that rezzes the spool when the kite has actually started floating.

Listing 9.6: The Flying Kite

```
string  SPOOL = "KiteSpool";
string  SPOOL_REZZED = "SpoolRezzed";
float   SENSOR_INTERVAL = 5.0;
float   MAX_SPOOL_DIST = 50.0;
float   MAX_WIND_STRENGTH = 0.75; // ratio of VecMag(wind) to string len

key       gSpoolID;
vector    gStartPos;
rotation  gStartRot;
float     gSpoolDistance = 5.0; // could listen to Chat to change
integer   gInitialKitePosHandle;
```

CHAPTER 9

▶ PARTICLE
EFFECTS

▶ TEXTURE
ANIMATION

LIGHT

SUMMARY

```
default {
    state_entry() {
        llSetStatus(STATUS_PHYSICS, TRUE);
        llSleep(0.1);
        gStartPos = llGetPos();
        gStartRot = llGetRot();
        vector targetPos = gStartPos + <0,0,2>; // float in the air
        llMoveToTarget( targetPos, 2.0 );
        gInitialKitePosHandle = llTarget( targetPos, 1.0 );
    }
    on_rez(integer param) {
        llResetScript();
    }
    at_target( integer targetHandle, vector targPos, vector currPos ) {
        if (targetHandle == gInitialKitePosHandle) {
            llRezObject(SPOOL,gStartPos, ZERO_VECTOR,ZERO_ROTATION, 1);
            llTargetRemove( gInitialKitePosHandle );
        }
    }
    object_rez(key id) {
        // message to other script in same prim
        llMessageLinked(llGetLinkNumber(), 0, SPOOL_REZZED, id);
        gSpoolID = id;
        llSensorRepeat(SPOOL, id, PASSIVE|ACTIVE, MAX_SPOOL_DIST,
                        TWO_PI, SENSOR_INTERVAL);
    }

    no_sensor() {
        llSay(0,"The spool has vanished. Returning home.");
        llSetStatus(STATUS_PHYSICS, FALSE);
        llMessageLinked(llGetLinkNumber(), 0, "", NULL_KEY);
        llSetPos(gStartPos); // or use moveTo() from Listing 2.4
        llSetRot(gStartRot);
        llSensorRemove();
    }
    sensor(integer num) {
        vector spoolPos = llDetectedPos(0);
        vector windDir = llWind( spoolPos );
        windDir.z = 0;
        float windStrength = llVecMag(windDir);
        if (windStrength > (gSpoolDistance * MAX_WIND_STRENGTH)) {
            windStrength = gSpoolDistance * MAX_WIND_STRENGTH;
        }
        float theta = llAsin( windStrength / gSpoolDistance );
        float height = gSpoolDistance * llCos( theta );
        vector posOffset = <windDir.x, windDir.y, height>;

        llMoveToTarget( spoolPos+posOffset, SENSOR_INTERVAL );
        llLookAt ( spoolPos, 1.0, 1.0 );
    }
}
```

When the spool has successfully rezzed, the `object_rez()` event is triggered; the *id* parameter contains the spool's key. The script sends out a link message announcing the spool's *id*. The message goes to all scripts in the same prim, namely those with the same `llGetLinkNumber()`.

Then the script sets up a periodic sensor repeat, looking for objects that are PASSIVE|ACTIVE. Although the spool is a completely passive object, you will probably want to be able to move it around; that motion makes the object active. While in general `llSensorRepeat()` is computationally expensive, this one is restricted to looking *only* for objects with a specific key. More information on sensing is found in Chapter 5, "Sensing the World."

When the kite fails to sense the spool, it returns to its initial location, turns off the sensor, and tells other scripts the spool has vanished. When a spool is detected, the `sensor()` event triggers and calculates the wind information at the spool's location. (More information about wind can be found in Chapter 10's "Air, Earth, Water, and Weather" section.) The strength of the wind determines how high the kite needs to fly: the stronger the wind, the lower the kite flies. The `sensor()` event uses a cap of `MAX_WIND_STRENGTH` to ensure the kite stays afloat. It then tells the kite to move to that target location and to rotate to look at the spool. `llLookAt()` is very specifically expecting the kite's root prim to be oriented so that its x-axis points correctly toward the spool.

You could augment this script by allowing users to change the string's length. Additionally, if you want your kite to travel with you, you will need to wear the spool. Because sensors cannot detect objects that are attached to an avatar, you will need to augment the scripts with communication: have the spool tell the kite where it is. You will also need to make sure the kite doesn't try to fly across sim boundaries or into parcels that don't allow outside objects; use `llGetParcelFlags()` and check for the flag `PARCEL_FLAG_ALLOW_ALL_OBJECT_ENTRY`.

CHAPTER 1
CHAPTER 2
CHAPTER 3
CHAPTER 4
CHAPTER 5
CHAPTER 6
CHAPTER 7
CHAPTER 8

CHAPTER 9

CHAPTER 10
CHAPTER 11
CHAPTER 12
CHAPTER 13
CHAPTER 14
CHAPTER 15
APPENDICES

TEXTURE ANIMATION

Texture placement, replacement, and animation are at the core of breathing life into textures. A prim's `PRIM_TEXTURE` property can be set with `llSetPrimitiveParams()` or retrieved with `llGetPrimitiveParams()`. Several other texture functions are available (many of which you've seen in other places in this book); these are shown in Table 9.1.

TABLE 9.1: FUNCTIONS THAT CONTROL TEXTURES

Function	Behavior
`string llGetTexture(integer face)`	Returns a string that is the name of the texture on `face`.
`llSetTexture(string texture, integer face)`	Sets the texture on the chosen `face` to the texture specified by `texture`, which is the name or the UUID.
`llRotateTexture(float rotation, integer face)`	Sets the texture `rotation` for the chosen `face`, in radians.
`llScaleTexture(float x, float y, integer face)`	Sets the texture `x` and `y` scales for the chosen `face`.
`vector llGetTextureOffset(integer face)`	Returns a vector that is the texture offset of `face` in the `x` and `y` components. The `z` component is ignored.
`float llGetTextureRot(integer side)`	Returns a float that is the texture rotation of `side`.
`vector llGetTextureScale(integer side)`	Returns a vector that is the texture scale of `side` in the `x` and `y` components.
`llOffsetTexture(float x, float y, integer face)`	Sets the texture `x` and `y` offsets for the chosen `face`.
`llSetLinkTexture(integer linknumber, string texture, integer face)`	Sets the `texture` on the chosen `face` of the prim with the specified `linknumber`.

The idea of texture *animation* is to move a texture in interesting ways to make it appear as though the object is moving. You simply choose an appropriate texture, then animate it to give the appearance of motion or change. (Linden Lab supplies an excellent assortment of textures in your Inventory's free

PARTICLE
EFFECTS

 TEXTURE
ANIMATION

LIGHT

SUMMARY

Library folder.) Animation might mean "jiggling" a single image (as in Chapter 6's water), or it might mean playing a sequence of "frames" in a movie (as in Listing 2.11's keyboard animator).

In some situations texture animation is a must. For instance, a combination of different particle effects must be complemented with a texture animation to make a volcano such as the one shown in Figure 9.6. A realistic volcano is hard to build—consider it your opportunity to enhance **SL**'s content by making more and more realistic ones!

Figure 9.6: This volcano at Lindeman's Design Beach <167, 123, 30> combines texture animation and particle effects to create a realistic volcano.

TEXTURE ANIMATION MODES

The function `llSetTextureAnim()` can do a variety of texture animations; it is flexible enough (and even intended) to power textures with multiple embedded frames. Figure 9.7 shows a texture often seen in campfires in **Second Life**. (Note that most graphics programs use the gray check pattern to indicate transparent areas of the image.) You may intuit why the arguments to `llSetTextureAnim()` have parameters for the number of rows (**x_frames**) and columns (**y_frames**) in the texture. For a texture like the flames, the "frames" need to be shown at a sufficiently rapid rate to create the well-known "persistence of vision" effect every filmgoer experiences. A digital slide show, in contrast, would have a very slow frame rate. `llSetTextureAnim()` can also rotate, slide, and zoom.

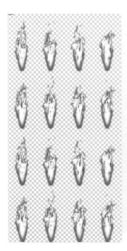

Figure 9.7: A four-by-four sequence of animations in a fire texture with a key of `150a5721-e27a-36f4-bf91-4d8d5ad781f7`.

Only one animation can be run per prim, although all sides of a prim can be animated at the same time by setting *face* to ALL_SIDES; the sides may have different textures, but will animate in the same way. llSetTextureAnim() works by changing the texture's scale and offset dynamically on the client side, overriding the server-side settings made with llScaleTexture() and the PRIM_TEXTURE component of llSetPrimitiveParams().

Seven *mode* flags (see Table 9.2) can be set for llSetTextureAnim(). These can be combined using the bitwise | operator, yielding interesting and complex results. However, there are four very different basic modes—Standard, Scale, Rotate, and Smooth—for llSetTextureAnim(). Because each mode causes quite different behavior and the parameters have different interpretations, each one is covered separately in this chapter. The Particle Laboratory, shown in Figure 9.8, demonstrates the complex effects of each of these values.

CHAPTER 1
CHAPTER 2
CHAPTER 3
CHAPTER 4
CHAPTER 5
CHAPTER 6
CHAPTER 7
CHAPTER 8

CHAPTER 9

CHAPTER 10
CHAPTER 11
CHAPTER 12
CHAPTER 13
CHAPTER 14
CHAPTER 15
APPENDICES

TABLE 9.2: MODE FLAGS FOR llSetTextureAnim()

Mode Flag	Value	Behavior
ANIM_ON	0x01	Turn on/off texture animation.
LOOP	0x02	Continuously loop the animation (or frames in the animation).
REVERSE	0x04	Play the animation (or frames in the animation) in reverse direction.
PING_PONG	0x08	Play the animation (or its frames) going forward, then backward.
SMOOTH	0x10	*Standard mode:* Slide in the x direction instead of playing separate frames. *Rotate or Scale mode:* Smoothly transition between ROTATE and SCALE animations.
ROTATE	0x20	Animate the texture rotation. Does not work with SCALE.
SCALE	0x40	Animate the texture scale. Does not work with ROTATE.

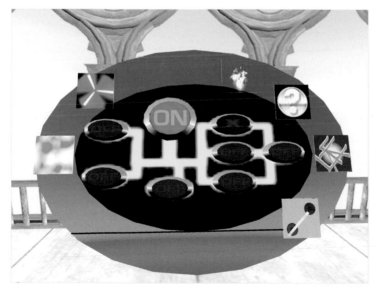

Figure 9.8: The interactive display at the Particle Laboratory allows you to explore the effects of all the convoluted combinations of the mode flags in Table 9.2. This demo is currently at Teal <245, 35, 291>, but you'll have to go searching for it; you can't teleport directly there.

Texture Animation: Standard Mode

The standard mode for llSetTextureAnim() plays the frames in the texture like a movie.

PARTICLE
EFFECTS

TEXTURE
ANIMATION

LIGHT

SUMMARY

DEFINITION

```
llSetTextureAnim(integer mode, integer face,
                 integer x_frames, integer y_frames,
                 float start, float length, float rate)
```

Standard mode. Animates the texture on the specified *face* at the specified *rate*. The texture is assumed to be a sequence of frames to be displayed like a movie, laid out in rows and columns specified by *x_frames* and *y_frames*, like the textures shown in Figures 9.7 and 9.9. The animation is row-wise, not column-wise.

> *mode* — ANIM_ON, plus optionally any combination of LOOP, REVERSE, or PING_PONG. (Not SMOOTH, ROTATE, or SCALE).
>
> *face* — Face number or ALL_SIDES.
>
> *x_frames* — Number of horizontal frames. Maximum value is 255.
>
> *y_frames* — Number of vertical frames. Maximum value is 255.
>
> *start* — Start position or frame number. The top-left corner is number 0.
>
> *length* — Number of frames to display. Setting *length* to 0 means animate all frames.
>
> *rate* — Frames per second. Must not be 0. Too high a value will be throttled to a lower-than-specified rate. Negative values are treated as a positive value with the REVERSE flag.

Chapter 2's keyboard texture (Listing 2.11) used the standard animation mode, as does the script in Listing 9.7, which shows the canonical example of how to create a fire for your firepit, campfire, or fireplace. This script puts the fire on the front and back of the prim, and animates the 4×4 texture at a rate of four frames per second. If the script didn't make the thin tops and sides completely transparent, you would be able to see just a thin suggestion of the texture on those sides. As that can be rather disconcerting, transparency is preferred.

Listing 9.7 Animating a Campfire

```
key fireTexture = "150a5721-e27a-36f4-bf91-4d8d5ad781f7";
default {
    state_entry() {
        llSetAlpha(0,ALL_SIDES);
        llSetAlpha(1,1);
        llSetAlpha(1,3);
        llSetTexture(fireTexture, ALL_SIDES);
        llSetTextureAnim(ANIM_ON | LOOP, // mode
                         ALL_SIDES,      // side
                         4, 4,           // x_frames, y_frames
                         0, 0,           // start, length frame
                         4);             // frame rate
    }
    on_rez( integer _n ) {
        llResetScript();
    }
}
```

CHAPTER 1
CHAPTER 2
CHAPTER 3
CHAPTER 4
CHAPTER 5
CHAPTER 6
CHAPTER 7
CHAPTER 8
CHAPTER 9
CHAPTER 10
CHAPTER 11
CHAPTER 12
CHAPTER 13
CHAPTER 14
CHAPTER 15
APPENDICES

BUILD NOTE

Create a cube of size <0.5, 0.01, 0.5> and place the code from Listing 9.7 in its inventory. Add your texture if you would prefer to use its name rather than its key. (If you use your texture's name rather than its key, a copy of the texture must be in your object's inventory.) Make two copies of the cube; all three copies should have the same position. Rotate one cube 60 degrees around the z-axis, and one cube 120 degrees around it, as shown in the image below, where an animated campfire is visible from all directions. The three prims will now look like an asterisk from above. Link them.

Texture Animation: Scale Mode

The second important mode for `llSetTextureAnim()` is the SCALE mode, which changes the size of the texture. The texture is no longer treated as a sequence of frames. This snippet zooms *out* from a single copy of the texture to nine copies, duplicating the original frame into a three-by-three-frame matrix:

```
llSetTextureAnim(ANIM_ON | LOOP | SMOOTH | SCALE,
                 ALL_SIDES, 1, 1, // side, ignored, ignored
                 1, 2,            // startRepeats, addRepeats
                 1);              // frame rate
```

In contrast, this snippet—with only one small difference— zooms *in* from three copies to one copy:

```
llSetTextureAnim(ANIM_ON | LOOP | SMOOTH | SCALE | REVERSE,
                 ALL_SIDES, 1, 1, // side, ignored, ignored
                 1, 2,            // startRepeats, addRepeats
                 1);              // frame rate
```

Note that very similar behavior can be achieved using negative values for the *startRepeats* value:

```
llSetTextureAnim(ANIM_ON | LOOP | SMOOTH | SCALE,
                 ALL_SIDES, 1, 1, // side, ignored, ignored
                 -3, 2,           // startRepeats, addRepeats
                 1);              // frame rate
```

The key difference is that the last snippet turns the texture upside down. Essentially, when the REVERSE flag is not used, then

- if *startRepeats* > 0, the final repeats-per-face value is
  start + llAbs(*length*).
- if *startRepeats* < 0, the final repeats-per-face value is
  llAbs(*start* - llAbs(*length*)).

In most instances, it is easier to use the REVERSE flag.

PARTICLE
EFFECTS

 TEXTURE
ANIMATION

LIGHT

SUMMARY

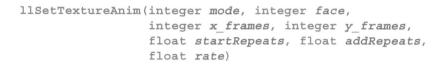

DEFINITION

```
llSetTextureAnim(integer mode, integer face,
                integer x_frames, integer y_frames,
                float startRepeats, float addRepeats,
                float rate)
```

SCALE mode. Causes the texture to zoom in or out at the specified *rate*. It always zooms toward or away from the center. In SCALE | SMOOTH mode, the zoom is smooth.

mode — ANIM_ON | SCALE, plus optionally any combination of LOOP, REVERSE, PING_PONG, or SMOOTH (not ROTATE).

face — Face number or ALL_SIDES.

x_frames — Ignored.

y_frames — Ignored.

startRepeats — Number of repeats per face of the texture at the beginning of the animation. The REVERSE flag will zoom in. A negative value will also zoom in, but turns the texture upside down.

addRepeats — If the REVERSE flag is not used, this is the number of repeats per face to *add* to the *startRepeats* value over the course of the animation. If the REVERSE flag is set, this is the number of repeats per face to *subtract* from the *startRepeats* value. The function ignores the negative sign.

rate — Animation speed, in integer scale changes per second. Does not work well for non-integer values of *start* and *length* unless the SMOOTH flag is also being used. Negative values are treated as positive values with the REVERSE flag.

Texture Animation: Rotate Mode

The third mode for llSetTextureAnim() is the ROTATE mode, which causes the texture to rotate. This mode is commonly used for making wheels that appear to turn. The following snippet makes a smooth, slow, continuous rotation all the way around the circle:

```
llSetTextureAnim(ANIM_ON | ROTATE | LOOP | SMOOTH,
        ALL_SIDES, 1, 1, 0, 2*PI, 1);
```

You want to make sure the wheel spins faster or slower depending on its speed.

DEFINITION

```
llSetTextureAnim(integer mode, integer face,
                integer x_frames, integer y_frames,
                float startAngle, float endAngle,
                float rate)
```

ROTATE mode. Causes the texture to rotate at the specified *rate*. In ROTATE | SMOOTH mode, the rotation is smooth.

mode — ANIM_ON | ROTATE, plus optionally any combination of LOOP, REVERSE, PING_PONG, or SMOOTH (not SCALE).

    face — Face number or ALL_SIDES.

    x_frames — Ignored.

    y_frames — Ignored.

    startAngle — The beginning angle, in radians.

    endAngle — The ending angle, in radians. An *endAngle* of TWO_PI indicates a full circle.

    rate — Animation speed in radians per second. Negative values will cause the texture to rotate in the opposite direction.

CHAPTER 1
CHAPTER 2
CHAPTER 3
CHAPTER 4
CHAPTER 5
CHAPTER 6
CHAPTER 7
CHAPTER 8

CHAPTER 10
CHAPTER 11
CHAPTER 12
CHAPTER 13
CHAPTER 14
CHAPTER 15
APPENDICES

Texture Animation: Smooth Mode

The fourth mode for `llSetTextureAnim()` is the SMOOTH mode. SMOOTH mode can also be used in conjunction with ROTATE or SCALE to make them work smoothly. When used by itself, SMOOTH mode scrolls the texture smoothly along the x-axis. Chapter 6's texture animations used SMOOTH mode, which is demonstrated here:

```
llSetTextureAnim( ANIM_ON | SMOOTH | LOOP, ALL_SIDES, 1, 1, 1.0, 1, 0.05);
```

DEFINITION

```
llSetTextureAnim(integer mode, integer face,
                 integer x_proportion, integer y_proportion,
                 float start, float length, float rate)
```

SMOOTH mode. This mode moves the texture smoothly between one frame and the next. In standard mode it scrolls in the x direction. (For smooth scrolling in the y direction on a prim, rotate the texture 90 degrees.)

    mode — ANIM_ON | SMOOTH, plus optionally any combination of LOOP, REVERSE, or PING_PONG (not ROTATE or SCALE).

    face — Face number or ALL_SIDES.

    x_proportion — 1/*x_proportion* of the texture will be seen at any one time.

    y_proportion — 1/*y_proportion* of the texture will be seen at any one time. In general, set to 1 or the number of rows. If *y_proportion* is greater than 1, the texture will scroll in rows; instantaneous (non-smooth) transitions happen from row to row.

    start — Start position or frame number. The top-left corner is number 0.

    length — Number of frames to display. Setting *length* to 0 means animate all frames.

    rate — Animation speed, in frames per second.

PARTICLE
EFFECTS

 TEXTURE
ANIMATION

LIGHT

SUMMARY

 # PICTURE FRAME

Another fun thing to do with texture animation is to make an electronic picture frame. One way is to create a single texture with multiple frames that you play at a slow rate, such as the one shown in Figure 9.9. With this approach, however, the set of images is fixed; you can't easily add another one.

Figure 9.9: You can create a digital picture frame by animating a single texture with multiple frames. However, you won't be able to add new textures.

The scripts in this section show a second approach: they grab textures in the object's inventory. This approach has a couple of variations. The variation you'll see in many places in **SL** has one big problem: it takes **time** for textures to load. The trick is to use prims that are invisible while they "preload" a texture, and then turn visible to show the image. If you create multiple prims, they can alternate preload and display to make an instantaneous transition between images.

 ## BUILD NOTE

The picture frame you'll create uses three prims; the root prim is the frame. Insert all the textures and the code from Listing 9.8 into the root prim's inventory. The script sets the hollow and cut, but not its size or rotation (so the user can adjust it). The image will appear in the frame's x-y plane (so make the z-axis the short one).

The two "image" prims are simply cubes. Place the code from Listing 9.9 in each one. You do not need to size, texture, or even place these—the script handles it all. Link the three prims together.

Listing 9.8 manages the frame and the inventory list. The `state_entry()` event handler calls `initFrame()` to set the prim parameters to create a hole in the middle of the frame (*hollow*) and taper the edges of the frame to make it look more like a real frame (*taper_b*). Other PRIM_TYPE_BOX parameters are their default values; Appendix A provides further explanation.

Listing 9.8: The Frame (Root Prim)

CHAPTER 1
CHAPTER 2
CHAPTER 3
CHAPTER 4
CHAPTER 5
CHAPTER 6
CHAPTER 7
CHAPTER 8

CHAPTER 10
CHAPTER 11
CHAPTER 12
CHAPTER 13
CHAPTER 14
CHAPTER 15
APPENDICES

```
float HOLLOW_SIZE = 0.75;

integer gNumTextures;
list gTextures;
integer gCurrentTexture;
integer gWhichFrame;

initFrame()
{
    float hollow = HOLLOW_SIZE;
    vector cut = <0,1.0,0>;
    vector twist = <0,0,0>;
    vector taper_b = <0.85,0.85,0>;   // a basic cube would be <1,1,0>
    vector topshear = <0.0,0.0,0>;
    llSetPrimitiveParams( [PRIM_TYPE, PRIM_TYPE_BOX, PRIM_HOLE_DEFAULT,
                           cut, hollow, twist, taper_b, topshear] );
}

default
{
    state_entry() {
        initFrame();
        gWhichFrame = 0;
        gNumTextures = llGetInventoryNumber( INVENTORY_TEXTURE );
        gCurrentTexture = 0;
        llSetTimerEvent(10);
    }
    on_rez(integer _n) {
        llResetScript();
    }
    timer() {
        string name = llGetInventoryName( INVENTORY_TEXTURE, gCurrentTexture );
        key id = llGetInventoryKey( name );
        vector size = llGetScale()*HOLLOW_SIZE;
        llMessageLinked(LINK_ALL_OTHERS, gWhichFrame, (string)size, id);
        gWhichFrame = !gWhichFrame;
        gCurrentTexture++;
        if (gCurrentTexture == gNumTextures) {
            gCurrentTexture = 0;
        }
    }
}
```

The work happens in the `timer()` event, which selects a texture from the inventory using `llGetInventoryName()` and iterates through however many textures were in the prim when the script was last reset. (Figure 9.10 shows a picture frame with a large suite of textures.) The `timer()` event then sends a linked message to the other prims. The parameter *gWhichFrame* alternates between 0 and 1, indicating which prim should load the texture. The third parameter, *size*, calculates how big the pictures need to be, based on the current size of the frame, `llGetScale()`, and how big the hollow is, HOLLOW_SIZE. The last parameter is the texture's key, *id*.

CHAPTER 9

PARTICLE
EFFECTS

 TEXTURE
ANIMATION

 LIGHT

SUMMARY

Figure 9.10: This digital picture frame has a long list of textures to display. Carefully managing prim position and transparency removes any apparent delays associated with loading textures.

 WARNING

`llGetInventoryKey()` works only on objects for which the script has *full* permissions. If you expect to be using textures for which your permissions are more limited, you'll need to change the script slightly so the texture's *name* is transmitted in `llMessageLinked()`; the receiver will have to parse the received message to separate the *size* from the *name*. This issue is problematic if you are building an object that will be sold: the textures in the object must be transferrable with full permissions.

Listing 9.9 manages the display of the images. The script manages the visibility of the prim and moves the visible prim to the front. (Technically, the move isn't necessary because the visibility trick will handle everything, but it will be useful for some of the extensions you'll see in a moment.)

Listing 9.9: The Images—One per Prim

```
default
{
    state_entry() {
        llSetPos(<0,0,0>);
        llSetLocalRot(llEuler2Rot(<0,0,PI>));
    }
    link_message(integer senderNum, integer num, string size, key id){
        vector v = (vector) size;
        float z = v.z / 2.0;
        if (num == llGetLinkNumber() - 2) {
            llSetPrimitiveParams(
                [PRIM_COLOR, ALL_SIDES, <1,1,1>, 0.0,
                 PRIM_POSITION, <0,0, -z>,
                 PRIM_SIZE, (vector)size,
                 PRIM_TEXTURE, ALL_SIDES, (string)id, <1,1,0>, <0,0,0>, 0.0]);
        } else {
            llSetPrimitiveParams(
                [PRIM_COLOR, ALL_SIDES, <1,1,1>, 1.0,
                 PRIM_POSITION, <0,0,z>,
                 PRIM_SIZE, (vector)size]);
        }
    }
}
```

Each of the two "image" prims contains a copy of Listing 9.9. The `state_entry()` handler simply places the prim at the same location as the frame.

When the message *num* matches the test, the script uses `llSetPrimitiveParams()` to do the following:

- Set the prim to transparent using `PRIM_COLOR`
- Move the prim to the back using `PRIM_POSITION`
- Resize the prim to what the root specified (in case the user changed the size of the frame) using `PRIM_SIZE`
- Tell the prim to load the texture using `PRIM_TEXTURE`

When the message *num* fails the test (meaning the other prim will be loading a texture), the script uses `llSetPrimitiveParams()` to make the prim visible, move it forward, and set the size.

Have fun with the various transitions you can make between images. For instance, you could make one image appear to "take over" the previous image with a zoom effect by making a texture with a 3×3 grid and placing the "real" image in the center, while the other 8 frames are transparent. The following snippet makes the texture zoom in from the full texture to the central 1/3:

CHAPTER 1
CHAPTER 2
CHAPTER 3
CHAPTER 4
CHAPTER 5
CHAPTER 6
CHAPTER 7
CHAPTER 8

```
llSetTextureAnim(ANIM_ON | LOOP | REVERSE | SMOOTH | SCALE,
            ALL_SIDES, 1, 1,  // side, ignored, ignored
            0.33, 0.66,       // startRepeats, addRepeats
            1);               // frame rate
```

CHAPTER 10
CHAPTER 11
CHAPTER 12
CHAPTER 13
CHAPTER 14
CHAPTER 15
APPENDICES

Another option might be to use a sequence of calls to `llSetAlpha()` to make the "old" image fade out. `llSetAlpha()` has a built-in 0.2 second delay, however, which may not be enough to make the fade work nicely. Alternatively, you could mimic a "wipe" effect by managing both the rotation and position of the images so they physically cross each other.

Another great extension to this object would be to allow inventory drops of textures from your friends. However, be aware of the permissions issue discussed previously: the textures need to be given with full permissions so that the script can get each texture's key and transmit it to the child prims.

LIGHT

Lighting design is an essential element of visual storytelling. It plays an important role in illumination, directing viewers' gazes to important locations and portraying visual tension. Lighting provides four functions:

- *Visibility:* Being able to see the objects
- *Modeling:* Light (and shadows) reveal the three dimensions
- *Focus:* Indicates what is important
- *Mood:* The emotional content of the scene

You can create light sources that affect other objects in the scene, as discussed next. You can also change the properties of prims so they respond differently to light.

PARTICLE
EFFECTS

TEXTURE
ANIMATION

LIGHT

SUMMARY

CREATING LIGHTS

SL allows for eight light sources; however, the sun and the moon are always on, so for all practical purposes only six matter. If more than six non-sun-and-moon light sources are present in a scene, only the closest six are shown. Face lights, torches, and street lights all count toward the six-light maximum. (**Bling** for shiny jewelry is usually a particle script, which doesn't count.) Recall that the size or shape of the light source makes no difference to how bright it can be.

Lights are created using the `PRIM_POINT_LIGHT` property of `llSetPrimitiveParams()`. A point light was the basis for the face light shown in Listing 2.7.

There are normally four properties of light: color, intensity, distance, and direction. With a point light you can easily control the color, intensity, and distance the light travels. The *color* is any RGB color vector. The *intensity* of light measures how strong in absolute terms the light is. *intensity* is a floating-point number ranging from 0.0 to 1.0, where 1.0 is fully on and 0.0 is equivalent to off. The *radius* controls distance, up to 20 meters, while *falloff* describes how fast the light decays as it travels away from the object; 0.01 is very slow and 2.0 is rapid. Remember that the size of the light source makes no difference to how bright it can be.

Direction is a little more awkward. Light in **Second Life** is spherical, in that all light is emitted in a 360-degree sphere, and light travels through objects, so you can't put up light blockers. Light is also shadowless (although LSL will one day support the `CAST_SHADOWS` constant or some other shadow implementation).

It is also useful to know that some users may not be able to see local point lights. Just as for particles, users can turn off local lights. (Go to Edit ▶ Preferences ▶ Graphics tab, click the check box for **Custom**, then choose whether to use **Sun and Moon Only** or **Nearby Local Lights**.)

Two other constants—`PRIM_GLOW` and `PRIM_FULLBRIGHT`—control an object's light properties, but instead of casting light they change how much light a prim's face gives off. (Chapter 3's Listing 3.9 shows a simple example of how to combine `PRIM_FULLBRIGHT` and `PRIM_POINT_LIGHT`.)

Figure 9.11 shows a simple example of how to use `PRIM_GLOW`. This arc of the covenant sits quietly in the chapel at SYW HQ. When touched, the lid opens and the top side begins to glow using the following command:

```
llSetPrimitiveParams([PRIM_GLOW, 0, 1.0]);
```

Figure 9.11: `PRIM_GLOW` helps give this arc of the covenant the aura it needs.

Baba Bu's Light Learning Lab at Bleaberry Tarn <225, 240, 272> has a few interesting examples of how light can be used in **SL**. At the very least you should change lighting properties for day and night, in a manner similar to the mechanism shown in Chapter 10's "Sim Time: Day, Night, and Shadows" section. But please use your creativity to do more!

Spotlight

Creating a spotlight in **SL** is an interesting exercise in coercing the available tools to make lighting appear realistic. In the real world a directional light has a bulb, a cone of light traveling through the air, and the actual light hitting the target. In **SL** the bulb and cone are just for show, and the point light is placed just in front of the target. Any shadows you want for effect need to be created manually. This contrast is illustrated in Figure 9.12.

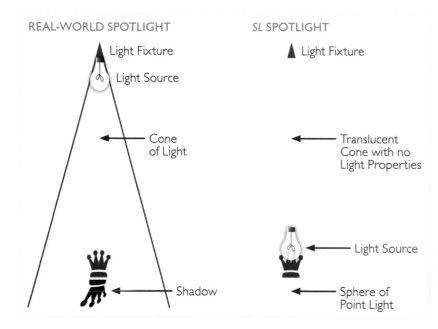

Figure 9.12: To get a spotlight effect in **Second Life**, you need to move the light source to the mouth of a translucent cone.

Listing 9.10 controls a basic spotlight. It selects a random display color on a timer interval and tells both the cone and the point light what color has been selected.

BUILD NOTE

An SL spotlight generally needs at least two prims: a cone and a light source. The cone prim is a cylinder with `taper=<1, 1, 0>`. If you apply a texture with a smooth gradient from opaque to transparent, the cone will appear more and more transparent toward its opening. (You can also chain together a sequence of prims to make a much larger cone.) The light-source prim is any small object placed just inside the mouth of the cone. (Nothing prevents you from using the cone itself as the light source, but because the light emanates from the prim's center, the lit area will appear differently than you'd expect from a real spotlight.) For visual effect you can add a bulb or other light fixture at the point of the cone; note that it doesn't actually emit light, however.

The scripts in this section expect a three-prim build of a spotlight, with the fixture as the root prim. Place Listing 9.10 inside the fixture, Listing 9.11 inside the cone, and Listing 9.12 inside the light source.

CHAPTER 1
CHAPTER 2
CHAPTER 3
CHAPTER 4
CHAPTER 5
CHAPTER 6
CHAPTER 7
CHAPTER 8

CHAPTER 9

CHAPTER 10
CHAPTER 11
CHAPTER 12
CHAPTER 13
CHAPTER 14
CHAPTER 15
APPENDICES

223

PARTICLE
EFFECTS

TEXTURE
ANIMATION

LIGHT

SUMMARY

Listing 9.10: Color-Changing Spotlight Controller (in the Bulb)

```
float TIMER_INTERVAL = 3.0;
float INTENSITY = 1.0;  // range 0.0 to 1.0
float RADIUS = 0.2;     // up to 20m
float FALLOFF   = 0.01; // range 0.01 (slow) to 2.0 (fast)
default
{
    state_entry() {
        llSetTimerEvent( TIMER_INTERVAL );
    }
    timer() {
        float r = llFrand(1.0);
        float g = llFrand(1.0);
        float b = llFrand(1.0);
        vector color = <r,g,b>;
        llSetPrimitiveParams([
            PRIM_POINT_LIGHT, TRUE, color, INTENSITY, RADIUS, FALLOFF,
            PRIM_FULLBRIGHT, ALL_SIDES, TRUE,
            PRIM_COLOR, ALL_SIDES, color, 0.75 ]);
        llMessageLinked( LINK_SET, 0, (string)color, NULL_KEY );
    }
}
```

The script for the cone of light (Listing 9.11) simply listens to link messages and sets the color of the prim. It also makes sure the prim is phantom so avatars can walk through it. Note that *all* prims in the object become phantom at the same time.

Listing 9.11: The Cone of Light

```
float TRANSPARENCY = 0.2;
default
{
    link_message(integer linknum, integer _n, string msg, key _id) {
        vector color = (vector)msg;
        llSetPrimitiveParams([PRIM_PHANTOM, TRUE,
                              PRIM_COLOR, ALL_SIDES, color, TRANSPARENCY]);
    }
}
```

The light-source script (Listing 9.12) also listens to link messages and uses the *color* to set the color of the PRIM_POINT_LIGHT property. This script also ensures this point light is transparent by setting the *alpha* parameter of PRIM_COLOR to 0.0. A spotlight's intensity is high, while falloff needs to drop slowly. The radius has been carefully selected to match the size of the cone's mouth. You could, of course, automatically calculate the radius by having the cone get its own size using llGetScale(), and then transmitting that information to the light source. (Recall that there is no llGetLinkPrimitiveParams() function.)

Listing 9.12: The Light-Emitting Prim

```
float INTENSITY = 1.0;  // range 0.0 to 1.0
float RADIUS    = 1.0;  // up to 20m
float FALLOFF   = 0.01; // range 0.01 (slow) to 2.0 (fast)
default
{
    link_message(integer linknum, integer _n, string msg, key _id) {
        vector color = (vector)msg;
        llSetPrimitiveParams(
            [PRIM_POINT_LIGHT, TRUE, color, INTENSITY, RADIUS, FALLOFF,
             PRIM_COLOR, ALL_SIDES, color, 0.0]);
    }
}
```

CHAPTER 1
CHAPTER 2
CHAPTER 3
CHAPTER 4
CHAPTER 5
CHAPTER 6
CHAPTER 7
CHAPTER 8

NOTE

At SYW HQ, the spotlight over the picture frame (shown here) uses a dialog menu that allows you to explore different settings of *color*, *intensity*, *radius*, and *falloff* for PRIM_POINT_LIGHT. The effect is client-dependent, so if you don't see anything, consider upgrading your graphics hardware.

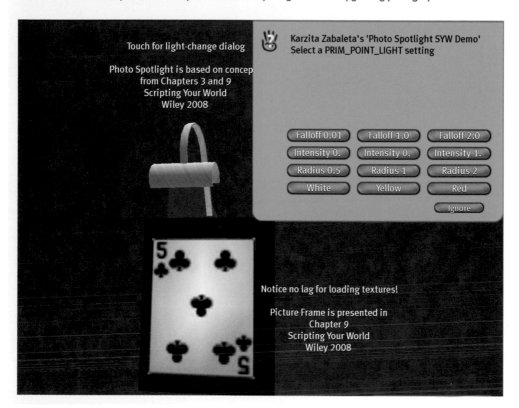

CHAPTER 9

CHAPTER 10
CHAPTER 11
CHAPTER 12
CHAPTER 13
CHAPTER 14
CHAPTER 15
APPENDICES

Filtered Light

Filtered light, such as light shining through stained glass, needs to be handled in a similar way as the spotlight's cone. If you're working with a stained-glass window, each piece of different-colored glass needs a similarly colored and shaped translucent prim that carries its light from the window onto the floor. On the floor you will want another prim with the same texture as the original stained glass. Depending on the exact effect you want, you will need to control the color, transparency, fullbright, and glow of each prim.

For added realism, the size and shape (elongation) of the prims should change depending on where the sun is. The technique for moving shadows shown in Chapter 10's "Sim Time: Day, Night, and Shadows" section can be adapted for this situation.

Figure 9.13 shows a build at Cubic Effects (Born East <165, 50, 39>). It has a series of keyhole-shaped windows with matching keyhole-shaped streams of light. The first image shows how the build looks to passersby, and the second image shows the build with Highlight Transparent turned on (**Ctrl+Alt+T**) so you can see the prims more clearly.

PARTICLE
EFFECTS

TEXTURE
ANIMATION

 LIGHT

 SUMMARY

Figure 9.13: Soft filtered light coming through a window adds realism and character to a room. The light is created by prims shaped similarly to the window.

REFLECTING LIGHT

Textures, colors, bumpiness, and shininess all contribute to an object's appearance and interaction with light. (The Material property does not.) The prim property PRIM_BUMP_SHINY affects how shiny each prim's face is and applies a bump texture that causes some shadowing. Appendix A describes these options in more detail.

The script in Listing 9.13 rezzes a set of spinning lights and changes the object's texture every second in the timer() event. Each of the lights is a different color, and *SL* will accurately mix them depending on how the light strikes the surface. The object in Figure 9.14 shows how the red and green mix to make oranges and yellows, and how red and blue mix to make pinks and purples. You can also see how the light travels through the sides of the object to strike the inside.

Listing 9.13: Texture-Changing Object

```
default
{
    state_entry() {
        vector currPos = llGetPos();
        llRezObject("Spinning Lights", currPos, ZERO_VECTOR, ZERO_ROTATION, 1);
        llSetTimerEvent(1);
    }
    timer() {
        integer bumpTexture = (integer)(llFrand(17));
        llSetPrimitiveParams([PRIM_BUMP_SHINY,ALL_SIDES,
                PRIM_SHINY_NONE, bumpTexture]);
    }
}
```

Figure 9.14: The light sources rotate around the column while the column changes its PRIM_BUMP_SHINY settings. You can see how the colors of light combine, how light travels through walls, and how the different settings change the texture's character.

"Reflection" in the sense of a mirror has not yet been implemented for **SL**. Partial implementations are available for some kinds of hardware via the **Debug** menu, by setting **Render Dynamic Reflections** to TRUE.

SUMMARY

Special effects are a wonderful way to create realism, surrealism, and interest in the environment. They are like the spices you put in an otherwise-bland meal. Be generous—after all, Kentucky Fried Chicken is only a dead bird without its 11 herbs and spices!

SCRIPTING THE ENVIRONMENT

If you're putting together an environment—whether it is a store, a school, or a rainforest—you need to think about *everything* in that environment. What things will make it come alive? Previous chapters showed how to make interesting characters and interactive objects. In this chapter you'll learn how to manage time, and how you can use time to make realistic day-and-night effects, as well as seasonal things. You'll see scripts for wind, water, and weather.

CHAPTER 10

 TIME

AIR, EARTH,
WATER, AND
WEATHER

SUMMARY

TIME

We all know time is important in our real lives. And it can be important in our second lives as well. LSL allows scripts to reason about time. You've already seen the `llSetTimerEvent()` and associated `timer()` event handler. These operate in seconds, as does almost everything in LSL.

Time can be relative to the script, the real world, or the sim. LSL functions return the time as an integer or formatted into a string. LSL can even report subsecond times, but given server lag and so forth, don't rely too much on the accuracy.

SCRIPT TIME: ELAPSED TIME

Script time is an indicator of how long the script has been running. A simple call to `llGetTime()` can tell you how long the object has been rezzed in a running sim, or, combined with `llResetTime()` or `llGetAndResetTime()` gives you elapsed time like a stopwatch. Timer events, `timer()`, are based on an independent timer of elapsed time; calls to `ll*ResetTime()` do not affect when the next `timer()` event will be triggered. Script time functions are shown in Table 10.1.

TABLE 10.1: SCRIPT TIME

FUNCTION	BEHAVIOR
`float llGetTime()`	Returns a float that is script time, in seconds, since the last sim reset, script reset, or call to either `llResetTime()` or `llGetAndResetTime()`.
`llResetTime()`	Resets the script-time timer to zero.
`float llGetAndResetTime()`	Returns a float that is script time, in seconds, and resets the script time to zero in a single step.
`llSetTimerEvent(float sec)`	Sets the timer event to be triggered every *sec* seconds.

REAL-WORLD TIME: ANALOG CLOCK

Real-world time, detailed in Table 10.2, is time you experience outside **SL**. You can use it to make a clock, to adjust the behavior of your dance ball based on the day of the week, or to adjust the environment based on the season.

TABLE 10.2: REAL-WORLD TIME

FUNCTION	BEHAVIOR
`string llGetDate()`	Returns a string that is the current date in GMT in the format yyyy-mm-dd.
`string llGetTimestamp()`	Returns a string that is the current date and time in GMT in an Internet-standard format, *yyyy-mm-ddThh:mm:ss.ssssssZ*. For instance, 6/12/2008 at 21:10:02 GMT would be 2008-06-12T21:10:02.000000Z.
`float llGetGMTclock()`	Returns a float that is the time in seconds since midnight GMT.
`float llGetWallclock()`	Returns a float that is the time in seconds since midnight *Second Life* Time (SLT), which is always the same as California time.
`integer llGetUnixTime()`	Returns an integer that is the number of seconds elapsed since midnight, Jan 1, 1970 GMT.

Listings 10.1 and 10.2 show how you might manage the hands of a clock like the one in Figure 10.1.

Figure 10.1: This classy wall clock is at SYW headquarters.

BUILD NOTE

If you build the clock so that midnight is zero degrees, the script can simplify the rotation calculation and set the hands to the exact setting. Create a small prim at the center of the clock; this will become the root prim. Create two prims for the clock's hands; name one MinuteHand, and the other HourHand. Optionally, create tick marks around the outside edge of the clock. Place the code from Listing 10.1 in the clock's root prim, and Listing 10.2's code in both of the clock's hands. Link the prims.

Listing 10.1: Clock Root Prim

```
vector getTime()
{
    integer t;
    integer hours;
    integer minutes;
    integer seconds;
    t = (integer)llGetWallclock(); // seconds since midnight

    hours = t / 3600;        // integer division removes decimals
    minutes = (t % 3600) / 60; // % is the modulo operator
    seconds = t % 60;        // get any remaining seconds

    return <hours, minutes, seconds>;
}

default
{
    on_rez(integer n) {
        llSetTimerEvent(58.0); // slighty less than once/min
    }
    state_entry() {
        llSetTimerEvent(58.0); // slighty less than once/min
    }
    timer() {
        vector time = getTime();
        llMessageLinked(LINK_ALL_CHILDREN, 0, time, NULL_KEY);
    }
}
```

231

CHAPTER 10

 TIME

AIR, EARTH,
WATER, AND
WEATHER

SUMMARY

Listing 10.2: Clock Hands

```
integer gCurrentHour;
integer gCurrentMin;

setHandPosition(integer hours, integer minutes) {
    integer degrees;
    if (llGetObjectName() == "MinuteHand") {
        float degreesPerMinute = 360.0 / 60.0;
        degrees = (integer)(minutes * degreesPerMinute);
    } else {
        if (hours>12) hours -= 12;
        integer degreesPerHour = 360 / 12;
        float degreesPerMinute = 360.0 / (12.0 * 60.0);
        degrees = hours * degreesPerHour + (integer)(minutes * degreesPerMinute);
    }
    rotation deltaRot = llEuler2Rot( <0,0,-degrees> * DEG_TO_RAD);

    // we know that midnight/noon is 0 degrees around the z axis
    // so we simply want to add minutes from zero
    vector currentOffset = ZERO_VECTOR;
    vector size = llGetScale();
    currentOffset.x += size.x / 2.0;
    vector newOffset = currentOffset * deltaRot;
    llSetLocalRot(deltaRot);
    llSetPos(newOffset);
}
default
{
    link_message(integer sender, integer _num, string msg, key id) {
        vector time = (vector)msg;
        gCurrentHour = msg.x;
        gCurrentMin = msg.y;
        setHandPosition(gCurrentHour, gCurrentMin);
    }
}
```

In the `timer()` event handler, the root prim works out what time it is and uses `llMessageLinked()` to transmit the information to the hands. The hands then calculate the angle, in degrees, at which they should be positioned. The script assumes that midnight is zero degrees and rotations happen around the z-axis. The rotational math used in `setHandPosition()` is described in detail in Chapter 4, "Making and Moving Objects."

The hour markers around the clock's edge can be manually generated, but this is a great place to use an automatic prim rezzer as described in Chapter 4.

SIM TIME: DAY, NIGHT, AND SHADOWS

There is no "real" way to calculate sim time. Nominally, there are four *SL* "days" per real-world day. However, estate owners can alter their sim's clock, and nights are shorter than days, so adjusting can be awkward. But you can calculate local time by working backward from the sun direction (see Table 10.3). You can use it to change the audio loop, alter wildlife behavior, or turn shadows on and off.

TABLE 10.3: SIM TIME

Function	Behavior
vector llGetSunDirection()	Returns a vector that is the direction of the sun in the region.
float llGetRegionTimeDilation()	Returns a float that is the current time dilation; the value range is [0.0, 1.0]—0.0 is full dilation and 1.0 is no dilation.
float llGetTimeOfDay()	Returns a float that is the time in seconds since *SL*–server midnight (or since server up-time, whichever is smaller).

CHAPTER 1
CHAPTER 2
CHAPTER 3
CHAPTER 4
CHAPTER 5
CHAPTER 6
CHAPTER 7
CHAPTER 8
CHAPTER 9

CHAPTER 10

CHAPTER 11
CHAPTER 12
CHAPTER 13
CHAPTER 14
CHAPTER 15
APPENDICES

Another thing to be aware of in sim time is time *dilation*: the ratio between script time change and real-world time. It occurs when the sim can't keep up with the processing of its tasks even after reducing the time allocated to scripts and physics. (So, the faster you move, the slower your time.) Avatars experience this as slow motion. If you have many scripts running in a sim, keep an eye on the time dilation; if it drops too low, it would be considerate to pause the script.

Listing 10.3 shows a sidewalk light that turns off when the sun comes up and turns on when the sun sets. It uses the z-axis from the call to llSunDirection() and sets the *gLightState* to TRUE or FALSE, depending on whether the sun is above or below the horizon. This script also allows an avatar to touch the lamp to turn it on or off, at least until the next timer() event.

Listing 10.3: Sidewalk Light

```
integer gLightState;

// lamplighter is almost identical to Chapter 3's Listing 3.8,
// with a one-line addition of messagelinked
lamplighter()
{
    if ( gLightState == 0) {
        llSetPrimitiveParams([PRIM_FULLBRIGHT,ALL_SIDES,FALSE,
                PRIM_COLOR,ALL_SIDES,<0.4,0.4,0.4>,1.0,
                PRIM_POINT_LIGHT, FALSE, <0.,0.,0.>,0.0,0.0,0.5]);
    } else {
        llSetPrimitiveParams([PRIM_FULLBRIGHT,ALL_SIDES,TRUE,
                PRIM_COLOR,ALL_SIDES,<1.0,1.0,0.0>,1.0,
                PRIM_POINT_LIGHT,TRUE,<1,1,1>,1.0,10.0,0.6]);
    }
    llMessageLinked(LINK_SET, gLightState, "", NULL_KEY);
}

default
{
    state_entry() {
        gLightState = FALSE;
        lamplighter();
        llSetTimerEvent(60);
    }
    timer() {
        vector sun = llGetSunDirection();
        if (sun.z <= 0) gLightState = TRUE; // Below the horizon
        else if (sun.z > 0) gLightState = FALSE; // Above the horizon
        lamplighter();
    }
    touch_start(integer total_number) {
        // allow avatar to toggle light
        // it will auto-turn on/off when timer goes off
        if (gLightState == FALSE) gLightState = TRUE;
        else gLightState = FALSE;
        lamplighter();
    }
}
```

Listing 10.4 shows the script for the light's shadow. The script sets the shadow properties depending on whether the light is on or off, and whether the sun or the moon is above the horizon. It assumes your light bulb is round, and casts a round or oval shadow depending on light conditions. The build only needs to make sure that the shadow is a sphere whose z value is at ground level; the script takes care of size, position, color, transparency, and rotation.

Listing 10.4: Sidewalk Light Shadow

```
setShadowToLight()
{
    vector pos = llGetLocalPos();
    llSetPrimitiveParams([PRIM_SIZE, <1,1,0.1>,          // circle
                           PRIM_POSITION, <0,0,pos.z>, // directly below root
                           PRIM_COLOR, ALL_SIDES, <0,0,0>, 0.5,
                           PRIM_ROTATION, ZERO_ROTATION]);
}

setShadowToSun()
{
    vector sunPosition = llGetSunDirection();
    vector sunDirection = llVecNorm(sunPosition);
    float sunAngle;
    float alpha;
    if (sunPosition.z > 0) {
        sunAngle=llAtan2(-sunPosition.y, -sunPosition.x);
        alpha = 0.5; // dark shadow
    } else {
        sunAngle=llAtan2(sunPosition.y, sunPosition.x);
        alpha = 0.2; // moonlight ; thin shadow
    }

    rotation currRotQ=llGetRootRotation();
    vector currRotE=llRot2Euler(currRotQ);
    float relativeSunAngle = sunAngle - currRotE.z;
    rotation rot = llEuler2Rot(<0, 0, relativeSunAngle >);

    float height = llFabs(sunDirection.z);
    float xsize = 1 / height;
    if (xsize > 20) xsize = 20; // can't move prim outside 10m radius
    vector size = <xsize, 1.0 , 0.1> ;

    vector currPos = llGetLocalPos();
    vector offset = <xsize/2, 0, currPos.z>;
    vector newOffset = offset * rot ;

    llSetPrimitiveParams([PRIM_POSITION, newOffset,
                           PRIM_SIZE, size,
                           //PRIM_ROTATION, rot, // what should work
                           //PRIM_ROTATION, rot/llGetRootRotation(), // workaround
                           PRIM_COLOR, ALL_SIDES, <0,0,0>, alpha]);
    llSetLocalRot(rot); // safer bug workaround
}

default
{
    link_message(integer sender_num, integer lightState, string msg, key id) {
        if (lightState==FALSE) { // light is off
            setShadowToSun();
        } else { // light is on; move shadow below light
            setShadowToLight();
        }
    }
}
```

The `default` state listens for linked messages then calls `setShadowToLight()` if the light is on, or `setShadowToSun()` if the light is off. The shadow under the light is easy. You need a circle about twice the size of the light bulb. It's a relatively dark shadow, so the black prim's alpha is 0.5.

The more interesting function is `set.ShadowToSun()`, which does three things: it makes the shadow rotate around the light depending on where the sun (or moon) is, it adjusts the shadow's size to be an oval scaled to the sun's height, and it changes the transparency (alpha) to make the shadow look appropriate for both moonlight and sunlight. Figure 10.2 shows these effects.

CHAPTER 1
CHAPTER 2
CHAPTER 3
CHAPTER 4
CHAPTER 5
CHAPTER 6
CHAPTER 7
CHAPTER 8
CHAPTER 9

CHAPTER 11
CHAPTER 12
CHAPTER 13
CHAPTER 14
CHAPTER 15
APPENDICES

Figure 10.2: The shadow the lamp casts is different when the light is on during the day, off during the day (shown here with the sun almost directly overhead), on in the evening, or off in the evening.

The first thing `setShadowToSun()` does is find the sun with `llGetSunDirection()`. In *SL*, the moon is **always** directly opposite the sun. (That means, of course, there is never an eclipse in *SL*.) We can therefore set the shadow's direction and transparency based on whether the sun is above the horizon. Using a positive `x` and `y`, you'll get the direction toward the sun (or shadow for moonlight), while a negative `x` and `y` gives you the direction toward the moon (or the shadow in sun). The script then sets the shadow's rotation to the ***relativeSunAngle***.

The script then resizes the shadow based on how high the sun is in the sky using a simple inverse relationship to the height: *1 ÷ height*. However, it also has to ensure the prim isn't longer than 20m—it can't set the prim's center to be more than 10m away. The last calculation is for the offset, using standard rotation math.

Finally, the script sets the properties of the shadow using `llSetPrimitiveParams()`. Note the commented lines for `PRIM_ROTATION`. There is a bug in this *SL* function: normally you would want to set the prim rotation to `rot`, but you can either set it to `rot / llGetRootRotation()` or use `llSetLocalRot(rot)` to get the correct behavior. The second workaround is probably safer because the defect may one day be fixed. This bug is documented as JIRA bug SVC-93.

AIR, EARTH, WATER, AND WEATHER

TIME

 AIR, EARTH,
WATER, AND
WEATHER

SUMMARY

Across cultures, environmental elements give you the power to understand and shape your world. *SL* models air (wind), earth, and water explicitly. (Fire, another of the ancient elements, is a particle effect.) By pulling these together, you create the fifth element—quintessence (also called idea, qi, aether, or energy).

AIR: WEATHER VANE

You have probably seen a picture of a weather vane—usually shaped like a farm animal such as a horse or a rooster—on top of a barn. A weather vane is just a flat piece of metal whose broad tail catches the wind and swivels to point toward the wind, as shown in Figure 10.3. You can use similar techniques to build a wind sock for your airfield, billow a flag in the right direction, or set your sailboat on a perfect broad reach.

Figure 10.3: The rooster swivels to always face the wind.

You can turn the sign post from Listing 4.7 into a weather vane by adding a timer to check the wind periodically, and a function call to `llWind()`.

DEFINITION

```
vector llWind(vector offset)
```

Returns the wind velocity, in meters per second, at *offset* relative to the object's position.

We care only about the horizontal wind direction, so the script calculates the wind direction, *windDir*, using the arctan (inverse tangent) of the x and y wind components:

```
float windDir = llAtan2(windVelocity.y, windVelocity.x);
```

Just as for the sun, using a positive **x** and **y** you'll get the direction the wind is blowing **to**, while a negative **x** and **y** will give you the direction the wind is blowing **from**.

In this script you also have to worry about the root prim's rotation relative to the wind. Therefore, in `calcWindAngle()`, the script uses `llGetRootRotation()` to get the root's rotation, and then subtracts its z-axis value from the wind direction. The function returns the current wind direction relative to the z-axis of the root prim.

The only other difference between the weather vane and the sign post is that you calculate the delta rotation by subtracting the current rotation of the vane from the current wind angle. Listing 10.5 shows the complete script.

Listing 10.5: Weather Vane

```
float gTimerInterval = 5.0; // check wind direction every 5 seconds
float calcWindAngle() {
    vector windVelocity = llWind(ZERO_VECTOR);
    float windDir = llAtan2(windVelocity.y,windVelocity.x);

    quaternion currRotQ = llGetRootRotation(); // adjust for rotation of root
    vector currRotE = llRot2Euler(currRotQ);
    float relativeWindAngle = windDir - currRotE.z;
    return relativeWindAngle;
}

default
{
    state_entry() {
        llSetTimerEvent( gTimerInterval );
    }
    timer() {
        float windAngle = calcWindAngle();
        rotation windAngleQ = llEuler2Rot(<0.0,0.0,windAngle>);
        rotation currentRotQ = llGetLocalRot();
        rotation deltaRotQ = windAngleQ / currentRotQ;

        quaternion newRotQ = currentRotQ * deltaRotQ;
        vector currentOffset = llGetLocalPos();
        vector newOffset = currentOffset * deltaRotQ;

        llSetLocalRot( newRotQ );
        llSetPos( newOffset );
    }
}
```

CHAPTER 1
CHAPTER 2
CHAPTER 3
CHAPTER 4
CHAPTER 5
CHAPTER 6
CHAPTER 7
CHAPTER 8
CHAPTER 9

CHAPTER 10

CHAPTER 11
CHAPTER 12
CHAPTER 13
CHAPTER 14
CHAPTER 15
APPENDICES

Adding a particle system to this script (during debugging) to show wind direction can be especially helpful. In SYW headquarters you'll find a weather vane with a smoke trail that demonstrates it is, in fact, turning correctly away from the wind. If you use more wind vector than we did here you can make lots of other things that fly. Try making a kite or a helium balloon. Just be careful not to lose it!

EARTH AND WATER: A FLOATING BOTTLE

You'll have many occasions to work with ground and water in **Second Life**, and you'll need a bit of knowledge to do it well. For instance, when you're building a boat you'll need to know the water level; you can find it with `llWater()`. Water is actually **everywhere** in **SL**, but sometimes you have to think of it as an underground spring, because there's ground above it. `llGround()` is the function that tells you at what height the ground is.

CHAPTER 10

TIME

 AIR, EARTH,
WATER, AND
WEATHER

SUMMARY

 DEFINITION

float llWater(vector *offset*)

Returns the water level (*z* coordinate) at *offset* relative to the object's position. The location must be in the same sim. Most sims have a water level of 20.0.

 DEFINITION

float llGround(vector *offset*)

Returns the ground level (*z* coordinate) at *offset* relative to the object position.

If water height is above ground height, your object's position is in the water; otherwise, it's above ground. If you want to get fancy with ground effects you can also use llGroundSlope(*offset*), which tells the script whether the position is on a hill; llGroundNormal(*offset*), which returns x and y components of llGroundSlope(), while the z component is 1.0; and llGroundContour(*offset*), which reveals the contour line (where elevation doesn't change). You can make your toboggan slide faster on a steeper hill or your stealth chat-relay bug fly close to the contour line. You can even make a lamp post's shadow change appropriately if there is a hill nearby.

Listing 10.6 shows the script for an object that floats at water level—at SYW HQ we placed it in a bottle. The script uses the physics engine to make the movements more realistic, and also sets the status flag STATUS_DIE_AT_EDGE to TRUE, just in case your object floats away. (Because it can be bumped, there's a very good chance it will.) You may also want to add a timer-based position reset in case the physics engine causes your object to get stuck somewhere you can't find it.

Listing 10.6: Water Floaty

```
float gTimerInt = 5.0; // how often to check water height

init()
{
    llSetTimerEvent( gTimerInt );
    llSetStatus(STATUS_PHYSICS, TRUE);
    llSetStatus(STATUS_DIE_AT_EDGE, TRUE);
}

integer setFloat()
{
    vector currPos = llGetPos();
    float waterLevel = llWater(ZERO_VECTOR);
    float groundHeight = llGround(ZERO_VECTOR);
    //float waterDepth = waterLevel - groundHeight;
    if (groundHeight > waterLevel) {
        return -1; // not OK
    }
```

```
        if ((currPos.z > waterLevel+0.1)) {          // fall to surface
            llStopMoveToTarget();
        } else if ((currPos.z < waterLevel-0.1)) {    // pop to surface
            llMoveToTarget(<currPos.x, currPos.y, waterLevel - 0.05>, 0.2);
        } else {
            llMoveToTarget(<currPos.x, currPos.y, waterLevel>, gTimerInt);
        }
        return 1; // OK
}

default
{
    state_entry() {
        init();
    }
    on_rez(integer n) {
        init();
    }
    timer() {
        if (setFloat() == -1) state on_land;
    }
}

state on_land
{
    state_entry() {
        llWhisper(0,"Not on Water. Move Me!");
        // may fall
    }
    moving_end() {
        state default;
    }
}
```

CHAPTER 1
CHAPTER 2
CHAPTER 3
CHAPTER 4
CHAPTER 5
CHAPTER 6
CHAPTER 7
CHAPTER 8
CHAPTER 9

CHAPTER 10

CHAPTER 11
CHAPTER 12
CHAPTER 13
CHAPTER 14
CHAPTER 15
APPENDIX

The function setFloat() first checks to see whether the object is in water; If It Is it has three tests. If the object is above the water height the object will fall to the water surface. If it's below the water height it will tell the floaty to "pop" to the surface. Otherwise, the script will tell the object to stay put. The motions are all controlled with llMoveToTarget() and llStopMoveToTarget(), rather than llSetBuoyancy(). As mentioned in Chapter 7, "Physics and Vehicles," buoyancy has little to do with water in **SL**. The llMoveToTarget() function sets a goal position and the speed to get there. The timer() handler is called on a periodic basis, allowing the object to "bob" depending on what the physics engine thinks its current motion is. Placing an llTarget() in this script is not necessary because the timer will reposition the object.

If the object isn't over water, the script changes state to on_land, tells the avatar to move the object, and returns to the default state when moved. Because this is a physical object, it can move just by being bumped, or it may move for other reasons (for example, it may roll down a hill).

Figure 10.4 shows the floating bottle. In Chapter 12, "Reaching outside *Second Life*," you'll learn how to have the bottle deliver the message it's carrying.

TIME

AIR, EARTH,
WATER, AND
WEATHER

SUMMARY

Figure 10.4: The bottle floats in water, eventually washing up on the shore of a desert island.

WEATHER: SNOWFALL

As you put these environmental elements together you will quickly realize you can create weather. While you can't control the wind or sun direction (unless you're an estate owner), you can use those elements to create just the right ambience for your scene. Rain? Yes. Thunder and lightning even. But falling snowflakes can make a really magical moment.

The simplest way to create a snowfall is with a particle emitter, as in Listing 10.7, which generates slow-moving particles in an explosion pattern. The script applies a snowflake texture and tells the particles to grow during their lifespan, generating 20 particles every 0.2 seconds. The particles move slowly with a gentle downward acceleration, falling to the ground. You'll want to place your emitter high in the sky so the flakes look more natural; make sure enough flakes live long enough to make it to the ground. You can make the emitter completely transparent or partially transparent in a gray cloud that follows you around.

Listing 10.7: Snowstorm

```
mySnowStorm() {
    list particle_parameters = [
      PSYS_PART_FLAGS, (PSYS_PART_INTERP_COLOR_MASK | PSYS_PART_INTERP_SCALE_MASK),
    // Appearance
      PSYS_SRC_TEXTURE,        "60ec4bc9-1a36-d9c5-b469-0fe34a8983d4",
      PSYS_PART_START_ALPHA,   1.0,
      PSYS_PART_END_ALPHA,     0.0,
      PSYS_PART_START_SCALE,   <0.2, 0.2, 0.0 >,
      PSYS_PART_END_SCALE,     <0.7, 0.7, 0.0 >,
    // Flow: how many, how quickly
      PSYS_PART_MAX_AGE,         10.0,  // 0.1 to 60
      PSYS_SRC_BURST_PART_COUNT, 20,    // 1 to 4096
      PSYS_SRC_BURST_RATE,       0.2,   // 0.0 to 60
      PSYS_SRC_MAX_AGE,          0.0,   // seconds 0.1-60; 0 always
    // Placement: where
      PSYS_SRC_PATTERN,        PSYS_SRC_PATTERN_EXPLODE,
      PSYS_SRC_BURST_RADIUS, 5.0,
      PSYS_SRC_OMEGA,          <0, 0, 0>, // rotate emitter
    // Movement
      PSYS_SRC_BURST_SPEED_MIN, 0.4,
      PSYS_SRC_BURST_SPEED_MAX, 1.0,
      PSYS_SRC_ACCEL,        <0.0, 0.0, -0.25>
    ];
    llParticleSystem( particle_parameters );
}
```

```
default
{
    state_entry() {
        mySnowStorm();
    }
    touch_start(integer i) {
        mySnowStorm(); // touch to reset/turn on the particles
    }
}
```

Unlike in the real world, not every snowflake in *SL* is unique. Each particle emitter can support only one texture. If you want variation in your flakes, make several emitters, each with a different texture, and place them a few meters apart from one another. Figure 10.5 shows the results of using three different emitters.

Figure 10.5: Three snowflake textures are used in this set of particle emitters.

You can augment this script by testing for cloud density using `llCloud()`. If the clouds are thick, turn on the snow. Going back to our earlier discussion of sunlight and shadows, you can also use this function to control how dark shadows are (more cloud density means less sunshine and therefore less shadow).

 DEFINITION

llCloud(vector *offset*)

Returns a float that is the cloud density (0.0 to 1.0) at the object position, plus *offset*.

Care to make your snow flurry more realistic? Have snowdrifts accumulate (grow) in corners when it's snowing, and melt (shrink, with watery particle effects) when it's not. If you're making a thunderstorm, *SL* has a built-in thunder sound that would be great (look for the key on the wiki page Internal_sounds).

SUMMARY

Manipulating time and weather are extremely useful techniques for creating an environment. An important part of an environment's ambience is the sounds you hear: bird noises, wind chimes, loud engines, and so on. The next chapter covers sound, but the ideas in this chapter help you make it interesting: make your sounds change or depend on things such as time of day, season, or what an object can sense.

CHAPTER 1
CHAPTER 2
CHAPTER 3
CHAPTER 4
CHAPTER 5
CHAPTER 6
CHAPTER 7
CHAPTER 8
CHAPTER 9

CHAPTER 11
CHAPTER 12
CHAPTER 13
CHAPTER 14
CHAPTER 15
APPENDICES

MULTIMEDIA

In this chapter you'll experience builds that use scripts to enliven *Second Life* with enhancements to the aural environment and with streamed audio and video from the Web to be viewed on any land you own or have group access to.

The ability to support sound and video media depends greatly on simulator issues, and thus is tied intimately to land ownership. Within the Media options on the About Land menu, subdialogs allow you to specify URLs for both video and audio streams (such as Internet radio from sources like `http://shoutcast.com`). In this chapter you will script things you ordinarily use the menu to do manually, and much more; it's the "much more" that is the primary focus of the chapter.

Many media elements are produced externally and used for in-world compositions. Externally produced and imported art-path elements might include textures in the form of JPEGs, Targa, and PNG files produced by GIMP, Photoshop, or other art programs; animations in the form of `.bvh` files produced by Blender* or QAvimator**; and, finally, sound clips in the form of `.wav` files produced by a sound editor such as Audacity***. Table 11.1 shows the media types *Second Life* supports.

TABLE 11.1: LSL MEDIA TYPES BY FILE EXTENSION

TYPE	FILE TYPE AND EXPECTED FILE EXTENSION
Video	Flash (`.swf`) QuickTime (`.mov`) AVI (`.avi`) Mpeg (`.mpg`, `.mpeg`) RealNetworks stream (`.smil`)
Images	Bitmap (`.bmp`) JPEG (`.jpg`) Mpeg (`.mpg`, `.mpeg`) Portable Network Graphics (`.png`) Macintosh PICT (`.pict`) Targa (`.tga`) Graphics Interchange Format (`.gif`) Silicon Graphics (`.sgi`) Tagged Image File Format (`.tiff`, `.tif`)
Text	Text (`.txt`)
Audio	MP3 (`.mp3`) WAV (`.wav`)

We'll start by building a few artifacts that demonstrate how to use sound in *Second Life*, then build a couple more that bring audio and video streams in-world from external web sources.

---

*   `http://www.blender.org`

** `http://www.qavimator.org`

*** `http://audacity.sourceforge.net`

WORKING WITH SOUND

Creating compelling soundscapes in *Second Life* involves both the science of scripting and the alchemy of capturing and manipulating sounds from the external world. The sounds you hear are often an important part of an area's ambience. Many of the builds in this book can be audio-enhanced; you'll find those enhancements on the SYW website and at the in-world SYW HQ.

One way to bring audio in-world is by uploading sounds created externally. LSL offers some sophisticated control mechanisms for tailoring the soundscape simply by playing the sounds in the inventory of one or more prims. This section discusses those mechanisms.

 ## AMBIENT-SOUND AUTOMATION: NORTHERN WINDS

As this chapter was being written it was winter in North America, and the authors, being from "northern tier" of the United States, wanted to bring the comforting howl of the winter winds into *Second Life* to accompany the writing effort. Multimedia and audio streaming are covered later in this chapter, but ambient-sound automation—the autonomous production of ambient noises—is an important addition to your efforts, and clearly sets you apart from other creators and scripters.

Listing 11.1 shows a basic approach for automating ambient sounds. You might want to hear people chatting inside a shopping mall, for example, or street noise in an urban setting. Controllers like these are usually embedded into other objects in the environment, like window shutters or plants. A prim may play only one sound at a time, irrespective of which LSL function is used.

Listing 11.1: Basic Sound Automation—Wind Effects

```
list gSounds = ["winter_wind1", "winter_wind2", "winter_wind3"];

default {
    state_entry() {
        llStopSound();
        llSetTimerEvent(2.0);
    }
    timer() {
        list soundMix = llListRandomize(gSounds, 1);
        llTriggerSound(llList2String(soundMix, 0), 1.0);
    }
}
```

Listing 11.1 assumes three sounds in the object's inventory*, specified in the list *gSounds*. Every two seconds the timer elapses, and when the `timer()` event fires, the list of sounds is shuffled using `llListRandomize()`. `llTriggerSound()` plays the first member of the shuffled list (at index zero). Note that the script could build the list of sounds automatically, using the following snippet:

---

* *Second Life* has a useful set of built-in sound clips that are available to your scripts by name or UUID. The wiki page Internal_sounds presents a comprehensive list.

```
integer numSounds = llGetInventoryNumber(INVENTORY_SOUND);
integer i;
list gSounds = [];
for (i=0; i<numSounds; i++) {
    gSounds += llGetInventoryName(INVENTORY_SOUND, i);
}
```

 DEFINITION

> ### llPlaySound(string *sound*, float *volume*)

Plays a sound clip once, emitting from the center of the object. Sounds played by this function from attached objects are audible only to the avatar wearing the object.

> ### llLoopSound(string *sound*, float *volume*)

Like llPlaySound() except the clip will repeat until stopped. Sounds played by this function from attached objects are audible only to the avatar wearing the object.

> ### llTriggerSound(string *sound*, float *volume*)

Plays a sound clip once, emitting from the place where the object was when it started. Triggered sounds are audible to others when caused by objects attached to avatars.

> ### llTriggerSoundLimited(string *sound*, float *volume*, vector *topNorthEast*, vector *bottomSouthWest*)

Similar to llTriggerSound(), but the sound is audible only when the listener is inside the three-dimensional box specified by the opposite corners *topNorthEast* and *bottomSouthWest*.

- *sound* — The name of an item in the inventory of the prim that's playing the sound, or the UUID of a sound clip anywhere.
- *volume* — A value with a min of 0.0 (silent) and max of 1.0 (as loud as possible).
- *topNorthEast* — The region coordinates of the upper northeast range of the sound (llTriggerSound() only).
- *bottomSouthWest* — The region coordinates of the lower southwest range of the sound (llTriggerSound() only).

For the most part, Listing 11.1 generates pure cacophony. Most of the sound clips are longer than the timer's interval of two seconds, so even the shorter pieces don't have time to complete before the next sound triggers. Just as in music, the silences are as much a part of the structure as the noisy bits. To create potential silences, you might consider lengthening the llSetTimerEvent() parameter, but you also want some overlaid sounds so there's not a sense of sharp cutoffs and startups. A better approach to ambient-sound automation might be to create a damper effect where there are sometimes gaps, and

CHAPTER 11

WORKING
WITH SOUND

STREAMING
MEDIA

SUMMARY

perhaps sometimes the equivalent of a pervasive ambient background for all the other sounds to play out against. You might think of a nearly continuous ambient sound as the melody line in a song, and the other sounds as harmony or punctuation. Listing 11.2 illustrates both the notions of an ambient background and random damping.

Listing 11.2: Better Sound Automation

```
float SOUND_PAUSE   = 0.80;
float SOUND_DENSITY = 0.90;
list gSounds = ["mm_wind", "winter_wind", "mm_wind_2", "windchimes"];
string gAmbient = "wind_in_trees";
default {
    state_entry() {
        llStopSound();
        llSetTimerEvent(5.0);
    }
    timer() {
        if (llFrand(1.0) > SOUND_PAUSE) {
            llStopSound();
        } else {
            llLoopSound(gAmbient, 1.0);
        }
        list soundMix = llListRandomize(gSounds, 1);
        if (llFrand(1.0) > SOUND_DENSITY) {
            llTriggerSound(llList2String(soundMix, 0), 1.0);
        }
    }
}
```

An ambient sound (in this case a soft rustle of wind through trees) is specified as a string, *gAmbient*. Its duration is a little more than five seconds; hence a `timer()` event firing at five-second intervals is just about right from the standpoint of providing continuous overlay of the basic ambient-sound clip (or clips). When the `timer()` fires, it uses `llFrand()` to roll a die. When the result is greater than `SOUND_PAUSE`, the sound is stopped with `llStopSound()`; otherwise the sound *gAmbient* is played in a loop with `llLoopSound()`.

The `timer()` finishes its activity by triggering one of the more interesting sounds (those in *gSounds*). Notice the second roll of the die, this time compared to `SOUND_DENSITY`, which means the script will sometimes choose to not trigger the sound, instead being silent.

When automating your ambient sounds, you'll need to do the following:

- Match the sounds thematically and for play volume.
- Provide for seamless overlay so that sounds appear to interweave.
- Provide "rest measures" in your ambient "symphony."
- Randomize the soundscape for a naturalistic mix.

A variety of functions allow you finer control over how sounds are played. `llAdjustSoundVolume()` and `llSetSoundRadius()` let you adjust the volume and range of the sound, while `llPreloadSound()` and `llStopSound()` give hints to the *SL* viewer that it should prepare to play a specific sound before it starts, or to stop a sound in progress.

DEFINITION

CHAPTER 1
CHAPTER 2
CHAPTER 3
CHAPTER 4
CHAPTER 5
CHAPTER 6
CHAPTER 7
CHAPTER 8
CHAPTER 9
CHAPTER 10

CHAPTER 11

CHAPTER 12
CHAPTER 13
CHAPTER 14
CHAPTER 15
APPENDICES

---

llAdjustSoundVolume(float *volume*)

Changes *volume* of the currently playing sound.

> *volume* — How loud the sound should be played, in the range 0.0 (silent) to 1.0 (loud).

---

llSetSoundRadius(float *radius*)

Sets a hard cut-off *radius* for the sound to be heard.

> *radius* — Distance from the point of origin the sound can be heard.

---

llPreloadSound(string *sound*)

Preloads *sound* on viewers within range, reducing the startup delays.

> *sound* — The name or UUID of the sound clip to preload.

---

llStopSound()

Stops playing the *sound* currently looping on the prim. Does not affect sounds started by collisions or llTriggerSound*() functions.

SOUND ORCHESTRATION: RAIN AND THUNDER

A more complex soundscape requires coordinating several sound-input sources. The general concept is that one of the prims acts as a sound "master" and other prims act as sound "slaves" that activate only when the master is active. Figure 11.1 shows a coordinated thunderstorm.

Figure 11.1: Three rainclouds, shown garishly tinted for greater visibility, coordinate the action.

247

Listing 11.3 enables the master cloud (green). This listing supports two states for the master cloud: a `default` state for when it's raining, and a `stormOff` state, both of which control the particle and sound systems. A storm or a period between storms can last a maximum of 120 minutes (*gTime*). The actual duration is somewhere in between, chosen by the function `llFrand()`, which returns a value between zero seconds and the ceiling specified by *gTime*. Turning the storm on and off visually is accomplished with the particle system (covered extensively in Appendix B, "The Particle System"); your purpose here is to create an orchestrated storm.

Listing 11.3: Storm Master

```
float  gTime = 7200.0;//ceiling duration of a given storm/no-storm
string SOUNDLOOP = "RainLoop";

makeStorm()
{
    llParticleSystem( [ // insert your storm particle system here
                      ] );
}
default {
    state_entry() {
        makeStorm()
        llLoopSoundMaster(SOUNDLOOP, 1.0);
        llSetTimerEvent(llFrand(gTime));
    }
    timer() {
        state stormOff;
    }
}
state stormOff {
    state_entry() {
        llParticleSystem([]);
        llStopSound();
        llSetTimerEvent(llFrand(gTime));
    }
    timer() {
        state default;
    }
}
```

When the storm is activated by `stormOn()` and the rain is coming down in buckets, the cloud also plays a continuous sound loop, `SOUNDLOOP`, contained in the cloud's inventory. Notice that in this case the sound-loop function is not `llLoopSound()` as seen in Listing 11.2, but a slightly different function, `llLoopSoundMaster()`.

Like `llLoopSound()`, `llLoopSoundMaster()` plays a sound in a continuous loop. In addition, if other sound emitters in the area are acting as sound slaves, the prim containing the sound master will either permit or deny the slave's ability to play. The slave can play only when the master is playing.

DEFINITION

CHAPTER 1
CHAPTER 2
CHAPTER 3
CHAPTER 4
CHAPTER 5
CHAPTER 6
CHAPTER 7
CHAPTER 8
CHAPTER 9
CHAPTER 10

llLoopSoundMaster(string *sound*, float *volume*)

Plays attached *sound* looping at *volume*. Declares this sound as a sync master. Sound synchronization happens at the client.

llLoopSoundSlave(string *sound*, float *volume*)

Plays attached *sound* looping at *volume*, synced to the most audible sync master. Must be in a different prim from the master.

llPlaySoundSlave(string *sound*, float *volume*)

Plays attached *sound* once at *volume*, synced to the next loop of the most audible sync master. Must be in a different prim from the master.

> *sound* — The name of an item in the inventory of the prim that's playing the sound, or a valid UUID.

> *volume* — A value with a min of 0.0 (silent) and max of 1.0 (as loud as possible).

CHAPTER 11

CHAPTER 12
CHAPTER 13
CHAPTER 14
CHAPTER 15
APPENDICES

This is precisely the behavior you want to see from the storm system overall. When it's raining you want random thunder, and when it's not you want overall calm. Listing 11.4, contained in the red and blue clouds in Figure 11.1, shows how random thunder is created in concert with the ambient rain. To create randomness (including the possibility that both slave clouds rumble at the same time), a random timer with a ceiling of *gCeiling* seconds is chosen. When the **timer()** event fires, the script calls **llPlaySoundSlave()**. *SL* checks whether a sound master is playing within earshot of the user; if so, the sound slave waits until the master starts the next iteration of its own sound loop, then plays the slave's audio clip once, starting at the same moment as the master's sound. **llLoopSoundSlave()** enables a slave to play a sound in a loop; this causes the slave sound to start playing at the beginning of a sync master loop, after which the slave sound loops normally (that is, as soon as it ends, it starts again).

Listing 11.4: Storm Slave

```
integer gStorm = 0;
string  SOUNDLOOP = "Thunder01";
float   gCeiling = 30.0;
default {
    state_entry() {
        llSetTimerEvent(llFrand(gCeiling));
    }
    timer() {
        llPlaySoundSlave(SOUNDLOOP, 1);
        llSetTimerEvent(llFrand(gCeiling));
    }
}
```

This script creates a sound system consisting of potentially many actors, each of whom has a well-defined role. The master's actions enforce turn-taking and temporal synchronization. You can cause a single sound to propagate in a coordinated fashion over long distances.

WORKING
WITH SOUND

STREAMING
MEDIA

SUMMARY

One final LSL sound-control function allows you to control how successive sounds get played by a single prim. If you call `11SetSoundQueuing(TRUE)`, then instead of successive calls to `11PlaySound()` or `11LoopSound()` starting immediately, they wait until the currently playing sound clip finishes. This function allows seamless, ordered playback of any number of audio clips. Scripters use this feature to build simple radio or tape playback devices and even musical instruments.

DEFINITION

`11SetSoundQueueing(integer queue)`

When *queue* is set to TRUE, calls to LSL functions in the `11PlaySound()` or `11LoopSound()` families will wait to start until the currently playing sound clip has finished. Only one sound can be queued at a time. State transitions disable sound queuing.

queue — Boolean; TRUE enables sound queuing, FALSE disables it.

SOUND CREATION AND EDITING

While this chapter is not intended to be a comprehensive treatise on working with sound, you should remember some important bits of general information.

- The correct sample size for any digital audio is 16 bits. At this rate you can achieve reasonable (though unremarkable) monaural and stereophonic sound for in-world use. Stereo digital audio is played at FM audio quality.

- The correct sampling rate for any digital audio you intend to upload is 44kHz. Even though your editor may work with a wide variety of internal sampling rates, you must export at 44kHz.

- If you are creating ambient effects such as those in Listing 11.1 (wind effects) or Listing 11.3 (rain for the orchestrated thunderstorm), you will be creating a sound loop. When working with sound loops, the ends must fit together seamlessly. Thus the first second of the loop will (in normal use) follow the final second; you never want a detectable pause or discontinuity between these critical points in the loop. You can do any number of manipulations to provide a transition at the sound's beginning and end.

- Match the sound levels in multiple sound cuts as closely as possible. Though your sounds may have been collected from different sources, you want to convey a cohesive soundscape.

- Remember that you can upload at most 10 seconds of digital sound. If you need to play something appreciably longer, such as a complete song, you will have to carefully chop the song into 10-second segments and sequence them. (The jukebox in SYW Old Town uses this approach.) If you want to offer a collection of complete songs, your best approach is to offer an audio stream. You can create an audio stream as a podcast, and have it hosted for free on a service such as SHOUTcast. (The Tunable Radio build in Listing 11.5 shows how streamed FM broadcast radio can be incorporated in-world.)

- For an excellent description of how to upload sound, consult Torley Linden's guide at `http://blog.secondlife.com/2008/02/14/tip-of-the-week-22-editing-and-uploading-sounds/`.

- Be warned that the *Second Life* Terms of Service (not to mention ever-watchful copyright monitors in some countries) enforce "digital rights management" laws. There may be harsh penalties for sharing music and even ambient sounds without the creator's permission. It's always preferable to use sounds hosted by royalty-free sites; searching the term "free ambient sound" will point you to a number of them.

CHAPTER 1
CHAPTER 2
CHAPTER 3
CHAPTER 4
CHAPTER 5
CHAPTER 6
CHAPTER 7
CHAPTER 8
CHAPTER 9
CHAPTER 10
CHAPTER 11
CHAPTER 12
CHAPTER 13
CHAPTER 14
CHAPTER 15
APPENDICES

STREAMING MEDIA

Second Life support for streamed content is excellent. An ordinary user with an understanding of the Web can use the World ▶ About Land dialog box (Figure 11.2) to set a URL to play in any parcel they own or have group access to.

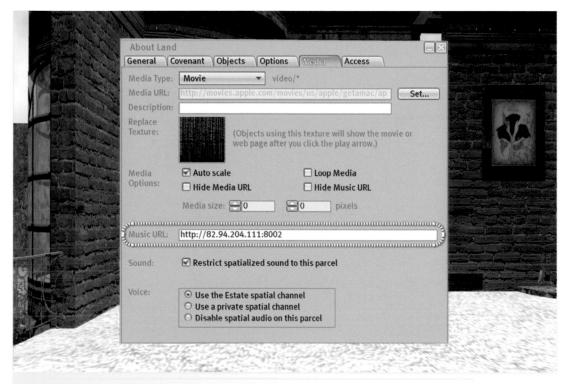

Figure 11.2: Use the World ▶ About Land ▶ Media dialog box to set a static music source.

The function `llSetParcelMusicURL()` allows you to stream audio into **SL** wherever you have permissions for the land's audio and video channels. Figure 11.3 and Listing 11.5 demonstrate a multichannel radio capable of tuning several streamcasts.

DEFINITION

`llSetParcelMusicURL(string url)`

Sets the streaming audio `url` for the parcel the object is on. Causes the script to sleep for 2.0 seconds. Setting the parcel URL to an empty string (" ") turns the stream off.

`url` — The URL of the streaming media source.

251

Figure 11.3: A vintage 1935 Atwater-Kent radio plays as well today as the day it was made. The current station is announced on the open chat channel.

Listing 11.5: Tunable Radio

```
integer STRIDE = 2;
list gStations = [
    "http://www.live365.com/play/wamu3",    "WAMU, Washington",
    "http://160.79.128.242:8054",           "Ambient Psi Music",
    "http://202.6.74.107:8060/triplej.mp3", "TripleJ Radio, Sydney",
    "http://205.234.188.21:80",             "WBUR, Boston",
    "",                                     "Silence" ];

integer gCurrentStation = 0;
integer gListLen;
change_station() {
    list newStation = llList2ListStrided(gStations, gCurrentStation,
                              gCurrentStation+STRIDE, 1);
    llSay(0, "You are listening to "+llList2String(newStation, 1)+".");
    llSetParcelMusicURL(llList2String(newStation, 0));
    gCurrentStation += STRIDE;
    if (gCurrentStation > gListLen - 1 ) { gCurrentStation = 0; }
}

default{
    state_entry() {
        llSay(0, "Resetting...");
        gCurrentStation = 0;
        gListLen = llGetListLength(gStations);
        change_station();
    }
    touch_start(integer total_number) {
        change_station();
    }
}
```

The strided list *gStations* contains source URLs for streaming audio and their accompanying descriptions. Replace these source URLs and descriptions with your own favorites. Algorithmically, the radio is fairly simple. When a resident touches the radio, `touch_start()` is fired, which invokes `change_station()`. In `change_station()`, `llList2ListStrided()` extracts one entry from *gStations*, consisting of a URL and its associated description. The script calls `llSetParcelMusicURL()` to set the parcel's music. Note also that this function has a two-second script delay.

The index of the current station, *gCurrentStation*, is then advanced by two so that the next call to `change_station()` selects the next station in the list. Note that setting the parcel URL to an empty string means "no URL," and is how this script turns off the radio.

WARNING

For a scripted object to set the audio or video streams using `llSetParcelMusicURL()` or `llParcelMediaCommandList()`, the object must be owned by the parcel owner. This is especially important to remember when controlling the media stream on group-owned land: your radio will have to be deeded to the group to control the music stream!

CHAPTER 1
CHAPTER 2
CHAPTER 3
CHAPTER 4
CHAPTER 5
CHAPTER 6
CHAPTER 7
CHAPTER 8
CHAPTER 9
CHAPTER 10

STREAMING VIDEO

Live video in-world is sometimes so arresting that new residents often have difficulty believing it is real. It's perhaps the most impactful method of bringing information in-world, and similar to uploaded sound, video creation and presentation are an art form. The topic of content creation (animation and machinima, for example) warrants its own book—and it has one: *Creating Your World: The Official Guide to Advanced Content Creation for Second Life*, Wiley, 2007. Therefore, this section concentrates on how to control existing media, whether for your creations or those in the inexhaustible trove of YouTube and its ilk.

The `llParcelMediaQuery()` function determines the object's various streaming-media properties. It can also determine whether the object, and by extension its owner, has sufficient parcel privileges to play the chosen media. In Listing 11.6 this function makes a quick query to determine whether it has permissions to command or query the parcel media; the constant `PARCEL_MEDIA_COMMAND_TEXTURE` will be empty (`[]`) when it does not have permissions. Any calls to `llParcelMediaCommandList()` will fail silently.

Generally you want to display the stream onto a flat surface such as a television, but certainly there is no restriction in the type of prim to use as a "screen."

DEFINITION

`list llParcelMediaQuery(list query)`

Returns a list, with the result of the query specified as a list of inputs. The elements in the returned list are in the same order as they were requested. Causes the script to sleep for 2.0 seconds.

> `list` — The list of query items of interest. Elements of the list are named constants, shown in the following table.

CONSTANT	RETURNS	DESCRIPTION
`PARCEL_MEDIA_COMMAND_DESC`	`string desc`	Gets the parcel's media description/ metadata.
`PARCEL_MEDIA_COMMAND_LOOP_SET`	`float loop`	Gets the parcel's media looping variable.
`PARCEL_MEDIA_COMMAND_SIZE`	A pair of integers: `integer x, integer y`	Gets the parcel's media pixel resolution.
`PARCEL_MEDIA_COMMAND_TEXTURE`	`key UUID`	Gets the parcel's media texture.
`PARCEL_MEDIA_COMMAND_TYPE`	`string mime_type`	Gets the parcel's media MIME type (for instance, "text/html").
`PARCEL_MEDIA_COMMAND_URL`	`string url`	Gets the parcel's media URL.

253

CHAPTER 11

WORKING
WITH SOUND

STREAMING
MEDIA

SUMMARY

Listing 11.6: SYW TV

```
integer DISPLAY_FACE = ALL_SIDES;
key     VIDEO_DEFAULT = "e35e5ff4-5a40-1b9b-3615-8e80d0c08259";
integer VIDEO_BRIGHT = TRUE;     //FULL_BRIGHT status for Video
list    MEDIA_URLS = [
"http://movies.apple.com/movies/us/apple/getamac/apple_getamac_office-➥
    stress_20080401_480x272.mov",
"http://movies.apple.com/movies/us/apple/getamac_ads4/boxer_480x272.mov"
];
integer gChannel = 986;
integer gListLength;

usage() {
    llWhisper(0, "Say \"/" + (string)gChannel + " play\"" +
                ", \"/" + (string)gChannel + " stop\"" +
                " or \"/" + (string)gChannel + " reset\"" );
}
reset() {
    if ( llParcelMediaQuery([PARCEL_MEDIA_COMMAND_TEXTURE]) == [] ) {
        llSay(0, "Lacking permission to set/query parcel media. "+
                "This object has to be owned by/deeded to the land owner.");
    }
    llParcelMediaCommandList( [
        PARCEL_MEDIA_COMMAND_TEXTURE, VIDEO_DEFAULT,
        PARCEL_MEDIA_COMMAND_STOP ] );
}
string cacheVideo() {
    integer randSelection = (integer)llFrand((float)(gListLength-1));
    return (llList2String(MEDIA_URLS, randSelection));
}
playVideo() {
    llParcelMediaCommandList( [
        PARCEL_MEDIA_COMMAND_AGENT,       llDetectedKey(0),
        PARCEL_MEDIA_COMMAND_URL,         cacheVideo(),
        PARCEL_MEDIA_COMMAND_AUTO_ALIGN, TRUE,
        PARCEL_MEDIA_COMMAND_PLAY ] );
    llWhisper(0, "Playing ...");
}
stopVideo() {
    reset();
}
default
{
    state_entry() {
        gListLength = llGetListLength(MEDIA_URLS);
        reset();
        llListen(gChannel, "", NULL_KEY, "");
    }
    touch_start(integer total_number) {
        usage();
    }
    listen(integer channel, string name, key id, string msg) {
        if (llToLower(msg) == "play")        { playVideo(); }
        else if (llToLower(msg) == "stop")   { stopVideo(); }
        else if (llToLower(msg) == "reset") { reset();      }
        else usage();
    }
}
```

The `llParcelMediaCommandList()` function, used in both `reset()` and `playVideo()`, uses a list to deliver a set of commands to the server. Some command constants are used in the sense of key-value pairs and require a parameter, and some do not. For example, the

PARCEL_MEDIA_COMMAND_PLAY and PARCEL_MEDIA_COMMAND_STOP commands are not followed by another argument, whereas the PARCEL_MEDIA_COMMAND_URL needs a string representing a URL source. In this case the result of the cacheVideo() function is the URL. Obviously some specifications don't make sense in the same llParcelMediaCommandList() function call; you wouldn't want to instruct the server to both play and stop a video in the same invocation, for instance.

DEFINITION

list llParcelMediaCommandList(list *commands*)

Controls the play of media (such as audio or videos streams) for a parcel or an agent attachment (a prim or a HUD). Causes the script to sleep for 2.0 seconds.

commands — A list whose elements are constants representing commands, and in some cases a following parameter, as shown in the following table.

Constant	Parameter	Description
PARCEL_MEDIA_COMMAND_AGENT	key *uuid*	Applies the media command to the specified agent only (not to the parcel).
PARCEL_MEDIA_COMMAND_AUTO_ALIGN	integer *boolean*	Sets/unsets the parcel's Auto Scale Content option.
PARCEL_MEDIA_COMMAND_DESC	string *desc*	Sets the parcel's media description/metadata.
PARCEL_MEDIA_COMMAND_LOOP	—	Starts the media stream playing from the position; when the end is reached, loops to the beginning and continues.
PARCEL_MEDIA_COMMAND_LOOP_SET	float *loop*	Sets the parcel's media looping variable.
PARCEL_MEDIA_COMMAND_PAUSE	—	Pauses the media stream (position remains at the current position in the stream).
PARCEL_MEDIA_COMMAND_PLAY	—	Starts the media stream playing from the current pointer position and stops when the end is reached.
PARCEL_MEDIA_COMMAND_SIZE	A pair of integers: integer *x*, integer *y*	Sets the parcel's media pixel resolution.
PARCEL_MEDIA_COMMAND_STOP	—	Stops the media stream and resets the position to the beginning of stream.
PARCEL_MEDIA_COMMAND_TEXTURE	string *UUID*	Sets the parcel's media texture.
PARCEL_MEDIA_COMMAND_TIME	float *time*	Moves the pointer in a media stream to a specific time relative to the zero point.
PARCEL_MEDIA_COMMAND_TYPE	string *mime_type*	Sets the parcel's media MIME type (such as, text/html).
PARCEL_MEDIA_COMMAND_UNLOAD	—	Unloads the media stream and restores the default texture.
PARCEL_MEDIA_COMMAND_URL	string *url*	Sets the parcel's media URL.

The SYW TV installed at SYW HQ is fairly simple; any resident can command it through chatting on the *gChannel*. Obviously there are many possibilities for control mechanisms, including dialogs, HUDs, and buttons on the radio or TV. When you begin exploring streaming media you're likely to find many uses, from advertising to enlivening a club with live entertainment to presenting educational material. Just remember that the server will support only a single stream per parcel.

WORKING
WITH SOUND
 STREAMING
MEDIA
 SUMMARY

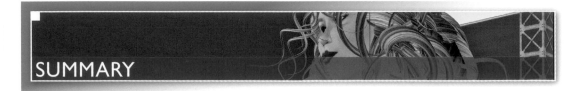

SUMMARY

Much of the effort in creating powerful objects in *Second Life* centers on building objects with a physical presence. Sound and video media sometimes receive only secondary consideration. In fact, some residents don't even turn their speakers on when in-world. In this chapter you've seen examples of scripts that incorporate powerful sound effects and media streams and give residents a reason to turn those speakers on. Sound will, at a minimum, augment the environment by adding ambience. Perhaps even more critically, automating sound and streaming both audio and video are a significant and superior method of creating an additional channel for information delivery.

CHAPTER 12

REACHING OUTSIDE *SECOND LIFE*

In Chapter 3, "Communications," you learned that LSL can communicate outside *Second Life* via email. In Chapter 11, "Multimedia," you learned how to stream audio from the Web. In this chapter you'll learn to use *Second Life* as part of a distributed application for conversations between scripted objects in-world and the 2D Web. *Second Life* supports XML-RPC and HTTP requests. Common uses for this include displaying Internet content in-world or allowing out-world programs to do things in-world.

Because LSL is an asynchronous event-handling language, it can get and receive asynchronous data from the Internet. Scripts issue requests for external Internet pages and handle the results when retrieved. LSL scripts can even act as servers, providing a way for the real world to interact more directly with *Second Life* objects, as illustrated in Figure 12.1.

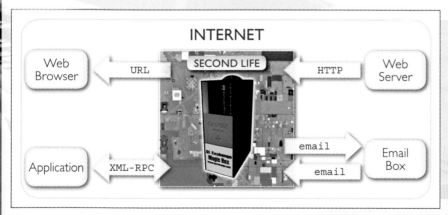

Figure 12.1: Scripts can communicate outside *Second Life*.

This chapter presents not only LSL code, but also examples of PHP and Perl code, as these are the lightweight languages commonly used by web programmers. The non-LSL languages are not explained exhaustively, but seeing the non-LSL code will give you a sense for what's entailed in writing distributed applications with one part residing in *Second Life* and one part on the Web— *it's not that scary*. The PHP example implements a simple web-server capability to generate messages for a "quote of the day." In the Perl example, you code a client that allows someone outside *SL* to control something in-world. You may be surprised at how easily you can set up interactions between the Internet and *Second Life*.

LOADING WEB PAGES IN-WORLD

▶ LOADING
  WEB PAGES
  IN-WORLD

▶ USING HTTP
  REQUESTS TO
  GET DATA
  FROM THE
  WEB

USING
XML-RPC
TO CONTROL
SL FROM THE
OUTSIDE

SUMMARY

Although it may seem out of step with the 3D nature of **Second Life**, it's quite easy to bring the flat world of web pages in-world. Suppose a visitor to your parcel is reading the news ticker's crawl, and would like more details. The button to the left of the news ticker, shown in Figure 12.2, pops up and a dialog box appears, offering to load a web page using the in-world browser. The script in Listing 12.1 is simple to implement, but has a huge payoff.

Figure 12.2. The URL loader dialog and the loaded page

Listing 12.1: URL Loader

```
default
{
    touch_start(integer total_number) {
        llLoadURL(llDetectedKey(0), "cnn", "http://cnn.com");
    }
}
```

The function `llLoadURL()` takes three arguments. The first is an avatar key, conveniently available in the `touch_start()` event handler via `llDetectedKey()`. The second argument is used to populate the information area of the dialog, and the third is the name of the HTML source itself. Be aware that the script penalty is 10 seconds, and the load time for the page can also be substantial.

CHAPTER 1
CHAPTER 2
CHAPTER 3
CHAPTER 4
CHAPTER 5
CHAPTER 6
CHAPTER 7
CHAPTER 8
CHAPTER 9
CHAPTER 10
CHAPTER 11

CHAPTER 12

CHAPTER 13
CHAPTER 14
CHAPTER 15
APPENDICES

DEFINITION

```
llLoadURL(key avatarID, string message, string url)
```

Shows a dialog, introduced with the *message*, that offers to load the web page. If the user clicks Yes, a page opens, either in the internal browser or their computer's default web browser, depending on preference settings and the *Second Life* client version. Causes the script to sleep for 10 seconds.

> *avatarID* — The UUID of the avatar to whom to display the dialog.
>
> *message* — The text shown at the top of the dialog box, up to 254 characters.
>
> *url* — A valid HTTP/HTTPS URL, up to 255 characters.

The **Second Life** in-world browser is minimalist in certain respects. For example, it does not support Flash applications or Java applets, and its QuickTime capabilities are extremely variable, ranging from "does not work at all" to "plays audio only" to "plays video and audio but fails to lay out the page correctly." Additionally, the in-world browser's handling of both JavaScript and cascading style sheets is extremely variable. Fortunately, there's a discreet little button labeled Open in My Web Browser tucked away at the bottom left of the browser window (see Figure 12.2). This will launch an external web browser, with the correct URL filled in.

USING HTTP REQUESTS TO GET DATA FROM THE WEB

Showing a web page in-world is a good first step to tying **Second Life** to applications elsewhere on the Internet, but there's still a lot more you can do. This section shows you how to pull data from an outside server and manipulate it in-world in interesting ways. Many objects are refreshed from the Web, and the Web is also frequently used as a persistent data-storage method.

GETTING DATA FROM A WEB SERVER

This example demonstrates how to access a very simple website and publish the results in-world. The script in Listing 12.2 waits for an avatar to touch its containing object, then goes to `http://secondlife.com` to get the current **Second Life** usage statistics. The specific data source that Listing 12.2 uses is simply a list of lines, alternating between the *name* of a statistic and the *value* of the statistic. For instance, a result like

```
logged60
1108840
exchange_rate
267.3433
inworld
51147
```

indicates that 1,108,840 avatars have been in-world in the last 60 days, the current exchange rate is about L$267 per US dollar, and 51,147 residents are logged on right now.

261

CHAPTER 12

LOADING
WEB PAGES
IN-WORLD

 USING HTTP
REQUESTS TO
GET DATA
FROM THE
WEB

USING
XML-RPC
TO CONTROL
SL FROM THE
OUTSIDE

SUMMARY

Listing 12.2: How Many Residents Are In-World?

```
string SL_STATS_URL = "http://secondlife.com/httprequest/homepage.php";
key gRequestid;

default
{
    touch_end(integer p) {
        gRequestid = llHTTPRequest(SL_STATS_URL, [HTTP_METHOD, "GET"], "");
    }
    http_response(key requestID, integer status, list metadata, string body) {
        if (requestID == gRequestid) {
            list lines = llParseString2List(body, ["\n"], []);
            integer i = llListFindList(lines, ["inworld"]);
            llSay(0, "There are currently "+llList2String(lines, i+1)+
                " residents online");
        }
    }
}
```

When the script gets a `touch()` event, it calls `llHTTPRequest()` to retrieve the contents of the web page at `http://secondlife.com/httprequest/homepage.php`. `llHTTPRequest()` returns a key that can be used to uniquely identify a particular outstanding request. When *SL* retrieves the page and is ready for the script, it triggers an `http_response()` event with the contents of the page. In this case, the page can be parsed by splitting up the response *body* at each newline character (`\n`), resulting in a strided list of alternating name-value pairs. Because the script needs only the value corresponding to how many residents are in-world, it uses `llListFindList()` to get the index of the `"inworld"` parameter and then prints the next element.

 EVENT DEFINITION

```
http_response(key requestHandle, integer status,
              list metadata, string body) {}
```

This event is invoked when an HTTP request fails or returns a value. Additional documentation can be found on the SYW website.

requestHandle — The handle that was returned by the specific `llHTTPRequest()` that initiated the call. Multiple requests can be pending.

status — The HTTP status code, either returned in the HTTP response or detailing the error that caused the request to fail. These values depend entirely on what the web server sends back[*]. The most important one is 200, which normally indicates success; anything else is most often a failure of some sort. In addition, *SL* may return a status of 499, which indicates either an *SL*-related failure or that you passed an illegal URL, usually due to spaces or other unescaped special characters.

metadata — This list is filled with alternating [*key*, *value*] pairs containing extra information about the response. The *key* will always be an integer LSL constant starting with `HTTP_`. The only *key* you will see in the current implementation is `HTTP_BODY_TRUNCATED`, indicating the body was truncated, with the *value* part of the pair indicating the character where the body was cut.

body — The body of the response. If the response is longer than 2,048 characters it will be truncated.

---

[*] The *status* values should conform to web standards. HTTP 1.1 result codes are defined by the W3C specification (`http://www.w3.org/Protocols/rfc2616/rfc2616-sec9.html`).

```
key llHTTPRequest(string url, list parameters, string body)
```

Sends an HTTP request to the specified URL with the body of the request and parameters. Returns a key (or *handle*) that uniquely identifies which HTTP request was made; the handle will be passed to `http_response()`. Handles survive state changes.

> *url* — A valid HTTP/HTTPS URL.

> *parameters* — HTTP request parameters in a strided list format [parameter1, *value1*, parameter2, *value2*, ..., parameterN, *valueN*]. The following table shows the valid parameter names and their types, values, and descriptions.

Name	Type	Default Value	Description
HTTP_METHOD	string	"GET"	One of four possible HTTP commands[*]: "GET", "POST", "PUT", and "DELETE".
HTTP_MIMETYPE	string	"text/plain;➡ charset=utf-8"	text/* MIME (Multipurpose Internet Mail Extensions) types should specify a character set. A MIME type is a way to specify whether the document contains text in character sets other than US-ASCII.
HTTP_BODY_MAXLENGTH	integer	2048	Setting HTTP_BODY_MAXLENGTH is not yet supported.
HTTP_VERIFY_CERT	integer	TRUE	If **TRUE**, the server SSL certificate must be verifiable using one of the standard certificate authorities when making HTTPS requests. If **FALSE**, any server SSL certificate will be accepted.

> *body* — The body of the HTTP request. This parameter is used only when the HTTP_METHOD is "POST" or "PUT".

---

* The World Wide Web Consortium specification offers a complete list of all HTTP commands; only these four are currently supported in LSL.

⛏ USING THE WEB FOR PERSISTENT STORAGE: **name2Key**

One of the big problems with scripting in *Second Life* is the lack of any way to effectively store persistent data. Scripts cannot even write into notecards. Keeping information in memory is rather limited, and worse, risks data loss if the script is reset. The most common way around this problem is to use websites to store and retrieve information for your scripts. There are many examples, but probably the single most useful examples are web databases that store the associations between avatar names and their keys.

263

LOADING
WEB PAGES
IN-WORLD

USING HTTP
REQUESTS TO
GET DATA
FROM THE
WEB

USING
XML-RPC
TO CONTROL
SL FROM THE
OUTSIDE

SUMMARY

You may have noticed that there is no `llName2Key()` function in LSL to match `llKey2Name()`. If the avatar you are interested in can be detected with `touch()` or `sensor()` events, you can use `llDetectedKey()` and `llDetectedName()` to get the key. However, if you can't explicitly sense the avatar, you need to use a script like the one in Listing 12.3.

Listing 12.3: Find the Key for an Avatar Name

```
string   N2KURL = "http://w-hat.com/name2key";
integer CHANNEL = 101;
string gPendingName;            // set during name2key lookup
key gHTTPKey;                   // key for http requests

lookupName(string name) {
    gPendingName = name;
    gHTTPKey = llHTTPRequest(N2KURL +
                "?terse=1&name="+llEscapeURL(gPendingName), [], "");
}

default
{
    on_rez(integer p) { llResetScript(); }
    state_entry() {
        llOwnerSay("Name2Key ready: Chat the full name of "+
                "the avatar you want to look up on channel "+CHANNEL);
        llListen(CHANNEL, "", llGetOwner(), "");
    }
    listen(integer ch, string name, key id, string m) {
        lookupName(m);
    }
    http_response(key id, integer status, list meta, string body) {
        if (status != 200) {
            llOwnerSay("name2key error "+ (string) status);
        } else {
            key k = (key) body;
            if (k == NULL_KEY) {
                llOwnerSay("Couldn't find key for "+gPendingName);
            } else {
                llOwnerSay(gPendingName+"'s key appears to be \""+(string)k+"\".");
            }
        }
    }
}
```

The site at `http://w-hat.com/name2key` maintains a big database of the associations between avatar names and keys. Your script simply needs to make the correct HTTP calls to retrieve the keys for most active avatars in *Second Life*. Note that the script isn't guaranteed to find a key, however!

The process here is very similar to that of Listing 12.2. First the script sets up a listener on channel 101 for the script's owner. Anything that it hears, it will look up using the following call:

```
gHTTPKey = llHTTPRequest(N2KURL +
                "?terse=1&name="+llEscapeURL(gPendingName), [], "");
```

It builds a query string to `llHTTPRequest()` composed of the base URL (`http://w-hat.com/name2key`) and a list of arguments. The argument list starts with a question mark (?) and a sequence of parameter pairs, such as `parametername=value`, separated by ampersands (&). The argument list for this query is `terse=1`, indicating to this particular web service that just the key should be returned rather than a big web page, and *gPendingName*. The call to `llEscapeURL()` ensures any special characters in the name are converted into HTTP argument strings. In this case `llEscapeURL()`

replaces the space in the name with the ugly but correct HTTP encoding for space, `%20`. When the query string has been constructed, the script calls `llHTTPRequest()` and waits for the response.

In the `http_response()` event handler, the script checks the status value. These are Internet-standard HTTP codes that every web server uses. The most critical one to know about is `200`, which indicates success. In addition to the usual possibilities, such as `404` for Not Found, *Second Life* also may return `499`, usually indicating a malformed query or a problem within *SL*. These values do not have LSL constants defined for them. If the handler gets a successful query, the string in the body will be the key from the `name2key` database; the string will be equal to `NULL_KEY` if the `name2key` service doesn't know the name. The script then uses `llOwnerSay()` to tell the owner what it discovered.

The section "Charity Collectors" in Chapter 13, "Money Makes the World Go Round," has an expanded version of this utility.

 ## CONSTRUCTING BOTH SIDES OF A REQUEST: MESSAGE IN A BOTTLE

The previous two examples showed how you can use `llHTTPRequest()` to get data from a web server. Neither example assumes you had anything to do with generating the information on the web server. This example takes the next step and teaches you to build both sides of the interaction. The client side (in *SL*) requests a message from a web server; the script is quite similar to the previous two examples. The server side (outside *SL*) generates a message. At SYW HQ, these scripts are in the form of a message in a bottle. Figure 12.3 shows an avatar retrieving a message from a bottle; the bottle contains Listing 12.4 while Listing 12.5 on the web server provides the quote.

Message in a Bottle whispers: Men occasionally stumble over the truth, but most of them pick themselves up and hurry off as if nothing ever happened. -- Sir Winston Churchill (1874-1965)

Figure 12.3: The message in this bottle is retrieved from an HTTP server.

The Client Side (LSL): Asking for the Message

Listing 12.4 shows the in-world side of the interaction. This script bears many similarities to the scripts in Listings 12.2 and 12.3 but adds significant parsing of commands from the user. The biggest change is in the calls to `llHTTPRequest()`. The function sends an HTTP request to the specified URL with a `"POST"` method, and the request *body* used by the http server. For a random quote, the *body* parameter is

CHAPTER 1
CHAPTER 2
CHAPTER 3
CHAPTER 4
CHAPTER 5
CHAPTER 6
CHAPTER 7
CHAPTER 8
CHAPTER 9
CHAPTER 10
CHAPTER 11
CHAPTER 12
CHAPTER 13
CHAPTER 14
CHAPTER 15
APPENDICES

"parameter1=random"

For a specific quote, the *body* parameter is

"parameter1=quote&parameter2="+quoteNum

`llHTTPRequest()` returns a handle that will be passed to the `http_response()` event when the data is ready.

Loading
Web Pages
In-World

► Using HTTP
Requests to
Get Data
From the
Web

Using
XML-RPC
to Control
SL from the
Outside

Summary

Listing 12.4: Message in a Bottle—The Client on the *SL* Side

```
key      gRequestid;
integer gCommandChannel = 989;
string  gMyServer = "http://abraxas-soft.com/phpscripts/quoter.php";
string  gOwner;
list gHttpParams = [HTTP_METHOD, "POST",
                    HTTP_MIMETYPE, "application/x-www-form-urlencoded"];
usage()
{
    string basicMessage = " Type: '/"+(string)gCommandChannel;
    llOwnerSay(basicMessage+" random!' to get a random quote");
    llOwnerSay(basicMessage+" quote! #' to get a specific quote");
}
default
{
    on_rez(integer param) {
        llResetScript();
    }
    state_entry() {
        gOwner = llGetOwner();
        llListen(gCommandChannel, "", gOwner, "");
        usage();
    }
    listen(integer channel, string name, key id, string message) {
        list messageContent = llParseString2List(message, [" "], []);
        integer len = llGetListLength(messageContent);
        message = llList2String(messageContent,0);

        if (message == "random!") {
            gRequestid = llHTTPRequest(gMyServer, gHttpParams, "parameter1=random");
        } else if (message == "quote!") {
            if (len < 2) {
                usage();
                return;
            }
            string quoteNum = llList2String(messageContent, 1);
            gRequestid = llHTTPRequest(gMyServer, gHttpParams,
                            "parameter1=quote&parameter2="+quoteNum);
        } else {
            usage();
        }
    }
    http_response(key requestID, integer status, list metadata, string body) {
        if (requestID == gRequestid) { // only the most recent HTTPRequest
            llInstantMessage(gOwner, "Quote of the day: " + body);
        }
    }
}
```

The Server Side (PHP): Generating the Message

The server side is almost as simple, and is implemented in PHP. PHP is one of several languages used to build websites. (Python and Perl are two others; an example of Perl follows in a later section of this chapter.*) All of the non-LSL languages discussed here are richly endowed with capabilities, especially in the handling of strings, and all are blessed with simple syntax that is even easier to follow than LSL code.

One thing PHP and Perl support that *isn't* supported in LSL is a data type called an `array`, which acts a lot like LSL's `list` structure; both are a sequence of items, but arrays are easier to access—instead of a function call `llList2String(myList, index)`, you can simply say `$myList[$index]`. (The $ is how PHP indicates the name of a variable.) Listing 12.5 shows a simple array of strings, `$arr`, that will be returned when the HTTP request is made.

Listing 12.5: Message in a Bottle—Server Side (PHP)

```php
<?
// Only works with PHP compiled as an Apache module
$arr = array(
0 =>"Welcome to the quote store",
    "Facts do not cease to exist because they are ignored. -- Aldous Huxley",
    "I'm altering our deal... pray I do not alter it further. -- Darth Vader",
    "Premature optimization is the root of all evil. - Donald Knuth",
    // ... expand the array of quotes to taste
    "Learn from yesterday, live for today, hope for tomorrow.",
    "The opposite of love is not hate, it's indifference -- Elie Wiesel"
);
// get things from $_POST[]
$parameter1    = $_POST["parameter1"];
$parameter2    = $_POST["parameter2"];

srand((double)microtime()*1000000);
if ($parameter1 == "quote")   {
    echo $parameter1. "\n". "\u";
    if ($parameter2 > sizeof($arr) ) $parameter2 = 0;
    $quote =  $arr[$parameter2];
} elseif ($parameter1 == "random") {
    $random = (rand()%sizeof($arr));
    $quote =  $arr[$random];
} else {
    $quote =  $arr[0];
}
echo $quote . "\n";
?>
```

The parameters are picked from the "POST" request and read. If the first parameter requests a specific quote from the stack, the second parameter is the specific quote number. If the first parameter matches the string "random", a random one is pulled off the stack. In either case, the quote is returned via the echo function.

When you decide to tackle writing web-server code, a myriad of language choices is available to you. This chapter presents only two examples—PHP and Perl—giving you a taste of what to expect. Pick the language that feels most comfortable to you, and run with it. The ability to use code outside *SL* will open many opportunities for you and enrich the interactions of every resident.

CHAPTER 1
CHAPTER 2
CHAPTER 3
CHAPTER 4
CHAPTER 5
CHAPTER 6
CHAPTER 7
CHAPTER 8
CHAPTER 9
CHAPTER 10
CHAPTER 11
CHAPTER 12
CHAPTER 13
CHAPTER 14
CHAPTER 15
APPENDICES

---

* You can get much more information on these languages from your local bookstore or on the Web at `http://php.net`, `http://python.org`, and `http://perl.org` for PHP, Python, and Perl, respectively.

LOADING
WEB PAGES
IN-WORLD

USING HTTP
REQUESTS TO
GET DATA
FROM THE
WEB

USING
XML-RPC
TO CONTROL
SL FROM THE
OUTSIDE

SUMMARY

RSS FEEDS IN *SECOND LIFE*

Another way to make a tighter coupling between the real world and the virtual world is to feature current headlines on an LED news ticker via RSS (Really Simple Syndication) feeds. This section pairs the `llHTTPRequest()` and its companion event handler `http_response()` to parse and display RSS feeds. The scripts in this section query an RSS news feed, in this case the site `http://slashdot.org`, and then display the query results on a scrolling news ticker. You can see it in action at SYW HQ (Figure 12.4).

Figure 12.4: All the news that's fit to scroll, from an RSS news feed

BUILD NOTE

Rez a box in front of you and name it `News Ticker`. Set Size to <1.5, 8.5, 1.5>. Set Rotation to <0, 0, 180>. Color the box black to make the faux LEDs to stand out. Place Listing 12.6 in its inventory.

For the LEDs, create another box and name it `LED`. Set Size to <0.25, 1.0, 1.0>. Set Rotation to <0, 0, 0>. It is important that each LED has the correct rotation, since in Listing 12.7 your script sets face number 2 (the "front" face in this case) to the textures representing the LED letters. Align the LED so that it's inset from the news ticker's left edge. Color the entire LED object white. Place Listing 12.7 in its Contents folder.

Using Shift-copy, make a line of seven copies of the first LED out to the right of the first LED, lining them up so there are no horizontal gaps. Next link the LEDs in a specific order: select each of the LEDs going back to the first one from right to left, starting with the last one you Shift-copied. Select the `News Ticker` last so it becomes the root prim, and link all nine prims together with *Control+L* or select Link under the Tools menu.

The news-ticker script contains the key of a texture (Figure 12.5) created by Corey Ondrejka, former CTO of Linden Lab. Corey also first implemented the algorithm for selecting which piece of the texture to display on the LEDs.

Figure 12.5: The **DISPLAY_LETTERS** constant in Listing 12.6 matches the layout of the Ondrejka Neon Letters texture. The **LETTERS_PER_ROW** constant in Listing 12.7 matches the number of letters per row.

CHAPTER 1
CHAPTER 2
CHAPTER 3
CHAPTER 4
CHAPTER 5
CHAPTER 6
CHAPTER 7
CHAPTER 8
CHAPTER 9
CHAPTER 10
CHAPTER 11

CHAPTER 12

Listing 12.6 controls the root prim. The `touch_start()` event handler makes an HTTP request, and the result is returned in `http_response()`. The function `getTitles()` parses the RSS data to extract the titles from the response and stores them in **gStories**. The `timer()` event works out which prim displays which letter of **gStories**, and uses `llMessageLinked()` to tell each one what to display.

Listing 12.6: RSS News Ticker

```
list DISPLAY_LETTERS = ["0","1","2","3","4","5","6","7","8","9",":",",","!",".","?",";",
                        "A","B","C","D","E","F","G","H","I","J","K","L","M","N","O","P",
                        "Q","R","S","T","U","V","W","X","Y","Z"];

float   TIMER_INTERVAL = 0.5;
string  RSS_LINK = " http://rss.cnn.com/rss/cnn_topstories.rss";
string  XML_ITEM_TAG = "<item>";
string  XML_TITLE_TAG = "<title>";
string  XML_TITLE_TAG_END = "</title>";
integer HTTP_OK = 200;
string  TEXTURE_FONT = "8b11c627-595a-bda4-b6f3-e2331255c280"; //alphaBlue

string  gStories = "And Now the News";
integer gLEDZero = 2;
integer gLEDS;
integer gCurrPos;

list getTitles(string bodyPart) {
    list rList = [];
    string title;
    bodyPart = chomp(bodyPart, XML_ITEM_TAG);  // find the item tag
    do { // extract titles
        bodyPart = chomp(bodyPart, XML_TITLE_TAG);
        title = extract(bodyPart, XML_TITLE_TAG_END);
        rList += title+"... ";
        bodyPart = chomp(bodyPart, XML_TITLE_TAG);
    } while (llStringLength(bodyPart) > 0);
    return rList;
}
string chomp(string input, string tag) {
    integer index = llSubStringIndex(input, tag);
    if (index == -1) return "";
    return llDeleteSubString(input, 0, index +llStringLength(tag) - 1);
}
```

LOADING
WEB PAGES
IN-WORLD

USING HTTP
REQUESTS TO
GET DATA
FROM THE
WEB

USING
XML-RPC
TO CONTROL
SL FROM THE
OUTSIDE

SUMMARY

```
string extract(string input, string tag) {
    integer index = llSubStringIndex(input, tag);
    if (index == -1) return "";
    return llGetSubString(input, 0, index - 1);
}
reset() {
    llMessageLinked(LINK_ALL_CHILDREN, -2, "", TEXTURE_FONT);
    gCurrPos = -gLEDS;
    gStories = llToUpper(gStories);
    llSleep(5.0); // give the LEDs time to "cool"
    llSetTimerEvent(TIMER_INTERVAL);
    gLEDS = llGetNumberOfPrims() - 1;
}

default
{
    state_entry() {
        reset();
    }
    touch_start(integer tnum) {
        llHTTPRequest(RSS_LINK, [], "");
        reset();
    }

    http_response(key request_id, integer status, list metadata, string body) {
        if (status == HTTP_OK) {
            gStories = "RSS News... " + (string) getTitles(body);
        } else {
            llOwnerSay("Unable to fetch "+RSS_LINK);
        }
        reset();
    }
    timer() {
        integer length = llStringLength(gStories);
        integer i;
        for (i = 0; i < gLEDS; i++) { // Tell each LED which letter to preload
            if (i + gCurrPos < 0) {    // No letter yet
                llMessageLinked(gLEDZero + i, 63, "", "");
            } else if (i + gCurrPos >= length) { // Finished
                llMessageLinked(gLEDZero + i, 63, "", "");
            } else {
                string temp = llGetSubString(gStories, i+gCurrPos, i+gCurrPos);
                integer position = llListFindList(DISPLAY_LETTERS, [temp]);
                if (position != -1) {
                    llMessageLinked(gLEDZero + i, position, "", "");
                } else {
                    llMessageLinked(gLEDZero + i, 63, "", "");
                }
            }
        }
        // tell all LEDs to display the new letter
        llMessageLinked(LINK_ALL_CHILDREN, -1, "", "");
        gCurrPos++;
        if (gCurrPos > length) {
            gCurrPos = -gLEDS;
        }
    }
}
```

The function `getTitles()` takes care of parsing the RSS data returned by `http_response()`. RSS data is structured XML for presenting news stories. RSS XML format is designed exclusively for machine understanding and processing; here is a sample pulled from `http://slashdot.org/slashdot.rdf`:

```
<item><title>Whitehouse Emails Were Lost Due to "Upgrade"</title><link>
http://rss.slashdot.org/~r/Slashdot/slashdot/to/~3/280835736/article.pl
  </link><description><p>
  <a href="http://rss.slashdot.org/~a/Slashdot/slashdot/to?a=uCeE9F">
  <img src="http://rss.slashdot.org/~a/Slashdot/slashdot/to?i=uCeE9F" border="0">
  </img></a></p>
  <img src="http://rss.slashdot.org/~r/Slashdot/slashdot/to/~4/280835736"
  height="1" width="1"/></description><feedburner:origLink>
  http://news.slashdot.org/article.pl?sid=08/04/30/1359209&from=rss
  </feedburner:origLink>
</item>
```

RSS feeds include a variety of XML tags in a feed, some of which are mandatory. Each item is delimited by the tags `<item>` *item content* `</item>`. Each item must contain the following:

- A headline, delimited by `<title>` *headline* `</title>`

- A link to a URL that contains the full story, delimited by `<link>` *URL* `</link>`

- A description containing something, often a few words, summarizing the story, delimited by `<description>` *descriptive text* `</description>`

LSL doesn't have a way to easily parse and pick out the salient elements of an RSS feed. Because parsing is often a significant challenge in LSL, it is useful to make a function that handles the details of how to extract the headline titles into a list.

`getTitles()` uses two utility functions, `chomp()` and `extract()`, to move from tag to tag, pulling out the important elements of the feed. `chomp()` *deletes* everything in the *input* string, up to and including the first *tag*, returning everything after the *tag*. For example, the line

```
bodyPart = chomp(bodyPart, XML_ITEM_TAG);
```

finds the starting `<item>` tag. The `extract()` function, meanwhile, *saves* everything in the *input* string, up to but not including the *tag*.

Therefore, the `do...while` loop in `getTitles()` nibbles away at the string, finding then discarding everything up to each `<title>` tag, then extracting each headline in turn, adding it to the growing list. Finally, it finds and discards the trailing newline character. The `do...while` loop terminates when it has exhausted the returned XML string. Note the use of `llSubStringIndex()` to find a string of interest, `llDeleteSubString()`, to discard a piece of text and return the residue back into the original string, and `llGetSubString()` to find the next headline and return it into its own string. The resulting string in *gStories* looks like this:

```
RSS News... Clinton, Obama decline to back loser as VP... Candlelight vigil caps
    Va. Tech anniversary... Elderly women guilty in murder-for-profit case... Bush
    climate change shift gets cool reception... Bumped fliers could get $800 with
    new rules...
```

Once *gTitles* has been constructed, Listing 12.6's `timer()` event manages the actual marching of letters from right to left across the face of the news ticker. Each time the `timer()` elapses, the news ticker updates each LED. The control loop traverses the set of LEDs specified in *gLEDS*. It calculates which letter each LED needs to display, extracting it from `DISPLAY_LETTERS` using the function `llListFindList()`, and reporting which letter with a call to `llMessageLinked()` to the specific LED. The last `llMessageLinked()` call goes to all the LEDs, causing them to update.

Each LED contains a copy of Listing 12.7; the `link_message()` event handler in each LED will receive the messages sent by the news ticker. Listing 12.7 calculates the offsets in the texture corresponding to the desired letter, then uses `llOffsetTexture()` to paint the face of each faux LED with the correct texture snippet. Note that `llScaleTexture(0.0625, 0.25, ALL_SIDES)` will scale the texture nicely regardless of the size of the LEDs themselves.

CHAPTER 1
CHAPTER 2
CHAPTER 3
CHAPTER 4
CHAPTER 5
CHAPTER 6
CHAPTER 7
CHAPTER 8
CHAPTER 9
CHAPTER 10
CHAPTER 11

CHAPTER 12

LOADING
WEB PAGES
IN-WORLD

➥ USING HTTP
REQUESTS TO
GET DATA
FROM THE
WEB

➥ USING
XML-RPC
TO CONTROL
SL FROM THE
OUTSIDE

SUMMARY

Listing 12.7: RSS News Ticker LED

```
integer LETTERS_PER_ROW = 16; // number of letters per row in texture
key     gTexture;
vector gOffset;
vector get_offset(integer num) { // prepares for the next letter
    integer s = num % LETTERS_PER_ROW;
    integer t = num / LETTERS_PER_ROW;
    float sf = (s - 8) * 0.0625 + 0.03175;
    float tf = (1 - t) * 0.25 + 0.124;
    return <sf, tf, 0.0>;
}

default {
    link_message(integer sender_num, integer num, string str, key id) {
        if (num == -2) { // when the key of the texture was sent
            llScaleTexture(0.0625, 0.25, ALL_SIDES);
            gTexture = id;
            llSetTexture(gTexture, 2);
        } else if (num == -1) { // move all letters
            llOffsetTexture(gOffset.x, gOffset.y, 2);
        } else { // when this prim needs to calculate offset
            gOffset = get_offset(num);
        }
    }
}
```

The RSS news ticker shown in Listings 12.6 and 12.7 has the virtue of being self-sufficient. That is, it takes the feed directly from the site specified and parses the result directly. Now for the bad news: currently, `llHTTPRequest()` returns only the first 2,048 characters of raw data from a web server. Given the wordiness of XML, that means you'll capture at most a few headlines. Unless you're easily satisfied, you'd probably prefer a longer set of headlines. One solution is to use a website as a proxy for your request—one that will do the heavy lifting of parsing and bundling for you. You will find scripts for a Python-based proxy server and an improved LSL news ticker on the SYW website.

USING XML-RPC TO CONTROL SL FROM THE OUTSIDE

In addition to using the `llHTTPRequest()` there is yet another way to access external resources. The XML-RPC (Remote Procedure Call) protocol uses XML to encode its calls by enabling synchronous data-centric exchange. This is the slowest way to get data in and out of **SL**, but it supports the largest amount of data. It is also the only way to establish a two-way, continuing conversation with something outside **SL**. In this section, we highlight the most significant benefit XML-RPC gives the LSL scripter: **the LSL side can become the server.**

In this build you create a flag whose texture can be changed by a Perl script outside **SL**. The flag implements an in-world XML-RPC server. The idea is that the out-of-world Perl script can cause the in-world flag to change its texture. There are some sophisticated uses for this remote-control capability. For example, you can have a remote script interrogate your vendors to ask them for a daily sales report. Scripted servers can also be important to the **SL** economy—for example, by allowing users of external applications such as OnRez or SL Exchange to buy virtual merchandise via their web browsers and have their purchases delivered directly to their account, even if they aren't logged in at the time. These websites work by using XML-RPC or email to instruct in-world inventory server objects to transfer objects from inventory to the target account.

THE SERVER SIDE (LSL): RECEIVING INSTRUCTIONS FROM OUT-WORLD

The flag shown in Figure 12.6 is initially textured with one of the flag textures in inventory. The server side of the conversation is implemented by the code in Listing 12.8.

CHAPTER 1
CHAPTER 2
CHAPTER 3
CHAPTER 4
CHAPTER 5
CHAPTER 6
CHAPTER 7
CHAPTER 8
CHAPTER 9
CHAPTER 10
CHAPTER 11

Figure 12.6: XML-RPC flag changer in its initial state

Listing 12.8: XML-RPC Flag Changer (LSL Server)

```
integer gListenChannel = 987;
list myTextures = ["USA", "Canada", "Rainbow", "Maryland" ];

integer changeFlag(key cID, key mID, integer idata, string texture) {
    integer i = llListFindList(myTextures, [texture]);
    if (i >= 0) {
        string reply += "Setting texture to "+texture;
        llRemoteDataReply(cID, mID, reply, idata);
        llSetTexture(texture,ALL_SIDES);
        return TRUE;
    } else {
        llRemoteDataReply(cID, mID, "Unknown texture", idata);
        return FALSE;
    }
}

default{
    state_entry() {
        llOwnerSay("Touch to listen on channel "+(string)gListenChannel);
        llSetTexture("totallyclear", ALL_SIDES);
        llSetTexture(llList2String(myTextures,0), 1); // front
        llSetTexture(llList2String(myTextures,0), 3); // back
    }
    touch_start(integer total_number) {
        llOwnerSay("Listening on channel "
                +(string)gListenChannel+" say 'START' or 'STOP'");
        llListen(gListenChannel,"", NULL_KEY,"");
    }
    listen(integer _channel, string _name, key _id, string message) {
        if (llToUpper(message) == "START") {
            llOpenRemoteDataChannel();
        } else {
            llCloseRemoteDataChannel(id);
        }
    }
```

LOADING
WEB PAGES
IN-WORLD

USING HTTP
REQUESTS TO
GET DATA
FROM THE
WEB

 USING
XML-RPC
TO CONTROL
SL FROM THE
OUTSIDE

SUMMARY

```
remote_data(integer event_type, key channelKey, key message_id,
        string sender, integer idata, string sdata) {
    if (event_type == REMOTE_DATA_CHANNEL) {
        llOwnerSay("Remote data channel available on " + (string)channelKey);
    } else if (event_type == REMOTE_DATA_REQUEST) {
        llOwnerSay("Got REMOTE_DATA_REQUEST. Changing to "+sdata);
        changeFlag(channel, message_id, idata, sdata);
    } else {
        llOwnerSay("Didn't understand remote data request");
    }
}
}
```

The script in Listing 12.8 sets up a private listener channel on **gListenChannel** for the owner to start the server. This is useful when a channel is lost or closed, for example when the sim is reset. Also, any channel not used for 14 days will be cleaned up. It is a good idea to check somewhat regularly (before expected use or on a regular schedule) that the channel is good; call llOpenRemoteDataChannel() and compare the returned handle to the previous one.

When the object gets a "START" message it invokes llOpenRemoteDataChannel(). The remote_data() event handler catches this invocation and checks to see whether the event was caused by the opening of the channel (**event_type** == REMOTE_DATA_CHANNEL), or a remote client invocation (**event_type** == REMOTE_DATA_REQUEST). Opening a channel returns a key, **channelKey**, that gets communicated in llOwnerSay(). This key will be needed on the client side, so keep track of it.

 ## EVENT DEFINITION

```
remote_data(integer event_type, key channel, key message_id,
        string sender, integer idata, string sdata) {}
```

Called whenever the script receives an XML-RPC message or is notified by *SL* of a successful channel registration resulting from a call to llOpenRemoteDataChannel().

event_type — The type of remote data event; valid values are shown in the following table.

EVENT_TYPE Constants	Description
REMOTE_DATA_CHANNEL	Indicates the channel handle is open and available for use, as requested by a call to llOpenRemoteDataChannel().
REMOTE_DATA_REQUEST	Indicates the event is a new request from outside the script.
REMOTE_DATA_REPLY	Indicates the event is a reply to a request issued by llSendRemoteData().

channel — The handle identifying the channel.

message_id — A unique identifier for the specific message.

sender — The name of the sender.

idata — An integer data item sent.

sdata — A string data item sent.

The valid flag textures are in the flag's inventory, and thus when one of them is received as an input string, the script calls `llSetTexture()` on the exposed faces of the flag, as shown in Figure 12.7.

CHAPTER 1
CHAPTER 2
CHAPTER 3
CHAPTER 4
CHAPTER 5
CHAPTER 6
CHAPTER 7
CHAPTER 8
CHAPTER 9
CHAPTER 10
CHAPTER 11

Figure 12.7: The XML-RPC flag changer receives change instructions from a remote channel.

Flag: Got REMOTE_DATA_REQUEST. Changing to Canada

Be aware that if an object moves from one region to another it must call `llRemoteDataSetRegion()` to reset the channel, or close and reopen the channel. The function `llCloseRemoteDataChannel()` also closes the XML-RPC channel. Table 12.1 outlines the functions supporting XML-RPC.

TABLE 12.1: XML-RPC FUNCTIONS

Function	Behavior
`key llSendRemoteData(key channel, string dest, integer idata, string sdata)`	Sends an XML-RPC request to *dest* through a channel with a payload of *channel*, *idata*, and *sdata*. Returns a key that is the *message_id* parameter for the resulting `remote_data()` events.
`llRemoteDataReply(key channel, key message_id, string sdata, integer idata)`	Sends an XML-RPC reply on *channel* to *message_id* with a payload of *sdata* and *idata*. Delays the script for three seconds.
`llOpenRemoteDataChannel()`	Creates a channel to listen for XML-RPC calls. Triggers a `remote_data()` event with *channel* identifier when results are available.
`llRemoteDataSetRegion()`	If a script using XML-RPC channels changes regions, you must call this function to re-register the remote data channels.
`llCloseRemoteDataChannel(key channel)`	Closes an XML-RPC channel.

WARNING

All inbound requests for any object acting as an XML-RPC server go through a common gateway (xmlrpc.secondlife.com). The current implementation of XML-RPC allows only *one* request for a given object to be queued on the gateway at a time. Any additional requests to the same data channel *overwrite* any pending requests. This has serious ramifications for the XML-RPC communication design where the in-world object can receive requests faster than it can respond to them. The three-second delay in `llRemoteDataReply()` exacerbates this problem even more.

LOADING
WEB PAGES
IN-WORLD

USING HTTP
REQUESTS TO
GET DATA
FROM THE
WEB

▶ USING
XML-RPC
TO CONTROL
SL FROM THE
OUTSIDE

▶ SUMMARY

▶ THE CLIENT SIDE (PERL): SEND INSTRUCTIONS INTO *SL*

Listing 12.9 shows a client-side script written in Perl (outside *SL*). Like PHP, Perl is a wonderfully tractable and useful language almost universally supported by ISPs. This XML-RPC client is meant to be invoked from the command line. It's liberally adapted from Richard Platel's example in the sister title in this series, *Creating Your World: The Official Guide to Advanced Content Creation in Second Life*. The wiki page on LSL_ XML-RPC has a longer description of XML-RPC, including server examples written in other languages.

Listing 12.9: *changeflag.pl*, an XML-RPC Flag Changer Client (Perl)

```perl
#!/usr/bin/perl  -w
use LWP::UserAgent;
use HTTP::Request::Common;
use CGI;

$XML_RPC_SERVER = "http://xmlrpc.secondlife.com/cgi-bin/xmlrpc.cgi";
$CHANNEL = CGI::escapeHTML(shift || "");
$FLAG_NAME = CGI::escapeHTML(shift || "");

$requestBody = "
<?xml version=\"1.0\"?>
<methodCall>
<methodName>llRemoteData</methodName>
<params>
  <param><value>
      <struct>
        <member><name>Channel</name>
                <value><string>$CHANNEL</string></value>
        </member>
        <member><name>StringValue</name>
                <value><string>$FLAG_NAME</string></value>
        </member>
      </struct>
  </value></param>
</params>
</methodCall>
";
$userAgent = LWP::UserAgent->new;
$userAgent->agent('SYW Perl XML-RPC Client');
$response = $userAgent->request( POST $XML_RPC_SERVER,
                                 Content_type => 'text/xml',
                                 Content      => $requestBody  );
print $response->error_as_HTML unless $response->is_success;
print $response->as_string;
```

The first few lines of Listing 12.9 show the required libraries being imported into the namespace of the Perl program. The line

```perl
$XML_RPC_SERVER = "http://xmlrpc.secondlife.com/cgi-bin/xmlrpc.cgi";
```

stores the URL of the *Second Life* XML-RPC gateway into a string. The channel key must be sent as part of the invocation for any LSL object; hence a command-line invocation for this particular client is of the form

```
perl filename.pl key-of-LSL-server-channel flag-name
```

and in this case, we use

```
perl changeflag.pl d5368b64-80c7-5d20-b517-d9902d744ee6 Maryland
```

CHAPTER 1
CHAPTER 2
CHAPTER 3
CHAPTER 4
CHAPTER 5
CHAPTER 6
CHAPTER 7
CHAPTER 8
CHAPTER 9
CHAPTER 10
CHAPTER 11

The variable *$requestBody* is filled in with several lines of data values in **SL**'s required XML format. The outer container `<params>` contains all parameters passed across the network. The single `<param>` here contains a composite object delimited by the `<struct>` tag pair. The `<struct>` has two element slots (each identified by a `<member>` tag), one being a string value for the channel, *$CHANNEL*, and the other being the flag you want to change to, *$FLAG_NAME*. The server invocation is packaged and sent, and the client waits for its reply.

SUMMARY

This chapter covered the basics of communicating into and out from **Second Life** using both Web techniques and the XML-RPC model. Email, a particularly useful method for external communications, was covered in Chapter 3, "Communications."

 ## WHEN TO USE EMAIL, HTTP, OR XML-RPC

Email is a fast way to get inter-object or inter-world communication. It supports one-way messages. Each call to *send* an email has a 20-second delay penalty to the script; you can reduce this penalty with a suite of worker scripts. *Reading* email can happen with no artificial script delay. Email is limited to 4,096 characters and queues up to 100 emails. Email is a sequence of one-shot messages between objects in-world, or an object in-world and something out-of-world.

HTTP is a call from *SL* to the real world, with a follow-up connected response. It can *not* be the server. It is the fastest way to interact. Requests are limited to 25 per 20 seconds; the delay comes from waiting for the web server to respond. Limited to 2,048 characters. HTTP is often used to store persistent data—the data is pushed to the server and retrieved when needed (as shown in Listing 12.3).

XML-RPC is the only way for *SL* to be the server side of the interaction. By allowing continuing conversations, it supports the largest amount of data transfer in and out of *Second Life*: each message is limited to 255 characters plus one 32-bit integer, but many messages can be transferred on the same channel. Only one message per channel can be queued at a time; by using the key returned by `llOpenRemoteDataChannel()`, you can manage multiple outstanding requests. This is the slowest of the three interactions. Each message has a three-second delay; your script cannot under any circumstances respond to more than one message every three seconds.

Note that both email and XML-RPC can be used point-to-point in-world. If you want to implement a server that responds to requests, email is often better than XML-RPC. (HTTP is not an option.) The wiki page `http://lslwiki.net/lslwiki/wakka.php?wakka=communications` has a useful summary that describes the tradeoffs in more detail.

For further reading, Chapter 15, "New and Improved," has a section on a new LSL feature that allows your script to act as an HTTP server to the rest of the Internet as well as for **SL** web clients. Finally, the SYW website has a bonus chapter that discusses interacting with the **Second Life** world through modified and alternative clients instead of with the official **SL** viewer.

CHAPTER 13

MONEY MAKES THE WORLD GO 'ROUND

Second Life gives you several ways to interact with other people and objects using money. You can give money directly to other avatars and automatically accept money given to you. (You don't script such interactions because they are avatar-to-avatar; there is no object involved to host a script.) You can also pay an object or have an object move money around on your behalf. In Chapter 13 we'll cover the scripting behind financial transactions.

TRANSACTION BASICS

 TRANSACTION
BASICS

 REDISTRIBUTING
WEALTH

SELLING IT!

RENTALS AND
SERVICES

GAMBL...
UH... GAMES
OF SKILL

SUMMARY

When you pay an object, you are transferring money from your account into the account of the person or group that owns the object. The scripts in a paid object are notified of the transfer details and can react to it, for example by giving an object to a paying avatar. Scripts may also give money to avatars by transferring money *out* of your account to theirs: you can program objects to give rewards, to pay salaries, or even to act as a bank teller by sharing a single account with multiple avatars.

Who gets the money? It's transferred to the object's owner. If the object is group-deeded, the money temporarily goes into the group's account, to be disbursed when there is enough to distribute to all members who have the Make/Receive Group Payments option enabled.

Figure 13.1 shows a pop-up menu you might see when you pay an object. This is the default menu, with four buttons and a box for entering your own amounts. You can change or hide any of these amounts if, for instance, you want to accept payment of only one specific price.

Figure 13.1: Paying an object

Second Life allows scripted objects to move money around on your behalf. Because you wouldn't want objects asserting free rein over your account without your knowledge, you'll be asked to grant objects special permissions before they request money from your account. Figure 13.2 shows how this looks: the menu's yellow background is clearly different from the rest of the permissions menus. If you grant permission, you really want to get it right; remember, you are playing with real money. You'll want to thoroughly debug your scripts before you grant permission, because one endless loop around a payment or one misplaced decimal point can clean out your account remarkably quickly.

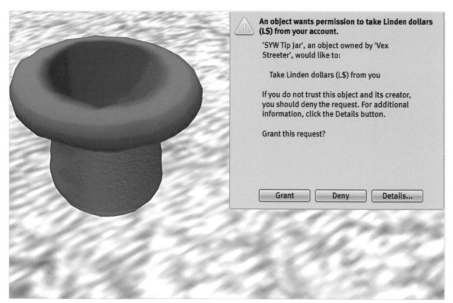

An object wants permission to take Linden dollars (L$) from your account.

'SYW Tip Jar', an object owned by 'Vex Streeter', would like to:

Take Linden dollars (L$) from you

If you do not trust this object and its creator, you should deny the request. For additional information, click the Details button.

Grant this request?

| Grant | Deny | Details... |

Figure 13.2: Granting debit permission

CHAPTER 1
CHAPTER 2
CHAPTER 3
CHAPTER 4
CHAPTER 5
CHAPTER 6
CHAPTER 7
CHAPTER 8
CHAPTER 9
CHAPTER 10
CHAPTER 11
CHAPTER 12

CHAPTER 13

CHAPTER 14
CHAPTER 15
APPENDICES

You also get feedback when these operations go through. All transactions are logged in your account's transaction history page*, and you'll see your account balance changing in the upper-right corner of your viewer window. Furthermore, when you grant debit permission you will get a message in your chat log indicating that you've done so.

REDISTRIBUTING WEALTH

This section is devoted to moving money around—accepting money from avatars, distributing money to other avatars, and even giving money away.

 **TIP JARS**

The simplest scripted money-transfer devices are tip jars. People rez these in all sorts of places as a way for residents to give thanks for a job well done, whether as a good tour guide or club host, or as a contributor to the maintenance of a beautiful or fun environment. Simply *pay* the tip jar, and your money is redirected to the correct place. There are, of course, lots of variations: simple personal ones like the hat that a street performer might pass, ones that perform a little service or put on a show, and ones that collect tips for different avatars depending on who is working or even split collected proceeds between collaborators. All you really need to make this work is a script with a **money()** event handler.

---

* https://secondlife.com/account/transactions.php

TRANSACTION
BASICS

 REDISTRIBUTING
WEALTH

SELLING IT!

RENTALS AND
SERVICES

GAMBL...
UH... GAMES
OF SKILL

SUMMARY

EVENT DEFINITION

$$money(key\ payer,\ integer\ amount)$$

This event handler is called whenever the object is paid. Without this event handler, the Pay menu is not available and the object cannot be paid.

payer — The key of the avatar that is making the payment.

amount — How many Linden dollars (L$) were paid.

Unlike with chat listeners, you do not need to explicitly tell the script to subscribe to money() events, and there aren't any filters. If a script has a money() event handler, it will be invoked when the object is paid. If the paid prim doesn't have a money() event handler, the scripts in the root prim receive the event.

NOTE

The money() event handler only notes payments. Like a bank transaction statement, it cannot change the transfer of funds in any way (such as refuse the transfer or accept only a portion), because it is only a notification that a transfer has *already happened*. Your script can undo the effect of a payment by refunding money, but it is important to remember you are then conducting a completely separate transaction, not changing the original one. (See the discussion of llGiveMoney() later in this chapter.)

Although a money() event handler alone is sufficient, it isn't very interesting. Listing 13.1 is a flexible personal tip jar that will be used as the basis for extensions later.

Listing 13.1: Simple Tip Jar

```
integer SUGGESTED = 50;          // the suggested donation

displayLabel()
{
    llSetText(llGetObjectName(), <1,0,0>, 1.0);
}
thankYou(key giver, integer love)
{
    llSay(0, "Thank you "+llKey2Name(giver) + "!");
    displayLabel();
    poof(giver, love);
}
poof(key giver, integer love)
{
    llParticleSystem([]);
    llParticleSystem([PSYS_PART_FLAGS, PSYS_PART_EMISSIVE_MASK,
                      PSYS_SRC_PATTERN,PSYS_SRC_PATTERN_EXPLODE,
                      PSYS_PART_START_COLOR, <1.0, 1.0, 1.0>]);
    llSleep(0.5);
    llParticleSystem([]);
}
```

```
default
{
    on_rez(integer p) {
        llResetScript();
    }
    state_entry() {
        llSetPayPrice(SUGGESTED,[SUGGESTED/2,SUGGESTED,SUGGESTED*2,SUGGESTED*4]);
        llSetClickAction(CLICK_ACTION_PAY);
        displayLabel();
    }
    money(key giver, integer love) {
        thankYou(giver, love);
    }
}
```

The `displayLabel()` function is a placeholder for any number of displays, mainly to let the tip jar indicate what is going on with it. This version puts only the name of the object in floating text.

The `thankYou()` function is called directly by the `money()` event handler to make the tip jar react in some way to getting tipped. This one calls `llSay()` to chat a thank-you message, calls `displayLabel()` to update the floating text label in case the text needs updating, and calls the `poof()` function to make a nice special effect.

The `poof()` function provides visible feedback, encouraging onlookers to tip. A nice, short, particle explosion is fine for this example, but anything fun will do: the lessons from Chapter 9, "Special Effects," could be especially useful here to launch fireworks for big tippers, or a particle stream of hearts toward the avatar that just paid you.

The main new element here is in the `state_entry()` event handler: it uses `llSetPayPrice()` to set up the payment menu to contain values of your choosing. If you do not call `llSetPayPrice()`, you will see a default menu like the one shown in Figure 13.1.

DEFINITION

`llSetPayPrice(integer entryDefault, list quickPays)`

Defines the options used in the payment menu when an avatar selects *Pay* from the pie menu, or when the default touch action is Pay and the object is clicked. The pay price is a persistent feature of the prim, not the script—once set, it remains set even if the script is removed.

> `entryDefault` — The default value to appear in the text-entry payment box, where the user may choose any amount to enter (in Figure 13.1, this is the box with the number 50 in it). If specified as `PAY_HIDE`, there will be no text-entry box.

> `quickPays` — A list of four integer values to be used as quick-payment buttons. Any or all may be specified as `PAY_HIDE` to avoid showing that specific button.

The **entryDefault** parameter allows you to set a default amount that displays when the user clicks Pay. (The user can change that amount.) The first call to `llSetPayPrice()` in the following code will produce a payment menu identical to the one shown in Figure 13.1:

```
// A dialog that is the same as the default
llSetPayPrice(1, [1,5,10,20]);

// A blank payment dialog.  You can't pay it!
llSetPayPrice(PAY_HIDE, [PAY_HIDE, PAY_HIDE, PAY_HIDE, PAY_HIDE]);
```

CHAPTER 1
CHAPTER 2
CHAPTER 3
CHAPTER 4
CHAPTER 5
CHAPTER 6
CHAPTER 7
CHAPTER 8
CHAPTER 9
CHAPTER 10
CHAPTER 11
CHAPTER 12

CHAPTER 13

CHAPTER 14
CHAPTER 15
APPENDICES

TRANSACTION
BASICS

 REDISTRIBUTING
WEALTH

SELLING IT!

RENTALS AND
SERVICES

GAMBL...
UH... GAMES
OF SKILL

SUMMARY

```
// A dialog with the entry box initialized to L$10 and no buttons.
llSetPayPrice(10, [PAY_HIDE, PAY_HIDE, PAY_HIDE, PAY_HIDE]);

// A dialog with one button for L$10
llSetPayPrice(PAY_HIDE, [10, PAY_HIDE, PAY_HIDE, PAY_HIDE]);
```

You can call `llSetPayPrice()` as many times as you need over an object's lifetime. This probably isn't useful for tip jars, but it is critical for advanced vendors that sell products of different prices.

 NOTE

 Keep in mind that limits on how many pending events can be queued are still in force (as discussed in Chapter 1, "Getting a Feel for the Linden Scripting Language"). This isn't much of a problem if avatars are paying your object unless your money event handlers take a long time to run. If you expect your object to deal with hundreds of payments per second, you must avoid using any functions that introduce long delays, or you risk losing events!

`state_entry()` also calls `llSetClickAction()`, so that a mouse click will pay the object instead of touch it. You can, of course, accomplish this using the *SL* build tools, but in viewers since version 1.19.1, you can also have your script do it for you.

 DEFINITION

`llSetClickAction (integer action)`

Sets the action to take when an avatar clicks on the prim that contains the script. The default behavior is CLICK_ACTION_TOUCH, indicating that a click should trigger the `touch()`, `touch_start()` and `touch_end()` event handlers.

action — A CLICK_ACTION_* value from the following table. CLICK_ACTION_PLAY and CLICK_ACTION_OPEN_MEDIA currently act by triggering the parcel media stream[*].

CONSTANT	VALUE	EFFECT OF CLICKING ON THE PRIM
CLICK_ACTION_NONE	0	Perform the default action.
CLICK_ACTION_TOUCH	0	Touch the prim.
CLICK_ACTION_SIT	1	Sit on the prim.
CLICK_ACTION_BUY	2	Buy the object.
CLICK_ACTION_PAY	3	Pay the prim.
CLICK_ACTION_OPEN	4	Open the prim, showing the contents.
CLICK_ACTION_PLAY	5	"Play" the parcel media stream on the prim, as though the media Play button in the viewer were pressed.
CLICK_ACTION_OPEN_MEDIA	6	Open the parcel media stream in the user's preferred browser.

---

[*] See the "Streaming Media" section of Chapter 11, "Multimedia" for details on setting up parcel media streams. Future *SL* releases may support per-prim media streams, in which case, the behavior of *action* may change.

As usual, the script itself is only part of the package. Figure 13.3 shows an unusual personal tip jar in the shape of a cow: if you tip it enough Linden dollars, the cow will actually tip over!

Figure 13.3: DJ Rocky's tipping cow at the Lonely Yak, BlaksleeWorld <224, 224, 24>

◥ A SHARED TIP JAR

The next example expands on the tip jar in a few ways: first, whereas the previous example is rezzed by the avatar who receives the tips, this one is intended to be placed by a club owner. The owner wants to make it easy to tip the club's hosts and DJs, and often wants to take a cut of the tips. To support this, all payments pass through the owner's account. The script in Listing 13.2 implements this mechanism, adding tip redistribution, a tax function, and a method for your hosts to log in and out of the tip jar.

Listing 13.2: A Shared Tip Jar

```
integer SUGGESTED = 50;        // suggested tip
integer TAX = 10;              // the house's tip tax (percent)

key gHost = NULL_KEY;
integer gLast = 0;
integer gHostTotal = 0;

displayLabel()
{
    if (gHost == NULL_KEY) {
        llSetText(llGetObjectName(), <1,0,0>, 1.0);
    } else {
        string text = llKey2Name(gHost)+"'s "+llGetObjectName()+"\n"+
                " Last tip "+ (string)gLast + ", total tips " + (string)gHostTotal;
        llSetText(text, <1,1,1>, 1.0);
    }
}

// poof() and thankYou() unchanged

login(key host) {
    gHost = host;
    gHostTotal = 0;
    gLast = 0;
    displayLabel();
}
```

285

TRANSACTION
BASICS

REDISTRIBUTING
WEALTH

SELLING IT!

RENTALS AND
SERVICES

GAMBL...
UH... GAMES
OF SKILL

SUMMARY

```
default
{
    on_rez(integer p) {
        llResetScript();
    }
    state_entry() {
        llRequestPermissions(llGetOwner(), PERMISSION_DEBIT);
    }
    run_time_permissions(integer perms) {
        if (perms & PERMISSION_DEBIT) {
            list buttons = [SUGGESTED/2, SUGGESTED, SUGGESTED*2, SUGGESTED*4];
            llSetPayPrice(SUGGESTED, buttons);
            displayLabel();
        } else {
            llOwnerSay("No debit permission");
        }
    }
    money(key giver, integer love) {
        gLast = love;
        if (gHost != NULL_KEY) {
            integer toHost = (love * (100 - TAX))/100;
            llGiveMoney(gHost, toHost);
            llInstantMessage(gHost,llKey2Name(giver)+" tipped you L$"+(string)love);
            gHostTotal += toHost;
        }
        thankYou(giver, love);
    }

    touch_start(integer count) {
        key id = llDetectedKey(0);
        if (llDetectedGroup(0)) {
            if (gHost == NULL_KEY) {
                login(gHost);
                llInstantMessage(id, "You are logged in");
            } else if (id == gHost) {
                llInstantMessage(id, "Thank you for hosting! You made L$"+
                                 (string) gHostTotal);
                login(NULL_KEY);
            } else {
                llInstantMessage(id, "Sorry, "+llKey2Name(gHost)+" is logged in");
            }
        }
    }
}
```

displayLabel() prints more information than before, including the size of the last tip and the running total—all the better to encourage more people to tip. The new integer variables *gLast* and *gHostTotal* support this additional information by tracking the values to be printed. The poof() and thankYou() functions are identical to those in the simple tip jar.

The next change is to support tip-jar-user login. This allows the host on duty to claim the tips generated during their shift. When someone touches the tip jar, the touch_start() event handler uses llDetectedGroup() to see if the person who touched it is a member of the same group as the jar. If so and the jar is unclaimed, it logs in that person by calling the login() function. If that person had already claimed the jar, it logs them out using the call login(NULL_KEY). Finally, if someone else already claimed the jar, it tells the current person that they may not log in. The login() function simply resets the tracking variables and sets the *gHost* variable to the specified key, either the new host key or NULL_KEY.

The most substantial change from the first tip jar is to redistribute payments to the logged-in avatar. To support this, the jar must be able to not only accept money from tipping customers, but also to pay money to the logged-in host out of the owner's account. This is accomplished by combining `PERMISSION_DEBIT` with the library function `llGiveMoney()`. `PERMISSION_DEBIT` is requested just like any other permission (see Chapter 2, "Making Your Avatar Stand Up and Stand Out"). Note that like permissions for attaching and changing links, a script may request the permission only from the owner of the containing object.

NOTE

A granted `PERMISSION_DEBIT` does not transfer with an object—a security measure that prevents inadvertently giving away objects that can take money from you whenever the new owner wants. It is a good idea to reset any script that uses `PERMISSION_DEBIT` in `on_rez()` or make certain the owner hasn't changed. If you don't take measures to address this issue, your script will stop working when transferred.

The script requests `PERMISSION_DEBIT` in the `state_entry()` event handler, and when the permission is granted, the `run_time_permissions()` event handler calls `llSetPayPrice()` to make it possible to pay the jar. Finally, in the `money()` event handler, instead of just thanking the tipper, the script pays the logged-in avatar the tip less **TAX** percent with the `llGiveMoney()` library function.

DEFINITION

```
integer llGiveMoney(key destination, integer amount)
```

Transfers the specified *amount* of money from the object owner's account of the into the *destination* avatar's account. The script must have already acquired the `PERMISSION_DEBIT` permission. Always returns 0.

> *destination* — The key of the avatar that will receive the money.
>
> *amount* — The number of Linden dollars to transfer; must be greater than zero (*amount* > 0).

One downside of this implementation is that the host will see tips coming from the tip-jar owner rather than the avatar who paid the tip jar. Therefore, to let the host know who originated each tip, the jar sends an IM to the host on each transaction.

Error-Checking for a Shared Tip Jar

What happens, though, when the host forgets to log out, or when their **SL** session crashes, or when the host abandons the club in a fit of pique? The preceding script would require the owner to reset the jar so another user could log into it. Listing 13.3 adds a check that automatically logs off the avatar if they disappear.

CHAPTER 13

Transaction
Basics

Redistributing
Wealth

Selling It!

Rentals and
Services

Gambl...
uh... Games
of Skill

Summary

Listing 13.3: Shared Tip Jar with Error Checking

```
// These are changes and additions only to Listing 13.2
float SCANRADIUS = 30.0;

login(key host) {
    gHost = host;
    gHostTotal = 0;
    gLast = 0;
    displayLabel();

    if (host != NULL_KEY) {  // ADD - keep track of the host
        llSensorRepeat("", gHost, AGENT, SCANRADIUS, PI, 30.0);
    } else {
        llSensorRemove();
    }
}

default
{
    no_sensor() {
        if (gHost != NULL_KEY && gHostTotal>0) {
            llInstantMessage(gHost, "Logged out, with L$"+
                        (string) gHostTotal+" in tips");
            login(NULL_KEY);
        }
    }
}
```

This variation adds a periodic scan for the logged-in host. If it fails to detect the avatar it will log them out automatically, freeing up the tip jar for a more dependable, or at least present, replacement host.

 NOTE

As with `llListen()`, any performance problems you see when using `llSensorRepeat()` are caused by not being specific enough in the filtering criteria. The script carefully looks for the one avatar logged into the tip jar, and scans only once every 30 seconds. If you expect to ever hit the maximum of 16 detected objects on a sensor scan, each scan will probably become expensive.

CHARITY COLLECTORS

In addition to keeping payments for the owner, objects can transfer the entire donation amount to a third party, such as a charity. Throughout *SL* you can find charity-collection boxes like the one for the American Cancer Society's 2008 Relay for Life, shown in Figure 13.4.

The money-handling parts of a charity box are no different from those of a tip jar. What does change is that the beneficiary of the payments is usually an account that doesn't have a real person attached to it—they are often solely used for donation collection. Large charity drives usually provide a charity box that has the target account written directly into the script so that it cannot be changed or tapped.

A useful alternative for smaller charity drives is a generic money collector the owner configures, indicating to which avatar payments should be directed. Listing 13.4 adds this feature during a configuration pass.

CHAPTER 1
CHAPTER 2
CHAPTER 3
CHAPTER 4
CHAPTER 5
CHAPTER 6
CHAPTER 7
CHAPTER 8
CHAPTER 9
CHAPTER 10
CHAPTER 11
CHAPTER 12

CHAPTER 13

CHAPTER 14
CHAPTER 15
APPENDICES

Figure 13.4: Collecting
for a good cause at the
Galleries of Camazotz
(Camazotz <243, 120, 104>).

Listing 13.4: A Charity-Collection Box

```
integer SUGGESTED = 50;          // suggested donation
string N2KURL = "http://w-hat.com/name2key";

integer gLast = 0;
integer gTotal = 0;

key gCharity = NULL_KEY;
string gCharityName;

string gPendingName;             // set during name2key lookup
key gPendingKey;                 // set while we're checking the key for accuracy

displayLabel() {
    string text = llGetObjectName()+"\nAll proceeds go to "+gCharityName+
        "\nLast donation L$"+(string)gLast+", Total donations "+ (string) gTotal;
    llSetText(text, <1,0,0>, 1.0);
}

// poof() is the same as in tip jars

thankYou(key giver, integer love) { // same as tipjar 1
    llSay(0, "Thank you for donating, "+llKey2Name(giver) + "!");
    displayLabel();
    poof(giver, love);
}

checkKey(key k) {
    llOwnerSay("Double checking the key. Please wait");
    gPendingKey = k;
    llRequestAgentData(gPendingKey, DATA_NAME);
}
```

CHAPTER 13

TRANSACTION
BASICS

REDISTRIBUTING
WEALTH

SELLING IT!

RENTALS AND
SERVICES

GAMBL...
UH... GAMES
OF SKILL

SUMMARY

```
default
{
    on_rez(integer p) {
        llResetScript();
    }
    state_entry() {
        llOwnerSay("Initializing");
        llListen(0, "", llGetOwner(), "");
        if (gCharity != NULL_KEY) {
            checkKey(gCharity);
        } else {
            llOwnerSay("Say the name of the charity avatar to start");
        }
    }
    listen(integer ch, string name, key id, string m) {
        if (m == "go") {
            if (gCharity == NULL_KEY) {
                llOwnerSay("Say the name of the charity avatar");
            } else {
                state running;
            }
        } else {
            gPendingName = m;
            llOwnerSay("Looking up key for "+m);
            llHTTPRequest(N2KURL + "?terse=1&name="+llEscapeURL(m), [], "");
        }
    }
    http_response(key id, integer status, list meta, string body) {
        if ( status != 200 ) {
            llOwnerSay("name2key error "+ (string) status);
        } else {
            key k = (key) body;
            if (body == NULL_KEY) {
                llOwnerSay("Couldn't find key for "+gPendingName);
            } else {
                llOwnerSay(gPendingName+"'s key appears to be "+(string)k);
                checkKey(k);
            }
        }
    }
    dataserver(key qid, string data) {
        if (gPendingName == "") {
            gPendingName = data;
        }
        if (gPendingName == data) {
            gCharity = gPendingKey;
            gCharityName = gPendingName;
            llOwnerSay("Charitable donations will go to " + gCharityName+
                       " ("+(string)gCharity+") say \"go\" to start.");
        } else {
            llOwnerSay("Warning! Name lookup mismatch. Expected "+gPendingName+
                       " but found "+data);
        }
    }
}
```

```
state running
{
    on_rez(integer p) {
        llResetScript();
    }
    state_entry() {
        llRequestPermissions(llGetOwner(), PERMISSION_DEBIT);
    }
    run_time_permissions(integer perms) {
        if (perms & PERMISSION_DEBIT) {
            list buttons = [SUGGESTED/2, SUGGESTED, SUGGESTED*2, SUGGESTED*4];
            llSetPayPrice(SUGGESTED, buttons);
            displayLabel();
        } else {
            llOwnerSay("No debit permission");
        }
    }
    money(key giver, integer love) {
        gLast = love;
        gTotal += love;
        llGiveMoney(gCharity, love);
        thankYou(giver, love);
    }
}
```

CHAPTER 1
CHAPTER 2
CHAPTER 3
CHAPTER 4
CHAPTER 5
CHAPTER 6
CHAPTER 7
CHAPTER 8
CHAPTER 9
CHAPTER 10
CHAPTER 11
CHAPTER 12
CHAPTER 13
CHAPTER 14
CHAPTER 15
APPENDICES

When this collection box is rezzed, it expects the owner to chat the name of the avatar that should receive the proceeds. It then uses an external **name2key** service to look up the named avatar's key (see Chapter 12, "Reaching outside *Second Life*," for a deeper discussion of this). Then, because the script will give lots and lots of money to the target, it uses a dataserver lookup to double-check that *Second Life* agrees the key is associated with the correct name. If it didn't do this, the external service could theoretically redirect funds to the wrong avatar, allowing that avatar to steal the funds. Your transaction logs would expose the fraud pretty quickly, but some damage could be done to your reputation. It is far better to keep everyone honest. The script needs to use **llRequestAgentData(*id*, AGENT_NAME)** because the much faster **llKey2Name(*id*)** will work only if the identified avatar is in the same sim as the charity collector.

When the owner is happy with the selected target account, they can chat ***go*** to switch the script to the running state. This is a perfect use for multiple states: the **default** state is now solely for configuration and the **running** state is nearly identical to any of the tip jar's **default** states. There is no need to turn off the listener, because the state transition to running will close the one set up by default. In every state, the script has an **on_rez()** event handler with **llResetScript()** so the owner can rerez the object and start over. An alternative would be to transition back to the **default** state without resetting, retaining the previously set beneficiary and running totals.

GOING ON THE DOLE: MONEY TREES

Another sort of charity is to support other avatars: one of the first things that new *Second Life* residents discover is that it costs money to do much of anything. While it is possible to get by on the cheap in *SL*, even the "freebie" products are more accurately described as "dollarbies," costing L$1 each. So, the first problem new residents are faced with is how to get enough money to get off the ground. The most straightforward way to get small amounts of money is to look for handouts—scripted objects that give you a Linden dollar or two just for asking. Our favorite example of this sort of thing is the money tree (Figure 13.5); we also have a pot of gold beneath the rainbow at SYW HQ.

CHAPTER 13

TRANSACTION
BASICS

REDISTRIBUTING
WEALTH

SELLING IT!

RENTALS AND
SERVICES

GAMBL...
UH... GAMES
OF SKILL

SUMMARY

Listings 13.5 and 13.6 illustrate one way to implement a simple money tree. The basic idea is first to accept donations such as with a tip jar, then every once in a while, rez a leaf, usually in the shape of a Linden dollar (Figure 13.5). If anyone clicks on the leaf it will give them a dollar. Listing 13.5 is the script for the trunk of the tree itself.

Listing 13.5: Money Tree

```
float   PERIOD = 600.0;   // seconds between leaf rez
integer LEAFMAX = 10;     // max number of leafs outstanding
string  LEAF = "leaf";    // inventory object to rez
list    gLeaves; // active leaves
integer gBalance = 0; // how much money left to give out
integer gChannel;

default
{
    on_rez(integer p) {
        llResetScript();
    }
    state_entry() {
        gChannel = -(10000 + (integer) llFrand(10000.0));
        llRequestPermissions(llGetOwner(), PERMISSION_DEBIT);
        llSetTimerEvent(PERIOD);
        llListen(gChannel, LEAF, NULL_KEY, "");
        llSetText("Pay to donate", <1,1,1>, 1.0);
    }
    money(key av, integer donation) {
        gBalance += donation;
        llSay(0, "Thanks for your contribution, "+llKey2Name(av));
    }
    timer() {
        if (gBalance>0 && llGetListLength(gLeaves) < LEAFMAX) {
            vector where = llGetPos() + <0.0, 0.0, 1.0>;
            vector offset = <llFrand(2.0), llFrand(2.0), llFrand(2.0)> - <1,1,1>;
            llRezObject(LEAF, where+offset, ZERO_VECTOR, ZERO_ROTATION, gChannel);
        }
    }
    object_rez(key leaf) {
        gLeaves += [leaf];
        gBalance--;
    }
    listen(integer ch, string name, key id, string message) {
        integer i = llListFindList(gLeaves, [id]);
        if (i!= -1) {
            gLeaves = llDeleteSubList(gLeaves, i, i);
            llGiveMoney((key) message, 1);
        }
    }
}
```

The donation part is similar to the personal tip jar: it collects money, accepting donations with the money() event handler, and adds it to the amount outstanding. In state_entry(), the script chooses a random channel to communicate with the leaves, starts a timer to go off every PERIOD seconds (10 minutes in this case), and also listens for communication from leaves that indicate they've been plucked.

If there is a positive balance in the account when the timer goes off, and too many leaves aren't already rezzed, the script rezzes a new leaf from inventory in a random spot above the tree. When it does choose to rez a new leaf, it watches for the rez to happen using the object_rez() event handler. When notified of the new object, it notes the leaf's key in its list of active leaves and decrements the balance in the account.

Figure 13.5: In **SL**, money **does** grow on trees.

The leaf script shown in Listing 13.6 gets the channel to speak on the `on_rez()` parameter. The only other thing the leaf does is wait for a `touch_end()` event when an avatar plucks the leaf. It will chat the key of the avatar that touched it on a communications channel and self-destruct.

Listing 13.6: Money-Tree Leaf

```
integer gChannel;

default
{
    on_rez(integer p) {
        gChannel = p;
    }
    touch_end(integer count) {
        llSay(gChannel, (string) llDetectedKey(0));
        llDie();
    }
}
```

When the tree hears a message from a leaf, it makes certain it is one of the leaves that it actually created. It then removes that leaf from the list and pays L$1 to the avatar identified by the chatted message. Just make certain the "leaf" object is placed in the inventory of the money tree.

WARNING

A word on security: always keep in mind that chat channels are insecure. If it is possible for someone to listen in on the right channel and steal from you, someone *will* do it. Even worse, if you sell a script that is not secure, the bad guys will steal from your customer, which is not very good for business.

This script depends on your rezzing being secure, and on the tree being certain that when an object says the right thing on the right channel, it is authorized to do so. It would be convenient to make each leaf pay the touching avatar, but that would require each individual leaf to have debit permissions.

CHAPTER 13

TRANSACTION
BASICS

REDISTRIBUTING
WEALTH

SELLING IT!

RENTALS AND
SERVICES

GAMBL...
UH... GAMES
OF SKILL

SUMMARY

Most money trees in *SL* give money only to new avatars. You can implement this restriction by firing off a call to `llRequestAgentData(id, DATA_BORN)`, parsing the resulting date string in the `dataserver` event handler, and only then paying the avatar if they are younger than 30 days (rather than paying the target directly in the `listen()` event handler). This is complicated because dataserver queries can take long enough that several people might click on different leaves before you can check for the age of the first avatar, so you need to keep track of outstanding age queries, paying only avatars that are young enough.

An even subtler problem is that avatars who are older than 30 days can waste the leaves—they will not get paid, but since the leaves die after the chat, nobody else can take them either. The simplest way to fix this is to add L$1 back to the balance if you refuse to pay the avatar. That way although the leaf has disappeared, it will eventually be replaced. Other options are to do the age check in the leaf and then have the leaf die only if the avatar passes your criteria, or having a more complex communications channel between leaf and tree to allow the tree to do all the complex work, and instruct the leaf when and if to die.

The topic of securing communications in *Second Life* could fill an entire chapter in a more advanced book than this. For more information, refer to Ordinal Malaprop's article on secure communications at `http://ordinalmalaprop.com/engine/2007/10/23/secure-inworld-password-nonsense/` or search the wiki for `llMD5String()`.

SELLING IT!

The easiest way to sell something is to mark it for sale (see Figure 13.6). You can specify the price and indicate whether the buyer gets the original object or a copy. There is nothing wrong with this approach, but it is limiting, mainly in that the actual object needs to be rezzed in-world for you to buy it, so you can easily run into prim limits: a high-quality prim hair unit can easily be over 200 prims! While there are no prim-limits on objects attached to avatars, rezzing more than a few in a typical storefront would quickly exhaust the prim allotments of even the largest store*.

That's where **vendors** come in; they're objects that sell other objects in *SL*, and they're pretty simple to create.

 NOTE

It is important to set the correct permissions on objects you sell or give away, no matter your method. We recommend giving away full-permission (*Copy/Mod/Trans*) scripted objects *only* when they are trivial or unsupported—it is impossible to provide support for full-permission items, and unless you are selling something specifically for resale, there is no reason for anyone to come back to you for repeat business. Of course, you need both Copy and Transfer permissions on an object to put it in a vendor.

Finally, always test everything before you go public: make an alternate avatar for testing purposes, who doesn't have any special rights, and have them buy your products and operate your vendors to make sure everything works properly.

* Vex's hair, for instance, is made from 221 prims, which would just barely be rezzable on a 1,024-square-meter region with a limit of 234 prims.

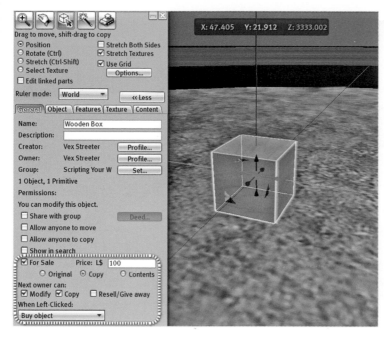

CHAPTER 1
CHAPTER 2
CHAPTER 3
CHAPTER 4
CHAPTER 5
CHAPTER 6
CHAPTER 7
CHAPTER 8
CHAPTER 9
CHAPTER 10
CHAPTER 11
CHAPTER 12

CHAPTER 13

CHAPTER 14
CHAPTER 15
APPENDIX

Figure 13.6: Setting an object for sale

A SIMPLE VENDOR

The first vendor script, shown in Listing 13.7, is really just a combination of an object giver (see Chapter 3, "Communications,") that is triggered by a money event rather than by touches or senses.

Listing 13.7: A Simple Vendor

```
integer gPrice = 100;  // price in Linden Dollars
string gProduct;

default
{
    on_rez(integer p) {
        llResetScript();
    }
    state_entry() {
        llSetPayPrice(PAY_HIDE, [gPrice, PAY_HIDE, PAY_HIDE, PAY_HIDE]);
        gProduct = llGetInventoryName(INVENTORY_OBJECT,0);
        string title = gProduct+"(L$"+(string)gPrice+")";
        llSetText(title, <1,1,1>, 1.0);
    }
    money(key customer, integer amount)
    {
        llInstantMessage(customer, "Thank you, "+llKey2Name(customer)+
                        "! Enjoy your purchase of "+gProduct);
        llGiveInventory(customer, gProduct);
    }
}
```

In state_entry(), the script sets up the payment menu so that only one *quickpay* button is active. It then identifies the first object in inventory as the product to sell, and sets the floating text to inform nearby avatars what is being sold. When a money() event occurs, the script needs to do nothing but give the product to the customer.

TRANSACTION
BASICS

REDISTRIBUTING
WEALTH

SELLING IT!

RENTALS AND
SERVICES

GAMBL...
UH... GAMES
OF SKILL

SUMMARY

 BUILD NOTE

The script is simple, but there are many variations on how to house the script. Because the object to be sold must be in inventory, you need to make certain that potential buyers know where to buy the items they want. Common approaches are to use an object that looks like the product itself, a placard displaying a picture of the product, or a "for sale" tag near the rezzed object.

This sort of vendor is great when you want to have one vendor rezzed per product to be sold, for instance at a clothing store or in an art gallery, as in Figure 13.7. The most common extension is to have the vendor figure look at a configuration notecard to find the object price, and perhaps a texture to display on the face of the vendor.

Figure 13.7:
The Riverbend Art
Gallery at Addu
<124, 195, 22> sells
copies of displayed
works of art using
simple vendors.

 NOTE

The best way to package a product for sale depends on the details of the product itself and the vendors you have available. It is convenient for buyers to receive multiple-part products (for example outfits) as a folder, so that their new purchase is ready to go straight from the vendor rather than the buyer having to rez a package that then needs to be unpacked. Single vendors that use `llGiveInventoryList()` are great for this sort of thing. However, most commercial vendor systems will not give object folders, because managing multiple collections in one vendor's inventory is difficult. The best solution is often to package everything in a gift box that a buyer can rez and open when they get home.

 ## A MULTIPRODUCT VENDOR

With the right script, you sell many different products from one vendor. Listing 13.8 uses a main panel to display a photo of the current product for sale, and two arrow buttons to advance through the products contained in the vendor (see Figure 13.8 for an example).

Listing 13.8: A Multiple-Product Vendor

```
key gOwner = NULL_KEY;

string CONFIGNOTE = ".config";
integer DISPLAYFACE = 0;
integer qLine = 0; // which config line are we on?

list gParameters; // [tag, product, price]
integer gParamLen = -1;

integer gCurrent = 0;
integer gPrice = -1;
string gProduct;
string gTag;

grokConfigLine(string data)
{
    if (llStringLength(data)==0 || "/" == llGetSubString(data,0,0)) {
        // ignore comments and empty lines
    } else {
        list kvl = llParseString2List(data, ["="], []);
        string tag = llList2String(kvl,0);
        list params = llParseString2List(llList2String(kvl,1), [","], []);
        string product = llList2String(params,0);
        integer price = llList2Integer(params,1);
        gParameters += [tag, product, price];
    }
}

displayProduct() {
    if (gCurrent >= gParamLen) {
        gCurrent = 0;
    }
    else if (gCurrent < 0) {
        gCurrent = gParamLen - 1;
    }
    integer i = gCurrent*3;
    gTag = llList2String(gParameters, i);
    gProduct = llList2String(gParameters, i + 1);
    gPrice = llList2Integer(gParameters, i + 2);
    llSetTexture(gProduct+".texture", DISPLAYFACE);
    llSetPayPrice(PAY_HIDE, [gPrice, PAY_HIDE, PAY_HIDE, PAY_HIDE]);
    llSetText(gTag+" (L$"+(string)gPrice+")", <1,0,0>, 1.0);
    llSetObjectName("Vendor for "+gTag);
}

default // default is unconfigured
{
    on_rez(integer p) {
        llResetScript();
    }
    state_entry() {
        state configuring;
    }
}
```

297

TRANSACTION
BASICS

REDISTRIBUTING
WEALTH

▶ SELLING IT!

RENTALS AND
SERVICES

GAMBL...
UH... GAMES
OF SKILL

SUMMARY

```
state configuring
{
    on_rez(integer p) {
        llResetScript();
    }
    state_entry() {
        gParameters = [];
        qLine = 0;
        llGetNotecardLine(CONFIGNOTE, qLine);
    }
    dataserver(key requested, string data) {
        if (data == EOF) {
            gParamLen = llGetListLength(gParameters) / 3;
            state running;
        } else {
            data = llStringTrim(data, STRING_TRIM);
            grokConfigLine(data);
            qLine++;
            llGetNotecardLine(CONFIGNOTE, qLine);
        }
    }
}


state running
{
    on_rez(integer p) {
        llResetScript();
    }
    state_entry() {
        gCurrent = 0;
        displayProduct();
    }
    money(key giver, integer amount) {
            llGiveInventory(giver, gProduct);
            llInstantMessage(giver, "Thank for purchasing "+
                            gProduct+" for L$"+(string) gPrice);
    }
    link_message(integer link, integer num, string m, key id) {
        if (m == "R") {
            gCurrent ++;
        } else if (m == "L") {
            gCurrent --;
        }
        displayProduct();
    }
}
```

Figure 13.8: A multiproduct vendor in action

The script reads a notecard that configures the products for sale, including their prices. Then it allows the user to view all options and purchase just the one desired. To support these modes, the script has three states: a `default` state solely to get things off the ground, a `configuring` state for use while the vendor is reading its configuration notecard, and a `running` state while the vendor is idling, waiting for a sale.

The list of products and attributes is kept in a strided list, *gParameters*, where each group of three elements is [*tag*, *ObjectNameInInventory*, *price*]. The notecard reader uses the `grokConfigLine()` function in the `configuring` state to parse each line of the configuration notecard and fill up *gParameters* with the product information. In the `configuring` state, the `state_entry()` and `dataserver()` event handlers implement a standard notecard reader, simply walking through the lines. The .config notecard might have a line like "Nice House=Victorian House 37,10000" which would result in the vendor describing the object "Victorian House 37" as a "Nice House" and setting the price at L$10,000. The `displayProduct()` function will look for a texture with the same name as the product name with a ".texture" suffix (such as Victorian House 37.texture) for display purposes. The function `grokConfigLine()` also ignores empty lines and lines starting with `//` to make it easy to format and control the contents.

The `displayProduct()` function figures out which product should be displayed, then looks for a texture in inventory that has the name of the tag, paints it on the vendor's face, sets the sales price, changes the floating text to describe the object, and changes the name of the vendor to include the product information in the payment dialog.

The `running` state is like previous vendors, simply reacting to `money()` events by giving the selected product to the purchaser. It also responds to "L" and "R" messages from the left and right button objects that are linked in as controls. The buttons, carefully named L and R, use the script in Listing 13.9.

Listing 13.9: Button Script for Multiple-Product Vendor

```
default
{
    touch_end(integer o) {
        llMessageLinked(LINK_ROOT, 0, llGetObjectName(), NULL_KEY);
    }
}
```

The button script simply link-messages the prim name to the main vendor when a button is touched. This allows the vendor to display the next or previous product in the list, resetting the prices and displaying texture as appropriate.

BUILD NOTE

The vendor object is made up of three prims. Make the main vendor out of a box shaped into a flat panel however large you'd like, containing the script from Listing 13.8. The two buttons should be triangles or arrows, each with the button script from Listing 13.9. One button should be named "L" (for left) and the other "R" (for right). Position the two buttons in front of the main panel and link the three prims together, making certain the main panel is the root. Load up the vendor with one of each of the products you want to sell, one texture for each product, and a .config notecard that holds it all together. Then reset the script in the vendor; the notecard should load and you should be ready for business. Figure 13.7 shows one example of this.

CHAPTER 1
CHAPTER 2
CHAPTER 3
CHAPTER 4
CHAPTER 5
CHAPTER 6
CHAPTER 7
CHAPTER 8
CHAPTER 9
CHAPTER 10
CHAPTER 11
CHAPTER 12

CHAPTER 13

CHAPTER 14
CHAPTER 15
APPENDICES

◥ NETWORKED VENDORS

TRANSACTION
BASICS

REDISTRIBUTING
WEALTH

◥ SELLING IT!

◥ RENTALS AND
SERVICES

GAMBL...
UH... GAMES
OF SKILL

SUMMARY

The previous chapter discussed using email, HTTP, and XML-RPC to allow in-world objects to communicate in both directions with the outside world. A number of scripters have built vendor systems that use these out-of-world communication paths to link up multiple sales points to object-distribution points for a much more flexible and portable system. The basic design looks something like Figure 13.9.

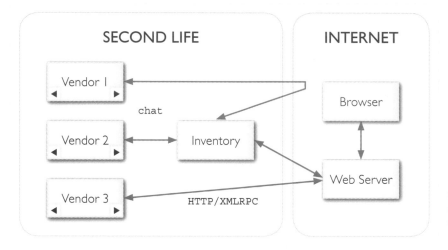

Figure 13.9: Design of a networked vendor system

The *Inventory* objects hold the products to be sold, along with the images, prices, and descriptions used to display them. The *Vendors* are very much like the vendor in Listing 13.8 except that instead of containing the objects to be sold in its own inventory, it asks the Inventory point for information on the products to display. When a purchase is made, it asks the Inventory point to give the item to the purchaser through its own inventory. There are several options for connecting vendors to Inventory points: they may send each other email using the `llEmail()` family of functions (Vendor 1), or they may use HTTP or XML-RPC to communicate with an external system acting as an intermediary (Vendor 3), or if they are near each other they can use chat commands like `llShout()` or `llRegionSay()` (Vendor 2). Often vendor systems use a combination of these options to balance performance with dependability.

Vendor networks that use an external system as an intermediary have the additional benefit that you can often manage the system from a web application with a standard browser, managing the inventory, tracking sales, and keeping your records without having to actually log into *Second Life*. Figure 13.10 shows several networked vendor systems that have been placed at SYW HQ as examples.

Figure 13.10: High-end networked vendors. The lower one, from OnRez, sells a variety of trees and special effects; the upper vendor, from Hippo Technologies, rents real estate.

CHAPTER 1
CHAPTER 2
CHAPTER 3
CHAPTER 4
CHAPTER 5
CHAPTER 6
CHAPTER 7
CHAPTER 8
CHAPTER 9
CHAPTER 10
CHAPTER 11
CHAPTER 12

CHAPTER 13

CHAPTER 14
CHAPTER 15
APPENDICES

RENTALS AND SERVICES

We've talked about passing money directly to another avatar, and about exchanging money for objects. The other main use for scripted money is to support rentals, either of services or of land.

◥ A TICKET TO RIDE

Paying for access to a ride is pretty common. Rezzable's Surfline sims at Surfline Aloha Rezzable <37, 141, 31> let you rent a surfboard to try out on their giant waves, you can go skydiving at Abbotts Aerodrome (Abbotts <160, 148, 71>) , practice batting at a re-creation of historic Ebbets Field (Ebbets Field <27, 169, 22>), or play golf at Holly Kai Golf Club (Hollywood <178, 236, 22>). Listing 13.10 implements a very simple example of a ride that will not let you play with it until you've paid.

Listing 13.10: Skyhook Ride

```
string gName;
key gKey = NULL_KEY;
integer gAltitude = 0;

displayLabel() {
    string text = llGetObjectName();

    if (gKey == NULL_KEY) {
        text += "\nPay me L$1 per 100 meters and then sit for a ride";
    } else {
        text += "\nReserved for "+gName+ ": sit for a ride!";
    }
    llSetText(text, <1,0,0>, 1.0);
}

// insert moveTo(vector origin, vector destination) {} from Listing 2.4
```

TRANSACTION
BASICS

REDISTRIBUTING
WEALTH

SELLING IT!

▶ RENTALS AND
SERVICES

GAMBL...
UH... GAMES
OF SKILL

SUMMARY

```
default
{
    state_entry() {
        displayLabel();
        llSetPayPrice(10, [PAY_HIDE, PAY_HIDE, PAY_HIDE, PAY_HIDE]);
        llSitTarget(<0,0,0.1>, ZERO_ROTATION);
    }
    money(key who, integer lindens) {
        gName = llKey2Name(who);
        gKey = who;
        gAltitude += lindens;
        llSay(0, "OK, "+gName+"! now sit and get a ride to "+
                    (string)(gAltitude*100) + " meters!");
        llSetTimerEvent(30.0);
        displayLabel();
    }
    changed(integer bits) {
        if (bits & CHANGED_LINK) {
            key av = llAvatarOnSitTarget();
            if (av == gKey && av != NULL_KEY) {
                llSay(0, "Hold on!!!");
                integer i;
                for (i=10; i>0; i--) {
                    llSay(0, (string)i+"...");
                    llSleep(1.0);
                }
                llShout(0, "Blast off!");
                vector home = llGetPos();
                vector dest = home+<0,0,gAltitude*100.0>;
                moveTo(home, dest);
                llUnSit(av);
                moveTo(dest, home);
                gKey = NULL_KEY;
                gName = "";
                gAltitude=0;
            } else {
                llSay(0, "Please pay me first");
                llUnSit(av);
            }
            displayLabel();
        }
    }
    timer() {
        if (gKey != NULL_KEY) {
            llSay(0, "Timing out: "+gName+" seems to have lost interest");
            gKey = NULL_KEY;
            gName = "";
            gAltitude = 0;
            displayLabel();
        }
        llSetTimerEvent(0.0);
    }
}
```

This is really just a high-altitude intrasim teleporter, using the `moveTo()` function from Chapter 2. The difference is that it won't operate until you've paid it. It sets up a payment box in `state_entry()` to reserve the device. Once an avatar has paid it, he can sit and be transported straight up 100 meters for every Linden dollar paid (to a maximum of 4,096m). When the avatar reaches the paid-for height, the script unsits the passenger and returns home to reset. You could slow it down and offer the passenger a parachute on the way up, or follow a path through a psychedelic panorama.

LAND RENTALS

Many residents want to have a region of the world to build a more permanent presence on. Build a house, open an office or an art gallery—the possibilities are endless. However, residents need to have a Premium account to actually own mainland real estate. Land isn't cheap, and you must pay a monthly maintenance fee (called *tier*) based on the amount of land you own over the course of the month. Due to the cost, the longer-term commitment, and the added complexity of owning land, many residents opt to rent instead of buy.

While rentals can certainly be handled manually by exchanging money avatar-to-avatar, most are handled automatically with rental boxes—scripted systems that accept payment for space, monitor use of the rented land, and offer the owner tools for managing rentals so they need not spend time in *Second Life* teleporting around the world taking care of rental properties.

Listing 13.11 illustrates how to institute a simple rental system.

Listing 13.11: Region Rental

```
float SCANRATE = 10.0;
float SCANRANGE = 30.0;

key     gRenter = NULL_KEY;
string  gName = "";
integer gRemain = 0;
string  gParcelName = "";

label() {
    if (gRenter == NULL_KEY) {
        llSetText("Pay L$1 per minute for region access", <1,1,1>, 1.0);
    } else {
        llSetText("Region rented by "+gName+" for another "+(string)gRemain
                +" minutes", <1,0,0>, 1.0);
    }
}

string parcelName(vector p) {
    return llList2String(llGetParcelDetails(p, [PARCEL_DETAILS_NAME]), 0);
}

default
{
    on_rez(integer p) {
        llResetScript();
    }
    state_entry() {
        llSensorRepeat("", NULL_KEY, AGENT, SCANRANGE, PI, SCANRATE);
        llSetPayPrice(10, [PAY_HIDE, PAY_HIDE, PAY_HIDE, PAY_HIDE]);
        label();
        llRequestPermissions(llGetOwner(), PERMISSION_DEBIT);
        gParcelName = parcelName(llGetPos());
    }
    money(key av, integer cash) {
        if (gRenter != NULL_KEY) {
            if (gRenter == av) {
                gRemain += cash;
            } else {
                llSay(0, "Sorry, region is already rented by "+gName);
                llGiveMoney(av, cash);
            }
```

TRANSACTION
BASICS

REDISTRIBUTING
WEALTH

SELLING IT!

RENTALS AND
SERVICES

GAMBL...
UH... GAMES
OF SKILL

SUMMARY

```
        } else {
            gRenter = av;
            gName = llKey2Name(av);
            gRemain = cash;
        }
        label();
    }
    sensor(integer n) {
        integer i;
        for (i=0; i<n; i++) {
            key k = llDetectedKey(i);
            if (k != gRenter) {
                vector pos = llDetectedPos(i);
                string pname = parcelName(pos);
                if (pname == gParcelName) {
                    // llEjectFromLand(k)
                    llSay(0, llKey2Name(k)+" is trespassing!");
                }
            }
        }
    }
    no_sensor() {
        gRenter = NULL_KEY;
        gName = "";
        gRemain = 0;
        label();
    }
}
```

This script is essentially a combination of a vendor and a security system. Like a vendor, it accepts payment, but instead of giving the purchaser a product, it gives them a metered amount of time as the official renter of the region the rental box is on. It also periodically scans the surrounding region, looking for trespassers. The `sensor()` event handler examines each detected avatar to see if they are on the same region as the rental box. Because the sensor range might cover other regions, it checks to see if the sensed avatar is over the same region as the rental box. If so, and it is anyone other than the currently active renter, it could use `llEjectFromLand()`—or in this case, it merely complains using `llSay()`. Of course, renters often like to have visitors, so such systems are more likely to coordinate land permissions such as building rights, track prim usage on the land, and give renters access to parcel-based controls such as media streams.

Figure 13.11 shows the in-world side of one of the popular rental systems put out by Hippo Technologies (`http://www.hippo-technologies.co.uk`) or in-world at Hippo Technologies Main Store at Hippo Technologies <116, 127, 44>. This starts with a system that works entirely in-world with rental boxes on the premises of each lot, and it also supports rental vendors that allow renters to pay their bills from central points, such as the rental vendor in Figure 13.11, as well as from a box on their rented land. Many of these systems can be extended with a suite of Internet-based management tools, allowing the land owner to manage a network of rentals from any web browser.

Figure 13.11: Real estate for rent

CHAPTER 1
CHAPTER 2
CHAPTER 3
CHAPTER 4
CHAPTER 5
CHAPTER 6
CHAPTER 7
CHAPTER 8
CHAPTER 9
CHAPTER 10
CHAPTER 11
CHAPTER 12

CHAPTER 13

CHAPTER 14
CHAPTER 15
APPENDICES

⤵ CAMPERS

New *Second Life* commercial enterprises must grapple with attracting a clientele. Classified ads and other sorts of advertising are great, and of course if they can get free coverage in blogs and news items, that's good too. One of the quirks of the *Second Life* search interface is that the ranking of results is biased by how popular a given place is, where "popular" is a combination of how often people put it in their Profile Picks tab and how much traffic there is at a given time. Although the importance of high traffic is slowly being eroded by more-advanced search algorithms, it remains true that nothing attracts a crowd of people better than a crowd of people.

Luckily, the needs of shop owners and new users who are often low on cash (many are initially reluctant to buy Linden dollars or register a credit card to their otherwise-free account) happily coincide: plenty of people in *Second Life* are willing to essentially rent their avatars as props. This sort of arrangement is known as *camping*: paying one or more avatars a little bit of money to just hang around boosting your traffic.

Probably the most common camping devices are simple animation balls (see the online chapter called "Dance") that keep track of how long someone has been sitting there, paying the seated avatar one Linden dollar every few minutes. There's an incredible variety of these camping devices: dance pads and chairs are the most common, but you'll also see avatars cleaning windows, sweeping, and scrubbing the floor. In horror sims you'll see tortured campers, and in adult-oriented sims you'll see avatars pole-dancing. Figure 13.12 is a nice example of the camping spots in front of Mischief Cove at The School of Mischief, Mischief <191, 124, 21>, where an avatar is serving hot dogs in the café, and another is playing the guitar.

CHAPTER 13

TRANSACTION
BASICS

REDISTRIBUTING
WEALTH

SELLING IT!

RENTALS AND
SERVICES

GAMBL...
UH... GAMES
OF SKILL

SUMMARY

Figure 13.12: Camping for income

A different approach is to allow visitors to wander around an extended area and still get paid. This encourages a much more realistic-looking atmosphere and makes it more likely that a camper will actually end up buying something from your store rather than just park their avatar someplace and go get lunch in the real world. Listing 13.12 is a simple example of this approach.

Listing 13.12: Traffic Rewarder

```
integer balance = 0; // how much money left to give out

float SCANRANGE = 50.0;    // how far around to look
float SCANRATE = 120.0;    // how often to scan
integer REWARD = 1;        // how much to pay

default
{
    on_rez(integer p) {
        llResetScript();
    }

    state_entry() {
        llRequestPermissions(llGetOwner(), PERMISSION_DEBIT);
        llSetText("Traffic rewarder\nPay to donate", <1,1,1>, 1.0);
        llSensorRepeat("", NULL_KEY, AGENT, SCANRANGE, PI, SCANRATE);
    }

    money(key av, integer donation) {
        balance += donation;
        llSay(0, "Thanks for your contribution, "+llKey2Name(av));
    }

    sensor(integer n) {
        if (balance>=REWARD) {
            integer pick = (integer)llFrand(n);
            key k = llDetectedKey(pick);
            llGiveMoney(k, REWARD);
            string n = llDetectedName(pick);
            llShout(0, n+" was paid L$1");
            balance -= REWARD;
        }
    }
}
```

Like the money-tree script earlier in this chapter, this script keeps track of expenditures to ensure it doesn't give out any more money than it has. The main behavior is to scan the surrounding 50 meters every two minutes. If the script detects an avatar, it picks one randomly and gives them a Linden dollar just for being there.

A real commercial implementation of this would warrant a few changes: certainly the scan rate, scan range, payout amount, and message to be chatted would be parameters. You might want to eliminate the need to pay into the traffic rewarder, instead preferring to pay directly out of your account. Additionally, you might choose to make the payout rate or amount vary depending on how many avatars the script senses—pay more when it is empty to attract more avatars, but don't bother when the region is full. If the goal is to attract new avatars, you might want to pay only newborns. Finally, you might want to keep track of the last few avatars paid to avoid paying the same ones over and over.

GAMBLI...UH...GAMES OF SKILL

CHAPTER 1
CHAPTER 2
CHAPTER 3
CHAPTER 4
CHAPTER 5
CHAPTER 6
CHAPTER 7
CHAPTER 8
CHAPTER 9
CHAPTER 10
CHAPTER 11
CHAPTER 12

Gambling has been officially disallowed in *Second Life* since July 25th, 2007. The precise implications of the policy have been discussed exhaustively, but the letter of the law is pretty clear (from `http://blog.secondlife.com/2007/07/25/wagering-in-second-life-new-policy`).

Policy

It is a violation of this policy to wager in games in the ***Second Life*** *environment operated on Linden Lab servers if such games:*

(1)   *(a) Rely on chance or random number generation to determine a winner,* ***OR***
        (b) Rely on the outcome of real-life organized sporting events,

AND

(2)   *Provide a payout in*

        (a) Linden Dollars, ***OR***
        (b) Any real-world currency or thing of value.

But as you might expect, an awful lot of people enjoy gambling. Venue owners, especially, like the traffic and income that gambling devices attract, so there have been many attempts to offer games that are gambling-like but that avoid falling afoul of the wagering policy. If you attempt to write such a game, consider the following attributes that appear to keep the policy enforcers happy:

- If the outcome of the game is determined **purely** by the skill or knowledge of the players, it is probably allowed: chess, wrestling, and trivia contests are all allowable.

- If you don't have to pay anything to play, it is probably OK: giveaways and gifts are probably fine, even if the winner is chosen randomly.

- If the winner gets nothing of tangible value, it is probably OK: accolades are fine.

TRANSACTION
BASICS

REDISTRIBUTING
WEALTH

SELLING IT!

RENTALS AND
SERVICES

▶ GAMBL...
uh... GAMES
OF SKILL

▶ SUMMARY

Any one of these is probably enough to make a game legal under *Second Life* policy*; therefore, for-money golf tournaments, free lotteries, and pay-to-play truth-or-dare games are probably all fine. It is a really good idea, however, to make it clear in documentation on your game how it conforms to the policy—for instance, with a notecard giver describing the game and its legal status. More than one game has been shut down not because it wasn't compliant, but because it wasn't *obviously* compliant.

SUMMARY

One of the features that sets *Second Life* apart from other virtual worlds is its rich economy, with an in-world currency that is exchangeable with real-world dollars and euros. As of June 2008, more than 1,100 residents are earning at least US$1,000 each month** from a mixture of product sales, real-estate development and rentals, and fees for services. Clearly, money is an important part of the *SL* environment. This chapter gives you the tools you need to play a part in the *Second Life* economy as a mover of money, rather than the much more common seller of products. Of course, you can also sell your scripts and scripted objects or offer your services as a scripter for an hourly fee. An excellent source of information on these aspects is *The Entrepreneur's Guide to Second Life: Making Money in the Metaverse* by Daniel Terdiman (Wiley, 2007), which focuses directly on the goal of making real money in *SL*.

---

*   But beware: your local laws may be stricter than *Second Life* policy. It is probably a good idea to treat gaming in *SL* as you would internet gaming—go beyond what your country's laws would allow in real life, and you might get a knock on your real door instead of simply having your object returned to your inventory.

**   See `http://secondlife.com/whatis/economy_stats.php` for the current *Second Life* economic statistics.

DEALING WITH PROBLEMS

Bugs happen. Nobody writes perfect code, so don't worry if you have problems. How do experts behave differently than novices? They don't get upset and they don't give up. Set up the conditions for success. Make sure you can tell when something is working and when it's not. Plan for dealing with problems. Learn from your mistakes and share your failures and successes with others.

There are two ways to write error-free programs; only the third one works.

—Alan J. Perlis

WHAT COULD POSSIBLY GO WRONG?

WHAT COULD POSSIBLY GO WRONG?

TOO SLOW?

BE PROACTIVE!

GETTING AND GIVING HELP

PRODUCT-IZING YOUR SCRIPT

SUMMARY

Script writing, and indeed all programming, is a matter of figuring out what you want to do in excruciating detail and writing it all down in a precise enough way that the computer **cannot** misinterpret your instructions. Despite our best efforts, even the most successful commercial software is full of bugs. According to Carnegie Mellon University's CyLab, typical commercial software has 20 to 30 bugs for every thousand lines of code. Even the IEEE standard for high-quality code suggests a goal of less than two defects per thousand lines of shipping code. When you consider that commercial software products contain millions of lines, you can see it adds up pretty quickly.

◥ COMPILER ERRORS

Compiler errors are the first kind of problems you'll encounter. These errors generally involve typos and violations of LSL syntax that are severe enough that the *Second Life* script editor will refuse to compile your script's text into something *SL* can actually run. The script-editor tool is not especially good at identifying these errors; often it identifies only one or two errors before giving up. Even worse, the error messages are sometimes obscure or deceptive. Figure 14.1 shows an attempt to compile a script with a trivial compiler error: **total_number** needs to be converted to a string, like this:

```
llOwnerSay("...deleted "+(string)total_number+" elements");
```

Note how the compiler gives the line number and column corresponding to its best guess at where the error is. However, keep in mind that while the compiler generally makes pretty good guesses, it can also be very wrong.

```
// This code shows a very buggy way
// to manage a list.

list myList = [0,1,2,3,4,5,6,7,8,9];

default
{
    state_entry()
    {
        integer i;
        integer total_number = 0;
        llOwnerSay("before: "+llDumpList2String(myList,","));
        for (i=0; i<llGetListLength(myList); i++) {
            myList = llDeleteSubList(myList,i,i);
            total_number ++;
        }
        llOwnerSay("after: "+llDumpList2String(myList,","));
        llOwnerSay("...deleted "+total_number+" elements");
    }
}
```

```
(17, 45) : ERROR : Type mismatch
```

Figure 14.1: Compiler error

Because most external editors have rich syntax highlighting, they are often better at identifying problems than the in-world script editor. Syntax highlighting refers to how the editor uses color to identify parts of the script the compiler reads, for instance making it clear what the compiler sees as a comment (orange), a literal string (dark green), an LSL library function (red), events (light blue), and reserved words like `integer` (green) or `for` (blue). This highlighting is extremely helpful for troubleshooting potential problems, letting you easily recognize run-on strings or mismatched braces. Additionally, most external editing tools ensure your script is correctly indented, which makes it easier to see how everything nests together and helps expose the **scope** of variables (where in the script the variable is visible). Several of the tools (LSLEditor and lslint, for example) check deeper into your script to expose the same sorts of errors the in-world compiler generates. Each tool helps you find a slightly different set of problems. If you are totally baffled by a compiler error, using a different tool may provide a more specific pointer to the problem. The SYW online chapter "Programming in the Out-World" and the LSL wiki both provide lists of external tools LSL scripters may find useful.

Following are some common causes of compiler errors:

CHAPTER 1
CHAPTER 2
CHAPTER 3
CHAPTER 4
CHAPTER 5
CHAPTER 6
CHAPTER 7
CHAPTER 8
CHAPTER 9
CHAPTER 10
CHAPTER 11
CHAPTER 12
CHAPTER 13

- Run-on strings, especially when you include double quotes in the string, as the following example shows (a double quote is missing at the end):

```
string bad = "run on \"string\";
```

- Missing or mismatched parenthesis, braces, or brackets

- Extra or missing arguments to functions

- Type mismatches, the most common of which is probably missing coercion to string types when building a string, as in this example:

```
integer x = 3;
llOwnerSay("x = "+x); // must be +(string)x
```

- Hard-to-see typos in names, such as `l1OwnerSay()`, where a numeral 1 is used instead of a second lowercase letter l

 RUNTIME ERRORS

When your script generates a runtime error (an error that occurs while the script is running), an alert icon appears over the object and another instance of the icon lights up in the upper-left part of your viewer. Clicking on either icon (or enabling the Show Script Warning/Error Window line on the viewer's Tools menu) opens a window that displays the complete error message. On this window you will see one tab for each object that is generating errors and an extra tab that shows error messages for all such objects combined. The latter reveals how errors generated by multiple interacting objects interleave with each other, which may provide valuable clues as to cause and effect. Figure 14.2 shows an object that reported a runtime error, with the alert icons highlighted in red.

What Could Possibly Go Wrong?

Too Slow?

Be Proactive!

Getting and Giving Help

Product-izing Your Script

Summary

Figure 14.2: A script generating a runtime error

Table 14.1 lists the most common runtime errors you'll encounter. See the LSL wikis* for more comprehensive lists.

TABLE 14.1: COMMON RUNTIME ERRORS

Runtime Error	Situation
Math error	The result of an operation is undefined, for example dividing by zero.
Heap error	Attempted to store the result of a function that returned no value.
Stack heap collision	Ran out of memory (see the "Memory" section of this chapter).
Too many listens	Tried to open too many (more than 64) listeners.
llSomeFunction error running rule #*n* unknown rule.	Element #n of the list argument to `llSomeFunction()` was an integer value that doesn't identify a legal rule. Similar error messages can happen at various index values with `llSetPrimitiveParams()` and `llGetPrimitiveParams()`.

LOGIC ERRORS

A lot of errors can arise from your program's logic. While there is no way we can predict all the ways you might get tripped up, it's worth highlighting the following logic errors that are easy to make and happen more frequently than others:

- Using integer arithmetic instead of float. In this example, the division is done with integer arithmetic and only then converted to a float:

```
float x = 1/2; // x = 0.0 not 0.5
```

- Using = instead of ==, & instead of &&, | instead of ||, etc. An example of using = instead of == is shown here:

```
if (x == 1) { doSomething(); }
if (x = 2) { doSomethingElse(); }    // x is set to 2 here!!
if (x == 3) { doYetSomeOtherThing(); }
```

---

* This is one example where the official and unofficial wikis are significantly different. We recommend that you look at both `http://wiki.secondlife.com/wiki/LSL_Errors` and `http://rpgstats.com/wiki/index.php?title=Errors`.

- Using nested `if` without braces:

```
if (x)
    if (y)
        foo();
        // baz();   // if you uncomment this, the else clause breaks!
    else            // most recent "if"
      bar();
```

- Indentation doesn't match actual structure:

```
if (x) {
  if (y) {
    foo();
} else {    // this is the else for the "if (y)" not the "if (x)"
  bar();
}
}
```

- Using `llGetListLength()` in a `for` loop that modifies the loop:

```
// this loop deletes every other item
for (i=0; i<llGetListLength(myList); i++) {
    myList = llDeleteSubList(myList,i,i);
}
```

- Difficult-to-see typos—for instance, using a comma instead of a period or the numeral 0 instead of the letter *O*. This example leads to an unintended heterogeneous list:

```
list positions = [<100.0, 10.00, 1.000>,  // vector
                   <123.4, 12.34, 1,234>]; // this item is a rotation!
```

CHAPTER 1
CHAPTER 2
CHAPTER 3
CHAPTER 4
CHAPTER 5
CHAPTER 6
CHAPTER 7
CHAPTER 8
CHAPTER 9
CHAPTER 10
CHAPTER 11
CHAPTER 12
CHAPTER 13

CHAPTER 14

CHAPTER 15
APPENDICES

 ## MEMORY

LSL scripts are rather limited in memory. Worse still, the scripts themselves occupy the same memory space used to hold the values of the scripts' variables. On top of all that, parameters are copied each time they are passed to functions, causing both speed and memory issues. One trick for reducing memory consumption while constructing large lists is to eschew

```
list a = a + b;
```

in favor of

```
list a = (a=[]) + a + b;
```

This trick works because LSL makes extra copies of intermediate values. The first expression makes copies of *a* and *b,* concatenates them, assigns the result to *a*, and only then discards the extra copies. The second expression discards the original value of *a* (but not the temporary copy!) before the concatenation is made, potentially saving a lot of temporary storage. Of course, for small amounts of list data you are unlikely to need these tricks. Furthermore, future versions of LSL are highly likely to make this sort of trick moot, if not actually counterproductive. A detailed article on script memory consumption is available at `http://wiki.secondlife.com/wiki/LSL_Script_Memory`. For some discussion of the next scripting engine, **Mono**, see Chapter 15, "New and Improved."

You can use function `llGetFreeMemory()` to work out the number of free bytes the stack can use; as the script executes, the stack grows and shrinks in size depending upon the complexity of the expressions being executed and which scripting engine you are using. Keep an eye on JIRA and the wiki for more discussion, as this function has some odd behavior.

WHAT COULD
POSSIBLY GO
WRONG?

 TOO SLOW?

BE PROACTIVE!

GETTING AND
GIVING HELP

PRODUCT-
IZING YOUR
SCRIPT

SUMMARY

ANNOYANCES

The following is a list of common problems, inconsistencies, and strange behaviors worth knowing about but that aren't technically bugs:

- The `==` operator on lists only compares the length of the lists, never looking at the contents.
- Generally there's no way to know when calls fail: `llGiveMoney()`, `llGiveInventory()`, and `llGiveInventoryList()` have no feedback mechanism to see if the transaction actually went through. `llRezObject()` is almost as silent, but failures here can be detected if the script never gets an `object_rez()` event.
- Only 64 events can be queued for delivery to a script. Any excess events silently disappear with no way to tell if you are losing events.
- Sensors return no more than 16 detected objects, no matter how many actually satisfy the filter criteria.
- `llSetPos()` and `llSetPrimitiveParams()` can move an object only 10 meters at a time.
- There is no good way to store large amounts of data locally: scripts cannot write to notecards.

The LSL wikis have other good lists, for instance by searching for Annoyances.

TOO SLOW?

You've written a nice script. It compiles and runs without error and even does what you want. But it doesn't run as fast as you were hoping due to inefficiency. Efficiency refers to how much effort or resources a particular script requires to execute. There are two kinds of efficiency relevant in LSL: efficiency of the actual code, such as speed of execution or memory usage, and efficiency to reduce "server lag," for example when there are too many scripts. LSL is not an optimizing compiler; therefore, you have to manage the efficiency of your own scripts.

How can you make it faster? Fixing a slow script is complicated business. First the bad news: sometimes the best you can do is file a bug report or feature request and look for an alternative approach. The good news is that not only are many speed problems fixable, but there are often many alternatives. But before you take any action, you need to think about what "too slow" really means.

NOTE

First make your code work, and then make it readable. Then, and only then, worry about efficiency. As Sir Tony Hoare said, "Premature optimization is the root of all evil." (This quote was popularized by Donald Knuth, renowned computer scientist.)

LAG

The first type of slowness is *lag*—the perception by a human user that things onscreen are visibly moving slowly: animation is slow, movement is sluggish, chat and IMs appear delayed, and so on.

Many things can make the world appear slow. The big factors are as follows:

Viewer lag: The user's computer is having trouble keeping up with the demands being placed on it. Examples include lots of particles and special effects; animated textures; shiny, glowing, spinning, or flexible objects; and local lights. These all add negligible load on the sim but can severely impact your viewer's performance.

Network lag: A slow network connection, either between you and the *Second Life* sims you can see or between the computers that make up the *Second Life* server farms. Lots of large textures in your field of view can severely impact performance even when you've got a good connection.

Simulator lag: The sim is having difficulty simulating the world, due to some combination of the sim's physics and the scripts running on objects in the sim. The function `llGetSimulatorHostname()` returns a string that is the hostname of the machine the script is running on. It causes the script to sleep for 10.0 seconds.

Overloaded common resources: There are several types of *SL* systems that cannot be easily duplicated, or *scaled* to support an unlimited-complexity world. For instance, you will often hear about *asset server* problems—an asset server is a cluster of computers that hold all the information about what objects look like, what they are called, etc. Similar systems deal with logins and user information, coordinate teleports to make sure you end up in only *one* place, and keep track of the money in your account.

Of all the lag varieties, *only simulator lag is directly impacted by scripting*.

  ## NOTE

The following URLs lead to excellent articles on the different forms of lag:

- `http://rpgstats.com/wiki/index.php?title=Lag`
- `http://wiki.secondlife.com/wiki/Help:Lag`
- `https://secondlife.com/community/support.php?questionID=4207`

 # LINEAR EXECUTION SPEED

Some operations simply take longer than others, even though they appear to do very similar things. In LSL, your best bet is generally to use the most straightforward approach. Don't use vectors if you can get away with integers. Avoid using lots of conversions between types. Conversions can be difficult to see because of the combination of LSL's implicit conversions and lack of automatic optimization. For instance, the vector `<0, 0, 0>` means the same thing as the vector `<0.0, 0.0, 0.0>`, but the latter is faster because vector components are already floats: specifying integers makes LSL convert each integer to a float every single time!

CHAPTER 14

What Could
Possibly Go
Wrong?

 Too Slow?

Be Proactive!

Getting and
Giving Help

Product-
izing Your
Script

Summary

Use as few calls to library functions as you can get away with. Many functions have extra delays built in (see the "Script-Speed Governors" section later in this chapter), and when *SL* is stepping though the lines of your script, it is just plain slower to use a library call, even when they are doing the very same operations!

The LSL wikis are, of course, full of good information on performance. For more detailed analysis on the speed of specific operations and tools for doing your own analyses, check out `http://wiki.secondlife.com/wiki/Efficiency_Tester` and `http://wiki.secondlife.com/wiki/LSL_Script_Efficiency`.

WARNING

The upcoming change from the current LSL script engine to the Mono engine has potentially dramatic effects on the speed at which LSL instructions are executed. Initial figures suggest it will be up to several hundred times faster! Be aware, however, that this directly improves only the linear execution speed of your script's instructions; it makes no changes to artificial delays in library functions and cannot do much with an extremely complex algorithm.

ALGORITHMS

An *algorithm* is a procedure for solving a problem. In scripting terms, an algorithm could be the recipe you use to shuffle a deck of cards, to find a particular avatar in a crowd, to coordinate a group of objects, to make a robot appear to walk, and so on. In computer science, as in the real world, some recipes are simply faster than others, but *there are always tradeoffs*. The single biggest concern is how much slower your algorithm becomes when the problem gets larger or more complicated.

Imagine the real-world problem of matching socks after doing the laundry. You could take the following approaches:

- Close your eyes and take two random socks out of the basket. If they match, you've got a pair to put away. If not, put both socks back and try again. Repeat.

- Take one sock at random. Take another sock at random. If it matches, great. If not, discard the second sock. Repeat until you find a match.

- Take a sock. Take another sock. If they match, great. If not, keep them out. Take another sock, see if it matches either of the other chosen socks. Repeat.

- Pre-sort all the socks into piles of the same sock size. Then sort each pile by color. Then use one of the other algorithms to find pairs within your now-much-smaller piles.

You can see how, even with such a simple task, there are tradeoffs to make—if all your socks are the same size and color, there might not be any difficulty using the first of the algorithms because every random pair will match. If you have lots of sizes and colors, then you might want something like the last option. Sometimes you can avoid needing to solve the problem: you could wash your socks in pairs, only have one pair of socks, or not wear socks at all!

Because an enormous amount of literature on algorithm complexity analysis is available, we won't go into depth here. However, it is worth remembering that the way you choose to go about solving a problem may affect your script's overall speed more than the slowness of *SL* will.

TIME DILATION

All scripts in objects rezzed in a sim or attached to avatars in a sim compete for execution time. When scripts are well-behaved and the sim is relatively unloaded, there are enough computational resources to run everything. When a sim becomes heavily loaded—for instance, due to the presence of many avatars, complex physical interactions, or runaway scripts—the sim will start falling behind. One way the simulator software deals with such slowdowns is to slow the delivery of events, including timers, to scripts. The term *time dilation* refers to the ratio of a sim's physical-model simulation speed to real time. For instance, a time dilation value of 0.5 means physical interactions are happening at half the speed they should. Although time dilation does not directly measure how slowly scripts are running in a sim, it is related. Your script can get the time dilation figure by calling `llGetRegionTimeDilation()`. You can also monitor it with your view by turning on the statistics bar (type Control+Shift+1).

You will see another figure in the statistics bar: *Script Perf.* This figure indicates how many compiled script instructions per second the sim is running, which is interesting but not generally useful, because a low value could mean either the sim is running slowly or the scripts in the sim aren't asking to run very often.

SCRIPT-SPEED GOVERNORS

Everything your script does in LSL takes time to execute: every function, operator, assignment, and event. However, many LSL functions impose *extra* delays to the calling scripts. These delays are an attempt to carefully balance calls that are either expensive for **SL** as a whole (even though not locally expensive) or that are easily abused. (The specific values are subject to change; check the LSL wiki for up-to-date figures.)

Some functions have high delays to slow down runaway or especially annoying scripts due to bugs or intentional abuse by griefers. Unfortunately, some functions are so useful that making **simple** delays high enough to keep them from severely impacting the grid isn't satisfactory because it would render them so slow as to be useless. To avoid this situation, there are several more-complicated limiters in place.

The `llHTTPRequest()` function (see Chapter 12) doesn't have a per-call delay at all! Instead it will allow only 25 calls in any 20-second period. This allows very high rates of communication as long it comes in bursts, but throttles back on continuous communications pretty dramatically.

The other limiter is called the **grey goo fence**. Taking its name from the science-fiction idea[*] that runaway self-replicating nanotechnology could turn everything into more self-replicating grey goo, the **SL** grey goo fence is a simulator-side limiter that blocks further scripted-object rezzing and object transfers when too much is going on. In particular, the current grey goo fence will stop an object or related group of objects when they've made more than 240 calls to `llRezObject()` or `llGiveInventory()` within six seconds, with extra penalties for rezzing physical objects. The actual algorithm is even more complicated and subject to change at any time. Search the LSL wiki for GreyGooFence to find more details and links to discussions of the topic.

SIMULTANEITY

Synchronizing events while using inherently asynchronous processes such as LSL scripts is always a difficult task. Even the double-door script in Chapter 3, "Communications," looks at first glance like it should be synchronized, but the function call and communication delays thwart the easy solutions.

---

* See the Wikipedia article on grey goo: `http://en.wikipedia.org/wiki/Grey_goo`

CHAPTER 1
CHAPTER 2
CHAPTER 3
CHAPTER 4
CHAPTER 5
CHAPTER 6
CHAPTER 7
CHAPTER 8
CHAPTER 9
CHAPTER 10
CHAPTER 11
CHAPTER 12
CHAPTER 13

CHAPTER 15
APPENDICES

CHAPTER 14

If you cannot directly affect multiple things at once, your best bet is to use a synchronizer script that triggers a group of separate scripts to accomplish the desired effect. The synchronized dances in the online chapter called "Dance" use a controller script that employs `llMessageLinked()` to instruct multiple scripts to animate their avatars at the same time. You still run the risk of the worker scripts running at slightly different speeds, but at least they will all get the start message at pretty much the same time.

What Could Possibly Go Wrong?

▼ Too Slow?

▼ Be Proactive!

Getting and Giving Help

Product-izing Your Script

Summary

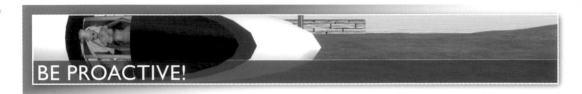

The knowledge and skills you use to *write* scripts are only part of what you need to be an effective scripter. You also need to acquire good practices to make it possible to debug, maintain, and document your code, especially when you start collaborating with other scripters or taking on large projects. The good news is that most of these techniques are very similar to the practices you use in any programming environment: if you are already a programmer, they'll come naturally; if LSL is your first language, the experience you gain here will translate to other languages.

DON'T BE OVERLY CLEVER

Everyone knows that debugging is twice as hard as writing a program in the first place. So if you are as clever as you can be when you write it, how will you ever debug it?

—Brian Kernighan

Always start out writing your script in the most straightforward way possible. Optimizing a script that is already working is far easier than fixing a confusing script that should run fast but has never worked!

DEBUGGING

What do you do if your script compiles correctly, doesn't generate any runtime errors, yet still doesn't work properly? Most programming languages have fancy debugging programs that allow you to watch the innards of your program as it runs—but not LSL. Therefore, most scripters insert debugging statements into their code to report on the script's progress as it runs. For simple cases, people usually just insert calls to `llOwnerSay()` or `llSay()` at the points in their script they suspect the problems lie. Running the annotated script gives you a string of reports about what the script is actually seeing rather than what you think it should be seeing. Figure 14.3 shows what this looks like.

Be aware of how many message you expect to see; a few thousand lines of debugging messages are unlikely to be very useful to you if the one line that matters is swamped by all the irrelevant ones. Add conditional code to print debugging messages only when it detects something unexpected. You can also use the special chat channel `DEBUG_CHANNEL`. Any chat sent to this channel goes to the debugging console in the viewer rather than the chat window—this is where runtime errors are printed.

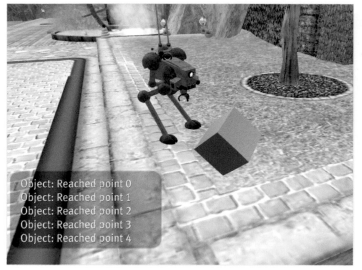

Object: Reached point 0
Object: Reached point 1
Object: Reached point 2
Object: Reached point 3
Object: Reached point 4

Figure 14.3: Tracing a script using `llOwnerSay()`

CHAPTER 1
CHAPTER 2
CHAPTER 3
CHAPTER 4
CHAPTER 5
CHAPTER 6
CHAPTER 7
CHAPTER 8
CHAPTER 9
CHAPTER 10
CHAPTER 11
CHAPTER 12
CHAPTER 13

CHAPTER 15
APPENDICES

CHAPTER 14

It is sometimes useful to leave debugging messages in your script in a way that lets you turn them on and off easily. This can make it easier to debug complex scripts, enabling messages only when you need to see what is going on, as in Listing 14.1.

Listing 14.1: Using a Debugging Function

```
// only a partial script
integer DEBUG = TRUE;

debug(string message) {
    if (DEBUG) {
        llOwnerSay("DEBUG. "+message);
    }
}

default
{
    state_entry() {
        debug("entered default state!");
    }
    touch_end(integer c) {
        if (DEBUG) {
            debug("current position = "+(string)pos+"\n"+
                "current rotation = "+(string)(llRot2Euler(rot)*RAD_TO_DEG)+"\n"+
                "current color = "+(string)color256(color));
        }
    }
}
```

The `debug()` function checks to see if the `DEBUG` constant is turned on before sending the passed message on to the script's owner. The `state_entry()` event handler uses the `debug()` function to print a progress message only if `DEBUG` is on. The `touch_end()` handler does an extra check to see if the message is going to be printed. If debugging is disabled, it will avoid the cost of constructing the big status string. This can be critical if you choose to leave debugging code in your script, especially when the calls to `debug()` are in parts of the code that might be called many times.

WHAT COULD POSSIBLY GO WRONG?

TOO SLOW?

 BE PROACTIVE!

GETTING AND GIVING HELP

PRODUCT-IZING YOUR SCRIPT

SUMMARY

You can adjust this pattern to suit your needs. One nice change is to treat DEBUG as a global variable instead of a constant and include a way to turn it on and off using a menu choice or chat listener; don't forget to change the name to *gDebug* instead of DEBUG to avoid confusing the constant with the variable. Then if you discover a situation where the script is acting up, you can turn on debugging and perhaps gain some insight into what is causing the problem. You can even do this with products you ship, but make certain it doesn't turn into a security hole for your clients!

Another option is to use llSay() on the DEBUG_CHANNEL rather than llOwnerSay(). This option lets others see the debugging messages, including in a product you've sold, but still keeps the messages out of the general chat window.

 BACKING UP YOUR SCRIPTS

It is all too easy to lose your scripts—and not only due to crashes at inopportune moments and inventory loss. You are much more likely to lose track of which inventory object or object rezzed in-world has the latest working version of your script. Or you may accidentally delete the object or transfer a no-copy object with your latest version to another avatar or deed it to a group, only to discover your script is no longer readable!

It is important to keep copies of your scripts around, especially when you are actively working on them. Two approaches are common. First, you can maintain copies of everything in your inventory; each time you make a substantial change, make a copy. Label your copies with a version number, keep them organized with folders, or use inventory features to sort by date. You should keep copies of complex scripts outside of the objects that will hold them. You can edit scripts directly from your inventory instead of editing in rezzed objects—this will keep them from running until you are ready to test, because scripts do not run unless rezzed.

The other good approach is to keep copies outside of *Second Life*. Do all of your scripting using external tools and use copy-and-paste to bring them into *SL*. The SYW website describes a number of external editors that are especially useful for editing LSL scripts, but you can use any editor you like, for instance Notepad in Windows, gedit or vi in Linux, or TextEdit in OS X. Many of these tools are much better than *SL*'s internal scripting tools (however, even the best of them aren't quite as good at finding errors).

Having your scripts outside *SL* means you can use external backup tools to keep your code safe. For large, complex products, and if you are collaborating with others, using a revision-control system such as Subversion not only gives you a simple backup solution, but also lets you keep track of all the differences between every version of your script. This is extremely helpful when you make a change and something stops working, or if a client has a problem with an old version of your product. You can always see what your scripts used to look like.

 VERSIONING

Any time you have a complicated project, you'll go through a lot of revisions. This is true not only during development; if you sell a product that people like, your customers will ask you to add features, make changes, and fix bugs. In a remarkably short period of time, you will have people using multiple versions of the same product. It is critical, therefore, to know which version someone is using so you can tell where to start. The version-control discussion in the online chapter "Programming in the Out-World" explains how this process can be automated.

Labeling both your products (objects) and scripts with version numbers is a good idea. The simplest option is to make the version number part of the name or description. We like to include a version number in the main script of an object. You can then have the script report the version using `llOwnerSay()` in the `on_rez()` event handler or, better yet, have a control mechanism—for instance, an `llListen()` on an unused channel or an `llDialog()` choice—that reports it only when asked.

When you have objects that communicate with each other, especially if they are sold as different objects (or at different times), it can be extremely useful to version the communication protocols. This allows the objects to detect when they are likely to be speaking subtly different languages or interacting with incompatible objects that happen to use the same messages. If you are signing messages using `llMD5String()` or encrypting them with `llXorBase64StringsCorrect()`, an easy option is to include the version number as part of the secret key: a version mismatch will be unintelligible.

TESTING

Test your scripts! It sounds obvious, but few scripters do as much testing as they should. The bottom line is that it takes much less time to fix problems when a script is still under your control.

You must know what behavior you expect to see before you can tell if something is working. Figure out how to test any expected behavior and make sure that that behavior works. When it works for you, give it to a friend (or an alternate avatar you create for yourself) to make certain it works for others. This is also a good time to check that permissions are set properly. *Unless you want to give your scripts away, always double-check the permissions of your scripts and objects before you sell them!*

Because many LSL functions work differently when they're in group-deeded objects, scripting such objects can be especially challenging. When working with group-deeded objects, remember the following:

- The process of *deeding* an object counts as a transfer.
- The owner of a deeded object is the *group*, not an avatar.
- `llOwnerSay()` has no effect on deeded objects.
- Groups cannot give permissions, so functions like `llGiveMoney()` cannot be used in group-deeded objects.

Chapter 11, "Multimedia," has some additional discussion of this in the Streaming Media section, for instance Listing 11.5.

Randomness is fine, maybe even desirable in some settings (art, games), but you even want to test randomness! For instance, if you are scripting a robot that is supposed to wander randomly around a region, let it run for a while and make certain it doesn't end up pressed against one side of the area, which might indicate a bias in your random-direction chooser.

Do you best to break your script. Try taking it into inventory while it is reading its configuration notecard, or rezzing an attachment on the ground. If it reacts to touches, try clicking on it dozens of times to see what happens. If it moves itself, try click-dragging it or use the edit tools to move or rotate it in different states. See what happens when you move it across sim boundaries.

If your script handles money, be extra diligent about testing. The vast majority of scripted objects don't do a lot of harm if they malfunction, but a buggy scripted object with debit permissions can transfer all your client's money to a third party remarkably quickly. Customers for money scripts are trusting you with real currency: respect their trust by being certain your code won't clean them out. One option for safely testing money-related scripts is to try them on the Beta Grid (see the following note) where major bugs cannot result in giving away the Linden dollars in your real account.

CHAPTER 1
CHAPTER 2
CHAPTER 3
CHAPTER 4
CHAPTER 5
CHAPTER 6
CHAPTER 7
CHAPTER 8
CHAPTER 9
CHAPTER 10
CHAPTER 11
CHAPTER 12
CHAPTER 13
CHAPTER 14
CHAPTER 15
APPENDICES

WHAT COULD
POSSIBLY GO
WRONG?

TOO SLOW?

BE PROACTIVE!

GETTING AND
GIVING HELP

PRODUCT-
IZING YOUR
SCRIPT

SUMMARY

NOTE

The *Beta Grid* is an alternate *Second Life* world. It is much smaller than the main grid, and resident accounts (inventory, Linden dollars, etc.) are copies, usually days or weeks old. You can download a different viewer for Beta Grid access from `http://secondlife.com/community/preview.php`. Everything that happens in the Beta Grid is transitory; all content and transactions are periodically discarded and never affect anything that happens on the main grid. The Beta Grid is useful for two purposes.

First, *Second Life* simulator software evolves and changes continually. When Linden Lab is preparing to roll out a new simulator revision with substantial changes, they advertise not only what the expected changes will be, but where you can try them in advance. Major simulator changes, especially those likely to affect scripting, are initially deployed to the Beta Grid, where you can safely test your scripts.

Second, you can safely test risky scripts on the Beta Grid. For the most part, this means you can test new scripts that have debit permissions without putting your real account on the line.

Unit testing (splitting up complex objects and scripts into their smallest components for testing) is very useful. You can simplify the testing process for a big, complicated system by testing all the pieces individually. When you are certain that all the pieces work properly, you assemble them together into larger and larger pieces until the whole thing is back together. One nice feature of this approach is that once unit-tested, the pieces are ready to be used in other products as well.

Sometimes it is impossible to manually test the pieces. You can get around that problem by building **test jigs**—other objects that appear to the test object to be "the rest of the system," but that are much simpler than the real thing, usually just a set of predefined tests. Test jigs can form the basis of **regression tests**, where any time you make a change to a script, you can rerun a set of scripted tests to make certain you haven't broken anything.

GETTING AND GIVING HELP

Just as **Second Life** itself is social, so is working with the **SL** platform. A great many communities in various forms are devoted to helping people create content in **Second Life**. This chapter is a categorized list of some of the high points. Like **SL** itself, things are constantly changing, but this section should offer you a good starting point to finding other scripters, builders, and **SL** developers.

EDUCATION

Scripting is not an especially easy skill to teach in-world. Unlike in building classes, it is relatively difficult for teachers to see their students' progress and put on demonstrations that have more pedagogical value than merely passing around scripts as text. There are some credible classes, however, that are particularly useful for beginning scripters. So far, few of these take advantage of the relatively new media features for slide shows and "live" presentations of traditional lectures. No doubt by the time you are reading this, there will be more choices.

A few people and places do offer group scripting classes, usually for free*. You can check out the Community Events section on the *Second Life* website at `http://secondlife.com/events/`, by selecting the Education category and searching for "scripting." Some specific classes to look for are any run by New Citizens Incorporated (NCI, various locations), the School of Mischief at Mischief Cove (Mischief <147, 160, 24>), or our own Scripting Your World classes at SYW Headquarters.

The *SL* wiki has an excellent list of LSL mentors at `http://wiki.secondlife.com/wiki/Category:LSL_Mentors`. These are people who have volunteered to be personal coaches to other scripters, generally in areas of their own expertise. They are not teachers as such, but are happy to help push you in the right direction. They also represent a treasure trove of information that is rather more personal than the mailing lists.

Additionally, there is a list of LSL teachers at `http://wiki.secondlife.com/wiki/Category:LSL_Teachers`. The list is often stale, with no guarantee of quality or style, but it is worth a look, especially if you are looking for more-formal personal instruction than a mentor will offer.

There is, of course, a variety of books available in addition to this one, even some in-world. Both *Second Life: The Official Guide* and *Creating Your World: The Official Guide to Advanced Content Creation for Second Life* (both from Wiley) have excellent scripting content. Check out your local book store or your favorite online store for real-world books, and *Second Life* stores such as SLExchange (`http://slexchange.com`) and OnRez (`http://onrez.com`) for in-world texts.

An ongoing project is aimed at creating a certification process for scripters. It is interesting to track the progress and see how your own scripting skills are likely to measure up on the *SL* wiki at `http://wiki.secondlife.com/wiki/Scripting_Certification`.

CHAPTER 1
CHAPTER 2
CHAPTER 3
CHAPTER 4
CHAPTER 5
CHAPTER 6
CHAPTER 7
CHAPTER 8
CHAPTER 9
CHAPTER 10
CHAPTER 11
CHAPTER 12
CHAPTER 13
CHAPTER 15
APPENDICES

CHAPTER 14

 ## ↘ IN-WORLD LOCALES

Many of the Linden movers and shakers hold regular in-world office hours. You can get a great deal of inside information on what is going on in *SL* and where it is heading by dropping by. Check the current list of Lindens, times, and locations at `http://wiki.secondlife.com/wiki/Office_Hours`.

There are a number of scripting-related regions in-world. Some of the standouts are as follows:

New Citizens Incorporated (NCI), many locations, including Nova Civis Caledon <173, 60, 36>: NCI offers classes, events, freebies, tutorials, and sandboxes. They also have a wide range of *SL* news publications and volunteers who assist visitors individually. NCI publishes their schedule in-world at all 11 of their classroom and information regions, and on the Web at `http://nci-sl.org`.

---

* However, be aware that most instructors in SL work for tips!

What Could
Possibly Go
Wrong?

Too Slow?

Be Proactive!

▶ Getting and
Giving Help

Product-
izing Your
Script

Summary

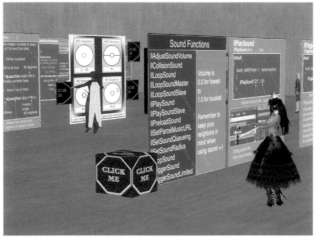

College of Scripting, Music, and Science, Horsa <26, 243, 84>: An excellent set of mainly self-guided tutorials on scripting. You literally start learning on the ground floor of a tower of increasingly advanced topics.

Academy of Second Learning, Eson <26, 164, 351>: Another major in-world school of content creation, with basic through relatively advanced scripting classes.

The Particle Laboratory, Teal <180, 73, 21>: The Particle Lab is the best way to explore the range of possible effects with `llParticleSystem()`. The region is both beautiful and highly educational with tutorials, sample scripts, and do-it-yourself particle control consoles modeled after the exhibits of the Exploratorium science museum in San Francisco.

Scripting Your World Headquarters, Hennepin <89, 144, 108>: You can play with in-world demonstrations of this book's scripts or get your own copies here. SYW also offers regular introductory classes and has a variety of support materials.

CHAPTER 1
CHAPTER 2
CHAPTER 3
CHAPTER 4
CHAPTER 5
CHAPTER 6
CHAPTER 7
CHAPTER 8
CHAPTER 9
CHAPTER 10
CHAPTER 11
CHAPTER 12
CHAPTER 13

As scripting and building is often so tightly coupled, it is also worth mentioning some of the more important building-related locations:

The Ivory Tower Library of Primitives, Natoma <207, 170, 25>: The Ivory Tower Library of Primitives is a complete, self-guided, self-paced in-world visual tutorial of the *Second Life* building interface.

CHAPTER 14

CHAPTER 15
APPENDICES

Robin (Sojourner) Wood's Texture Tutorials, Livingtree <127, 99, 25>: This locale offers a comprehensive, in-world, self-paced set of nine tutorial stations that teach you how to work with textures in *Second Life*.

WHAT COULD
POSSIBLY GO
WRONG?

TOO SLOW?

BE PROACTIVE!

 GETTING AND
GIVING HELP

PRODUCT-
IZING YOUR
SCRIPT

SUMMARY

↘ GROUPS

Joining one of the many active in-world scripting groups is probably the best way to get access to scripter peers. Most of these mainly offer group IM so that people can ask questions of other in-world scripters. Some groups give members access to special script libraries, business opportunities, or the ability to build and run scripts in group-private sandbox regions. You will probably want to join a few to see which ones fit your style and level of expertise. Note that some require payment or additional steps in order to join. Here are a few you may want to look at (they are free and offer open enrollment unless noted otherwise):

Scripters of _Second Life_: This group is willing to exchange information and provide scripting help to anyone. This is currently the largest free scripting group in _SL_ with an active membership. To join, send an IM to any online group member who has the role "Inviter."

College of Scripting, Music, and Science: This group has a huge library of scripts and tutorials. Currently the second largest of the scripting groups, this is an excellent choice for new scripters. You need to join in person at their College at Horsa <26, 243, 84>.

GNU Scripters of _Second Life_: This group of scripters is dedicated to the spread of free software scripts licensed under the GNU GPL v3 or later. Excellent for people interested in open source scripting, it may be problematic if you want to sell scripts. This is a low-traffic group with a nice script library.

Linden Script Tutorial Group: This is a group associated with the in-world Linden Script Tutorial Exhibition, and supports members helping each other with scripting problems. It has a large membership but isn't especially busy in IM.

Script Academy: This group of volunteer teachers helps you learn how to script through tutorials, group IM discussions, and _SL_ get-togethers. Similar to the College of Scripting Music Science, this is a nice group with good IM discussion.

Script Crypt: This group gives members access to several libraries of full-perm scripts of somewhat higher quality than the typical freebies. There is no IM traffic.

Script Database Group: This is another good in-world script library group.

Scripts: Members help each other with scripting problems and provide LSL scripts to members. This is a moderately large and active group, excellent for beginners.

Advanced Scripters of _Second Life_: This group is for advanced scripters only but can make for fascinating reading for moderate-level scripters who aren't ready to participate in the discussion. The group has a very low tolerance for naïve questions; if a question can be answered by wikis or other information sources, it shouldn't be asked here. The membership fee is L$600.

Scripting Your World: This group combines support for this book with announcements for related events and scripting access to the sandbox at SYW HQ.

CHAPTER 1
CHAPTER 2
CHAPTER 3
CHAPTER 4
CHAPTER 5
CHAPTER 6
CHAPTER 7
CHAPTER 8
CHAPTER 9
CHAPTER 10
CHAPTER 11
CHAPTER 12
CHAPTER 13

MAILING LISTS AND FORUMS

In addition to in-world group membership, there are several ways to communicate directly with other scripters via email and online forums. With both email lists and forums, a great many interested people will see anything you post and, unlike with in-world group IMs, discussions are usually archived for later viewing.

Scripting Tips Forum: The best place outside of *SL* to ask scripting questions is on the Scripting Tips forum. A forum is similar to a mailing list, albeit one that resides entirely within the confines of a web page. Either visit `http://forums.secondlife.com/forumdisplay.php?f=54` or begin from the main *SL* website, and choose Community from the menu at the top, Forums from the menu on the left, and then Scripting Tips at the bottom of the page in the Content Creation section. There are lots of other forums of secondary interest to scripters as content developers, including ones focused on building, animation, and business-related classified ads.

Secondlifescripters: Of interest to many scripters is a traditional email list at `secondlifescripters@lists.secondlife.com`. Secondlifescripters is usually pretty low volume, but it's a great way to ask questions to a broad audience. The traffic on this list dropped dramatically in early 2008 when all unmoderated Linden Lab–hosted email lists were closed. This particular list was reopened fairly quickly with a new moderator, but has not, at the time of this writing, recovered completely. You can join the list by visiting `https://lists.secondlife.com/cgi-bin/mailman/listinfo/secondlifescripters`. Archives are available here, as well.

CHAPTER 14

SLDev: If you are interested in the guts of *Second Life*, the `sldev@lists.secondlife.com` list is probably of interest. Discussion centers on viewer development, but touches on some scripting-related bugs and workarounds on occasion. Sign up at `https://lists.secondlife.com/cgi-bin/mailman/listinfo/sldev`.

WEBSITES

Websites are critical to keeping up with *Second Life* happenings. First there are the official sites:

`http://secondlife.com`: This website is the *Second Life* home page of course.

`http://blog.secondlife.com`: This website has lots of good information, not the least of which are the video tutorials published by Torley Linden. Few are directly scripting related, but many blog entries are relevant, including viewer and simulator updates.

`http://jira.secondlife.com`: This website houses the public JIRA, where you can report bugs and request new features.

`http://wiki.secondlife.com`: This website is the entry point to the official *Second Life* wiki pages. A wealth of information, not only for scripting, but all types of content creation, volunteering, marketing, and behind-the-scenes software that makes up the entirety of *Second Life*.

There are two additional important sources of useful LSL documentation: `http://rpgstats.com/wiki` and `http://lslwiki.net/lslwiki`. Think of them as private alternatives to the official LSL Portal, with slightly different organization and slants on scripting.

Finally, don't forget that Scripting Your World has a website of its own at `http://syw.fabulo.us`. SYW on the Web will not be a general resource for LSL or scripting, but will act as support for the book—an easy way to get the scripts from all the chapters and an Internet index of news and events going on at SYW HQ.

What Could
Possibly Go
Wrong?

Too Slow?

Be Proactive!

 Getting and
Giving Help

 Product-
izing Your
Script

Summary

SCRIPT LIBRARIES

The best way to learn any new computer language, including LSL, is to look at lots of examples then start modifying them to suit your own purposes. This book offers you a comprehensive set of scripts that cover most of LSL, but it represents a tiny fraction of what can be done in *SL*. Most of the scripts from in-world products aren't accessible to purchasers, but there are still a lot of scripts freely available for your use. Some examples of where to find these are listed here:

- The wikis each have sections for examples and libraries. The examples section is mainly intended to be educational, much like the scripts in this book. The library sections, which can be very educational as well, tend to be more advanced or are carefully tuned to be used in conjunction with other scripts or other products.

- Scripts from the educational in-world regions are usually excellent and useful (see the "Education" section in this chapter).

- Group scripts are often good, though the quality depends highly on the individual groups in question. The groups mentioned in this chapter are all pretty high-quality, but there are other *SL* groups that are devoted to collecting *all* scripts, regardless of quality, and still others that focus on scripts useful for annoying others.

- There is an officially maintained Scripting Library section of the *SL* forums at `http://forums.secondlife.com/forumdisplay.php?f=15` (in the same place as the Scripting Tips forum) with a large set of useful scripts, either as forum messages or as links to other places, mainly the Scripting Tips section.

- A vast number of scripts is available for free or for very little money inside *Second Life*. Be aware that the overall quality of these scripts is often pretty low, so read them without assuming they do anything in the best way, or even that they work properly at all.

WARNING

Be careful when taking scripting code from someone else. LSL code, like most other *Second Life* content, can be copyrighted, so you must abide by the terms of the license the author has granted you. Conveniently, most of the samples referenced in this chapter, as well as all the code in this book, come with a no-strings-attached license or are public domain. It is polite, if not required, to reference your sources.

BUGS? IN *SECOND LIFE*?!

The software that makes up *Second Life* is itself in constant development, incorporating bug fixes and new features at every release. Of course, with new features come new bugs, so sometimes the reason your scripts aren't behaving the way you expect isn't your code, but rather a bug in *SL*! Reading about *SL* bugs that other people have found and reporting those that you find yourself are important ways to get and give help.

Linden Lab has a site at `http://jira.secondlife.com` where you can report any bugs you find. The site runs the popular JIRA bug-tracking software from Atlassian software. Often called the PJIRA, for *public JIRA*, this is the official way that *SL* users can report bugs, request features, and communicate with Linden developers on software issues. Be aware that Linden Lab has an entirely separate JIRA for internal use: often PJIRA bugs will be assigned an additional "Linden Lab Issue ID" that cross-references the two systems.

There are two good tutorials for how to report *SL* bugs. The *SL* wiki contains a document that describes the process at `http://wiki.secondlife.com/wiki/Bug_Reporting_101`. Torley Linden also produces a nice, less-formal blog entry on the topic at `http://blog.secondlife.com/2007/07/05/how-to-report-bugs-better/`.

The most critical things about reporting bugs, in *Second Life* or any other software, are as follows:

- Be as specific as possible. If a problem happens in only one situation or environment, mention that. Also mention if it always happens!

- Avoid reporting bugs that have already been reported. There is some art involved in finding bugs in JIRA, but give it a try before submitting a new one. At least look at `http://wiki.secondlife.com/wiki/Issue_tracker` to see if it is well-known.

- Include sample code, snapshots, and workarounds if you can.

- Try to identify if the bug is really in *Second Life* or if it is a documentation problem. LSL documentation can lag quite far behind development. Luckily, most of the documentation is on wikis that allow user contributions; if you find that the documentation is missing or incorrect, fix it!

CHAPTER 1
CHAPTER 2
CHAPTER 3
CHAPTER 4
CHAPTER 5
CHAPTER 6
CHAPTER 7
CHAPTER 8
CHAPTER 9
CHAPTER 10
CHAPTER 11
CHAPTER 12
CHAPTER 13

CHAPTER 14

CHAPTER 15
APPENDICES

PRODUCTIZING YOUR SCRIPT

You've written the next big thing in scripted objects and have made so many Linden dollars that you are considering quitting your day job. Congratulations! Don't get cocky, though; making a product **work** is just the first step. You also need to do the following.

Write good documentation: No matter how cool your product is, it will fail if your customers cannot figure out how to operate it.

Package for sale: A pile of scripts is difficult to sell. You need a nice build with all the pieces packed together so that you can sell it as a unit through networked vendor systems.

Market it: Word of mouth is awfully productive in *Second Life*, but judicious use of classified advertisements and Internet-based sales are also great ways to generate sales.

Offer support: Especially for expensive or complicated products, people will want to be able to contact you for help and to request new features.

Fix bugs: You must fix not just bugs in your scripts, but also problems that take advantage of new features when *SL* changes.

Offer updates: Most expensive scripted objects include free updates. At minimum, customers will expect you to fix bugs that crop up.

At the time of this writing, scripters are still madly scrambling to update products after the change from the Havok1 to the Havok4 physics engine. Although Linden Lab attempted to keep most things working as before, changing to a more realistic simulation broke a huge number of scripts that depended

WHAT COULD
POSSIBLY GO
WRONG?

TOO SLOW?

BE PROACTIVE!

GETTING AND
GIVING HELP

PRODUCT-
IZING YOUR
SCRIPT

SUMMARY

on bugs in the original simulator. By publication time, most of these issues will probably have been resolved, but it is an excellent reminder: nothing in **Second Life** stands still, so even if your scripts are perfect today, they might be broken tomorrow.

NOTE

The simplest option for updating products is to be prepared to give people updates on request—assuming, of course, that you keep records of who has copies of your products. You can also set up a group for customers and announce updates as group notices. Many products use `llHTTPRequest()` to check a website for updates periodically, and if there is one it suggests the owner request an update. Finally, if the build doesn't need to be updated, scripted objects can make use of `llRemoteLoadScriptPin()` to upgrade just the script(s). See the LSL wiki entry for LibrarySelfUpgradingScriptAlt for an example of how to do this.

SUMMARY

Remember that nobody writes perfect code, even the best of the best. It's normal—**you will have mistakes, bugs, and problems**. Be persistent and it will become easier over time.

Online environments like **Second Life** are notoriously dynamic. Use this chapter as a guide for finding information and for seeking out other scripters, but don't worry if some highly regarded site or region has seemingly disappeared: two or three equally good options have probably taken their place.

Finally, as you become an expert in LSL, don't forget to give some time and effort back to the scripting community. More great scripters means more great scripts, which means a more interesting **Second Life**.

NEW AND IMPROVED

Just as the world inside *Second Life* is constantly changing and evolving, the platform that runs it never stands still. Over the months we've worked on *Scripting Your World*, there have been some major changes in *Second Life* and the scripting environment. The deployment of the upgraded Havok4 physics engine has been the most recent major change on the simulator side, but increased support of sculpted prims and even the WindLight viewer have had some impact on scripts.

There are bigger things still in the works. By the time you read this, the new Mono virtual machine will be deployed to the main grid, leading to faster execution for scripts that take advantage of the upgrade. Changes to LSL itself will probably be implemented to make it easier to program in, and a bunch of neat library functions are waiting in the wings.

THE *SECOND LIFE* VIRTUAL MACHINE: ON TO MONO!

▶ THE *SECOND LIFE* VIRTUAL MACHINE: ON TO MONO!

▶ RECENT CHANGES TO LSL

ANNOUNCEMENTS OF NEW FEATURES

ONWARD!

Scripts are executed within the hosting sim by a part of the simulator software called a *virtual machine* or *VM*. A VM is a "machine" because it implements something that, to the programs it runs, looks very much like a real computer. It is "virtual" because the machine is implemented entirely within software. Virtual machines are useful because they protect the computer and its programs from the programs that run inside the virtual machines, not just for security reasons (a major reason to use VMs on the Web!) but also to simplify allocating resources carefully to each VM (so that the other programs get fair amounts of memory and time to run) and so the programs can be considered separately from the host computer.

This last point is especially useful for portability: platforms like Sun's Java rely on this feature, compiling the source programs to instructions that can be run on any Java VM installed on any operating system you are running (for instance, Linux, Windows, or Mac OS X). Wikipedia describes this as a *process* or *application virtual machine*, which "runs as a normal application inside an OS and supports a single process." It further states, "It is created when that process is started and destroyed when it exits. Its purpose is to provide a platform-independent programming environment that abstracts away details of the underlying hardware or operating system, and allows a program to execute in the same way on any platform."*

When you compile an LSL script, you are converting your program's human-readable text into an intermediate form called LSO (LSL Object file)**. The sim's virtual machine runs LSO instructions to make the script execute. The problem is that the LSO virtual machine wasn't designed for the stressful environment of the current *Second Life* grid. Other virtual machines have been built from the ground up for flexibility and performance, which much wider audiences than even *Second Life* provides. Java paved the way for broad acceptance of VMs, but Linden Lab couldn't embed Java into the guts of *SL*. Microsoft implemented a direct Java competitor called .NET, but it was even more encumbered by licensing issues and less portable than Java.

Enter Mono! Mono is a relatively complete implementation of .NET that is available as open source software. According to the Mono website, "Mono provides the necessary software to develop and run .NET client and server applications on Linux, Solaris, Mac OS X, Windows, and UNIX. Sponsored by Novell, the Mono open source project has an active and enthusiastic contributing community and is positioned to become the leading choice for development of Linux applications."*** The Mono VM is what Linden Lab was looking for: a high-quality and high-performance virtual machine that is well supported in the industry and can be embedded legally in the *Second Life* grid.

For scripters and *SL* residents, the major improvement is speed: in terms of raw processing power, scripts can run several hundred times faster under Mono than under the old VM. Of course, Mono does not change any of the artificial delays that many of the LSL library functions impose, so complex scripts that interact with the world might not seem dramatically speedier than before. Even so, there is a major benefit: faster execution when scripts are running means less server lag! A nice bonus is that the Mono compiler and VM are much more specific about detected problems, making Mono scripts easier to debug than they were with the old VM.

---

*   `http://en.wikipedia.org/wiki/Virtual_machine`

**   `http://wiki.secondlife.com/wiki/LSO`

*** `http://mono-project.com/Main_Page`

Mono's integration into **SL** won't affect LSL; the scripting language is staying exactly the same for the foreseeable future (see the following note). Furthermore, the old VM isn't going away any time soon; old scripts will continue to run under the old VM, and initially, at least, you will need to choose if you want to compile for Mono or for the old VM (sometimes called LSL2 VM). The in-world script-editor window has a check box labeled Mono: simply check the box and save the script, and you've got a Mono-compiled script!

NOTE

The incorporation of Mono into *Second Life* does not render all you know about LSL and scripting invalid! In some ways, just the opposite: since Mono doesn't change the language at all yet is faster and less stressful on the *SL* servers, it will *extend the life* of LSL.

Mono was first deployed to the **SL** beta grid at the end of January 2008[*], where it underwent extensive public testing for approximately six months. The list of bugs residents found during the beta trial is interesting background reading (see JIRA issue SVC-1276). You can find more details by searching for Mono on the **SL** wiki.

CHAPTER 1
CHAPTER 2
CHAPTER 3
CHAPTER 4
CHAPTER 5
CHAPTER 6
CHAPTER 7
CHAPTER 8
CHAPTER 9
CHAPTER 10
CHAPTER 11
CHAPTER 12
CHAPTER 13
CHAPTER 14
CHAPTER 15
APPENDICES

RECENT CHANGES TO LSL

There are always calls to make LSL syntax more expressive, to fix what appear to be design bugs in the language, or to allow the compiler to produce more-efficient code. You can participate in the ongoing campaign for changes to LSL on the **SL** wiki at `http://wiki.secondlife.com/wiki/LSL3` and through the JIRA issue SVC-1657.

This section highlights some of the changes that have happened since the related chapters in this book were finalized: no doubt more changes will show up between now and when you read the book.

◥ TOUCH POSITION

One upcoming LSL feature allows scripts to not only see *that* a prim has been touched, but exactly *where* it was touched. Fairlight Lake made a formal proposal to implement such a feature in early 2007[**] and Qarl Linden introduced an expanded version of the concept in March 2008.[***] An implementation of Qarl's proposal has been committed to the official server and viewer trees, and may appear around the same time as this book is published.

---

[*]   `http://blog.secondlife.com/2008/01/29/mono-beta-launch`
[**] `http://wiki.secondlife.com/wiki/Touch_Coordinates`
[***] `http://wiki.secondlife.com/wiki/LSL_Touch_Position`

CHAPTER 15

THE *SECOND
LIFE* VIRTUAL
MACHINE: ON
TO MONO!

 RECENT
CHANGES TO
LSL

ANNOUNCE-
MENTS OF NEW
FEATURES

ONWARD!

Qarl describes the new functions as follows:

> *An extension of the detected LSL functions to determine surface information for touch events. Each of the following functions is valid only inside* `touch_start`, `touch`, *and* `touch_end` *events. In the case of* `touch` *events, which are triggered repeatedly while the mouse button is held down, the surface information is valid (and is updated correctly) as long as the mouse remains over the surface of the object (allowing pseudo GUI builds with sliders, levers, dials, etc.).*

Once you can use these functions, you can dramatically simplify many types of interactive objects. Any time additional prims are used only to let the script know where on the build a touch happens, the extra prims can be removed and replaced with touch-position feedback. The following definition box presents the supporting set of functions added to *Second Life* at the end of July 2008:

DEFINITION

vector llDetectedTouchPos(integer *number*)

Returns the position touched by touch event *number* in region coordinates.

> *number* — The specific touch event to get information about. This is exactly like all other functions in the `llDetected*()` family of functions, allowing you to select which of up to 16 touches to examine.

integer llDetectedTouchFace(integer *number*)

Returns the face of the prim touched by touch event *number*.

vector llDetectedTouchUV(integer *number*)

Returns the position touched by touch event *number* as texture coordinates. Texture coordinates are of the form `<u, v, 0>` where *u* and *v* are the coordinates of a point (here the location of the touched point) on the texture itself, regardless of how the texture was scaled, rotated, or positioned on the prim's face. For instance, `<0.1, 0.5, 0.0>` would indicate a point 10% in from the left side of the texture image and halfway down it.

vector llDetectedTouchST(integer *number*)

Returns the surface coordinates of the position touched by the detected touch event *number*. Surface coordinates are of the form `<x, y, 0>` where *x* and *y* are the coordinates of a point (here the location of the touched point) on the face of the prim that was touched.

CHAPTER 1
CHAPTER 2
CHAPTER 3
CHAPTER 4
CHAPTER 5
CHAPTER 6
CHAPTER 7
CHAPTER 8
CHAPTER 9
CHAPTER 10
CHAPTER 11
CHAPTER 12
CHAPTER 13
CHAPTER 14

```
vector llDetectedTouchNormal(integer number)
```

Returns the surface normal of the position detected by touch event number *number*. A surface normal is a vector that points directly away from the surface at the specified point.

```
vector llDetectedTouchBinormal(integer number)
```

Returns the surface binormal of the position detected by touch event *number*. A binormal in this context is a vector tangent to the surface that points along the u direction of tangent space.

AVATAR INFORMATION

Linden Lab has added two functions, shown in Table 15.1, that provide more information about avatars.

TABLE 15.1: NEW AVATAR-INFORMATION FUNCTIONS

Function	Description
`integer llGetRegionAgentCount()`	Returns the number of agents (avatars) in the current region.
`string llGetAgentLanguage(key avatar)`	Returns the language code of the avatar's language preference. These values are lowercase versions of standard internationalization locales—for instance "en-us" for US English or "de" for German.

HTTP SERVER

Chapter 12, "Reaching outside *Second Life*," discussed some of the problems with the existing mechanisms that scripts can use to communicate with the outside world and with each other. XML-RPC is useful but has serious performance and scalability problems. Email is good, but it is very slow as implemented. HTTP is excellent, but scripts may be clients only, not servers. As a result, scripters often use a complicated combination of methods to achieve the level of reliability and performance they are looking for.

One way to solve the problem might be to allow scripts to become HTTP *servers* as well as clients. That proposal started with a public JIRA entry (SVC-913) in November 2007 by Sean Linden and was followed up in December with a JIRA entry (SVC-1086) made by Kelly Linden and an associated wiki entry (`http://wiki.secondlife.com/wiki/LSL_http_server`). The wiki entry describes the goal of the new feature as follows: to "Create an alternative to the XML-RPC server and email gateway for communication with LSL scripts initiated from outside *Second Life* that is easy to use and scalable. Extra bonus for enabling LSL ▶ LSL communication at the same time." The HTTP server functionality is predicted to hit the main grid around the end of 2008.

THE *SECOND LIFE* VIRTUAL MACHINE: ON TO MONO!

RECENT CHANGES TO LSL

 ANNOUNCEMENTS OF NEW FEATURES

ONWARD!

ANNOUNCEMENTS OF NEW FEATURES

There are always more features coming. In addition to reading the **Second Life** blog at `http://blog.secondlife.com` for new-release information and watching the public JIRA for interesting discussions and feature requests, you can read the Feature Requests[*] (this category includes touch position) and Design Discussions[**] (including topics such as HTTP server) pages on the **SL** wiki. Of course, there is always interesting discussion on the various email lists and in the **SL** forums (see the SYW website for some pointers).

Second Life will continue to evolve rapidly, no doubt becoming faster, growing more stable, and supporting a richer virtual world. Certainly much of the evolution will involve scripting changes. Perhaps the most intriguing of potential shifts will be the transformation of **SL** into a true **metaverse**. The idea of the metaverse was put forth by Neal Stephenson in his 1992 novel **Snow Crash**, a major acknowledged source of inspiration for **Second Life**'s creators. (Perhaps because of that inspiration, **SL** is already often referred to as a metaverse.) One of the crucial differences from the current **SL** implementation is that the metaverse concept doesn't depend on a particular vendor, but is constructed more like the Internet: a conglomeration of peer servers, each owned and operated by different entities.

This metaverse vision is edging toward fruition as **Second Life**'s competitors and interested third parties extend and implement other protocols. Already there are working alternative and largely compatible sim implementations from the OpenSimulator project[***], and there have been demonstrations of avatars teleporting between **SL** and OpenSimulator sims. **SL**'s metamorphosis into a true metaverse will introduce new scripting challenges, as your scripts may end up running in a very different environment than they were designed for, might not operate at all in some worlds, or might be at risk of theft from unscrupulous sim owners.

ONWARD!

We hope you've found **Scripting Your World** both useful and enjoyable. **Second Life** can always use more (and better) scripters to make more cool stuff, to lend their creativity to expanding the world, and to help push **SL** into even more compelling areas. As is true in all of **Second Life**, it's up to you to make the world a fascinating, social, wonderful place. So go out and do it!

---

[*]   `http://wiki.secondlife.com/wiki/Category:Feature_Requests`
[**] `http://wiki.secondlife.com/wiki/Category:Design_Discussions`
[***] `http://opensimulator.org`

APPENDICES

The first two appendices describe in detail the parameters and options of the `ll*PrimitiveParams()` and `llParticleSystem()` functions. They are structured very differently than the rest of the language in that they take complex lists of parameters. The third appendix is the *Second Life* Community Standards, which describe how *SL* residents, including scripters, are expected to conduct themselves in-world. The SYW website has an additional appendix of all events, functions, and constants defined by LSL.

APPENDIX A: SETTING PRIMITIVE PARAMETERS

APPENDIX A

APPENDIX B

APPENDIX C

The three functions `llSetPrimitiveParams()`, `llGetPrimitiveParams()`, and `llSetLinkPrimitiveParams()` all operate on a list of property-value tuples. Many of the specific properties have an alternate function call that will set or get the value. Note that there is no `llGetLinkPrimitiveParams()` function; instead you have to use the call `llGetLink<property>()`. Both of the "set" functions cause the script to pause for 0.2 seconds, irrespective of the number of properties being set; note that this can be significantly cheaper than a sequence of several calls to the alternate functions.

Table A.I lists the properties that can be set, alternative functions (if available), and the values that need to appear for each property. The table uses alphabetical order, but specific properties can be listed in any order in a function call. Each property is discussed in further detail after the table.

TABLE A.I: PRIMITIVE PROPERTIES THAT CAN BE SET OR RETRIEVED

Property	Description	Usage	Alternate Functions

`PRIM_BUMP_SHINY`	Sets the face's shiny & bump.	`[ PRIM_BUMP_SHINY,`
		`integer face,`
		`integer shiny,`
		`integer bump ]`	

`PRIM_COLOR`	Sets the face's color.	`[ PRIM_COLOR,`
		`integer face,`
		`vector color,`
		`float alpha ]`
			`llSetColor()`
			`llSetAlpha()`
			`llGetColor()`
			`llSetColor()`
			`llSetLinkAlpha()`
			`llSetLinkColor()`

`PRIM_FLEXIBLE`	Sets the prim as flexible.	`[ PRIM_FLEXIBLE,`
		`integer boolean,`
		`integer softness,`
		`float gravity,`
		`float friction,`
		`float wind,`
		`float tension,`
		`vector force ]`	

`PRIM_FULLBRIGHT`	Sets the face's fullbright flag.	`[ PRIM_FULLBRIGHT,`
		`integer face,`
		`integer boolean ]`	

`PRIM_GLOW`	Sets the face's glow attribute.	`[ PRIM_GLOW,`
		`integer face,`
		`float intensity ]`	

`PRIM_MATERIAL`	Sets the prim's material.	`[ PRIM_MATERIAL,` `integer type ]`	
`PRIM_PHANTOM`	Sets the object's phantom status.	`[ PRIM_PHANTOM,` `integer boolean ]`	
`PRIM_PHYSICS`	Sets the object's physics status.	`[ PRIM_PHYSICS,` `integer boolean ]`	`llSetStatus()` `llGetStatus()`

Property	Description	Usage	Alternate Functions

PRIM_POINT_LIGHT	Sets the prim as a point light.	[PRIM_POINT_LIGHT,
		  integer *onOff*,
		  vector *color*,
		  float *intensity*,
		  float *radius*,
		  float *falloff*]	

PRIM_POSITION	Sets the prim's position.	[PRIM_POSITION, vector *position*]	llSetPos() llGetPos()
PRIM_ROTATION	Sets the prim's rotation. **(Note: This is buggy. Use the alternate functions.)**	[PRIM_ROTATION, rotation *rot*]	llSetRot() llGetRot()
PRIM_SIZE	Sets the prim's size.	[PRIM_SIZE, vector *size*]	llGetScale() llSetScale()
PRIM_TEMP_ON_REZ	Sets the object's temporary status.	[PRIM_TEMP_ON_REZ, integer *boolean*]	

PRIM_TEXGEN	Sets the face's texture mode.	[PRIM_TEXGEN,
		  integer *face*,
		  integer *type*]	

PRIM_TEXTURE	Sets the prim's texture attributes.	[PRIM_TEXTURE,
		  integer *face*,
		  string *texture*,
		  vector *repeats*,
		  vector *offsets*,
		  float *rot*]
			llSetTexture()
			llScaleTexture()
			llOffsetTexture()
			llRotateTexture()
			llSetLinkTexture()
			llGetTexture()
			llGetTextureRot()
			llGetTextureScale()

PRIM_TYPE	Sets the prim's shape.	[PRIM_TYPE, integer *typeflag*] + *flag_parameters*	

CHAPTER 1
CHAPTER 2
CHAPTER 3
CHAPTER 4
CHAPTER 5
CHAPTER 6
CHAPTER 7
CHAPTER 8
CHAPTER 9
CHAPTER 10
CHAPTER 11
CHAPTER 12
CHAPTER 13
CHAPTER 14
CHAPTER 15

APPENDICES

WARNING

These functions may silently fail in several different ways. Examples include missing a value in a long sequence or using a position value such as <56.3,158,0,106.8> (which, you'll note, is actually a 4D rotation and *not* a 3D vector). If something isn't working the way you expect, double-check your parameter lists and types! It also helps to pull values out of the list and into their own typed parameters.

PRIM_BUMP_SHINY

PRIM_BUMP_SHINY is used in Listing 9.13.

- integer *face* is the number of the face. ALL_SIDES affects the entire object.
- integer *shiny* values are PRIM_SHINY_NONE, PRIM_SHINY_LOW, PRIM_SHINY_MEDIUM, PRIM_SHINY_HIGH.
- integer *bump* values are shown in Table A.2.

TABLE A.2: VALUES FOR THE *bump* PROPERTY OF `PRIM_BUMP_SHINY`

CONSTANT	VALUE	DESCRIPTION
PRIM_BUMP_NONE	0	None: no bump map.
PRIM_BUMP_BRIGHT	1	Brightness: generate bump map from highlights.
PRIM_BUMP_DARK	2	Darkness: generate bump map from lowlights.
PRIM_BUMP_WOOD	3	Wood grain.
PRIM_BUMP_BARK	4	Bark.
PRIM_BUMP_BRICKS	5	Bricks.
PRIM_BUMP_CHECKER	6	Checker.
PRIM_BUMP_CONCRETE	7	Concrete.
PRIM_BUMP_TILE	8	Crusty tile.
PRIM_BUMP_STONE	9	Cut stone blocks.
PRIM_BUMP_DISKS	10	Disks: packed circles.
PRIM_BUMP_GRAVEL	11	Gravel.
PRIM_BUMP_BLOBS	12	Petri dish: blobby amoebalike shapes.
PRIM_BUMP_SIDING	13	Siding.
PRIM_BUMP_LARGETILE	14	Stone tile.
PRIM_BUMP_STUCCO	15	Stucco.
PRIM_BUMP_SUCTION	16	Small rings that look like suction cups.
PRIM_BUMP_WEAVE	17	Weave.

PRIM_COLOR

PRIM_COLOR is used in Listings 2.7, 3.9, 7.3, 9.9, 9.10, 9.11, 9.12, and 10.3.

- integer *face* is the number of the face. ALL_SIDES affects the entire object.
- vector *color* is the color of the object, in RGB: <red, green, blue>. Each value is scaled from 0.0 to 1.0, but often scaling the values from 0 to 255 can be useful since each component of the color vector is represented with 8 bits (2^8=256). The following snippet illustrates possible formats:

```
vector red    = <1.0, 0.0, 0.0>;              // most efficient
vector green  = <0., 1., 0.>;                 // equally efficient
vector blue   = <0,0,1>;          // conversion to float is inefficient
vector purple = <1,0,1>;
vector yellow = <255.0, 255.0, 0.0> / 255.0;  // divide is not efficient
vector cyan   = <255,0,255>/255;              // extremely inefficient
```

- float *alpha* is the translucency of the face, ranging from 0.0 (fully transparent) to 1.0 (fully opaque).

You can create a list of colors, but the parser sometimes has trouble with the order. Logically, the following snippet would make all faces white, and then face number 1 red, but you cannot always predict the order in which the parser will apply the transitions:

```
llSetPrimitiveParams([PRIM_COLOR, ALL_SIDES, <1,1,1>, 1.0,
                PRIM_COLOR, 1, <1,0,0>, 1.0]);
```

This error can be especially disconcerting if some of the sides are intended to be transparent. You can either specify each individual side, or make two sequential calls to llSetPrimitiveParams().

PRIM_FLEXIBLE

Flexible prims are discussed throughout this book.

- `integer` *boolean* is TRUE when the prim is flexible, and FALSE when rigid.
- `integer` *softness* affects how floppy the object is. Ranges from 0 to 3.
- `float` *gravity* indicates how much gravity will affect the prim. Ranges from −10.0 to 10.0.
- `float` *friction* acts like a damper on motion. Ranges from 0.0 to 10.0.
- `float` *wind* indicates how much the wind should cause the object to move. Ranges from 0.0 to 10.0.
- `float` *tension* indicates how much bounce or spring the object has. Ranges from 0.0 to 10.0.
- `vector` *force* indicates how much force to apply to the prim. Each component of the vector ranges from −10.0 to 10.0.

Flexible prims (**flexiprims**) are a client-side effect and are automatically made **phantom** and **nonphysical**. However, flexiprims can be linked to a solid, physical root prim and will thus take on some of those properties as well (though it's buggy). See Chapter 7, "Physics and Vehicles," for more discussion.

CHAPTER 1
CHAPTER 2
CHAPTER 3
CHAPTER 4
CHAPTER 5
CHAPTER 6
CHAPTER 7
CHAPTER 8
CHAPTER 9
CHAPTER 10
CHAPTER 11
CHAPTER 12
CHAPTER 13
CHAPTER 14
CHAPTER 15

APPENDICES

PRIM_FULLBRIGHT

PRIM_FULLBRIGHT is used in Listings 3.9, 9.10, and 10.3.

- `integer` *face* is the number of the face. ALL_SIDES affects the entire object.
- `integer` *boolean* is TRUE when the prim is at its maximum brightness, and FALSE otherwise.

PRIM_GLOW

PRIM_GLOW is used in the "Creating Lights" section of Chapter 9, "Special Effects."

- `integer` *face* is the number of the face. ALL_SIDES affects the entire object.
- `float` *intensty* is the strength of the glow, from 0.0 to 1.0.

If your compiler complains about this named constant, use its integer value of 25 instead. (Linden Lab is in the process of updating the software for the compilers, viewers, and editors.)

PRIM_MATERIAL

- `integer` *type* is one of the following: PRIM_MATERIAL_STONE, PRIM_MATERIAL_METAL, PRIM_MATERIAL_GLASS, PRIM_MATERIAL_WOOD, PRIM_MATERIAL_FLESH, PRIM_MATERIAL_PLASTIC, and PRIM_MATERIAL_RUBBER.

Material affects a physical object's friction but not its mass. Glass has the least friction, followed by metal, plastic, wood, stone, rubber, and flesh. Material also affects an object's collision sounds and its bounce (collision handling).

347

PRIM_PHANTOM

PRIM_PHANTOM is used in Listings 4.6 and 9.11.

- `integer` *boolean* is TRUE if the object is phantom, and FALSE otherwise. Note that if one prim is phantom, the entire object is phantom.

PRIM_PHYSICS

- `integer` *boolean* is TRUE if physics is enabled, and FALSE otherwise.

PRIM_POINT_LIGHT

PRIM_POINT_LIGHT is used in Listings 2.7, 3.8, 9.10, and 9.12.

- `integer` *onOff* is TRUE when the prim is a light source, and FALSE otherwise. Other properties are irrelevant when *onOff* is FALSE.
- `vector` *color* is the color of the light, in RGB <red, green, blue>.
- `float` *intensity* is the intensity of the light, and ranges from 0.0 to 1.0.
- `float` *radius* is the radius of the light, and ranges from 1.0 to 10.0 meters.
- `float` *falloff* is the rate of falloff of the light source, and ranges from 0.01 to 1.0.

PRIM_POSITION

PRIM_POSITION is used in Listings 2.3, 2.4, 4.4, 9.9, and 10.4. The listings in Chapter 2, "Making Your Avatar Stand Up and Stand Out," are particularly interesting because they supply a *sequence* of PRIM_POSITION items.

- `vector` *position* is the position of the prim.
  - In `llSetPrimitiveParams()`, the coordinates are local to the attachment point (the region, the avatar, or the root prim).
  - In `llGetPrimitiveParams()`, the coordinates are regional.

PRIM_ROTATION

PRIM_ROTATION is used in Listing 10.4.

- `rotation` *rot* is the prim's rotation.

This property is buggy—it does not handle rotations correctly. Chapter 10, "Scripting the Environment," describes the bug, and Listing 10.4 shows an example of the workaround. Normally if you want to set the prim rotation to *rot*; you can either set it to *rot*/`llGetRootRotation()` in `llSetPrimitiveParams()` or use `llSetLocalRot(rot)` to get the right behavior.

PRIM_SIZE

PRIM_SIZE is used in Listings 9.9 and 10.4.

- **vector** *size* is the size of the object.

PRIM_TEXGEN

- **integer** *face* is the number of the face. ALL_SIDES affects the entire object.
- **integer** *type* is either PRIM_TEXGEN_DEFAULT or PRIM_TEXGEN_PLANAR. The default maps to curves better, but the planar maps to larger objects better.

PRIM_TEMP_ON_REZ

PRIM_TEMP_ON_REZ is used in Listings 4.4 and 5.4, and in the code snippet on page 170.

- **integer** *boolean* is TRUE if the object will die approximately 60 seconds after setting this property, and FALSE otherwise.

PRIM_TEXTURE

PRIM_TEXTURE is used in Listing 9.9. It refers to an image that is placed on the specified *face* of the object, as in Figure A.1.

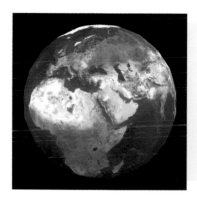

Figure A.1: This texture of the Earth has key
`ec751148-03b4-7876-78a4-b360884d1262`.

- **integer** *face* is the face's number. ALL_SIDES affects the entire object.
- **string** *texture* is the name of a texture in inventory, or a UUID. If it is not a texture or a UUID and it is missing from the prim's inventory, then an error is shouted on DEBUG_CHANNEL.
- **vector** *repeats* indicates how many repeats of the texture to place on each of the x and y axes (z is ignored). Negative values will flip the texture. There appears to be no compiler limit on x or y (you will hit visual limits much faster).
- **vector** *offsets* is the texture offset on each of the x and y axes (z is not used). Range is −1.0 to 1.0 for both x and y.
- **float** *rot* is rotation of the texture in radians.

CHAPTER 1
CHAPTER 2
CHAPTER 3
CHAPTER 4
CHAPTER 5
CHAPTER 6
CHAPTER 7
CHAPTER 8
CHAPTER 9
CHAPTER 10
CHAPTER 11
CHAPTER 12
CHAPTER 13
CHAPTER 14
CHAPTER 15

APPENDICES

PRIM_TYPE

PRIM_TYPE is used in Listing 9.8, the code snippet later in this section, and the sidebar at the end of this appendix.

 Appendix A

Appendix B

Appendix C

- integer *typeflag* is any one of the constants in Table A.3.
- list *flag_parameters* is the list from the Parameters column of Table A.3.

TABLE A.3: **PRIM_TYPE** FLAGS

Constant	Value	Parameters
PRIM_TYPE_BOX	0	integer *holeshape*, vector *cut*, float *hollow*, vector *twist*, vector *taper_b*, vector *topshear*
PRIM_TYPE_CYLINDER	1	integer *holeshape*, vector *cut*, float *hollow*, vector *twist*, vector *taper_b*, vector *topshear*
PRIM_TYPE_PRISM	2	integer *holeshape*, vector *cut*, float *hollow*, vector *twist*, vector *taper_b*, vector *topshear*
PRIM_TYPE_SPHERE	3	integer *holeshape*, vector *cut*, float *hollow*, vector *twist*, vector *dimple*
PRIM_TYPE_TORUS	4	integer *holeshape*, vector *cut*, float *hollow*, vector *twist*, vector *holesize*, vector *topshear*, vector *profilecut*, vector *taper_a*, float *revolutions*, float *radiusoffset*, float *skew*
PRIM_TYPE_TUBE	5	integer *holeshape*, vector *cut*, float *hollow*, vector *twist*, vector *holesize*, vector *topshear*, vector *profilecut*, vector *taper_a*, float *revolutions*, float *radiusoffset*, float *skew*
PRIM_TYPE_RING	6	integer *holeshape*, vector *cut*, float *hollow*, vector *twist*, vector *holesize*, vector *topshear*, vector *profilecut*, vector *taper_a*, float *revolutions*, float *radiusoffset*, float *skew*
PRIM_TYPE_SCULPT	7	string *map*, integer *sculpttype*

 NOTE

You can find good tutorials on making sculpty prims (prims of the type PRIM_TYPE_SCULPT) at http://amandalevitsky.googlepages.com/sculptedprims and http://bentha.net/sculpted-tuto/Blender-export-template-tut.html.

The following snippet shows two example calls to llSetPrimitiveParams() for **PRIM_TYPE**.

```
// this is a pyramid
float hollow = 0.0;
vector cut = <0,1,0>;
vector twist = <0,0,0>;
vector taper_b = <0,0,0>;  // a basic cube would be <1,1,0>
vector topshear = <0,0,0>;
llSetPrimitiveParams([PRIM_TYPE, PRIM_TYPE_BOX, PRIM_HOLE_CIRCLE,
                      cut, hollow, twist, taper_b, topshear]);
```

```
// this makes a nice expanding spiral
vector cut = <0,1,0>;                    // 0.0 to 1.0
float hollow = 0.0;                      // 0.0 to 0.95
vector twist = <0, 0.0, 0.0>;            // -1.0 to 1.0
vector holesize = <1.0, 0.05, 0.0>;      // max X:1.0 Y:0.5
vector topshear = <0.0, 0.0, 0.0>;       // -0.5 to 0.5
vector profilecut = <0.0, 0.0, 0.0>;     // 0.0 to 1.0
vector taper_a = <0.0, 0.0, 0.0>;        // 0.0 to 1.0
float revolutions = 3.0;                 // 1.0 to 4.0
float radiusoffset = 1.0;                // -1.0 to 1.0
float skew = 0.0;                        //
llSetPrimitiveParams( [PRIM_TYPE, PRIM_TYPE_TORUS, PRIM_HOLE_DEFAULT,
                       cut, hollow, twist, holesize, topshear,
                       profilecut, taper_a, revolutions,
                       radiusoffset, skew] );
```

NOTE

Prim torture is the art of shaping a prim and then changing its type, producing shapes that are otherwise impossible. You essentially take advantage of the strange (possibly buggy) way that properties transfer from one shape to another. Look on the wiki for LibraryPrimTorture for a discussion and scripting examples.

The following list indicates the behavior of each parameter in Table A.3, in alphabetical order by parameter name.

- *cut* (all shapes except PRIM_TYPE_SCULPT) is a **vector** that causes a pie shape to be cut out of the shape around the z-axis; the removed portion ranges from **x** to **y** (think of **x** as the start and **y** as the end of the pie slice). **x** and **y** range from 0.0 to 1.0; **x** must be at least 0.05 smaller than **y** (**z** is ignored). Figure A.2 shows a torus with a *cut* of <0.20, 1.0, 0.0>. On a sphere, the official mathematical name for a cut is **spherical wedge**.

Figure A.2: A cut removes a pie slice from the object.

- *dimple* (only spheres) is a **vector** that removes pie slices around the sphere's x-axis. **x** and **y** range from 0.0 to 1.0; **x** must be at least 0.05 smaller than **y** (**z** is ignored). Figure A.3 shows a sphere with *dimple* = <0.1, 0.75, 0.0> (and *cut* = <0.25, 1, 0>). The official mathematical name for a dimple is **spherical cone.**

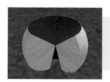

Figure A.3: Dimples remove spherical cones around a sphere's x-axis.

CHAPTER 1
CHAPTER 2
CHAPTER 3
CHAPTER 4
CHAPTER 5
CHAPTER 6
CHAPTER 7
CHAPTER 8
CHAPTER 9
CHAPTER 10
CHAPTER 11
CHAPTER 12
CHAPTER 13
CHAPTER 14
CHAPTER 15

APPENDICES

APPENDIX A
APPENDIX B
APPENDIX C

- **holeshape** (all shapes except `PRIM_TYPE_SCULPT`) is an `integer` that must be one of the following constants: `PRIM_HOLE_DEFAULT`, `PRIM_HOLE_SQUARE`, `PRIM_HOLE_CIRCLE`, `PRIM_HOLE_TRIANGLE`. It controls the shape of the hollow area inside the object, as shown in Figure A.4.

Figure A.4: A **PRIM_HOLE_SQUARE** can cause interesting effects in a torus.

- **holesize** (torus, tube, and ring) is a `vector` that indicates the size of the empty part in the middle. `x` ranges from 0.05 to 1.0; think of it a bit like the thickness of a torus, or the vertical gap between revolutions. `y` controls the size of the inside hole, and ranges from 0.05 (large hole) to 0.50 (no hole), as shown in Figure A.5 (`z` is ignored). A corkscrew might have `x = 0.50` and `y = 0.25`, with 3 **revolutions** (similar to what's shown in Figure A.11).

Figure A.5: The tube on the left has a **holesize.**`y` of 0.25, while the tube on the right has a **holesize.**`y` of 0.05.

- **hollow** (all shapes except `PRIM_TYPE_SCULPT`) is a `float` that ranges from 0.0 (solid) to 0.95 (thin shell). Figure A.6 shows six prims with different **hollow** values and different effects. In boxes, cylinders, and prisms the hole goes all the way through the object (acting sort of like the **holesize** for tori, tubes, and rings). In spheres, tori, tubes, and rings, the hollow stays entirely within the outer shell. Any number greater than 0.95 is treated as 0.95; watch for accidental use of the GUI's 0.0-to-95.0 scale.

Figure A.6: From left to right, these objects have **hollow** = 0.0, 0.25, and 0.75.

 NOTE

hollow is not the same as **holesize**; the object in Figure A.4 has **holesize**=`<0,0,0>`, while the objects in Figure A.5 could easily be **hollow**—the space would be inside the shell, where you can't see it. Just to make sure Linden Lab's naming scheme is sufficiently confusing, **holeshape** deals with the shape of the *hollow*, not the *hole*. The child's toy shown here is a series of tori with increasing size and increasing **holesize**. All of them are **hollow** = 0.95. To keep the walls of the tori approximately the same width, they have increasing **holesize.**`y` values. For comparison, the purple torus has the same **holesize.**`y` as the orange one; you can see that its walls are fatter.

- **map** (only `PRIM_TYPE_SCULPT`) is the `string` name of a displacement map (Figure A.7) in inventory or a UUID `key` of a displacement map*. If **map** is not a displacement map or if it is named and missing from the prim's inventory, then an error is shouted on `DEBUG_CHANNEL`.

CHAPTER 1
CHAPTER 2
CHAPTER 3
CHAPTER 4
CHAPTER 5
CHAPTER 6
CHAPTER 7
CHAPTER 8
CHAPTER 9
CHAPTER 10
CHAPTER 11
CHAPTER 12
CHAPTER 13
CHAPTER 14
CHAPTER 15

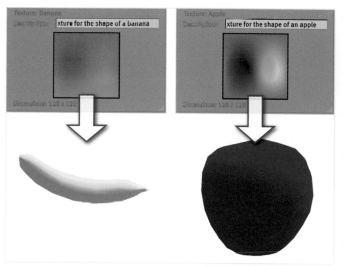

Figure A.7: Displacement maps for sculpted prims are uploaded as textures; each color channel represents an axis in 3D space, where red, green, and blue map to x, y, and z respectively. The apple and banana displacement maps are in your Inventory's Library folder.

- **profilecut** (torus, tube, and ring) is a `vector` that slices away parts of the shape around the x-axis from **x** to **y** (think of **x** as the start and **y** as the end of the pie slice). The center of the pie lies where the center of the hole would be if the object were hollow. Figure A.8 shows the results for a range of **profilecut.x** values, and Figure A.9 shows the results for a range of **profilecut.y** values. **x** and **y** range from 0.0 to 1.0; **x** must be at least 0.05 smaller than **y** (z is ignored).

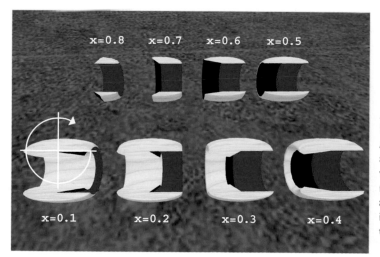

Figure A.8:
A profilecut starts at the angle specified by the **x** value. Increasing values rotates the cut clockwise around the x-axis. All tori in this image are exactly the same size.

---

* A good source for experimenting with displacement map textures is `http://wiki.secondlife.com/wiki/Sculpted_Prims_Textures`

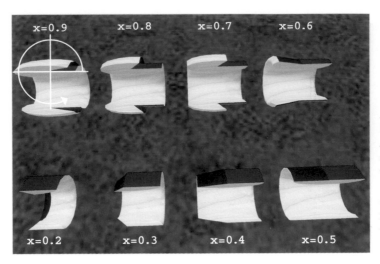

x=0.9   x=0.8   x=0.7   x=0.6

x=0.2   x=0.3   x=0.4   x=0.5

Figure A.9:
A profilecut ends at the angle specified by the **y** value. Increasing values rotates the cut counter-clockwise around the x-axis. All tori are exactly the same size.

- **radiusoffset** (torus, tube, and ring) is a `float` that controls the distance between where an arc starts and where it ends, from the perspective of the y-axis. Zero means that it is a circle; 1.0 has the arc start very near the center and end at the size of the torus (as shown in Figure A.10); −1.0 has the arc start at the size of the torus and end at the center. Its effect depends on **holesize.y** and **revolutions**.

Figure A.10: **radiusOffset** controls how far apart the torus start and end points are, around the y-axis.

- **revolutions** (torus, tube, and ring) is a `float` that indicates how many times to rotate the object around the x-axis, as shown in Figure A.11. Valid values range from 1.0 to 4.0.

Figure A.11: This tube has three revolutions. (**holesize.x** is 0.5; if **holesize.x** were 1.0, then from this angle you would see none of the internal portions of the spiral.)

- **sculpttype** (only PRIM_TYPE_SCULPT) is an `integer` that is one of the following constants: PRIM_SCULPT_TYPE_SPHERE, PRIM_SCULPT_TYPE_TORUS, PRIM_SCULPT_TYPE_PLANE, PRIM_SCULPT_TYPE_CYLINDER.

- **skew** (torus, tube, and ring) is a `float` that controls the distance between where an arc starts and where it ends, from the perspective of the x-axis. It ranges from −0.95 to 0.95. Figure A.12 shows the middle of that range.

Figure A.12: Skew controls how far apart the torus start and end points are, around the x-axis. This figure has **skew = 0.5**.

- **_taper_a_** (torus, tube, and ring) is a `vector` that adjusts the height (**x**) or thickness (**y**) of the side walls of the torus, ring, or tube. **x** and **y** range from 0.0 to 1.0. Figure A.13 shows the effect of **_taper_a_** on a cylinder.

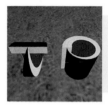

Figure A.13: The tube on the left shows **_taper_a_** = <1,0,0>; the tube on the right shows **_taper_a_** = <0,1,0>. This parameter does interesting things when interacting with **_revolutions_** in the GUI: try adding 3 revolutions, then returning to 1—you won't get what you started with.

- **_taper_b_** (box, cylinder, and prism) is a `vector` that adjusts the size of the top of the object, ranging from 0.0 (no top) to 2.0 (no bottom); **z** is ignored. For example, a cube with **_taper_b_** = <0, 0, 0> appears as a pyramid. *Note that the GUI values are different; they range from −1.0 (no bottom) to 1.0 (no top)*. Figure A.14 shows an example of a tapered cube.

Figure A.14: This cube has **_taper_b_** = <0.0,0.25,0>. The red side meets at the top (0.0) while the blue side doesn't (0.25). Note that the GUI shows these values as **x** = **1.0** and **y** = **0.75**.

- **_topshear_** (box, cylinder, prism, torus, tube and ring) is a `vector` that controls an object's tilt, and ranges from −0.5 to 0.5 for both **x**, and **y** (**z** is ignored). Figure A.15 shows the effect of **_topshear_** on a cube.

Figure A.15: A **_topshear_** of <0.25,0.25,0.0> tilts this cube into a parallelogram.

- **_twist_** is a `vector`; each component is a multiplier of a full rotation around the z axis (1.0 = 360 degrees). Component use depends on prim type, but **x** is always how much to twist the beginning end of the prim (usually minimum **z**) and **y** is how much to twist the opposite end (usually maximum **z**):
  - *Box, cylinder, and prism:* Ranges from −0.5 to 0.5. Figure A.16 shows the effect of **_twist_** on a cube.
  - *Sphere:* Ranges from −0.5 to 0.5. When **_twist_** = <0.5, 0.5, 0>, the sphere turns inside out; this trick can be used to make tiny prims (see the sidebar "Making Tiny Prims"). Values outside this range cause strange shapes rather than errors.
  - *Tube, torus, and ring:* Ranges from −1.0 to 1.0. Twists in these objects do beautiful things.

Figure A.16: **_twist_** causes the cube to turn on itself.

The Ivory Tower Library of Primitives (Figure A.17) at Natoma <207, 170, 25> has wonderful examples of each of these settings.

CHAPTER 1
CHAPTER 2
CHAPTER 3
CHAPTER 4
CHAPTER 5
CHAPTER 6
CHAPTER 7
CHAPTER 8
CHAPTER 9
CHAPTER 10
CHAPTER 11
CHAPTER 12
CHAPTER 13
CHAPTER 14
CHAPTER 15

Figure A.17: The second floor of the Ivory Tower Library of Primitives has samples of the effects of all primitive parameters.

MAKING TINY PRIMS

Careful use of primitive parameters can yield prims that are significantly smaller than the <0.01, 0.01, 0.01> minimum size. Torley Linden has a wonderful video tutorial at http://wiki. secondlife.com/wiki/Video_Tutorials (search for "How to make tiny prims"). Natalia Zelmanov has a good web tutorial at http://www.mermaiddiaries.com/2006/11/build. html (look for "Jewelry Part 3"). Both tutorials use the object editor in the GUI, but you can accomplish the same thing with scripts.

The following code snippet makes the flat triangle shown here: 10mm tall by 2mm wide, and a scant .2mm thick! The box on the left is a plain <0.01, 0.01, 0.01> cube. The box on the right shows that it has been hollowed to the maximum value, then cut and taper make it into a triangle that measures only <0.002, 0.0002, 0.01>.

```
makeTinyTriangle() {
    float hollow = 0.95;
    vector cut = <0.85,0.9,0>; // edge 2mm wide
    vector twist = <0,0,0>;
    vector taper_b = <1,0,0>;  // make triangular
    //vector taper_b = <1,1,0>;  // make square
    vector topshear = <0,0,0>;
    llSetPrimitiveParams(
            [PRIM_SIZE, <0.01, 0.01, 0.01>,
             PRIM_TYPE, PRIM_TYPE_BOX, PRIM_HOLE_DEFAULT,
                            cut, hollow, twist, taper_b, topshear]);
}
```

This next code snippet makes a sphere about 5mm in diameter. It creates a tiny hollow and then turns the sphere inside out with *twist*. The outside shell is made transparent in a second call to llSetPrimitiveParams() because the parser sometimes gets confused about when to do it.

```
makeTinySphere() {
    vector cut = <0, 1, 0>;
    float hollow = 0.05;  // bigger hollow means bigger sphere
    vector twist = <0.5,0.5,0>;
    vector dimple = <0, 1, 0>;
    llSetPrimitiveParams([
        PRIM_TYPE, PRIM_TYPE_SPHERE, PRIM_HOLE_DEFAULT,
                cut, hollow, twist, dimple,
        PRIM_SIZE, <0.01, 0.01, 0.01>,
        PRIM_COLOR, ALL_SIDES, <1,1,1>, 1.0
        ]);
    llSetPrimitiveParams([  // not part of first call
        PRIM_COLOR, 0, <1,1,1>, 0.0 // outside of sphere
        ]);
}
```

APPENDIX B: PARTICLE SYSTEM

CHAPTER 1
CHAPTER 2
CHAPTER 3
CHAPTER 4
CHAPTER 5
CHAPTER 6
CHAPTER 7
CHAPTER 8
CHAPTER 9
CHAPTER 10
CHAPTER 11
CHAPTER 12
CHAPTER 13
CHAPTER 14
CHAPTER 15

Second Life's particle system allows you to create a wide variety of effects, including shiny jewelry; flames and smoke; water splashes and bubbles; falling leaves and petals; and weather effects such as rain, snow, fog, and lightning. You can stretch it further to make butterflies, rainbows, or the string of a kite.

The `llParticleSystem()` function creates a particle system within the prim that contains the script. Each prim has only one particle emitter, located at its geometric center and aligned along the z-axis. Multiple scripts in the same prim all operate on the same emitter; therefore if you want to make one object appear to have multiple particle systems, you need to make multiple prims. A particle system is saved in the object's state, which means deleting the script does not stop the particle flow.

DEFINITION

APPENDICES

`llParticleSystem(list rules)`

Defines a particle system for the containing prim based on a list of `rules`. Turn the emitter off using `llParticleSystem([])`.

> `rules` — Particle-system rules list in the format [`property_1, data_1, property_2, data_2, ..., property_n, data_n`]

This appendix lists the various properties and their potential data values. The wiki lists several unimplemented properties—both flags and constants. Example use occurs in Listings 9.1, 9.2, 9.4, 9.5, and 10.7.

Jopsy Pendragon has developed a wonderful tutorial at the Particle Laboratory at Teal <200, 60, 21>. The lab has many free scripts and many interactive displays like the one in Figure B.1. Torley Linden also has a good video tutorial in his "Tip of the Week" series that samples some particle-system ideas; search for Particle Editing Magic! at `http://wiki.secondlife.com/wiki/Video_Tutorials`.

Figure B.1: One of many interactive particle-system demonstrations at the Particle Laboratory. This one shows what happens **with** a **PSYS_SRC_TARGET_KEY** (green particles travel toward a target) and **without** (red particles float free).

357

↘ FLAGS

Various flags control the particle system's behavior. There is only one named property; its values are a bitmask.

PSYS_PART_FLAGS

An `integer` value specified as one or more values from Table B.I ORed together (using the | operator).

TABLE B.I: PARTICLE-SYSTEM FLAGS (BITMASK)

Flag	Description	Value
PSYS_PART_INTERP_COLOR_MASK	When set, particle color and alpha transition from PSYS_PART_START_COLOR to PSYS_PART_END_COLOR (and PSYS_PART_START_ALPHA to PSYS_PART_END_ALPHA) during the particle's lifetime. The transition is a smooth interpolation.	0x001
PSYS_PART_INTERP_SCALE_MASK	When set, particle scale transitions from its PSYS_PART_START_SCALE to PSYS_PART_END_SCALE setting during the particle's lifetime.	0x002
PSYS_PART_BOUNCE_MASK	When set, particles bounce off a plane at the emitter's z height. On bounce, each particle reverses velocity and angle. Particles must be emitted upward so they can fall down to the plane.	0x004
PSYS_PART_WIND_MASK	When set, wind affects particle movement. Wind is applied as a secondary force on the particles.	0x008
PSYS_PART_FOLLOW_SRC_MASK	When set, particles move relative to the emitter's position. Otherwise, the emitter's position and movement do not affect particle position and movement. This flag disables the PSYS_SRC_BURST_RADIUS rule.	0x010
PSYS_PART_FOLLOW_VELOCITY_MASK	When set, particles rotate to orient their "top" toward the direction of movement. Otherwise, particles always face up.	0x020
PSYS_PART_TARGET_POS_MASK	When set, emitted particles change course during their lifetime, attempting to move toward the target specified by the PSYS_SRC_TARGET_KEY rule by the time they expire.	0x040
PSYS_PART_TARGET_LINEAR_MASK	When set, emitted particles move in a straight line toward the target specified by the PSYS_SRC_TARGET_KEY rule. In this mode, PSYS_SRC_ACCEL, PSYS_SRC_BURST_RADIUS, and possibly other rules are ignored.	0x080
PSYS_PART_EMISSIVE_MASK	When set, particles are fullbright and are unaffected by global lighting (sunlight). Otherwise, particles are lit depending on the current global lighting conditions. Note that point lights do illuminate nonemissive particles.	0x100

 ## ✋ WARNING

Particle system `float` values need to be floats, and `integer` values need to be integers. This is one place where LSL will not cast implicitly. Vectors, however, can still be mixed `integer` and `float`, since vector components are always cast to float.

PARTICLE PLACEMENT

The five properties in this section control the pattern and initial placement of particles.

PSYS_SRC_PATTERN

Specifies the general emission pattern, using one (and only one) of the `integer` constants shown in Table B.2. The explode pattern tends to be overused, in the sense that often particles are lost into the ground or behind a wall (and therefore wasted). In these cases, use the angle cone instead and focus your particles where they can be seen.

TABLE B.2: PARTICLE-SYSTEM PATTERNS (NOT A BITMASK, DESPITE APPEARANCES)

Constant	Behavior	Value
PSYS_SRC_PATTERN_DROP	Presents particles by dropping them at the emitter position with no force. Ignores the PSYS_SRC_BURST_RADIUS, PSYS_SRC_BURST_SPEED_MIN, and PSYS_SRC_BURST_SPEED_MAX rules.	0x01
PSYS_SRC_PATTERN_EXPLODE	Presents particles by shooting them out in all directions according to the burst motion rules. Ignores PSYS_SRC_ANGLE_BEGIN, PSYS_SRC_ANGLE_END, and PSYS_SRC_ANGLE_OMEGA.	0x02
PSYS_SRC_PATTERN_ANGLE	Presents particles in a 2D circular section as defined by PSYS_SRC_ANGLE_BEGIN and PSYS_SRC_ANGLE_END, as shown in Figure B.2. The plane lies on the emitter's y-axis.	0x04
PSYS_SRC_PATTERN_ANGLE_CONE	Presents particles in a 3D spherical section, as defined by PSYS_SRC_ANGLE_BEGIN and PSYS_SRC_ANGLE_END.	0x08

APPENDICES

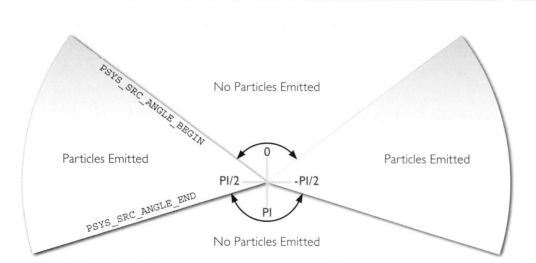

Figure B.2: **PSYS_SRC_PATTERN_ANGLE** emits particles on the y-axis between **PSYS_SRC_ANGLE_BEGIN** and **PSYS_SRC_ANGLE_END**. 0.0 radians is "up" on the z-axis. For a **PSYS_SRC_PATTERN_ANGLE_CONE** pattern, rotate the emitter zone around the z-axis.

PSYS_SRC_BURST_RADIUS

A `float` that specifies the distance in meters from the emitter where particles will be created. This rule is ignored when the **PSYS_PART_FOLLOW_SRC_MASK** flag is set. Maximum value is 50.00.

359

PSYS_SRC_ANGLE_BEGIN

A `float` that specifies a half angle, in radians, of a circular or spherical "dimple," or conic section, starting from 0.0 degrees on the emitter's z-axis within which particles will **not** be emitted. Valid values are 0.0 to π (PI). 0.0 causes no dimple, and π would allow only a straight line in the direction opposite where the emitter is facing. If the pattern is `PSYS_SRC_PATTERN_ANGLE`, the presentation is a 2D flat circular section. If `PSYS_SRC_PATTERN_ANGLE_CONE` is used, the presentation is a 3D spherical section. Note that the value of `PSYS_SRC_ANGLE_BEGIN` and `PSYS_SRC_ANGLE_END` are reordered internally such that `PSYS_SRC_ANGLE_BEGIN` gets the smaller of the two values.

PSYS_SRC_ANGLE_END

A `float` that specifies a half angle, in radians, of a circular or spherical "dimple," or conic section, starting from 0.0 degrees on the emitter's z-axis, within which particles *will* be emitted. Valid values are 0.0 to π (PI); 0.0 results in particles being emitted in a straight line in the direction the emitter is facing, and π results in particles being emitted in a full circular or spherical arc around the emitter, not including the dimple defined by `PSYS_SRC_ANGLE_BEGIN`. If the pattern is `PSYS_SRC_PATTERN_ANGLE`, the presentation is a 2D flat circular section. If `PSYS_SRC_PATTERN_ANGLE_CONE` or `PSYS_SRC_PATTERN_ANGLE_CONE_EMPTY` is used, the presentation is a 3D spherical section. Note that the value of `PSYS_SRC_ANGLE_END` and `PSYS_SRC_ANGLE_BEGIN` are reordered internally such that `PSYS_SRC_ANGLE_END` gets the larger of the two values.

PSYS_SRC_OMEGA

A `vector` that specifies the emitter's rotational spin in radians per second along each axis. Prim spin (via `llTargetOmega()`) has no effect on emitter spin because the spin defined by `PSYS_SRC_OMEGA` is relative to the region coordinate system, not the prim's local coordinate system. There is no way to **set** the emitter's orientation.

 PARTICLE FLOW

Four properties control the flow rate of particles: the emitter's age, the particles' age, particle-burst frequency, and number of particles per burst. A single particle system can manage only 4,096 particles at a time. The total number of concurrent particles is calculated by the following equation:

```
PSYS_PART_MAX_AGE ÷ PSYS_SRC_BURST_RATE × PSYS_SRC_BURST_PART_COUNT
```

With multiple emitters (especially textured ones), your viewer may suffer. Particles are a client-side effect, so they do not cause sim lag. You can set an internal particle-count limit in your viewer preferences: Edit ▶ Preferences ▶ Graphics tab and using the Max Particle Count slider. The default value is 4,096, and can be raised to 8,192 directly. It can also be increased in `settings.ini`.

PSYS_SRC_MAX_AGE

A `float` that specifies the length of time, in seconds, for which the emitter will operate upon coming into view range (if the particle system is already set) or upon execution of this function (if already in view range). Upon expiration, no more particles will be emitted, except as specified in the next paragraph. An emitter age of 0.0 gives the particle system an infinite duration.

When using particle systems that have a nonzero emitter age, the particle system may restart without any scripted trigger going off. This is due to a bug that causes the emitter to reset when any of the prim properties are updated or otherwise sent to the viewer. As a result, you may have to use a timer or a forced sleep and then clear the particle system using `llParticleSystem([])` once the age has expired.

PSYS_PART_MAX_AGE

A `float` that specifies the lifetime, in seconds, of each particle emitted. Maximum is 30.0 seconds. During this time the particle will appear, change appearance, move according to the parameters specified in the other sections, then disappear.

PSYS_SRC_BURST_RATE

A `float` that specifies the time interval, in seconds, between bursts of particles being emitted. Specifying a value of 0.0 causes particles to emit as fast as the viewer can support.

PSYS_SRC_BURST_PART_COUNT

An `integer` that specifies the number of particles emitted in each burst.

 PARTICLE APPEARANCE

Three flags affect the appearance of the particles:

- PSYS_PART_INTERP_COLOR_MASK
- PSYS_PART_INTERP_SCALE_MASK
- PSYS_PART_EMISSIVE_MASK

By using these flags along with the following seven properties, you can control the glow, size, color, transparency, and texture of your particles.

PSYS_PART_START_SCALE

A `vector` that specifies the scale or size of the particles upon emission. Valid values for each direction are 0.03125 to 4.0, in meters. The vector's `z` component is ignored and can be set to 0.0.

PSYS_PART_END_SCALE

A vector that specifies the particles' scale or size at the end of their lifespan. Used only if the `PSYS_PART_INTERP_SCALE_MASK` flag is set. Valid values are the same as `PSYS_PART_START_SCALE`.

PSYS_PART_START_COLOR

A color `vector` that specifies the particles' color upon emission.

PSYS_PART_END_COLOR

A color `vector` that specifies the particles' color at the end of their lifetime. Used only if the `PSYS_PART_INTERP_COLOR_MASK` flag is set.

CHAPTER 1
CHAPTER 2
CHAPTER 3
CHAPTER 4
CHAPTER 5
CHAPTER 6
CHAPTER 7
CHAPTER 8
CHAPTER 9
CHAPTER 10
CHAPTER 11
CHAPTER 12
CHAPTER 13
CHAPTER 14
CHAPTER 15

APPENDIX A
APPENDIX **B**
APPENDIX C

PSYS_PART_START_ALPHA

A `float` that specifies the particles' alpha upon emission. Valid values are in the range 0.0 (transparent) to 1.0 (opaque).

PSYS_PART_END_ALPHA

A `float` that specifies the particles' alpha at the end of their lifespan. Used only if the `PSYS_PART_INTERP_COLOR_MASK` flag is set. Valid values are the same as `PSYS_PART_START_ALPHA`.

PSYS_SRC_TEXTURE

A `string` that specifies the name of a texture in the prim's inventory to use for each particle. Alternatively, you may specify an asset key UUID for a texture. An emitter emits particles with only one texture at a time. The default texture is a white circle, with not *quite* transparent corners.

NOTE

Your Inventory's Library contains interesting textures in the Textures folder, and a couple of sample particle scripts in the Waterfalls folder. Jopsy Pendragon has some excellent particle textures for sale at the Particle Laboratory at Teal <200, 60, 21>. Textures are available all over *SL*, but it might take some work to find freebies that are good for particles. The following table shows a handful of useful textures. They are all Trans/Copy/Mod, given out as freebies.

Name	Creator	Key
Red Arrow	— (Library)	a990f9a1-ab01-5071-444e-552b0f3f4983
Water	— (Library)	4c6bee64-0869-63da-e2ba-71c984721a23
Mist	— (Library)	dcab6cc4-172f-e30d-b1d0-f558446f20d4
Smoke	— (Library)	b4ba225c-373f-446d-9f7e-6cb7b5cf9b3d
Snowflake	Kinn Gray	60ec4bc9-1a36-d9c5-b469-0fe34a8983d4
Lightning	Chrischun Fassbinder	a9b196ef-d358-e3bf-240f-c5773bfd4e05
Lava	Thili Playfair	9db6a042-add2-5352-08c5-af70899ee86c
Sparks	Jopsy Pendragon	181c6b1d-c2d0-70ba-bbf2-52ccc31687c6
Clown Fish	Arazael Maracas	13c20952-8cce-27a8-8e18-05c19bc59147
Fern Leaf	Karzita Zabaleta	b404c9f4-74d2-1f91-abc9-d36e5da0f263
Ghost	Karzita Zabaleta	7b0f3873-ff44-fd8c-fa6c-c813dd0501b7
Pink Rose Petal	Vex Streeter	7d03784c-38f7-b722-7c9f-5f7fa6fde53d
Smiley Face	Vex Streeter	6b4c8a9d-e51c-109f-e266-375738afc1bc
Red Heart	Jopsy Pendragon	5b3f3df0-b20b-5dc4-b49e-377c5805a0e3
Be Mine! Valentine Message	Karzita Zabaleta	2047827b-65ae-cad0-9f4a-267480b03f86
Question Mark	Vex Streeter	377d2ee4-2394-0f73-aaf5-be7113c438e9

Don't forget that an emitter can use the name of a texture in its inventory—that's usually much easier than dealing with keys.

CHAPTER 1
CHAPTER 2
CHAPTER 3
CHAPTER 4
CHAPTER 5
CHAPTER 6
CHAPTER 7
CHAPTER 8
CHAPTER 9
CHAPTER 10
CHAPTER 11
CHAPTER 12
CHAPTER 13
CHAPTER 14
CHAPTER 15

↘ PARTICLE MOTION

Six of the flags in Table B.1 control particle motion:

- `PSYS_PART_FOLLOW_VELOCITY_MASK`
- `PSYS_PART_WIND_MASK`
- `PSYS_PART_BOUNCE_MASK`
- `PSYS_PART_TARGET_LINEAR_MASK`
- `PSYS_PART_TARGET_POS_MASK`
- `PSYS_PART_FOLLOW_SRC_MASK`

Additionally, there are four properties that control the particle's speed, acceleration, and final position.

PSYS_SRC_TARGET_KEY

Specifies the `key` of a target object or agent toward which the particles will travel. They attempt to end up at the target's geometric center at the end of their lifetime. Particles will track a moving target. Requires the `PSYS_PART_TARGET_POS_MASK` flag to be set.

Particles moving toward a humanoid avatar end at the geometric center of the avatar's bounding box, which, unfortunately, makes them appear to be striking the avatar in the groin. If you want them to end up at another point on a target avatar, you have to place a target prim where you wish them to end up, and use that prim's key.

If `PSYS_PART_TARGET_LINEAR_MASK` is set, the particles will move evenly in a straight line toward the target, ignoring velocity and acceleration. If no target is specified, the target moves out of range, or an invalid target is specified, the particles target the prim itself.

PSYS_SRC_BURST_SPEED_MIN

A `float` that specifies the minimum value of a random range of values that is selected for each particle in a burst as its initial speed upon emission, in meters per second. Note that the value of `PSYS_SRC_BURST_SPEED_MIN` and `PSYS_SRC_BURST_SPEED_MAX` are reordered internally such that `PSYS_SRC_BURST_SPEED_MIN` gets the smaller of the two values.

PSYS_SRC_BURST_SPEED_MAX

A `float` that specifies the maximum value of a random range of values that is selected for each particle in a burst as its initial speed upon emission, in meters per second. Note that the value of `PSYS_SRC_BURST_SPEED_MAX` and `PSYS_SRC_BURST_SPEED_MIN` are reordered internally such that `PSYS_SRC_BURST_SPEED_MAX` gets the larger of the two values.

PSYS_SRC_ACCEL

A `vector` that specifies a directional acceleration vector applied to each particle as it is emitted, in meters per second. Valid values are 0.0 to 100.0 for each direction, as region coordinates.

APPENDICES

APPENDICES

PARTICLE-SYSTEM CHEAT SHEET

The following code snippets are complete particle systems, albeit not very exciting ones. If you're having trouble seeing how the particles change, add `PSYS_SRC_ACCEL, <0, 0, 0.2>` to the rule.

APPENDIX A
APPENDIX B
APPENDIX C

Respond to Wind

```
llParticleSystem([PSYS_PART_FLAGS, PSYS_PART_WIND_MASK]);
```

Respond to Gravity

```
llParticleSystem([PSYS_SRC_ACCEL, <0,0,-1>]);
```

Change Size

```
llParticleSystem([
    PSYS_PART_FLAGS, PSYS_PART_INTERP_SCALE_MASK,
    PSYS_PART_START_SCALE, <0.04, 0.04, 0.0>,
    PSYS_PART_END_SCALE, <4.0, 4.0, 0.0>]);
```

Change Color

```
llParticleSystem([
    PSYS_PART_FLAGS, PSYS_PART_INTERP_COLOR_MASK,
    PSYS_PART_START_COLOR, <1.0, 0.0, 0.0>,
    PSYS_PART_END_COLOR, <0.0, 1.0, 0.0>]);
```

Change Transparency

```
llParticleSystem([
    PSYS_PART_FLAGS, PSYS_PART_INTERP_COLOR_MASK,
    PSYS_PART_START_ALPHA, 1.0,
    PSYS_PART_END_ALPHA, 0.0]);
```

Use a Texture

```
llParticleSystem([PSYS_SRC_TEXTURE, "My Particle Texture"]);
```

```
llParticleSystem([
    PSYS_SRC_TEXTURE, a990f9a1-ab01-5071-444e-552b0f3f4983"]);
```

Make a Spiral

```
llParticleSystem([
    PSYS_SRC_PATTERN, PSYS_SRC_PATTERN_ANGLE,
    PSYS_SRC_BURST_PART_COUNT, 10,
    PSYS_SRC_ANGLE_BEGIN, PI_BY_TWO,
    PSYS_SRC_ANGLE_END,   PI_BY_TWO,
    PSYS_SRC_OMEGA, <0,0,20>]);
```

Travel toward a Target

```
llParticleSystem([
      PSYS_PART_FLAGS, PSYS_PART_TARGET_POS_MASK,
      PSYS_SRC_TARGET_KEY, llGetOwner()]);
```

Stop Emitting

```
llParticleSystem([]);
```

DEFAULT VALUES

You can create a particle system that relies on the default values for many parameters (as evidenced by the simple examples just provided). Many people write their code to make changes to default values easy to see, as in this snippet:

```
llParticleSystem([
      PSYS_SRC_PATTERN, PSYS_SRC_PATTERN_ANGLE, // DROP
      PSYS_SRC_BURST_PART_COUNT, 10,            // 1
      PSYS_SRC_ANGLE_BEGIN, PI_BY_TWO,          // 0.0
      PSYS_SRC_ANGLE_END,   PI_BY_TWO,          // 0.0
      PSYS_SRC_OMEGA, <0,0,20>                  // <0,0,0>
]);
```

CHAPTER 1
CHAPTER 2
CHAPTER 3
CHAPTER 4
CHAPTER 5
CHAPTER 6
CHAPTER 7
CHAPTER 8
CHAPTER 9
CHAPTER 10
CHAPTER 11
CHAPTER 12
CHAPTER 13
CHAPTER 14
CHAPTER 15

APPENDICES

Also common in particle scripts is a complete list of the parameters, as shown in Listing B.1. Scripters often alter a few specific ones of interest to change the particle system's behavior. This approach has two advantages. First, scripters never have to go hunting for the precise spelling of a parameter they weren't previously using—it's already there in the script with its default value. Second, if Linden Lab ever changes the default settings, the particle system won't change.

Create a script in your inventory named **Complete Particle Script**, put Listing B.1 inside, and it will be there for the next time you want to make particles. If you run this directly, it makes an extremely unexciting glowing white ball—the particles don't even move. Many of the particle scripts floating around **SL** are (rightly) based off a template by Jopsy Pendragon. There are two differences between his and listing B.1: Jopsy's template defines **all** the values for the properties as variables before the `llParticleSystem()` call, and includes many more comments about the behavior of each property.

Listing B.1: A Complete Particle System with Only Default Values

```
makeParticleSystem()
{
    integer InterpColorMask     = FALSE;
    integer InterpScaleMask     = FALSE;
    integer EmissiveMask        = FALSE;
    integer FollowSrcMask       = FALSE;
    integer FollowVelocityMask  = FALSE;
    integer WindMask            = FALSE;
    integer BounceMask          = FALSE;
    integer TargetPosMask       = FALSE;
    integer TargetLinearMask    = FALSE;
```

```
        llParticleSystem([
            PSYS_PART_FLAGS, (
                    (       EmissiveMask * PSYS_PART_EMISSIVE_MASK ) |
                    (         BounceMask * PSYS_PART_BOUNCE_MASK ) |
                    (    InterpColorMask * PSYS_PART_INTERP_COLOR_MASK ) |
                    (    InterpScaleMask * PSYS_PART_INTERP_SCALE_MASK ) |
                    (           WindMask * PSYS_PART_WIND_MASK ) |
                    (      FollowSrcMask * PSYS_PART_FOLLOW_SRC_MASK ) |
                    ( FollowVelocityMask * PSYS_PART_FOLLOW_VELOCITY_MASK ) |
                    (   TargetLinearMask * PSYS_PART_TARGET_LINEAR_MASK ) |
                    (      TargetPosMask * PSYS_PART_TARGET_POS_MASK ) ),

    //Placement
        PSYS_SRC_PATTERN,        PSYS_SRC_PATTERN_DROP,
        PSYS_SRC_BURST_RADIUS, 0.00,
        PSYS_SRC_ANGLE_BEGIN,  0.00,
        PSYS_SRC_ANGLE_END,    0.00,
        PSYS_SRC_OMEGA,        < 0.00, 0.00, 0.00 >,

    //Flow
        PSYS_SRC_MAX_AGE,         0.0,
        PSYS_PART_MAX_AGE,        10.00,
        PSYS_SRC_BURST_RATE,      0.10,
        PSYS_SRC_BURST_PART_COUNT, 1,

    //Appearance
        PSYS_PART_START_SCALE,  < 1.0, 1.0, 0.0 >,
        PSYS_PART_END_SCALE,    < 1.0, 1.0, 0.0 >,
        PSYS_PART_START_COLOR,  < 1.0, 1.0, 1.0 >,
        PSYS_PART_END_COLOR,    < 1.0, 1.0, 1.0 >,
        PSYS_PART_START_ALPHA,  1.00,
        PSYS_PART_END_ALPHA,    1.00,
        PSYS_SRC_TEXTURE,       "",

    //Movement
        PSYS_SRC_BURST_SPEED_MIN, 1.00,
        PSYS_SRC_BURST_SPEED_MAX, 1.00,
        PSYS_SRC_ACCEL,          < 0.00, 0.00, 0.00 >,
        PSYS_SRC_TARGET_KEY,     llGetKey() // come back to itself
    ]);
}

init(integer delay)
{
    makeParticleSystem();      // turn on the particle system
    llSetTimerEvent( delay ); // set up a timer to turn it off
}
default {
    state_entry() {
        init( 30 );
    }
    on_rez(integer t) {
        llResetScript();
    }
    timer() {
        llParticleSystem([]); // turn off the particle system
        llSetTimerEvent( 0 ); // turn off the timer
    }
}
```

CHAPTER 1
CHAPTER 2
CHAPTER 3
CHAPTER 4
CHAPTER 5
CHAPTER 6
CHAPTER 7
CHAPTER 8
CHAPTER 9
CHAPTER 10
CHAPTER 11
CHAPTER 12
CHAPTER 13
CHAPTER 14
CHAPTER 15

COMMON PROBLEMS

Extracted from a notecard by Jopsy Pendragon, Particle Laboratory, Teal <200,60,21>

Particles too small?

- Particles must be at least 0.04 wide and tall at some point in their life to be displayed.
- Make sure you have INTERP_SCALE_MASK enabled.

Particles too faint?

- Is your ALPHA setting really low (below 0.1)?
- Make sure you have INTERP_COLOR_MASK enabled.

Particle drought?

- Is MAX_AGE really small? Is PART_COUNT = 0? Is your BURST_RATE really long? These can trip you up too.
- Try setting your emitter prim transparent, the particles may just be trapped inside!

APPENDICES

Particles going nowhere?

- Unless you use PATTERN_DROP, particles must have a SPEED_MIN and SPEED_MAX of at least 0.01, or they don't appear.

Particles going too far, too fast to be seen?

- What's your SPEED_MIN set to? They might be too fast to see.
- Check your BURST_RADIUS setting. Look further away from the emitter for your particles.

Emitter not being rendered?

- Small prims far from the viewer often don't get drawn, and when they don't, neither do the particles on that prim. You can use this to your advantage! Make small delicate particle effects on small prims so that they don't show up unless someone is nearby and can appreciate it!

Particle overload?

- Each client can only display so many particles at a time. If there are several emitters near a viewer all pumping out lots of particles, your emitter may be creating so few that it seems broken. Give a hoot, don't pollute!

Typo?

- If all else fails, look for misplaced decimal points.

APPENDIX C: *SL* COMMUNITY STANDARDS

Welcome to the Second Life *world!*

We hope you'll have a richly rewarding experience, filled with creativity, self expression and fun.

The goals of the Community Standards are simple: treat each other with respect and without harassment, adhere to local standards as indicated by simulator ratings, and refrain from any hate activity which slurs a real-world individual or real-world community.

Behavioral Guidelines—The "Big Six"

Within **Second Life**, we want to support Residents in shaping their specific experiences and making their own choices.

The Community Standards sets out six behaviors, the "Big Six," that will result in suspension or, with repeated violations, expulsion from the **Second Life** community.

All **Second Life** Community Standards apply to all areas of **Second Life**, the **Second Life** Forums, and the **Second Life** website.

1. Intolerance

Combating intolerance is a cornerstone of **Second Life**'s Community Standards. Actions that marginalize, belittle, or defame individuals or groups inhibit the satisfying exchange of ideas and diminish the **Second Life** community as whole. The use of derogatory or demeaning language or images in reference to another Resident's race, ethnicity, gender, religion, or sexual orientation is never allowed in **Second Life**.

2. Harassment

Given the myriad capabilities of **Second Life**, harassment can take many forms. Communicating or behaving in a manner which is offensively coarse, intimidating or threatening, constitutes unwelcome sexual advances or requests for sexual favors, or is otherwise likely to cause annoyance or alarm is Harassment.

3. Assault

Most areas in **Second Life** are identified as Safe. Assault in **Second Life** means: shooting, pushing, or shoving another Resident in a Safe Area (see Global Standards below); creating or using scripted objects which singularly or persistently target another Resident in a manner which prevents their enjoyment of **Second Life**.

4. Disclosure

Residents are entitled to a reasonable level of privacy with regard to their **Second Life** experience. Sharing personal information about a fellow Resident—including gender, religion, age, marital status, race, sexual preference, and real-world location beyond what is provided by the Resident in the First Life page of their Resident profile is a violation of that Resident's privacy. Remotely monitoring conversations, posting conversation logs, or sharing conversation logs without consent are all prohibited in **Second Life** and on the **Second Life** Forums.

5. Indecency

Second Life is an adult community, but Mature material is not necessarily appropriate in all areas (see Global Standards below). Content, communication, or behavior which involves intense language or expletives, nudity or sexual content, the depiction of sex or violence, or anything else broadly offensive must be contained within private land in areas rated Mature (M). Names of Residents, objects, places, and groups are broadly viewable in *Second Life* directories and on the *Second Life* website, and must adhere to PG guidelines.

6. Disturbing the Peace

Every Resident has a right to live their *Second Life*. Disrupting scheduled events, repeated transmission of undesired advertising content, the use of repetitive sounds, following or self-spawning items, or other objects that intentionally slow server performance or inhibit another Resident's ability to enjoy *Second Life* are examples of Disturbing the Peace.

Policies and Policing

Global Standards, Local Ratings

All areas of *Second Life*, including the `www.secondlife.com` website and the *Second Life* Forums, adhere to the same Community Standards. Locations within *Second Life* are noted as Safe or Unsafe and rated Mature (M) or non-Mature (PG), and behavior must conform to the local ratings. Any unrated area of *Second Life* or the *Second Life* website should be considered non-Mature (PG).

Warning, Suspension, Banishment

Second Life is a complex society, and it can take some time for new Residents to gain a full understanding of local customs and mores. Generally, violations of the Community Standards will first result in a Warning, followed by Suspension and eventual Banishment from *Second Life*. In-World Representatives, called Liaisons, may occasionally address disciplinary problems with a temporary removal from *Second Life*.

Global Attacks

Objects, scripts, or actions which broadly interfere with or disrupt the *Second Life* community, the *Second Life* servers or other systems related to *Second Life* will not be tolerated in any form. We will hold you responsible for any actions you take, or that are taken by objects or scripts that belong to you. Sandboxes are available for testing objects and scripts that have components that may be unmanageable or whose behavior you may not be able to predict. If you chose to use a script that substantially disrupts the operation of *Second Life*, disciplinary actions will result in a minimum two-week suspension, the possible loss of in-world inventory, and a review of your account for probable expulsion from *Second Life*.

Alternate Accounts

While Residents may choose to play *Second Life* with more than one account, specifically or consistently using an alternate account to harass other Residents or violate the Community Standards is not acceptable. Alternate accounts are generally treated as separate from a Resident's principal account, but misuse of alternate accounts can and will result in disciplinary action on the principal account.

Buyer Beware

Linden Lab does not exercise editorial control over the content of *Second Life*, and will make no specific efforts to review the textures, objects, sounds, or other content created within *Second Life*. Additionally, Linden Lab does not certify or endorse the operation of in-world games, vending machines, or retail locations; refunds must be requested from the owners of these objects.

Reporting Abuse

Residents should report violations of the Community Standards using the Abuse Reporter tool located under the Help menu in the in-world tool bar. Every Abuse Report is individually investigated, and the identity of the reporter is kept strictly confidential.

CHAPTER 1
CHAPTER 2
CHAPTER 3
CHAPTER 4
CHAPTER 5
CHAPTER 6
CHAPTER 7
CHAPTER 8
CHAPTER 9
CHAPTER 10
CHAPTER 11
CHAPTER 12
CHAPTER 13
CHAPTER 14
CHAPTER 15

APPENDICES

INDEX A: KEY TERMS (EXCLUDING LSL CODE)

A

About Land menu: 243
Academy of Second Learning: 326
acceleration: 159, 160-162
access list: 148
active object: 210
add: 11
Advanced Scripters of *Second Life*: 328
aether: 236
air: 236-237
airplanes: 176
AJAX: 96
algorithms: 318
Altassian software: 330-331
alternate accounts: 369
alternate avatar: 323
ambient sounds: 244-250
American Cancer Society: 288-298
Animania: 129
animation: 57-63; of textures 211-221; of water 144-147
animation balls: 305
animation overrides: 57-63
annoyances: 316; *see also* problems
AO: *see* animation overrides
application virtual machine: 336; *see also* virtual machine
arc of the covenent: 222
arctan (inverse tangent): 236
articulation: 121, 123
ASCII: 19
assault: 368
asset server: 317
associating prims with link numbers: 88
associative arrays: 15
asynchronous communications: 25
asynchronous data: 259
asynchronous request: 92, 93
attached objects: 53
attaching objects to body parts: 53

attachment points: 46-47
attachments: 46-57
Audacity: 243
audio: streamed 243; *see also* sound
autogeneration: 100
automatic prim rezzer: 232
automation: 139
avatar death: 169
avatar health: 169
avatar information: 339
avatar name: 254-265
AVI: 243
axel: making 166
axial orientation: 113
axis: 114-123
axis-aligned textured polygon: 206

B

backslash: 74
backup: 322
balloons: 176
banishment: 369
banking: 180-181
bee: 129-130
Beta Grid: 323-324
Big Six, the: 368 369
bitmap: 243
bitwise arithmetic: 42
Blender: 57, 243
bling: 22, 200, 201
blocks: 5
blogHUD: 83
boats: 176
body parts: attaching objects to 53
books: 325
Boolean operators: 21, 86-87
Boolean values: 73
bowling: 46
braces: 5, 19, 20; mismatched 313
brackets: 33; mismatched 313
browsers: in-world 260, external 261
Bu, Baba: 223

bugs: 235, 312, 330-331, 345, 348; bug reporting 316, 330-331
built-in functions: *see* functions
bumpiness: 226
buoyancy: 159, 162, 181, 239
butterflies: 200
buttons: 77-79
buyer beware: 369

C

C family of languages: 8
California time: 230
calling cards: 188, 195
camera: 182-184; controls 183-184; property constants 184
campers: 305-307
campfire: *see* fire
cannon: for fireworks 203
Carnegie Mellon University's CyLab: 312
cars: 176
Case, Max
channels: 9, 68
charity: 288-291
chat catcher: 83
chat channels: 68
chat relay: 82-83
chess: 307
child prim: 4, 87, 134
client-dependent effect: 225
client-side effect: 113, 158, 201
clock: 120-122, 230-232
clouds: 240-241, 247-250
club host: 285, 287-288
club owner: 285
coding styles: 33
coercion: *see* type coercion
College of Scripting, Music, and Science: 326
collision: 134-137, 158, 169
color: 205, 222, 223, 224, 225, 226-227; interpolation 205; parsing 50
common denominator casing: 76

communication: 67-96; among objects 79-83; channels 106, 107-108; email and IM 89-96; in dialogs 77-79; inside an object 83-89; to objects 68-76; protocols: 323
community standards: 368
competitions: 307
compiler errors: 312-313
conditionals: 20-21
constants: **5**, 7; attach points 53; avatar status 63; link number 84; link set 86; names vs. values 55; permissions 56
contacts roster: 89
container: 192-193
containing prim: 39
Content folder : 4, 39, 102, 107
contour line: 238
conversational interfaces: 67-96
coordinates: 11-12
copyright laws: 250, 330
Creating Your World: The Official Guide to Advanced Content Creation: 325
Cubic Effects: 225
customer bell: 89-90

D

damage: 169-170
damage-enabled land: 169
dance: 320
dance ball: 305
databases: 263
day: 223, 232-235
death: 169
debit permission: 280-281
debugging: 29, 68, 280, 320-322, 336
degrees: 12, 115-116
delays: in scripts 319
delta rotation: 117-118
Design Discussion: 340
destination coordinates: 40
detected objects: 52-53
dialogs: 77-79
digger: 145-147

digital rights management laws: 250; *see also* copyright

disclosure: 368

disturbing the peace: 369

DJ: 285

documentation for scripts: 331

door opening: 80-81, 127-128

double quote: 74

Dr. Dobb's Journal: 83

drag effects: 144

duplicate keys: 151

dust devil: 113-114

E

Earth: 122-123, 237-239

ECHOCHANNEL: 82-83

economy: 279-308; statistics: 308

Edit tab: 39

education: 324-325

efficiency: 316-

ejecting avatars: 150-151

email: 89-96, 259, 273, 277, 300, 339; object to object 94-96; retrieving: 95

emitter: 200, 201, 204, 205, 206

energy: 159, 175, 236; drain: 175

enkythings: 46

Entrepreneur's Guide to Second Life: Making Money in the Metaverse: 209

environment: 229-241

error: checking for tip jars 287-288; icon 313; in listeners: 73; messages: 312-314; *see also* problems, bugs; *specific error*

escape characters: 74

Euler rotation: 12, 115-116

event-driven finite state machines: 26

events: 25; counters: 9; excess queued 316; handlers: 5, **7**, 25

explicit casting: 8

exponent: 10

external backup: 322

external editors: 322

external web browser: 261

external web server: 191

F

face light: 48-50, 54, 222

fade: 221

failed calls: 316

Fairlight Lake: 337

Fassbinder, Chrischun: 362

Feature Requests: 340

filtered light: 225-226

fire: 199, 200, 212, 214-215

firepit: *see* fire

fireplace: *see* fire

fireworks: 201-204

flame: *see* fire

Flash: 243, 261

flexible prims: *see* flexiprims

flexiprims: 143-144, 158, 185, 207, 208, 347; physics hack 185

flight: 170-172

flip tag: 47-48

floating: 239

floating text: 47

flow control: 20-21

flower petals 103-104

Flying Tako Sailboat: 182

flying vehicle: 176-178

focus: 221

Fonzarelli, Guzar: 92

force functions: 163

force: 159

forums: 329, 330, 368-369

fountains: 142; *see also* water

Fowler, Martin: 32

frame rate: 212

free money: 291-294

freebies: 291; textures 362

friction: 159, 347

Frog Prince: 46

function length: 3

functions: **5**, 23-24; animation overrides 60; built in 23; detected objects 52-53; llSay family 68; math 22-23; naming 34; that convert lists to strings 16; that extract list elements 15; that manipulate lists 16; that manipulate strided lists 18; that manipulate strings 14; that use keys 13; user defined 23

G

Galleries of Camazotz: 289

gambling: 307-308

games: 307-308

garbage-collection system: 106, 108, 110

GBIV: 205-207

gedit: 322

generator prim: 100

GIMP: 113, 243

giveaways: 307

global attacks: 369

global constants: *see* constants

global coordinates: *see* coordinates

global standards: 369

global variables: *see* variables

GMT: 230

GNU Scripters of *Second Life*: 328

golf: 301

Graphics Interchange Format: 243

gravity: 159, 160

Gray, Kinn: 362

green type: 76

greeters: 136-139

GreyGooFence: 110, 319

griefer/griefing: 73,76, 93, 110, 150, 195

ground: 237-238; ground repel 159

group privileges: 152

group-deeded object: 195, 197, 280, 322, 323

H

hack: 185

harassment: 368

Havok1 physics engine: 157, 185

Havok4 physics engine: 157, 185, 331, 335

heads up display: *see* HUD

health: 169

help: getting and giving 324-331

heterogeneous: 15

highlight transparent: 225

hill: 238

Hippo Technologies: 301, **304**

Hoare, Sir Tony: 316

hollow prims: 175

Holly Kai Golf Club: 201

hopping balls: 106-107

hover: 159, 162, 173-174, 180-181

hovering:

HTML source: 260

HTTP: 277, 300; requests 89; server 339

HUD: 46-47, 53, 54, 60, 64-65, 152, 169; attach points 64

human cannon ball: 167-169

I

idea: 236

IEEE: 312

IM *see* instant messaging

implicit casting: 8

implicit permissions: 55, 64

impulse functions: 163

impulse: 159

indecency: 368

indentation: 33

instant messaging: 89-96

integer: 9-10

integer arithmetic: 314

intermediate values: 315

intolerance: 368

intrasim teleports: 44-46

inventory 186-197; giving 189-193; permissions 195-197; taking 193-195

Inventory folder: 30

Inventory:Trash: 103

inverse tangent (arctan): 236

in-world browser: 260

in-world help: 325-327

Ivory Tower Library of Primitives: 327, 355

JK

Jabber (XMPP): 96

Java/JavaScript: 8, 261, 336

jet pack: 169, 174

JIRA bug: 235

JIRA: 35, 185, 315, 329, 330, 337, 339

JPEG: 243

key: 9, 13

kite: 200, 207-211

Knuth, Donald: 316

L

lag: 68, 126, 201, 316, 317, 336

land ban list: 150

land design: 141-155

land information functions: 152-155

land management: 141-155

land ownership: 108, 243, 253, 303

land pass list: 150

land rental: 303-305

land security: 141, 147-155

land settings: 169

landmark 45; objects: 188
leaves: 20
LED news ticker: 267-272
legal issues: 208
libraries: of scripts 330
Library folder: 142, 212
library functions: 318
Light Learning Lab: 223
light: 221-227; properties 222
Lindeman's Design Beach: 212
Linden dollars: 282, 285, 287, 291,
  292, 295, 302, 305, 307
Linden office hours: 325
Linden Script Tutorial Group: 328
Linden, Kelly: 339
Linden, Qarl: 337
Linden, Sean: 339
Linden, Torley: 250, 356, 357
line wrap: 33
linear execution speed: 317-318
linear motor: 179
link messages: 83-89, 219
link number: 84; associating prims
  with 88
linked prims: 84
link-number constants: 84
linkset 104-105
Linux: 83, 322, 336
list: 9, 15-18
listen: 68-96; filters 70-72;
  handles 9
local coordinates: see coordinates
local ratings: 369
logic errors: 314-315
login: for tip jar users: 286-287
Lo-Jack beacon: 182
loop rezzers: 100-105
LSL math functions: 22-23
LSL media types: 243
LSL Object file: 336
LSL style: 32-34
LSL teachers: 325
LSL wiki: **3**, 8, 45, 59, 73, 78, 84,
  313-333
LSLEditor: 312
lslint: 313
LSO: 336

M

Mac OS X: 336
Macintosh PICT: 243
magic carpet: 177-178, 182, 185
mailbox: 193-195, 204
mailing lists: 329

Malaprop, Ordinal: 294
mantissa: 10
Maracas, Arazael: 362
marketing scripts: 331
mass: 159, 175
master/slave sounds 247-250
Media options menu: 243
media types: 243
memory errors: 315
menu: for payments 280, 283-
  284
message in a bottle: 265-268
metaverse: 340
Microsoft: 336
mimic: 75-76
Mischief Cove: 305-306, 325
missing arguments: 313
modeling: 221
modularity: 34, 207
money: 279-308; debit
  permissions 280-281;
  safeguarding in scripts 323-
  324; trees 291-294; see also
  Linden dollars
Mono scripting engine: 315, 318,
  335-337
mood: 221
moon: 122-123, 222,: 235
Morane, Danna 75-76
mouse click: 284
mouselook: 182-184
movement limits: 43
MP3: 243
Mpeg: 243
multimedia: 243-256
multiple states: 28
multiproduct vendor: 296-299

N

naming conventions: for
  constants 7, for variables 7
NCI: 325
negative channels: 68, 77
.NET: 336
network lag: 317
networked vendor: 300-301
New Citizens Incorporated: 325
new line: 74
new residents: 291, 294, 305, 307
New Script command: 39
news feeds: 89
news ticker: 260
night: 223, 232-235
nonphysical objects: 134;

controlling motion of 112-123
normalizing axis: 52
notecards: 148-150, 189-191, 193,
  195, 204, 299, 316
Notepad: 322
Novell: 336

O

objects: 4; attaching to body
  parts 53; communicating with
  67-96; controlling motion
  of 112-123; detaching 55;
  inventory 187-197, 218; mass
  159; object to object email:
  94-96
offset: 74, 118-119
omega: 159
Online Status Indicator: 92
OnRez: 272-273, 301, 325
OpenSimulator project: 340
open-source software: 336
operations, mathematical: 11
operators: 21-23, 42, 57, 59, 63,
  74, 76
optical illusions: 165-167
OS X: 322
overloaded common resources:
  317

P

paid object: 280
parachute: 174
paraglider: 174
parallel execution: 207
parcel flags: 153
parcel information: 152-153
parentheses: mismatched 313
parser: 73, 76
particle: count 203-204; effects
  200-211; emitters 240-241
Particle Laboratory, the: 213, 326,
  357, 367
particle scripts: 182
particle system: 236, **357-367**
passive object: 210
paying: see money
paying campers: 305-307
payment menu 280-283-284
pending events: 894
Pendragon, Jopsy: 357, 362, 367
periodic sensor repeat: 210
Perl: 259, 267-268, 272, **276-277**
Perlis, Alan J: 311

permissions: 54-57: animation
  override 59-60; debiting
  money 280-281; explicit 64;
  for inventory 195-197; for
  objects 195; for scripts 195;
  for textures 220, 211; implicit
  55; to attach objects 54; who
  granted 56-57
persistence of vision: 212
persistence: in listeners 72; of
  particle effects 201
persistent data: 263
persistent features: 40, 48, 48
personalizing greeters: 137-139
petals: 200
phantom: 113
phantom objects: 133, 135, 136,
  158
phantom prim: 224
Photoshop: 113, 243
PHP: 259, 267-268
Physical check box: 158
physical objects: 134, 157-175;
  moving 163-164, monitoring
  163-164
physical properties, setting: 162
physics engine: 157, 185, 166
physics hack: 185
physics: 157-185
picture frame: 218-221, 225
pie menu: 38-40; changing text
  in 39-40
pitch: 115-116
PJIRA: 330-331; see also JIRA
Playfair, Thili: 362
point light: 222-223
policing: 369
policy: 307-308, 369
polygon: 206
pool: 145-147
pools: see water
popularity: 305-307
pop-up window: 77
port key: 148
portable network graphics: 243
Poser: 57
postures: 59
practical joke: 75-76
pranks: 75-76
preload texture: 218
Premium account: 303
prims: **4**, 84; associating with
  link numbers 88; budget 100;
  clothing 46; hair 46; persistent
  features of 48; torture 351
prim-local: 41; converting from
  sim-local: 41

problems: in scripts: 310-333
projectile aiming: 121
push: 162, 169
push-limited land: 169; *see also* assault
Python: 267-268, 272

Q

QAvimator: 243
quaternion: *see* rotation
query string: 264
qui: 236
QuickTime: 243, 261
quintessence: 236

R

radar: 151-152
radians: 12, 115-116
radio: 251-252
rain: *see* water
rainbows: 200, 205-207
random floating point number: 143
random number: 74,77
randomness: for sounds 247-250
readability: 3
RealNetworks stream: 243
recent changes to LSL: 337-340
reflection: 227
region coordinates: *see* coordinates
region flags: 153
region information: 152-153
regression tests: 324
Relay for Life: 288-298
remote control: 272-277
removing listens: 73
rentals: land 303-305
renting: 301-309
reporting abuse: 369
reporting bugs: 330-331
rezzing: 100-110; failure to rez 102-103
rides: 301-302
Riverbend Art Gallery: 296,
rivers: *see* water
Robin (Sojourner) Wood's Texture Tutorials: 327
roll: 115-116
Roomba: 130-133
root prim: 4, 12, 38, 84, 87, 134
Rosedale, Philip: 3

rotate mode (texture animations): 216-217
rotation: 9, 12-13, 162; combining Target Omega and quaternions 122-123; shortcuts for 121;using quaternions 115; with Target Omega 113-114
rotational math: 323
ROY: 205, 207
royalties: 250
RSS feeds: 89, 268-272
runtime errors: 313-314

S

scale mode (texture animations): 215-216
scaling issues: 317
School of Mischief: 305-306, 325
scope: 19
Script Academy: 328
Script Crypt: 328
Script Database Group: 328
script editor: 312; external 313
script inventory: 187-197
script libraries: 330
script pauses: 43
script placement: 47
scripted objects, managing: 29
Scripters of *Second Life*: 328
scripting groups: 328
Scripting Tips Forum: 329
Scripting Your World Headquarters: **3**, 46, 47, 48, 52, 53, 60, 64, 65, 69, 81, 86, 93, 103, 113, 130, 136, 142, 182, 185, 204, 222, 225, 238, 244, 256, 268, 300, 325, 327, 328, 329; website 38, 42, 121, 123, 134, 144, 164, 194, 197, 244, 262, 322,: 329, 340
Scripts (group): 328
scripts: multiple 30-31; resetting 31-32; worker scripts 34
scripts in this book: access-controlled teleport 148-149; animating a campfire 214; automatic doors 80-81; basic mailbox 194; basic sound automation--wind effects 244; bee 129; better sound automation 246; button script for multiple-product vendor 299; chain of temporary hopping balls 106-107; *changeflag.pl*, an XML-RPC flag changer client (Perl) 276;

charity collection box 289; chatty light switch 71; clock hands 232; clock root prim 231; collisions 134; color changing spotlight controller 224; complete particle system with only default values: 365-366; cone of light 224; customer bell: 90-91; default new script 4; dialog-based colorizer 77; dying leaf 131-132; face light 49; find a key for an avatar name 264; fireworks cannon 204; fireworks--a big ball of small, slow-moving particles 203; fireworks--an explosion of red shooters 201; flip tag 47; flower loop rezzer 100-101; flower petal 103; flying kite 209 210; getting properties of inventory items: 188-189; giving a list of inventory 192; giving usage hints 74; how many residents are in-world 261; HUD in AO 65; improved water animation 143; intrasim teleport 44; intersim teleport assistant 45; kite string 208-209; land monitor and ejector 151; leaf rezzer 131; light controlled by touch relay link message 85; light-emitting prim 224; linking objects 105; local teleporter 41; long-distance chat relay 82; making a clock face using a rotation shortcut function 122; managing records in a strided list 18; message in a bottle--server side (php) 267; message in a bottle--the client on the SL side 266; mimic someone 75-76; money tree 292; money-tree leaf 293; multiple-product vendor 297; neon texture flipper as multiple states: 28; notecard giver 189; object to object email 95-96; optimized intrasim teleport 45; perpetual temp rezzer 109; personalized memory greeter 138-139; picture frame 219; picture frame images 220-221; rainbow 205-206; region rental 303; retrieving email 95; Roomba 132-133; rotate around a point 120; rotating a sign around a post 117; RSS news ticker 269-270; RSS news ticker LED 271; self-attaching face light 54;

shared tip jar 285; shared tip jar with error checking 288; sidewalk light 233; sidewalk light shadow 234; simple greeter--using sensing 137; simple tip jar 282; simply sitting 39; simple vendor 295; skyhook ride 301; sliding doors 127; small strided list 17; storm master 248; storm slave 249; SYW-TV 254; terraforming pool digger 145-146; texture changing object 227; texture flipper 6; the moon's rotation 123; touch relay in a linked set 85; traffic rewarder 306; tunable radio 252; typing animator 61-62; URL loader 260; using a debugging function 321; using a timer to reset and object's position and orientation 29; water animation 142; water floaty 238-239; watery pool controller 147; waving waters 144; whirling trash using Target Omega 114; wind-up key 51; XML-RPC flag changer (LSL server) 273; yoga float animation override 58-59
script-speed governors: 319
sculpted prims: 335
sculpty prims: 350
search interface: 305
Second Life blog: 329, 340
Second Life days: 232
Second Life time: 230
Second Life wiki: 340
Second Life: The Official Guide: 325
Secondlifescripters: 329
securing communications: 294
selling scripts: 331-332
selling: 294-301; services 301-308; *see also* money
sensors: 125-139
services, selling 301-308
shadow variable: 20
shadows: 222, 223, 225, 232-235
shininess: 226
short-circuiting: 21
shortcuts: rotational 121
sidewalk light: 233-235
signs: 113
Silicon Graphics: 243
sim boundaries: 211
sim-local: 41; converting to prim-local: 41
simulator lag: 317

simulator revision: 324
simultaneity: 319-320
sit balls: 40
Sit Here option: 39
sitting: 38-40; sit offsets 40
skyhook: 301-302
SL GUI: 145
SLDev: 329
sleds: 176
slerp: 121
SLExchange: 272-273, 325
slow scripts: 316-320
smooth mode (texture
    animations): 217
snow: 240-241
Snow Crash: 340
Solaris: 336
sound: 244-250; built in clips
    244; creation and editing 250;
    emitters 248soundscapes
    244-250; volume 246-247;
    wind 244, 246
spam: 93
special effects: 199-227
spherical linear inerpolation: 121
spin: 162,165
spiral texture: 165
spotlight: 223-225
sprites: 206-207
stained glass: 225
standard mode (texture
    animations): 213-215
states: 4, 5, 7, 26-28
statistics bar: 319
Stephenson, Neal: 340
storm: 247-250
streaming media: 251-256
streaming video: 253-256
Streeter, Vex: 362
stride: 17
strided list: 17-18, 77-78, 88, 110,
    262-263, 299
string: 9, 14, 313
style: 32-34
subtract: 11
suggestion box: 193
sun: 122-123, 222; sun direction
    232-233
Sun Microsystems: 336
support: for your marketed
    scripts 331
surface binormal: 338
surface coordinates: 338
surface normal: 338
surfboard: 301

Surfline Aloha Rezzable: 128, 301
suspension: 369
synchronizing events: 319-320
syntax highlighting: 313
SYW: *see* Scripting Your World
SYW-TV: 254-256

T

tab: 74
Tagged Image File Format: 243
taking controls: 172-173
Targa: 243
tax: 285, 287; *see also* money
teachers: 325
teleport: 41-46; intrasim 44-46;
    speed limitations 43
temporary objects 106-110
temporary rezzer: 106-110
Terdiman, Daniel: 208
Terms of Service: 74, 150, 250,
    307-308
Terra, Cubey: 182
terraforming: 145-147
test jigs: 324
testing: 323-324
text display color: 48
text files: 243
TextEdit: 322
textures: 192-193, 195, 196;
    animation 62, 211-22;
    coordinates 338; modes: 213-
    217; permissions: 220, 221
theft: 293, 340
thunder: 247-250
time dilation: 233, 319
time: 230-235; of day 138
time-limited restrictions: 150
timeout interval: 93
timescales: 179-180
tiny prims: 356
tip jar user login: 286-287
tip jars: *see* tipping
tipping: 281-288; for teachers
    325; tipping cow: 285
torque: 159
touch position: 337-339
traffic: 306-307
transaction basics: 280-281
transaction history: 281
transition effects: 221
transparency: 212, 214
transparent prim: 87-88
trivia: 307
tuples: 43, 344

tutorials: 68, 176, 325-329, 331,
    350, 357
Twitterbox: 83
type coercion: 8
type mismatches: 313
types: 8-9
typing animator: 61-62
typos: 313, 315

U

uniqueness: 37
unit testing: 324
Universal Unique Identifier: *see*
    UUID
UNIX: 336
unsitting: 40, 42
updates: for your marketed
    scripts 331-332
user preferences: 201, 222
user-defined functions: 5; *see also*
    functions
user-defined state: 5
UUID: 13, 42, 52, 55, 63, 92, 104,
    105, 149, 151, 152, 211, 244,
    245, 247, 261, 349, 353, 362

V

variables: **5**, 7-9, 19-20; naming
    33-34
vector: 9-12
vector cross product: 11
vector dot product: 11
vehicles: 176-185; direction 179;
    efficiency 180; flags 181-182;
    properties 178-181; rotation
    179
velocity: 159
vendor script:
vendors: 97, 196, 295-301; simple
    295-296; multiproduct 296-
    299; networked 300-301;
    vending machines 193
versioning: 322-323
vi: 322
video, streamed 243
viewer lag: 317
Vint's primskirtbuilder sandbox:
    100
virtual machine: 335-337
visibility: 221
VM: *see* virtual machine
Volcán Tenorio: 200
volcanoes: 200, 212

W

warning: 369
water: 141-144, 237-239;
    animation: 142-144; effects
    200; mill 142; waterfalls 141-
    144
WAV: 243
waves: *see* water
weather: 240-241; effects 200;
    sounds 244-250; vane 236
web: 89, 260-277; for scripting
    help 329
wheels: 216
whirlwind: 113-114
Wikipedia: 73, 121, 336,
wildcard: 72, 94
wildlife: 128
wind: 211; direction 236-237;
    effects 144
winding key script: 50-51
WindLight viewer: 335
Windows: 322, 336
wipe: 221
worker scripts: 34
World Wide Web Consortium:
    263
wrestling: 307
Wright, Steven: 110

XYZ

XML: 270-277
XML-RCP: 259, 272-277, 300,
    339
XMPP (Jabber): 96
yaw: 115-116
yoga float 68-69
YouTube: 253
Zabaleta, Karzita: 362
ZHAO-II scripts: 60
zoom effect: 221

RETURNTYPE	CODE	PAGE(S)
	-- (Decrement)	22
	- (Subtract)	11, **22**, 117
	! (Not)	21, **22**
	!= (Comparison not equal)	22
	% (Modulus, Cross Product)	11, **22**
	%= (Assignment)	22
	& (Bitwise AND)	**22**, 63, 173, 314
	&& (Comparison AND)	**22**, 314
	* (Multiply, Dot Product, Add)	11, **22**, 117
	*= (Assignment)	22
	. (Dot)	22
	/ (Divide, Subtract)	**22**, 117
	// (Comment)	7
	/= (Assignment)	22
	\" (Quoted Quotation mark)	14, 74
	\\ (Quoted Backslash)	14, 74
	\n (Quoted Newline)	14, 74
	\t (Quoted Tab)	14, 74
	^ (Bitwise XOR)	22
	| (Bitwise OR)	**22**, 59, 128, 129, 132, 213, 314
	|| (Comparison OR)	**22**, 314
	~ (Bitwise complement)	21, **22**, 173
	+ (Add, Concatenate)	11, 16, **21-22**, 117
	++ (Increment)	22
	+= (Assignment)	16, **22**
	< (Less than)	22
	<< (Left Shift)	22
	<= (Less than or equal to)	22
	= (Assignment)	**22**, 76
	-= (Assignment)	**22**, 314
	== (Comparison equal)	**22**, 314, 316
	> (Greater than)	22
	>= (Greater than or equal to)	22
	>> (Right Shift)	22
	ACTIVE (0x2)	53, 126, 129, 132, 133
	AGENT (0x1)	53, 126
	AGENT_ALWAYS_RUN (0x1000)	63
	AGENT_ATTACHMENTS (0x0002)	63
	AGENT_AWAY (0x0040)	63
	AGENT_BUSY (0x0800)	63
	AGENT_CROUCHING (0x0400)	63
	AGENT_FLYING (0x0001)	**63**, 171
	AGENT_IN_AIR (0x0100)	63
	AGENT_MOUSELOOK (0x0008)	63
	AGENT_ON_OBJECT (0x0020)	63
	AGENT_SCRIPTED (0x0004)	63
	AGENT_SITTING (0x0010)	63

RETURNTYPE	CODE	PAGE(S)
	AGENT_TYPING (0x0200)	62, **63**
	AGENT_WALKING (0x0080)	63
	ALL_SIDES (-1)	49, 62, 213, 214-217, 221, 234, 271
	ANIM_ON (0x1)	213, 214, 215-217, 221
	at_rot_target() event	164,
	at_target() event	25, **164**, 209
	attach() event	55, 170, 171
	ATTACH_BACK (9)	53
	ATTACH_BELLY (28)	53
	ATTACH_CHEST (1)	53
	ATTACH_CHIN (12)	53, 54
	ATTACH_HEAD (2)	53
	ATTACH_HUD_BOTTOM (37)	53
	ATTACH_HUD_BOTTOM_LEFT (36)	53
	ATTACH_HUD_BOTTOM_RIGHT (38)	53
	ATTACH_HUD_CENTER_1 (35)	53
	ATTACH_HUD_CENTER_2 (31)	53
	ATTACH_HUD_TOP_CENTER (33)	53
	ATTACH_HUD_TOP_LEFT (34)	53
	ATTACH_HUD_TOP_RIGHT (32)	53
	ATTACH_LEAR (13)	53
	ATTACH_LEYE (15)	53
	ATTACH_LFOOT (7)	53
	ATTACH_LHAND (5)	53
	ATTACH_LHIP (25)	53
	ATTACH_LLARM (21)	53
	ATTACH_LLLEG (27)	53
	ATTACH_LPEC (30)	53
	ATTACH_LSHOULDER (3)	53
	ATTACH_LUARM (20)	53
	ATTACH_LULEG (26)	53
	ATTACH_MOUTH (11)	53
	ATTACH_NOSE (17)	53
	ATTACH_PELVIS (10)	53
	ATTACH_REAR (14)	53
	ATTACH_REYE (16)	53
	ATTACH_RFOOT (8)	53
	ATTACH_RHAND (6)	53
	ATTACH_RHIP (22)	53
	ATTACH_RLARM (19)	53
	ATTACH_RLLEG (24)	53
	ATTACH_RPEC (29)	53
	ATTACH_RSHOULDER (4)	53
	ATTACH_RUARM (18)	53
	ATTACH_RULEG (23)	53
	CAMERA_ACTIVE (12)	184
	CAMERA_BEHINDNESS_ANGLE (8)	184
	CAMERA_BEHINDNESS_LAG (9)	184
	CAMERA_DISTANCE (7)	184
	CAMERA_FOCUS (17)	184

RETURNTYPE	CODE	PAGE(S)
	CAMERA_FOCUS_LAG (6)	184
	CAMERA_FOCUS_LOCKED (22)	184
	CAMERA_FOCUS_OFFSET (1)	184
	CAMERA_FOCUS_THRESHOLD (11)	184
	CAMERA_PITCH (0)	184
	CAMERA_POSITION (13)	184
	CAMERA_POSITION_LAG (5)	184
	CAMERA_POSITION_LOCKED (21)	184
	CAMERA_POSITION_THRESHOLD (10)	184
	changed() event	**42**, 104, 177, 178, 182, 194, 195
	CHANGED_ALLOWED_DROP (0x40)	194-195
	CHANGED_COLOR (0x2)	
	CHANGED_INVENTORY (0x1)	194-195
	CHANGED_LINK (0x20)	42
	CHANGED_OWNER (0x80)	
	CHANGED_REGION (0x100)	
	CHANGED_SCALE (0x8)	
	CHANGED_SHAPE (0x4)	
	CHANGED_TELEPORT (0x200)	
	CHANGED_TEXTURE (0x10)	
	CLICK_ACTION_BUY (2)	284
	CLICK_ACTION_NONE (0)	284
	CLICK_ACTION_OPEN (4)	284
	CLICK_ACTION_OPEN_MEDIA (6)	284
	CLICK_ACTION_PAY (3)	284
	CLICK_ACTION_PLAY (5)	284
	CLICK_ACTION_SIT (1)	284
	CLICK_ACTION_TOUCH (0)	284
	collision() event	135, 136, 160, 168
	collision_end() event	135
	collision_start() event	135, 136
	control() event	59, 60, 172, **173**, 176, 177, 178, 183
	CONTROL_BACK (0x2)	172
	CONTROL_DOWN (0x20)	172, 174
	CONTROL_FWD (0x1)	172
	CONTROL_LBUTTON (0x10000000)	172
	CONTROL_LEFT (0x4)	172
	CONTROL_ML_LBUTTON (0x40000000)	172
	CONTROL_RIGHT (0x8)	172
	CONTROL_ROT_LEFT (0x100)	172
	CONTROL_ROT_RIGHT (0x200)	172
	CONTROL_UP (0x10)	172, 174
	DATA_BORN (3)	92, 294
	DATA_NAME (2)	92
	DATA_ONLINE (1)	92
	DATA_PAYINFO (8)	92
	DATA_RATING (4)	92
	DATA_SIM_POS (5)	
	DATA_SIM_RATING (7)	
	DATA_SIM_STATUS (6)	
	dataserver() event	91, 92, **93**, 150, 294, 298, 299
	DEBUG_CHANNEL (2147483647)	68, 320, 321
	default state	5, 19, 23, 26, 28, 31, 75, 92, 170, 291, 297, 298

RETURNTYPE	CODE	PAGE(S)
	DEG_TO_RAD (0.0174532925199 ➡ 43295769236907684886)	12-13, 115
	do...while	20-21, 271
	email() event	95
	EOF (\n\n\n)	149-150
	Events	
	at_rot_target()	164
	at_target()	25, **164**, 209
	attach()	55, 170, 171
	changed()	**42**, 104, 177, 178, 182, 194, 195
	collision()	135, 136, 160, 168
	collision_end()	135
	collision_start()	135, 136
	control()	59, 60, 172, **173**, 176, 177, 178, 183
	dataserver()	91, 92, **93**, 150, 294, 298, 299
	email()	95
	http_response()	25, **262**, 264, 265, 266, 268, 269, 270, 290
	land_collision()	135, 168, **169**
	land_collision_end()	169
	land_collision_start()	169
	link_message()	85, **86**, 208, 232, 271, 298
	listen()	7, 23, 25, 48, 50, **69**, 70, 71, 72, 73, 76, 77, 79, 81, 82, 93, 102, 294
	money()	25, 281, **282**, 283, 286, 287, 292, 295, 299, 303
	moving_end()	**112**, 164
	moving_start()	**112**, 164
	no_sensor()	127, 129, 288
	not_at_rot_target()	164
	not_at_target()	133, **164**
	object_rez()	101, **102**, 210, 316
	on_rez()	**31**, 32, 83, 92, 102, 120, 171, 207, 291, 293, 323
	remote_data()	274
	run_time_permissions()	54, 55, **56**, 59, 177, 178, 287

RETURNTYPE	CODE	PAGE(S)
	sensor()	127, 128, 129, 130, 132, 137, 138, 151, 211, 264, 304
	state_entry()	4, 7, **26-28**, 30, 32, 41, 75, 92, 110, 120, 143, 170, 171, 172, 176, 202, 209, 219, 221, 283, 284, 287, 292, 295, 299, 302, 303, 321
	state_exit()	**26-27**, 170, 173
	timer()	7, **30**, 52, 60, 63, 79, 93, 110, 122, 152, 160, 172, 173, 219, 226, 230, 246, 271
	touch()	7, 45, **52**, 135, 262, 264, 338, 339
	touch_end()	7, 45, 51, **52**, 79, 293, 321, 338
	touch_start()	4, 7, 30, 45, **52**, 93, 108, 122, 160, 252, 269, 286, 338
	FALSE (0)	9, 17, 21, 64, 73, 86
	float	10
	for	20-21
	HTTP_BODY_MAXLENGTH (2)	263
	HTTP_BODY_TRUNCATED (0)	
	HTTP_METHOD (0)	263, 266
	HTTP_MIMETYPE (1)	263, 266
	http_response() event	25, **262**, 264, 265, 266, 268, 269, 270, 290
	HTTP_VERIFY_CERT (3)	263
	if...else	20, 315
	integer	
	INVENTORY_ALL (-1)	188
	INVENTORY_ANIMATION (20)	188
	INVENTORY_BODYPART (13)	188
	INVENTORY_CLOTHING (5)	188
	INVENTORY_GESTURE (21)	188
	INVENTORY_LANDMARK (3)	188
	INVENTORY_NONE (-1)	188
	INVENTORY_NOTECARD (7)	188, 190
	INVENTORY_OBJECT (6)	188
	INVENTORY_SCRIPT (10)	188
	INVENTORY_SOUND (1)	188

RETURNTYPE	CODE	PAGE(S)
	INVENTORY_TEXTURE (0)	188
	jump	21
	key	13
	land_collision() event	135, 168
	land_collision_end() event	
	land_collision_start() event	
	LAND_LARGE_BRUSH (Do not use this named constant; use the value instead: 3)	147
	LAND_LEVEL (0)	147
	LAND_LOWER (2)	147
	LAND_MEDIUM_BRUSH (Do not use this named constant; use the value instead: 2)	147
	LAND_NOISE (4)	147
	LAND_RAISE (1)	147
	LAND_REVERT (5)	147
	LAND_SMALL_BRUSH (Do not use this named constant; use the value instead: 1)	147
	LAND_SMOOTH (3)	147
	LINK_ALL_CHILDREN (-3)	84, 86, 231, 270
	LINK_ALL_OTHERS (-2)	84, 86, 219
	link_message() event	85, **86**, 208, 232, 271, 298
	LINK_ROOT (1)	84, 86
	LINK_SET (-1)	84, 86, 87, 88, 89
	LINK_THIS (-4)	84, 86, 88, 89
	list	15
	LIST_STAT_GEOMETRIC_MEAN (9)	
	LIST_STAT_MAX (2)	
	LIST_STAT_MEAN (3)	
	LIST_STAT_MEDIAN (4)	
	LIST_STAT_MIN (1)	
	LIST_STAT_NUM_COUNT (8)	
	LIST_STAT_RANGE (0)	
	LIST_STAT_STD_DEV (5)	
	LIST_STAT_SUM (6)	
	LIST_STAT_SUM_SQUARES (7)	
	listen() event	7, 23, 25, 48, 50, **69**, 70, 71, 72, 73, 76, 77, 79, 81, 82, 93, 102, 294
integer	llAbs(integer val)	**22**, 215
float	llAcos(float val)	23
	llAddToLandBanList(key avatar, float hours)	150
	llAddToLandPassList(key avatar, float hours)	150
	llAdjustSoundVolume(float volume)	246, **247**
	llAllowInventoryDrop(integer add_boolean)	194, **195**
float	llAngleBetween(rotation a, rotation b)	121
	llApplyImpulse(vector force, integer local_boolean)	162, 163, 168, 169, 175
	llApplyRotationalImpulse(vector force, integer local_boolean)	162, 163, 165, 166, 175
float	llAsin(float val)	23
float	llAtan2(float y, float x)	23
	llAttachToAvatar(integer attachPoint_named_constant)	54

RETURN TYPE	CODE	PAGE(S)
key	llAvatarOnSitTarget()	40, 41, **42,** 44, 177
rotation	llAxes2Rot(vector fwd, vector left, vector up)	121
rotation	llAxisAngle2Rot(vector axis, float angle)	121
integer	llBase64ToInteger(string str)	
string	llBase64ToString(string str)	
	llBreakAllLinks()	104
	llBreakLink(integer linknum)	104
integer	llCeil(float val)	**22,** 74
	llClearCameraParams()	183
	llCloseRemoteDataChannel(key channel)	273, **275**
float	llCloud(vector offset)	241
	llCollisionFilter(string name, key id, integer accept_boolean)	134
	llCollisionSound(string impact_ sound, float impact_volume)	134
	llCollisionSprite(string impact_ sprite)	
float	llCos(float theta)	23
	llCreateLink(key target, integer parent_boolean)	104, 105
list	llCSV2List(string src)	16
list	llDeleteSubList(list src, integer start, integer end)	16, 292
string	llDeleteSubString(string src, integer start, integer end)	14, 271
	llDetachFromAvatar()	54
key	llDetectedCreator(integer number)	52
vector	llDetectedGrab(integer number)	53, 286
integer	llDetectedGroup(integer number)	52, 134, **152**
key	llDetectedKey(integer number)	13, 52, 132, 190, 260, 264
integer	llDetectedLinkNumber(integer number)	53
string	llDetectedName(integer number)	52, 130, 134, 137, 264
key	llDetectedOwner(integer number)	52, 134,
vector	llDetectedPos(integer number)	52, 130, 134
rotation	llDetectedRot(integer number)	52, 130, 134
vector	llDetectedTouchBinormal(integer number)	339
vector	llDetectedTouchFace(integer number)	338
vector	llDetectedTouchNormal(integer number)	338
integer	llDetectedTouchPos(integer number)	338
vector	llDetectedTouchST(integer number)	338
vector	llDetectedTouchUV(integer number)	338
integer	llDetectedType(integer number)	53
vector	llDetectedVel(integer number)	52, 134
	llDialog(key avatar, string message, list buttons, integer channel)	77, **78,** 323
	llDie()	102, **103,** 132, 202
string	llDumpList2String(list src, string separator)	16, 17, 84
integer	llEdgeOfWorld(vector pos, vector dir)	153,

RETURN TYPE	CODE	PAGE(S)
	llEjectFromLand(key pest)	150, 151, 197, 304
	llEmail(string address, string subject, string message)	91, 93, **94,** 95, 300
string	llEscapeURL(string url)	14, 264
rotation	llEuler2Rot(vector v)	12, 110, **115**
float	llFabs(float val)	22
integer	llFloor(float val)	22
	llForceMouselook(integer mouselook_boolean)	183
float	llFrand(float mag)	**23,** 74, 76, 143, 246
vector	llGetAccel()	160, 161
string	llGetAgentLanguage(key avatar)	339
integer	llGetAgentInfo(key id)	62, **63,** 170, 171
vector	llGetAgentSize(key id)	160
float	llGetAlpha(integer face)	111
float	llGetAndResetTime()	230
string	llGetAnimation(key id)	58, **60**
list	llGetAnimationList(key id)	60
integer	llGetAttached()	**53,** 54, 58, 171
list	llGetBoundingBox(key object)	160
vector	llGetCameraPos()	183
rotation	llGetCameraRot()	183
vector	llGetCenterOfMass()	160
vector	llGetColor(integer face)	111
key	llGetCreator()	13, 134
string	llGetDate()	230
float	llGetEnergy()	159, **160**
vector	llGetForce()	160
integer	llGetFreeMemory()	315
vector	llGetGeometricCenter()	160
float	llGetGMTclock()	230
key	llGetInventoryCreator(string item)	189, 220
key	llGetInventoryKey(string name)	189, 219
string	llGetInventoryName(integer type_ named_constant, integer number)	109, 149, **189,** 190, 192, 295
integer	llGetInventoryNumber(integer type_ named_constant)	109, **189,** 192
integer	llGetInventoryPermMask(string item, integer mask_named_constant)	196, **197**
integer	llGetInventoryType(string name)	189
key	llGetKey()	13, 88
key	llGetLandOwnerAt(vector pos)	90, **153**
key	llGetLinkKey(integer linknum)	**88,** 105
string	llGetLinkName(integer linknum)	88, **89,** 105
integer	llGetLinkNumber()	105, 210
integer	llGetListEntryType(list src, integer index)	15
integer	llGetListLength(list src)	16
vector	llGetLocalPos()	112, **113,** 121
rotation	llGetLocalRot()	115, 117
float	llGetMass()	159, **160,** 165, 166
	llGetNextEmail(string address, string subject)	**94,** 95
key	llGetNotecardLine(string name, integer line)	13, **149,** 298
key	llGetNumberOfNotecardLines(string name)	149, 150
integer	llGetNumberOfPrims()	88, 105, **106**

RETURNTYPE	CODE	PAGE(S)
integer	llGetNumberOfSides()	111
string	llGetObjectDesc()	111
list	llGetObjectDetails(key id, list list_of_named_constant_params)	83, 132, **133**
float	llGetObjectMass(key id)	159, **160**, 163
string	llGetObjectName()	75, 89, **111**
integer	llGetObjectPermMask(integer mask_named_constant)	196, **197**
integer	llGetObjectPrimCount(key object_id)	105
vector	llGetOmega()	160
key	llGetOwner()	13, 32, 47, **48**, 54, 90, 92, 105, 171, 182, 197, 286, 291, 292, 303
key	llGetOwnerKey(key id)	13, 134
list	llGetParcelDetails(vector pos, list list_of_named_constant_params)	153, 303
integer	llGetParcelFlags(vector pos)	152-153, 154, 211
integer	llGetParcelMaxPrims(vector pos, integer sim_wide_boolean)	153
integer	llGetParcelPrimCount(vector pos, integer category_named_constant, integer sim_wide_boolean)	153
list	llGetParcelPrimOwners(vector pos)	153
integer	llGetPermissions()	56, **57**, 105
key	llGetPermissionsKey()	56
vector	llGetPos()	30, 41, 103, 112, **113**, 122
list	llGetPrimitiveParams(list list_of_named_constant_params)	40, 42, 111, **113**, 115, 158, 211, 344
integer	llGetRegionAgentCount()	339
vector	llGetRegionCorner()	11, **153**
integer	llGetRegionFlags()	152-153, 154, 170
float	llGetRegionFPS()	153
string	llGetRegionName()	153
float	llGetRegionTimeDilation()	233, 319
vector	llGetRootPosition()	113
rotation	llGetRootRotation()	115, 235, 237
rotation	llGetRot()	30, 41, **115**, 128
vector	llGetScale()	40, 111, 219, 224
string	llGetScriptName()	34, **111**, 192
integer	llGetScriptState(string name)	111
string	llGetSimulatorHostname()	317
integer	llGetStartParameter()	102, **103**, 106, 107, 202
integer	llGetStatus(integer status_bitwise_named_constant)	158, **159**
string	llGetSubString(string src, integer start, integer end)	14, 76, 271
vector	llGetSunDirection()	233, 234, 235
string	llGetTexture(integer face)	211
vector	llGetTextureOffset(integer face)	211
float	llGetTextureRot(integer side)	211
vector	llGetTextureScale(integer side)	211
float	llGetTime()	161, **230**
float	llGetTimeOfDay()	233
string	llGetTimestamp()	230
vector	llGetTorque()	160
integer	llGetUnixTime()	230
vector	llGetVel()	160
float	llGetWallclock()	230
	llGiveInventory(key destination, string inventory)	189-190, **191**, 296, 316, 319
	llGiveInventoryList(key avatar, string folder, list inventory)	192, **193**, 316
integer	llGiveMoney(key destination, integer amount)	286, **287**, 292, 303, 316, 323
	llGodLikeRezObject(key inventory, vector pos)	
float	llGround(vector offset)	237, **238**
vector	llGroundContour(vector offset)	238
vector	llGroundNormal(vector offset)	238
	llGroundRepel(float height, integer water_boolean, float tau)	162, 175
vector	llGroundSlope(vector offset)	238
key	llHTTPRequest(string url, list parameters_strided, string body)	13, 25, 262, **263**, 264, 265, 266, 270, 272, 290, 319, 332
string	llInsertString(string dst, integer pos, string src)	14
	llInstantMessage(key user, string message)	68, 90, 91, **94**, 266, 286, 288
string	llIntegerToBase64(integer number)	
string	llKey2Name(key id)	13, 134, 153, 264, 291, 302
string	llList2CSV(list src)	16
float	llList2Float(list src, integer index)	15
integer	llList2Integer(list src, integer index)	15
key	llList2Key(list src, integer index)	15
list	llList2List(list src, integer start, integer end)	16
list	llList2ListStrided(list src, integer start, integer end, integer stride)	17, 77, 78, 252
rotation	llList2Rot(list src, integer index)	15
string	llList2String(list src, integer index)	15, 17, 252, 297
vector	llList2Vector(list src, integer index)	15, 79
integer	llListen(integer channel, string name, key id, string msg)	9, 25, 48, 69, 70, 71, 72, 73, 76, 77, 80, 81, 91, 93, 106, 108, 110, 288, 292, 323
	llListenControl(integer number, integer active_boolean)	69, **73**

RETURNTYPE	CODE	PAGE(S)
	llListenRemove(integer number)	69, **73**, 77, 91, 94
integer	llListFindList(list src, list test)	16, 79, 88, 138, 262, 271, 292
list	llListInsertList(list dest, list src, integer start)	16
list	llListRandomize(list src, integer stride)	17, 244
list	llListReplaceList(list dest, list src, integer start, integer end)	16
list	llListSort(list src, integer stride, integer ascending_boolean)	17
float	llListStatistics(integer operation_named_constant, list src)	16
	llLoadURL(key avatar_id, string message, string url)	260, **261**
float	llLog(float val)	23
float	llLog10(float val)	23
	llLookAt(vector target, float strength, float damping)	163, 210, 211
	llLoopSound(string sound, float volume)	245, 246, 250
	llLoopSoundMaster(string sound, float volume)	248, **249**
	llLoopSoundSlave(string sound, float volume)	249
	llMapDestination(string simname, vector pos, vector _look_at_ignored)	45
string	llMD5String(string src, integer nonce)	323
	llMessageLinked(integer linknum, integer num, string str, key id)	83, 85, **86**, 87, 209, 219, 220, 231, 232, 269, 270, 271, 320
	llMinEventDelay(float delay)	25
	llModifyLand(integer action_named_constant, integer brush_0_to_2)	145, 146, **147**
integer	llModPow(integer base, integer exponent, integer mod)	23
	llMoveToTarget(vector target, float tau)	130, 132, 133, **163**, 165, 166, 174, 175, 209, 210, 239
	llOffsetTexture(float u, float v, integer face)	211, 271, 272
	llOpenRemoteDataChannel()	273, 274, **275**
integer	llOverMyLand(key id)	151
	llOwnerSay(string msg)	8, 20, 23, **68**, 74, 197, 265, 274, 289, 320, 321, 322, 323
	llParcelMediaCommandList(list commandList)	253, 254, **255**
list	llParcelMediaQuery(list query)	253
list	llParseString2List(string src, list separators, list spacers)	16-17, 49, 84, 297
list	llParseStringKeepNulls(string src, list separators, list spacers)	16

RETURNTYPE	CODE	PAGE(S)
	llParticleSystem(list rules)	10, 178, **200**, 202, 208, 326, 357
	llPassCollisions(integer pass_boolean)	134
	llPassTouches(integer pass_boolean)	87
	llPlaySound(string sound, float volume)	245, 250
	llPlaySoundSlave(string sound, float volume)	249
	llPointAt(vector pos)	
float	llPow(float base, float exponent)	23
	llPreloadSound(string sound)	246, **247**
	llPushObject(key target, vector impulse, vector ang_impulse, integer local_boolean)	154, **162**, 163, 169, 170, 172, 175
	llRefreshPrimURL()	
	llRegionSay(integer channel, string msg)	**68**, 82, 300
	llReleaseCamera(key avatar)	
	llReleaseControls()	172, **173**, 178
	llRemoteDataReply(key channel, key message_id, string sdata, integer idata)	273, **275**
	llRemoteDataSetRegion()	275
	llRemoteLoadScript(key target, string name, integer running, integer start_param)	
	llRemoteLoadScriptPin(key target, string name, integer pin, integer running_boolean, integer start_param)	111, 195, 332
	llRemoveFromLandBanList(key avatar)	150
	llRemoveFromLandPassList(key avatar)	150
	llRemoveInventory(string item)	196
	llRemoveVehicleFlags(integer flags_bitwise_named_constants)	181, **182**
key	llRequestAgentData(key id, integer data_named_constant)	13, 90, 289, 291, 294
key	llRequestInventoryData(string name)	188, **189**
	llRequestPermissions(key agent, integer perm_bitwise_named_constants)	54, 55, **56**, 58, 59, 104, 105, 171, 172, 286, 291, 292, 303
key	llRequestSimulatorData(string simulator, integer data_named_constant)	11
	llResetLandBanList()	150
	llResetLandPassList()	150
	llResetOtherScript(string name)	32, 291
	llResetScript()	26, **31**, 32, 55, 83
	llResetTime()	230
	llRezAtRoot(string inventoryname, vector position, vector velocity, rotation rot, integer startparam)	101, **102**

ReturnType	Code	Page(s)
	llRezObject(string inventoryname, vector pos, vector vel, rotation rot, integer startparam)	101, **102**, 107, 108, 110, 131, 146, 204, 210, 292, 316, 319
float	llRot2Angle(rotation rot)	121
vector	llRot2Axis(rotation rot)	121
vector	llRot2Euler(rotation rot)	12, 115, **116**
vector	llRot2Fwd(rotation rott)	121, 122
vector	llRot2Left(rotation rott)	121
vector	llRot2Up(rotation rot)	121
	llRotateTexture(float rotation, integer face)	211
rotation	llRotBetween(vector start, vector end)	121
	llRotLookAt(rotation target, float strength, float damping)	132, **163**
integer	llRotTarget(rotation rot, float error)	163, 164
	llRotTargetRemove(integer number)	163, 164
integer	llRound(float val)	22
integer	llSameGroup(key agent)	151, **152**
	llSay(integer channel, string msg)	**68**, 75, 79, 80, 81, 82, 283, 304, 320, 321
	llScaleTexture(float u, float v, integer face)	211, 213, 271, 272
integer	llScriptDanger(vector pos)	
key	llSendRemoteData(key channel, string dest, integer idata, string sdata)	275
	llSensor(string name, key id, integer type type bitwise_named_constants, float range, float arc)	25, **126**, 127, 128, 133
	llSensorRemove()	126, 288
	llSensorRepeat(string name, key id, integer type type_ bitwise_named_constants, float range, float arc, float rate)	25, **126**, 127, 128, 131, 135, 136, 137, 138, 151, 210, 303, 304
	llSetAlpha(float alpha, integer face)	62, 63, 75, 221
	llSetBuoyancy(float buoyancy)	162, 181, 239
	llSetCameraAtOffset(vector offset)	183
	llSetCameraEyeOffset(vector offset)	183
	llSetCameraParams(list rules_ strided)	183
	llSetClickAction(integer action_ named_constant)	283, **284**
	llSetColor(vector color, integer face)	
	llSetDamage(float damage)	169, 170
	llSetForce(vector force, integer local_boolean)	160, **162**, 163, 169, 175
	llSetForceAndTorque(vector force, vector torque, integer local_ boolean)	162, 163, 175
	llSetHoverHeight(float height, integer water_boolean, float tau)	162, 175
	llSetInventoryPermMask(string item, integer mask_named_ constant, integer value)	
	llSetLinkAlpha(integer linknumber, float alpha, integer face)	105
	llSetLinkColor(integer linknumber, vector color, integer face)	105
	llSetLinkPrimitiveParams(integer linknumber, list rules)	105, **113**, 115, 144, 344
	llSetLinkTexture(integer linknumber, string texture, integer face)	105, **211**
	llSetLocalRot(rotation rot)	115, 117, 122, 232, 235
	llSetObjectDesc(string desc)	111
	llSetObjectName(string name)	75, **111**
	llSetParcelMusicURL(string url)	197, **251**, 252
	llSetPayPrice(integer price, list four_quick_pay_buttons)	283, 284, 286, 287, 291, 295, 302, 303
	llSetPos(vector pos)	30, **43**, 112, **113**, 118, 121, 128, 144, 178, 232, 316
	llSetPrimitiveParams(list rules)	43, 44, 49, 50, 106, 107, 111, **113**, 115, 119, 158, 167, 170, 178, 211, 221, 222, 224, 233, 234, 235, 316, 344
	llSetRemoteScriptAccessPin(intege r pin)	111
	llSetRot(rotation rot)	30, **115**
	llSetScale(vector scale)	147
	llSetScriptState(string name, integer run_boolean)	32, **111**
	llSetSitText(string text)	39, **40**
	llSetSoundQueueing(integer queue_ boolean)	250
	llSetSoundRadius(float radius)	246, **247**
	llSetStatus(integer status_ bitwise_named_constants, integer value_boolean)	158, 160, 161, 165, 167, 170, 177, 178, 185, 238
	llSetText(string text, vector color, float alpha)	48, 108, 192
	llSetTexture(string texture, integer face)	23, **211**, 272
	llSetTextureAnim(integer mode_ bitwise_named_constants, integer face, integer sizex, integer sizey, float start, float length, float rate)	61, **62**, 142, 143, 144, 212-213, **214-217**
	llSetTimerEvent(float sec)	7, 28, **30**, 128, 129, 143, **230**
	llSetTorque(vector torque, integer local_boolean)	162, 163, 166, 181
	llSetTouchText(string text)	40

RETURNTYPE	CODE	PAGE(S)
	llSetVehicleFlags(integer flags_ bitwise_named_constants)	176, 181, **182**, 183
	llSetVehicleFloatParam(integer param_named_constant, float value)	176, 178
	llSetVehicleRotationParam(integer param_named_constant, rotation rot)	178,
	llSetVehicleType(integer type)	176, 177
	llSetVehicleVectorParam(integer param_named_constant, vector vec)	177, 178-179, 183
	llShout(integer channel, string msg)	**68**, 82, 300
float	llSin(float theta)	23
	llSitTarget(vector offset, rotation rot)	39, **40**, 44
	llSleep(float sec)	25, 42, 158
	llSound(string sound, float volume, integer queue_boolean, integer loop_boolean)	
	llSoundPreload(string sound)	
float	llSqrt(float val)	23
	llStartAnimation(string anim)	58, **60**
	llStopAnimation(string anim)	58, **60**
	llStopHover()	162
	llStopLookAt()	163
	llStopMoveToTarget()	163, 174, 239
	llStopPointAt()	
	llStopSound()	244, 246, **247**, 248
integer	llStringLength(string str)	14, 269
string	llStringToBase64(string str)	
string	llStringTrim(string src, integer type_named_constant)	14
integer	llSubStringIndex(string source, string pattern)	14, 271
	llTakeCamera(key avatar)	
	llTakeControls(integer controls_ bitwise_named_constants, integer accept_boolean, integer pass_on_boolean)	59, 171, **172**
float	llTan(float theta)	23
integer	llTarget(vector position, float range)	25, 132, 133, **163**, 164, 239
	llTargetOmega(vector axis, float spinrate, float gain)	51, 113, **114**, 122-123, **162**
	llTargetRemove(integer number)	163, 164
	llTeleportAgentHome(key agent)	150, 170
string	llToLower(string src)	14, 76
string	llToUpper(string src)	14
	llTriggerSound(string sound, float volume)	81, 244, **245**
	llTriggerSoundLimited(string sound, float volume, vector top_north_east, vector bottom_south_west)	245
string	llUnescapeURL(string url)	14
	llUnSit(key id)	41, **42**, 168
float	llVecDist(vector vec_a, vector vec_b)	12
float	llVecMag(vector vec)	**12**, 168
vector	llVecNorm(vector vec)	12
	llVolumeDetect(integer detect_ boolean)	135, 136, 151

RETURNTYPE	CODE	PAGE(S)
float	llWater(vector offset)	237, **238**
	llWhisper(integer channel, string msg)	68
vector	llWind(vector offset)	236, 237
string	llXorBase64StringsCorrect(string str1, string str2)	323
	LOOP (0x2)	213, 214-217, 221
	MASK_BASE (0)	197
	MASK_EVERYONE (3)	197
	MASK_GROUP (2)	197
	MASK_NEXT (4)	197
	MASK_OWNER (1)	197
	money() event	25, 281, **282**, 283, 286, 287, 292, 295, 299, 303
	moving_end() event	**112**, 164
	moving_start() event	**112**, 164
	no_sensor() event	127, 129, 288
	not_at_rot_target() event	164
	not_at_target() event	133, **164**
	NULL_KEY (00000000-0000-0000-0000-000000000000)	13, 15, 42, 48, 55, 69, 129, 132, 133, 231, 265, 285, 286, 288, 289, 292, 303, 304
	OBJECT_CREATOR (8)	134
	OBJECT_DESC (2)	134
	OBJECT_GROUP (7)	134
	OBJECT_NAME (1)	132
	OBJECT_OWNER (6)	83
	OBJECT_POS (3)	132
	object_rez() event	101, **102**, 210, 316
	OBJECT_ROT (4)	132
	OBJECT_UNKNOWN_DETAIL (-1)	
	OBJECT_VELOCITY (5)	
	on_rez() event	**31**, 32, 83, 92, 102, 120, 171, 207, 291, 293, 323
	PARCEL_COUNT_GROUP (2)	153
	PARCEL_COUNT_OTHER (3)	153
	PARCEL_COUNT_OWNER (1)	153
	PARCEL_COUNT_SELECTED (4)	153
	PARCEL_COUNT_TEMP (5)	153
	PARCEL_COUNT_TOTAL (0)	153
	PARCEL_DETAILS_AREA (4)	153
	PARCEL_DETAILS_DESC (1)	153
	PARCEL_DETAILS_GROUP (3)	153
	PARCEL_DETAILS_NAME (0)	153, 303
	PARCEL_DETAILS_OWNER (2)	153
	PARCEL_FLAG_ALLOW_ALL_OBJECT_ENTRY (0x8000000)	154, 211
	PARCEL_FLAG_ALLOW_CREATE_GROUP_ OBJECTS (0x4000000)	154
	PARCEL_FLAG_ALLOW_CREATE_OBJECTS (0x40)	154
	PARCEL_FLAG_ALLOW_DAMAGE (0x20)	154
	PARCEL_FLAG_ALLOW_FLY (0x1)	154

RETURNTYPE	CODE	PAGE(S)
	PARCEL_FLAG_ALLOW_GROUP_OBJECT_ ENTRY (0x10000000)	154
	PARCEL_FLAG_ALLOW_GROUP_SCRIPTS (0x2000000)	154
	PARCEL_FLAG_ALLOW_LANDMARK (0x8)	154
	PARCEL_FLAG_ALLOW_SCRIPTS (0x2)	154
	PARCEL_FLAG_ALLOW_TERRAFORM (0x10)	154
	PARCEL_FLAG_LOCAL_SOUND_ONLY (0x8000)	154
	PARCEL_FLAG_RESTRICT_PUSHOBJECT (0x200000)	154
	PARCEL_FLAG_USE_ACCESS_GROUP (0x100)	154
	PARCEL_FLAG_USE_ACCESS_LIST (0x200)	154
	PARCEL_FLAG_USE_BAN_LIST (0x400)	154
	PARCEL_FLAG_USE_LAND_PASS_LIST (0x800)	154
	PARCEL_MEDIA_COMMAND_AGENT (7)	254, **255**
	PARCEL_MEDIA_COMMAND_AUTO_ALIGN (9)	254, **255**
	PARCEL_MEDIA_COMMAND_DESC (12)	253, **255**
	PARCEL_MEDIA_COMMAND_LOOP (3)	255
	PARCEL_MEDIA_COMMAND_LOOP_SET (13)	253, **255**
	PARCEL_MEDIA_COMMAND_PAUSE (1)	255
	PARCEL_MEDIA_COMMAND_PLAY (2)	254, **255**
	PARCEL_MEDIA_COMMAND_SIZE (11)	253, **255**
	PARCEL_MEDIA_COMMAND_STOP (0)	254, **255**
	PARCEL_MEDIA_COMMAND_TEXTURE (4)	253, 254, **255**
	PARCEL_MEDIA_COMMAND_TIME (6)	255
	PARCEL_MEDIA_COMMAND_TYPE (10)	253, 255
	PARCEL_MEDIA_COMMAND_UNLOAD (8)	255
	PARCEL_MEDIA_COMMAND_URL (5)	253, 254, **255**
	PASSIVE (0x4)	53, 126, 129, 132, 133
	PAY_DEFAULT (-2)	
	PAY_HIDE (-1)	283, 295, 302, 303
	PAYMENT_INFO_ON_FILE (1)	
	PAYMENT_INFO_USED (2)	
	PERM_ALL (0x7FFFFFFF)	196
	PERM_COPY (0x8000)	196
	PERM_MODIFY (0x4000)	196
	PERM_MOVE (0x80000)	196
	PERM_TRANSFER (0x2000)	196
	PERMISSION_ATTACH (0x20)	54, 55, **56**
	PERMISSION_CHANGE_JOINTS (0x100)	
	PERMISSION_CHANGE_LINKS (0x80)	**56**, 105
	PERMISSION_CHANGE_PERMISSIONS (0x200)	
	PERMISSION_CONTROL_CAMERA (0x800)	**56**, 183
	PERMISSION_DEBIT (0x2)	**56**, 286, 287, 291, 292, 303
	PERMISSION_RELEASE_OWNERSHIP (0x40)	
	PERMISSION_REMAP_CONTROLS (0x8)	
	PERMISSION_TAKE_CONTROLS (0x4)	56, 59, 171, 172
	PERMISSION_TRACK_CAMERA (0x400)	**56**, 183
	PERMISSION_TRIGGER_ANIMATION (0x10)	56, 59
	PI (3.14159265358979323846264343832795)	5, 128, 129, 132, 133, 303, 304
	PI_BY_TWO (1.5707963267948966192313216916398)	79
	PING_PONG (0x8)	213, 214-217
	PRIM_BUMP_BARK (4)	346
	PRIM_BUMP_BLOBS (12)	346
	PRIM_BUMP_BRICKS (5)	346
	PRIM_BUMP_BRIGHT (1)	346
	PRIM_BUMP_CHECKER (6)	346
	PRIM_BUMP_CONCRETE (7)	346
	PRIM_BUMP_DARK (2)	346
	PRIM_BUMP_DISKS (10)	346
	PRIM_BUMP_GRAVEL (11)	346
	PRIM_BUMP_LARGETILE (14)	346
	PRIM_BUMP_NONE (0)	346
	PRIM_BUMP_SHINY (19)	226, 227, **344**, 345-346
	PRIM_BUMP_SIDING (13)	346
	PRIM_BUMP_STONE (9)	346
	PRIM_BUMP_STUCCO (15)	346
	PRIM_BUMP_SUCTION (16)	346
	PRIM_BUMP_TILE (8)	346
	PRIM_BUMP_WEAVE (17)	346
	PRIM_BUMP_WOOD (3)	346
	PRIM_CAST_SHADOWS (24)	
	PRIM_COLOR (18)	49, 50, 221, 224, 234, **344**, 346
	PRIM_FLEXIBLE (21)	344, 347
	PRIM_FULLBRIGHT (20)	222, **344**, 347
	PRIM_GLOW (25)	222, **344**, 347
	PRIM_HOLE_CIRCLE (0x10)	352
	PRIM_HOLE_DEFAULT (0x00)	352
	PRIM_HOLE_SQUARE (0x20)	352
	PRIM_HOLE_TRIANGLE (0x30)	352
	PRIM_MATERIAL (2)	344, 347
	PRIM_MATERIAL_FLESH (4)	347
	PRIM_MATERIAL_GLASS (2)	347
	PRIM_MATERIAL_METAL (1)	347
	PRIM_MATERIAL_PLASTIC (5)	347
	PRIM_MATERIAL_RUBBER (6)	347
	PRIM_MATERIAL_STONE (0)	347
	PRIM_MATERIAL_WOOD (3)	347
	PRIM_PHANTOM (5)	344, 348
	PRIM_PHYSICS (3)	344, 348
	PRIM_POINT_LIGHT (23)	49, 50, 222, 224, **345**, 348
	PRIM_POSITION (6)	43, 44, 221, 234, **345**, 348
	PRIM_ROTATION (8)	235, **345**, 348
	PRIM_SCULPT_TYPE_CYLINDER (4)	354
	PRIM_SCULPT_TYPE_PLANE (3)	354
	PRIM_SCULPT_TYPE_SPHERE (1)	354
	PRIM_SCULPT_TYPE_TORUS (2)	354
	PRIM_SHINY_HIGH (3)	345
	PRIM_SHINY_LOW (1)	345
	PRIM_SHINY_MEDIUM (2)	345
	PRIM_SHINY_NONE (0)	345
	PRIM_SIZE (7)	234, **345**, 349

RETURNTYPE	CODE	PAGE(S)
	PRIM_TEMP_ON_REZ (4)	107, 108, 131, 170, 221, **345**, 349
	PRIM_TEXGEN (22)	345, 349
	PRIM_TEXGEN_DEFAULT (0)	349
	PRIM_TEXGEN_PLANAR (1)	349
	PRIM_TEXTURE (17)	211, 213, 221, **345**, 349
	PRIM_TYPE (9)	345, 350-355
	PRIM_TYPE_BOX (0)	350
	PRIM_TYPE_CYLINDER (1)	350
	PRIM_TYPE_PRISM (2)	350
	PRIM_TYPE_RING (6)	350
	PRIM_TYPE_SCULPT (7)	350
	PRIM_TYPE_SPHERE (3)	350
	PRIM_TYPE_TORUS (4)	350
	PRIM_TYPE_TUBE (5)	350
	PSYS_PART_BOUNCE_MASK (4)	10, **358**, 363
	PSYS_PART_EMISSIVE_MASK (256)	201, 202, **358**, 361
	PSYS_PART_END_ALPHA (4)	201, **362**
	PSYS_PART_END_COLOR (3)	201, 206, 207, **361**
	PSYS_PART_END_SCALE (6)	203, 206, 207, 209, **361**
	PSYS_PART_FLAGS (0)	202
	PSYS_PART_FOLLOW_SRC_MASK (16)	209, **358**, 363
	PSYS_PART_FOLLOW_VELOCITY_MASK (32)	201, 202, 205, 206, 209, **358**, 363
	PSYS_PART_INTERP_COLOR_MASK (1)	201, 205, **358**, 361, 362
	PSYS_PART_INTERP_SCALE_MASK (2)	203, 205, **358**, 361
	PSYS_PART_MAX_AGE (7)	
	PSYS_PART_START_ALPHA (2)	201, **362**
	PSYS_PART_START_COLOR (1)	201, 206, 207, **361**
	PSYS_PART_START_SCALE (5)	203, 206, 207, 209, **361**
	PSYS_PART_TARGET_LINEAR_MASK (128)	**358**, 363
	PSYS_PART_TARGET_POS_MASK (64)	**358**, 363
	PSYS_PART_WIND_MASK (8)	10, 202, 209, **358**, 363
	PSYS_SRC_ACCEL (8)	202, **363**, 364
	PSYS_SRC_ANGLE_BEGIN (22)	203, **360**
	PSYS_SRC_ANGLE_END (23)	203, **360**
	PSYS_SRC_BURST_PART_COUNT (15)	361
	PSYS_SRC_BURST_RADIUS (16)	203, 206, 207, **359**
	PSYS_SRC_BURST_RATE (13)	361
	PSYS_SRC_BURST_SPEED_MAX (18)	363
	PSYS_SRC_BURST_SPEED_MIN (17)	363
	PSYS_SRC_MAX_AGE (19)	361
	PSYS_SRC_OMEGA (21)	360
	PSYS_SRC_PATTERN (9)	359
	PSYS_SRC_PATTERN_ANGLE (4)	205, **359**

RETURNTYPE	CODE	PAGE(S)
	PSYS_SRC_PATTERN_ANGLE_CONE (8)	203, **359**
	PSYS_SRC_PATTERN_DROP (1)	359
	PSYS_SRC_PATTERN_EXPLODE (2)	202, **359**
	PSYS_SRC_TARGET_KEY (20)	208, 209, **363**
	PSYS_SRC_TEXTURE (12)	362
	PUBLIC_CHANNEL (0)	
	quaternion: see rotation	
	RAD_TO_DEG (57.2957795130823208➥ 76798154814105)	12-13, 115
	REGION_FLAG_ALLOW_DAMAGE (0x1)	154
	REGION_FLAG_ALLOW_DIRECT_TELEPORT (0x100000)	154
	REGION_FLAG_BLOCK_FLY (0x80000)	154
	REGION_FLAG_BLOCK_TERRAFORM (0x40)	154
	REGION_FLAG_DISABLE_COLLISIONS (0x1000)	154
	REGION_FLAG_DISABLE_PHYSICS (0x4000)	154
	REGION_FLAG_FIXED_SUN (0x10)	154
	REGION_FLAG_RESTRICT_PUSHOBJECT (0x400000)	154
	REGION_FLAG_SANDBOX (0x100)	154
	remote_data() event	274
	REMOTE_DATA_CHANNEL (1)	274
	REMOTE_DATA_REPLY (3)	274
	REMOTE_DATA_REQUEST (2)	274
	return	7, 21, 24
	REVERSE (0x4)	213, 214-217, 221
	ROTATE (0x20)	213, 214-217
	rotation	9, 12-13, 98-123
	run_time_permissions() event	54, 55, **56**, 59, 177, 178, 287
	SCALE (0x40)	213, 214-217, 221
	SCRIPTED (0x8)	53, 126
	sensor() event	127, 128, 129, 130, 132, 137, 138, 151, 211, 264, 304
	SMOOTH (0x10)	213, 214-217, 221
	SQRT2 (1.414213562373095048801➥ 6887242097)	
	state	21, **26-28**
	state_entry() event	4, 7, **26-28**, 30, 32, 41, 75, 92, 110, 120, 143, 170, 171, 172, 176, 202, 209, 219, 221, 283, 284, 287, 292, 295, 299, 302, 303, 321
	state_exit() event	**26-2**7, 170, 173
	STATUS_BLOCK_GRAB (0x40)	158
	STATUS_CAST_SHADOWS (0x200)	158

RETURN TYPE	CODE	PAGE(S)
	STATUS_DIE_AT_EDGE (0x80)	158, 170, 238
	STATUS_PHANTOM (0x10)	158
	STATUS_PHYSICS (0x1)	5, **158**, 165, 168, 177, 178, 185, 238
	STATUS_RETURN_AT_EDGE (0x100)	158
	STATUS_ROTATE_X (0x2)	158
	STATUS_ROTATE_Y (0x4)	158
	STATUS_ROTATE_Z (0x8)	158
	STATUS_SANDBOX (0x20)	158
	string	**9**, 14
	STRING_TRIM (3)	14
	STRING_TRIM_HEAD (0x01)	14
	STRING_TRIM_TAIL (0x02)	14
	TEXTURE_BLANK (5748decc-f629-461c-9a36-a35a221fe21)	
	TEXTURE_DEFAULT (8b5fec65-8d8d-9dc5-cda8-8fdf2716e361)	
	TEXTURE_PLYWOOD (89556747-24cb-43ed-920b-47caed15465)	
	TEXTURE_TRANSPARENT (59facb66-4a72-40a2-815c-7d9b42c56f60)	
	timer() event	7, **30**, 52, 60, 63, 79, 93, 110, 122, 152, 160, 172, 173, 219, 226, 230, 246, 271
	touch() event	7, 45, **52**, 135, 262, 264, 338, 339
	touch_end() event	7, 45, 51, **52**, 79, 293, 321, 338
	touch_start() event	4, 7, 30, 45, **52**, 93, 108, 122, 160, 252, 269, 286, 338
	TRUE (1)	5, 9, 17, 21, 63, 73, 86, 87
	TWO_PI (6.28318530717958647692➡5286766559)	12, 210, 217
	TYPE_FLOAT (2)	10, 15
	TYPE_INTEGER (1)	15
	TYPE_INVALID (0)	15
	TYPE_KEY (4)	15
	TYPE_ROTATION (6)	15
	TYPE_STRING (3)	15
	TYPE_VECTOR (5)	15
	vector	10-12
	VEHICLE_ANGULAR_DEFLECTION_EFFICIENCY (32)	180
	VEHICLE_ANGULAR_DEFLECTION_TIMESCALE (33)	180
	VEHICLE_ANGULAR_FRICTION_TIMESCALE (17)	180
	VEHICLE_ANGULAR_MOTOR_DECAY_TIMESCALE (35)	180
	VEHICLE_ANGULAR_MOTOR_DIRECTION (19)	177, **179**

RETURN TYPE	CODE	PAGE(S)
	VEHICLE_ANGULAR_MOTOR_TIMESCALE (34)	176, **180**
	VEHICLE_BANKING_EFFICIENCY (38)	180
	VEHICLE_BANKING_MIX (39)	181
	VEHICLE_BANKING_TIMESCALE (40)	176, **180**
	VEHICLE_BUOYANCY (27)	176, **181**
	VEHICLE_FLAG_CAMERA_DECOUPLED (0x200)	181, 183
	VEHICLE_FLAG_HOVER_GLOBAL_HEIGHT (0x10)	181
	VEHICLE_FLAG_HOVER_TERRAIN_ONLY (0x8)	181
	VEHICLE_FLAG_HOVER_UP_ONLY (0x20)	181
	VEHICLE_FLAG_HOVER_WATER_ONLY (0x4)	181
	VEHICLE_FLAG_LIMIT_MOTOR_UP (0x40)	179, **181**
	VEHICLE_FLAG_LIMIT_ROLL_ONLY (0x2)	176, **181**
	VEHICLE_FLAG_MOUSELOOK_BANK (0x100)	181
	VEHICLE_FLAG_MOUSELOOK_STEER (0x80)	181
	VEHICLE_FLAG_NO_DEFLECTION_UP (0x1)	181
	VEHICLE_HOVER_EFFICIENCY (25)	180
	VEHICLE_HOVER_HEIGHT (24)	181
	VEHICLE_HOVER_TIMESCALE (26)	180
	VEHICLE_LINEAR_DEFLECTION_EFFICIENCY (28)	180
	VEHICLE_LINEAR_DEFLECTION_TIMESCALE (29)	180
	VEHICLE_LINEAR_FRICTION_TIMESCALE (16)	179, **180**
	VEHICLE_LINEAR_MOTOR_DECAY_TIMESCALE (31)	179, **180**
	VEHICLE_LINEAR_MOTOR_DIRECTION (18)	177, **179**
	VEHICLE_LINEAR_MOTOR_OFFSET (20)	179
	VEHICLE_LINEAR_MOTOR_TIMESCALE (30)	180
	VEHICLE_REFERENCE_FRAME (44)	179
	VEHICLE_TYPE_AIRPLANE (4)	176
	VEHICLE_TYPE_BALLOON (5)	176
	VEHICLE_TYPE_BOAT (3)	176
	VEHICLE_TYPE_CAR (2)	176
	VEHICLE_TYPE_NONE (0)	176
	VEHICLE_TYPE_SLED (1)	176
	VEHICLE_VERTICAL_ATTRACTION_EFFICIENCY (36)	180
	VEHICLE_VERTICAL_ATTRACTION_TIMESCALE (37)	180
	while	20-21
	ZERO_ROTATION (<0.0,0.0,0.0,1.0>)	12-13, 15, 40, 42, 107, 210, 292
	ZERO_VECTOR (<0.0,0.0,0.0>)	11, 15, 40, 42, 107, 210, 292

385